Poverty and Welfare in Modern German History

New German Historical Perspectives

Series Editors: Paul Betts (Executive Editor), Timothy Garton Ash, Jürgen Kocka, Gerhard Ritter, Nicholas Stargardt and Margit Szöllösi-Janze

Established in 1987, this special St. Antony's series on New German Historical Perspectives showcases pioneering new work by leading German historians on a range of topics concerning the history of Modern Germany and Europe. Publications address pressing problems of political, economic, social and intellectual history informed by contemporary debates about German and European identity, providing fresh conceptual, international and transnational interpretations of the recent past.

Poverty and Welfare
in Modern German History

Edited by
Lutz Raphael

berghahn
NEW YORK · OXFORD
www.berghahnbooks.com

First published in 2017 by
Berghahn Books
www.berghahnbooks.com

© 2017, 2020 Lutz Raphael
First paperback edition published in 2020

Library of Congress Cataloging-in-Publication Data

Names: Raphael, Lutz, 1955- editor.
Title: Poverty and welfare in modern German history / edited by Lutz
    Raphael.
Description: New York : Berghahn Books, 2017. | Series: New German
    Historical perspectives ; volume 7 | Includes bibliographical references
    and index.
Identifiers: LCCN 2016026102 | ISBN 9781785333569 (hardback :
    alk. paper)
Subjects: LCSH: Public welfare--Germany--History. | Poverty--
    Germany--History. | Germany--Social conditions. | Germany--
    Social policy.
Classification: LCC HV275 .P68 2017 | DDC 362.5/80943--dc23 LC
    record available at https://lccn.loc.gov/2016026102

British Library Cataloguing in Publication Data
A catalogue record for this book is available from the British Library

ISBN 978-1-78533-356-9 hardback
ISBN 978-1-78920-515-2 paperback
ISBN 978-1-78533-357-6 ebook

Contents

Tables and Figures

Acknowledgements

This book has a rather long history. It started with an invitation to organize a conference at the European Studies Centre, at St Anthony's college in Oxford, on problems of German contemporary history. During my stay at this marvellous place of interdisciplinary scholarship and debate on Europe's past, present and future as a visiting professor in 2011/2012, I invited colleagues to prepare papers on a subject that has been at the heart of a large research project at my home university of Trier since 2001: the long-term history of the politics of poverty in Europe. The overarching focus of this interdisciplinary project's research agenda was the interplay between exclusion and inclusion and its intellectual, social, economic and political underpinnings. Therefore the book is strongly linked to this project funded by the Deutsche Forschungsgemeinschaft. As many of the studies realized in this project have opened new perspectives on the German history of welfare and poverty relief, the chapters in this book owe a great deal to the new paradigm of exclusion/inclusion. It has become a major approach in German historiography on poverty and welfare during the last decade and this book tries to present a first synthesis to the English-speaking reader.

My thanks go to Jane Caplan, fellow of St Anthony's College and professor of German History at Oxford University and to Paul Betts, her successor, for their kind invitation to publish this book in the series 'New German Historical Perspectives' and for all their support along the way, not least in helping me to overcome such problems as translation and delays.

Two reviewers gave valuable comments on first drafts of this book and all chapters and their authors have profited greatly from their critical remarks and suggestions. Finally I want to thank Thomas Brodie, who took over the always tricky and complicated task of translating four chapters written in German. Anyone who has stepped into the field of German social policy and welfare administration knows about the kind of twisted professional jargon full of technical and juridical terms that have no equivalent in English – or in British or American welfare settings.

Introduction

Poverty and Welfare in Modern German History – Recent Trends and New Perspectives in Current Research

Lutz Raphael

The history of the welfare state has been one of the main themes in contemporary European history and, together with Britain and the Scandinavian countries, the history of welfare and social policy in Germany has always been at the centre of comparative interest. But in sharp contrast to the British historiographical tradition, the link between research on poverty and that on welfare policies has been rather weak in German historiography. The welfare reforms in 2001 and 2004 and the impact of problems like rising levels of (relative) poverty and inequality, the spread of low-wage jobs and the accumulation of social risks for parts of the German population have shifted perspectives among historians of welfare, and the complex relationship between poverty and welfare has come into view.

Recent Trends in the Historiography of Poverty and Welfare: the Particularities of the German Case

Historical research on welfare and poverty is strongly informed by national particularities. Institutional settings of the national welfare regimes and intellectual traditions in social philosophy and welfare doctrine have an impact on how historians and social scientists approach the problems of social policy in the past and present. In the German case, three aspects are striking, Firstly, the dividing line within the welfare system created by the passage of the 1880s reform laws, separating the world of social insurance (*Sozialversicherungen*) from that of social assistance and social welfare (*Fürsorge* or *Wohlfahrtspflege*) has become a pattern for the intellectual division of labour in historical and social scientific research. Academic specialization has given further support to this trend, as has the extensive focus on the problems of social insurance provision by the political mainstream in East and West Germany. As a consequence, the so called lower levels of German welfare regimes – the system of social assistance for the poor and the politics of poverty – were marginalized as topics of contemporary history when (West) German social history was at its peak during the 1970s and 1980s. Public debates addressing the 'new poverty' during the 1980s and 1990s, later the reforms of the Schröder government in social policy, blurred this well-established border between the worlds of social assistance and social insurance. The return of social assistance as a necessity for millions of people in contemporary Germany has raised interest in historical studies on poverty and welfare in the recent past.[1] Different research teams have started to work on new historical and social studies of poverty more or less simultaneously. One group gathered in Munich around Hans Günther Hockerts, who launched a series of studies on welfare and poor relief covering the whole period from the Weimar Republic to the recent past of the Federal Republic.[2] In Trier, a series of historical studies on poverty and welfare started in 2001, linking for the first time the early modern and contemporary periods.[3] In 2006, another project on poverty and welfare in Germany after the Second World War was established at Freiburg University. Together with other individual studies, they served to compensate for the slower development of research on poverty in Germany compared to Britain or France, and to re-establish the link between historical studies on poverty and those on welfare regimes.

A second demarcation line separates studies on social policy and welfare written by political scientists on the one side and historians on the other. Again, this intellectual division has been established over a long period and is still very strong: political scientists and sociologists dominate the field of welfare state studies, particularly when it comes to comparative research and the period after the Second World War. The Centre of Social Policy Research at Bremen University has become a vital centre for new empirical and theoretical approaches in these fields of scholarship.[4] German historians have intervened only reluctantly in the debates over the European welfare model and the three or four 'worlds of welfare' invented by Esping-Andersen. From Kaufmann to Leisering, most of the authors of seminal contributions to the debates about the particularities of the German welfare system and its embeddedness in political and economic systems since the end of the nineteenth century have been social scientists by training.[5] The exception to this is the long-standing tradition of bilateral Anglo-German comparisons of welfare regimes composed on both sides of the Channel since the pioneer studies of Ritter and Hennock.[6]

The third particularity of German welfare historiography has to do with the impact of the Christian denominations on the field of welfare and care. Since the Reformation, Germany has been divided into Catholic and Protestant territories and the competition between the two main Christian Churches has been strong for more than four centuries. Confessional institutions such as the Protestant

Diakonie or Innere Mission and the Catholic Caritas have been central institutions in the field of social services from the *Kaiserreich* to the contemporary Federal Republic of Germany.[7] They have always been an important element in the institutional framework of private and public poor relief, establishing themselves since the nineteenth century as a kind of third party between private philanthropy and public services. Since the Weimar Republic the Churches have been institutionally integrated into the public system of welfare provision, delivering their services autonomously but being financed largely by the state when fulfilling regular services stipulated by law. Social Catholicism and Protestantism have strongly informed the historiography on poverty and welfare in Germany and many studies have been initiated in the context of Church history. The contributions of scholars with a background in social Catholicism, such as Hockerts or Kaufmann, have had a particularly strong impact far beyond their own sociopolitical milieu.[8]

Historical studies on poverty and welfare in the nineteenth and twentieth centuries have mainly followed the periodization of political history, centring on one of the many changing political regimes Germany has known since the 1870s; studies covering only one period, whether it be the Weimar Republic, Third Reich, GDR or West Germany, still dominate. Approaches transgressing these established political demarcation lines are rarer, with most of these studying both the period of the late Empire and that of the Weimar Republic.[9] Thus, Sachße and Tennstedt's four volume overview covering the whole period from 1800 to the middle of the twentieth century is still the best synthesis and reference work when it comes to the relation between poverty and welfare in contemporary German history.[10]

From a mere quantitative point of view, most recent studies have been focused on the German Empire and Weimar Republic, with the Third Reich attracting a smaller number of scholars and studies. The Weimar period is still the best studied when it comes to welfare and poverty. The attention devoted to these topics reflects the importance that economic deficiency and social misery had during these years, with the social and economic consequences of the First World War confronting the social promises and legal entitlements to social protection opened up by the new democracy. The Weimar welfare regime and its collapse during the years of the great slump must be seen as central explanations for the establishment of the Nazi dictatorship in 1933. Existing studies have concentrated on urban situations of social assistance and the different local regimes of urban welfare. Other research has focused on the different groups of war victims who constituted one part of the Weimar welfare regime's large new clientele.[11] Other studies have come back to the problem of unemployment as one of the central problems of interwar welfare policies. New research confronts us with a social reality in interwar Germany quite different from what one might expect. Women's work and rural work, in particular, were not separated sharply enough from private services and household or subsistence activities to count in legal and social terms as 'unemployment'; and various kinds of informal work still shaped the social existence of large numbers of the lower classes, especially in the countryside. Under these circumstances, the new legal frameworks for assistance when laid off from work were strongly disputed or subverted by the authorities in rural areas. They refused the new rights of assistance to large numbers of people who had lost their regular jobs.[12]

Studies focusing on the problem of poverty and social assistance during the Third Reich are still rare, with other aspects of the Nazi welfare regime, such as health care and the politics of work, standing in the centre of interest.[13] Currently, the corresponding policies of discrimination, criminalization and extermination of those excluded from the racially defined national community (*Volksgemeinschaft*) are on top of the agenda of historical research on this period.[14] Specific studies on social assistance and poverty after 1945 remain rare, in marked contrast to the institutional and legal frameworks of the two welfare regimes in West and East Germany, which have been studied in detail.[15]

In sharp contrast to the recent interest concerning the twentieth century, new research on the earlier periods of the nineteenth century is still urgently missing. The history of poverty in nineteenth-century Germany remains largely unwritten and the lists of available literature is short if compared with the rich historiography available for the early modern period and Holy Roman Empire.

New Perspectives on Poverty and Welfare

The intellectual outcome of historical studies on poverty and welfare has changed fundamentally in the last two decades. A new paradigm has started to orientate recent studies on poverty and welfare in modern Germany. It is the level of inclusiveness that different welfare regimes were prepared to offer their clients and beyond that to all citizens that is now the focal point of critical inquiry. Responsiveness to the personal needs of people at the margins or in danger of dropping out of society has become a kind of yardstick for historical studies. Across the range of institutional settings and behind all the political, moral or religious ideas about help and welfare, vulnerability and exclusion have become constant themes. Protection and recognition are nowadays the two key dimensions that historians of German welfare regimes have in mind, as well as the individual as the person in need and as recipient of assistance.

Under the impact of this new paradigm, three themes have dominated debate: the politics of inclusion and exclusion; the impact of biological and racial concepts; and, strongly linked to the last point, the role of social experts in the formation of social policies.

German historians have been late in taking up the common European social science research agenda on poverty that was launched in the 1990s as an initiative of the European Commission.[16] This impulse for new empirical research on contemporary poverty went together with new theoretical perspectives. Problems of economic hardship and social assistance have been integrated into the larger problem of 'social exclusion'. The notion itself was first developed in the French debate but was soon taken up by German scholars both in the social sciences and in history. When the notion entered the political debate about the social consequences of mass unemployment and the lack of social recognition in a moment of financial crisis of the welfare state, the debate in sociology and history turned to a broader and more nuanced use of the term, linking it in the German case to its positive antonym: inclusion.[17] In this dialectic view, both terms designate the two different sides of one and the same operation that links the individual to a social unit. In this perspective poverty and welfare are strongly connected: economic deficiency turns into a social phenomenon when it generates operations of neglect and of marginalization. When this happens, lack of work, food and shelter create social groups or individuals whose social status is defined by their need for assistance or their deviance from 'normal' life. Inclusion and exclusion are seen in this model as a fact of both social structure and of language and communication. The use of the pair of words reminds us of the historical fact that they rarely exist in pure form as radical exclusion or complete inclusion but more often in a complex relationship, where a first step of exclusion may lead to a second step of inclusion, or vice versa. Welfare systems are the best examples of this social logic: unemployment insurance or social assistance start when people have been excluded from labour markets. Exclusion and inclusion are often strongly interrelated with regard to different social groups, the exclusion of the one being the precondition for the inclusion of the other. Beggars and vagrants on the one hand, widows and orphans on the other, are examples of this kind. Workhouses and mean tests have been classic instruments in order to operate a social selection separating the 'deserving' from the 'undeserving' poor, giving poor relief to the one and defining legal procedures of control for the other. The perspective of social exclusion/inclusion has largely replaced an approach underlining the dimension of social control or *Sozialdisziplinierung* as a central element of state building from the beginning of the early modern period.

Poverty as a social phenomenon is strongly linked to an asymmetric relationship between those in need and depending on help, and those providing assistance. The cultural and political representations of poverty are strongly linked to the problem of how to deal with the salience of non-reciprocity inherent in this kind of social relationship. Starting from this theoretical perspective, studies of poverty and welfare in modern Germany have been redirected towards new problems and new fields of interest. One such field is that of the relationship between welfare institutions, poverty and deviance.[18] The poor and deviant share the risk of marginalization and becoming an object of social operations linking inclusion and exclusion, such as the obligatory workhouse in the case of recidivist beggars and vagrants in Germany until 1945, or the English paupers going to a workhouse and subscribing to the disciplinary regime inside that institution. The history of deviance and poverty is best analysed in terms of the *longue durée* because the relevant cultural representations and elementary codes of labelling are of astonishingly long-standing continuity. The 'sturdy' beggar – able bodied, conscious of his rights and an outsider – has been a social and cultural figure stigmatized since the early modern era and handed down to later periods (well into the twentieth century) before transformation into the figure of the 'workshy' unemployed, profiting illegitimately from social assistance.[19] Recent studies on the lower rungs of the German welfare system have brought to the surface a large number of different cases where the labelling processes have been prominent elements in the social logic of exclusion. This is particularly true for the group of vagrants or travellers addressed as 'gypsies' (*Zigeuner*) by the authorities of the German states. Their exclusion via administrative interventions (prohibition of trading, control of mobility, expulsion and black lists) is part of a very long history culminating during the Nazi period in their internment in concentration camps and outright extermination.[20]

On the other side stands the group of elderly women, particularly widows, or wives with children who have lost their husbands and lack sufficient support from their family group. Again one can observe a *longue durée* of inclusion via entitlement for local poor relief and later social assistance. But this group shares with the aforementioned category of vagrants a high degree of uncertainty about the level of help it could expect from local authorities, whose benevolence was often linked to perceptions of the moral respectability and deference of the women in need.[21]

These historical studies of social exclusion have turned the focus of social history writing on poverty away from a mere economic understanding of the phenomenon, but they do not fall into the pitfalls of purely cultural analysis by ignoring the impact of elementary deficiencies and their social consequences. They have introduced into historical research the notion of vulnerability, taking up the findings of French sociologists such as Castel and others about the social consequences of unemployment and the deregulation of labour markets.[22] Thus the history of poverty is not only restricted to the registered clients of poor relief and other social services, but it includes the lives of those who are living more or less constantly on the verge of depending on makeshift economies to make ends meet and who are reluctant to address the local authorities for relief. It is only recently that statistical data is available concerning contemporary Germany which allows us to measure how large this group is. Unlike their British counterparts, German social historians cannot use social enquiries into poverty like those of Booth or Rowntree from the 1900s, 1930s and 1950s to reconstruct this area of precariousness and vulnerability essential to the understanding of poverty and the logics of including or excluding those in need from the welfare system and its services and economic support.

The second topic takes up the particularly strong and long-lasting influence of socio-biological and racial concepts on welfare policies in contemporary German history. Eugenics and racial hygiene had growing support in Germany among medical experts at their beginnings as an international movement at the turn of the nineteenth century. Both disciplines presented themselves as hard sciences distanced from legal or moral discourses on poverty. They pushed forward a socio-biological worldview where the social could only be changed profoundly by interventions in the genetic code of the population and a strong guidance of the individual. Both profited from the upheaval caused by the First World War and racial hygiene became one of the favourite disciplines whose argument the radical right used to attack the Weimar welfare system. Welfare specialists nevertheless also evoked these disciplines in their struggle for reform and rationalization of welfare services and expenditure.[23] This resulted in the establishment of racial hygiene as the core scientific support for welfare policies during the Nazi dictatorship. It legitimized the exclusion of a growing number of welfare clients from standard services and initiated a trend towards repression and violence in dealing with all those clients of welfare services regarded as deviant or racially different. Medicine was the academic discipline most directly involved in these trends, but physicians got strong support from lawyers and social scientists in putting the new racial doctrine of welfare into practice.[24]

The third new approach is strongly connected with these studies on the interplay between welfare, political ideology and scientific knowledge. This approach studies the role of experts more generally in the transformation of German welfare policies in the modern period. Since the late 1990s, the 'scientization of the social' has become a particularly innovative field of interdisciplinary research in Germany. 'The continuing presence of experts from the human sciences, their arguments and the results of their research had in administrative bodies and in industrial firms, in parties and parliaments'[25] has been particularly strong in the field of social and penal policy. Taking a long-term view, the presence of social 'experts' in the nineteenth and twentieth centuries stood in a line of continuity from the roles of theologians and lawyers in the construction of poor laws during the early modern period. But this early presence was much more limited in time and number, designating both the routine business of poor relief and the administrative supervision to clerks without academic knowledge. This changed dramatically in the last decades of the nineteenth century when psychologists, psychiatrists and economists entered the arena of political debate concerning welfare policies. They relied on their own knowledge regarding particular aspects of poor relief, vagrancy or delinquency to intervene in the field.[26] Human sciences – this originally French term encompasses medicine, socio-biology and the social sciences – were embedded in the institutional settings of the welfare regime in different ways: one was the establishment of consultative boards of scientific scholars giving regular advice to governments; the second was the professionalization of the personnel engaged in providing the various services for the poor. In Germany, schools for social workers and social assistants were created before the First World War, but it was the Weimar period that witnessed the decisive steps towards the creation of new professions in the field of social services. The academic social sciences took rather a long time to really get in touch with this new field of expertise largely controlled by men and women combining practical knowledge and various combinations of academic and practical training.[27] Social engineering became a particularly strong trend in German welfare politics concerning poor relief and social assistance between 1920 and 1960. After the defeat of the Nazi regime, social engineering inspired by socio-biological approaches lost much of its public support and intellectual legitimacy but nevertheless survived well into the 1960s. It was only in the 1980s that a new generation of social scientists shaped the field of poverty policy formation. Between 1960 and 1975 poverty more or less disappeared from the agenda of the social sciences leaving the field open to experts who were mostly qualified as clerks or managers of social institutions or communal services having studied law, economics or administration. They largely defended the legal status quo and ignored the dramatic shifts resulting from social change under the conditions of de-industrialization and globalization since the 1970s. The political debates on 'the new social question' in the mid 1970s launched by the CDU and those concerning the 'new poverty' launched by the Trade Union Association (DGB) assisted by the SPD served party interests to start strong anti-government campaigns, but both shed light on a new mass phenomena of poverty. It was social scientists giving evidence and advice to political parties who kept the theme on the agenda of German public affairs.[28] Most of these experts defined themselves as defenders of the poor and their claims. Under these circumstances the field of social expertise kept a distance to established administrative interests and government views, largely giving advice and research support for those institutions such as the associations of care and social assistance which defended the interests of the poor.[29] But we still need detailed research into the relationship between the new academic professionals in the field of social work or assistance and their clientele.

The renewal of this field of historiography profits from the opening up of social history towards cultural history and of a change in methods: most of the recent studies are case studies using the procedures of microhistory to focus on interactions at the local or regional level and strongly interested in writing a history 'from below', attentive to the agency and voice of the poor themselves. These studies deliberately take their cue from the microhistory movement of the 1980s, seizing opportunities for new insights that can be gained by changing the focal point of the inquiry and by zooming closer in to the events and contexts in order to get a clearer view of single actors and specific situations. Microstudies have always been wary of master narratives and tend to stick to their critical function – to debunk certainties on the macro level or to deconstruct large periodizations and general models. They have been instrumental in the shift to a new paradigm in focusing on the local, the individual and the agency of the poor and the marginal. The 'cultural turn' has imposed a sharp social constructivist eye on the many languages used to define and describe poverty and social politics. Discourse analysis and microstudies are the two most innovative trends in the recent literature on our subject. Normative orientations have attracted particular attention and the new studies on poverty and welfare underline the historical impact of norms and perceptions.

A last feature common to current research on the 'new' history of welfare is the insistence on agency. It has become a central category in most of the recent studies and it stands against any perspective transforming those in need or without power into passive objects of state regulations or welfare interventions. 'Negotiation' is the term used to cover the bargaining spaces always, to some degree, at the disposal of the vulnerable and poor. Nowadays the agency of the poor and the vulnerable has become a moral and political claim in itself and has been transformed into a kind of compulsory hypothesis for the historian.

Long-term Trends: Continuity and Change

This book has chosen a long time span – covering the period from the eighteenth century to the early twenty-first. It starts from two observations that have come to the fore in many of the recent studies discussed above. First, that change in the policies of poverty did not follow the short periods of political change characteristic of the twentieth century, nor the much longer periods of nineteenth-century political history in Germany. Second, that there exist striking continuities when we consider local regimes and the languages of welfare and poor relief during the nineteenth and twentieth centuries.

The normative orientations and intellectual frameworks underpinning German welfare regimes followed their own developmental timescales as they adapted to changing social and political contexts. The categories of 'deserving' and 'undeserving' are examples in kind. For centuries entrenched in German, as in most European, regulations on assistance for the poor they have had a very long life: even in the 1980s social researchers still found their traces not only in the self-images of unemployed people but in public opinion regarding unemployment in general. This dichotomy established in the early modern period has adapted itself to very different social situations. Thus the history of the different terminology underpinning the welfare regimes in Germany since the nineteenth century must take into account the *longue durée* of mental and emotional frameworks. Deservingness and belonging are two complementary categories of social assistance and welfare interventions and they are linked to different 'languages' or 'discourses' legitimizing welfare. The language of 'deservingness' clearly emphasized the element of exclusion, in contrast to the overall recognition of inclusion inherent in the Christian language relating to poverty. The language of 'belonging' took up the social ties of family, neighbourhood or place (village, parish or town) and kept a key place in the regulation of social assistance throughout the nineteenth and twentieth centuries. The argument of belonging was renewed and strengthened by the idea of national solidarity which came to the fore in the long nineteenth century; this culminated in the period of the two world wars, when the idea of *Volksgemeinschaft* became a strong argument in defence of legitimate demands for help from those who could metaphorically claim the German nation as their 'home'. The flip side of this inclusionary rhetoric was the exclusion of all those declared aliens to this political body – national socialist ideology pushed this logic to its extreme, legitimizing a welfare regime defined by sharp demarcation lines between insiders and outsiders. The prominence of these operations of exclusion and inclusion in German society under the Nazi dictatorship has been strongly underpinned by recent studies on the idea and practice of 'national community' *(Volksgemeinschaft)* during this period.[30] Even after the murderous consequences of such a welfare regime had been revealed between 1933 and 1945, postwar Germany has known continuities of this exclusionary language of national belonging, which is now critically and aggressively turned against labour migrants and asylum seekers, with both groups accused of fiddling social benefits.

The concept of the welfare state has its own history and there exists a particular German tradition of thinking about social policy.[31] Key notions like *Wohlfahrt* (welfare) and *Fürsorge* (social assistance) were until very recently confined to the bottom rungs of the German welfare state, whereas the concepts of *Soziale Sicherheit* (social security) and *Sozialstaat* (social state) were used when it came to the realm of social insurance and general problems of social policy. *Wohlfahrtsstaat*, the German equivalent of the English term 'welfare state' had to wait until the early 1970s before it lost its negative connotations linking it to any form of light-handed social spending and the doctrine of a paternalistic provision of the citizen with all kinds of social service. In the German tradition the state has been the central point of reference in public debates on welfare politics. Both socialist/social democratic and Christian, particularly Catholic thought, have also extensively informed the traditions of German welfare since the middle of the nineteenth century, ensuring that the connotations and meanings of German concepts in this field frequently diverge markedly from liberal Anglo-Saxon understandings of the same terms.

Another long-term factor to consider is the cooperation of Church and state in the realm of social assistance, and particularly poor relief, within the German states. Its roots can be found in the early modern period when the territorial states of the Holy Roman Empire sought to get control over welfare institutions, but in fact had to cooperate with their established Churches when it came to handling current affairs, be that local poor relief, the running of asylums or the administration of foundations and charities. This cooperation survived the liberal reforms of the nineteenth century and became a central element of the Weimar welfare regime that survived the Nazi period and was fully re-established within the West German model. The experience of the Nazi and SED dictatorships has strongly delegitimized any attempt to change this mixed welfare system. Religious arguments concerning the spiritual dimensions of poverty and individual help have coexisted with a political discourse outlining the elimination of poverty via useful work for the commonweal.

Themes: an Introduction to the Following Chapters

The following chapters do not give a comprehensive overview of the history of poverty and welfare in Germany and do not cover all periods within the selected timeframe. They explore the history of welfare and poverty through discrete case studies. In the first chapter, Sebastian Schmidt discusses the denominational dualism established in Germany since the Reformation, and the political compromise of 1550 ending the first wave of religious wars inside the Holy Roman Empire. This chapter presents a new reading of the differences in poor relief administration between Catholic and Protestant authorities inside the Empire. Schmidt shows that the organization of poor relief was built in both cases on new theological interpretations of *caritas* revising the scholastic Thomist orthodoxy of the thirteenth century. Both confessions preferred centralizing poor relief and welfare activities in the hands of public authorities. But in Catholic territories they had to cope with long-standing traditions and theologies of private alms giving and philanthropy. In the eighteenth century, the political doctrines of the Enlightenment brought together Protestant and Catholic reformers in their will to define poverty as a sign of bad government and to redefine the phenomenon in mainly economic and pedagogic terms.

The next chapter by Andreas Gestrich presents us with a case study in one of the newest fields in the German history of welfare and poverty. In sharp contrast to the English case, the collection and study of pauper letters and other ego documents of the poor has been neglected in German historiography until recently. The chapter offers pioneering insights into the findings of this ongoing research from a sample of documents covering a time span from the early nineteenth century to the middle of the twentieth. This study of petitions and 'pauper' letters shows the impact the established rhetoric of deference had on the vulnerable and the silent rise of more self-confident languages of demand as the twentieth century progressed. This chapter also studies social networks, local connections and the worldviews of the poor revealed in these documents.

The third chapter, by Beate Althammer, considers the field of welfare and social intervention in around 1900 where the mix of old and new approaches can be best observed for the German case. Vagrancy or homelessness is an old problem of welfare. Before and after 1900, German states were familiar with high rates of migration, largely caused by economic distress and the search for work opportunities. Though liberal legislation encouraged the mobility of work much more than had previously been the case, the legal framework still criminalized begging and vagrancy. Althammer convincingly shows that legislation and administrative practice in the German Empire tended to switch from the paradigm of pauperism (and the old image of social danger from vagrant groups) to new perspectives. In these new views, the economic problem was separated from the psychological or medical one. Unemployment on the one hand, and moral or medical deficiency on the other, became the new categories 'explaining' an irregular geographical mobility and an implicit move to the bottom of the social scale that worried and irritated social reformers and Christian philanthropists active in this field alike. The vagrant became the most visible element of a socio-biologically defined 'underclass' from which all other social groups took care to distance themselves. This social construction generated normative orientations that have had a long, robust life throughout the twentieth century and into the twenty-first. This prepared the ground for the growing attractiveness of repressive 'solutions', later including eugenic and 'racial hygiene' proposals, during the first half of the twentieth century.

Wilfried Rudloff's chapter on the German urban welfare regime reflects on the particularities of the municipal administration of welfare services during the Weimar years. Summing up recent studies it clearly shows the strong tensions inherent in the dual welfare system under the stress of new social expectations and the ongoing instability of the economy after the First World War. The social, political and economic outcome of these short-lived urban welfare regimes is still open to historical debate, but Rudloff insists on the variety of political options and potential manifested in them during these twelve years.

Nicole Kramer's chapter discusses the outcomes of new approaches to the historiography of welfare during the Nazi dictatorship. Firstly, Götz Aly's provocative description of a regime bribing its 'Aryan' population with a series of welfare grants, particularly during the war years, has attracted much public attention but also strong intellectual criticism underlining that the economic transfers in terms of welfare allowances were rather small and never compensated the relative hardships the regime's wartime mobilizations imposed on the German population. Secondly, the new *Volksgemeinschaft* approach equally underlines the regime's strategic and ideological interest in the politics of inclusion for the majority of its loyal citizens, having its counterpart in a deliberate and propagated politics of exclusion towards all those defined as political or racial enemies or outsiders to the German *Volk*. Kramer insists on the priority Nazi welfare gave to all kinds of assistance directly useful and functional to the military aims of the regime – first the symbolic and material uplifting of the victims of the First World War, the younger and the able bodied during the years before 1939 and then, during the war, soldiers' wives and the evacuees. Social assistance was strongly limited when it came to the elderly and the deficient and it was cut entirely when it came to the marginal and deviant. This chapter reopens the debate about the long-term impact of the Nazi period, and particularly the war years, on the development of German welfare regimes after 1945.

Chapters 6 to 8 deal with postwar Germany, concentrating on developments and problems in the Federal Republic. From very different perspectives, all three chapters take up the public debate on the 'new social question' and 'new poverty' during the 1970s and 1980s as a kind of turning point in the relationship between poverty and welfare in West German social policy. After the first years of hunger and general shortage immediately after the Second World War, poverty seemed to disappear from the agenda of welfare politics, but it came back with a vengeance when the limits to industrial growth and welfare expenditure entered the front stage of political debate during the 1970s. Again poverty became a highly controversial theme of social policy.

In Chapter 6, Christiane Kuller gives an overview of the gendered dimensions of the West German welfare state. She reminds us that in the dual German welfare regime (insurance/social assistance) established since the 1880s, women have been the classical clients of social assistance – but they have been systematically marginalized in the social insurance system. As happened in the aftermath of the First World War, after 1945, widows, single mothers and their children constituted a large group whose care became a responsibility of the state and its services of social assistance. Paradoxically, this situation did not challenge the de facto exclusion of most women from the system of social protection via social insurance. West Germany re-established the male breadwinner model, a model adapted to the new economy of consumerism by including an ever growing number of married women into the labour markets as part-time employees. This model became very popular from the 1960s onwards, but still deprived women legally of many social rights, strengthening the dependency on their husband's entitlements to pensions and health care. Kuller shows that it was only in the 1970s and the 1980s that feminist criticism of this gender model, combined with the return of female poverty for elderly widows and young single mothers, challenged this state of affairs.

Winfried Süß's study of the return of poverty to the agenda of West German welfare policies focuses on the interactions between social expertise, political agendas and party politics since the 1970s. The chapter starts from the remarkable fact that poverty had been pushed to the margins of political debate in the 1960s and early 1970s as a result of general affluence and the depoliticization of the new system of social assistance which was introduced in 1961 with a federal law and implemented by a silent coalition of local administrators and social experts. Government and opposition reopened the political agenda on poverty, generating new social expertise concerning its causes and manifestations, but it took more than two decades before the first official report on poverty was published, in 2001.

Olaf Groh-Samberg gives a critical account of the concepts that informed the debate about the new poverty among social scientists and he contrasts that debate with the social data available for the last three decades (since 1984) on the spread of social vulnerability and relative poverty in West and later reunified Germany. This chapter relativizes the discovery of the new qualities of poverty since the 1970s, showing that the risks of accumulating insufficient income, bad housing conditions and a lack of financial reserves continued to cluster socially among the lower (working) classes. Groh-Samberg's quantitative approach is based on social data available only since 1984 thanks to the new panel data of the *Socio-Oeconomische Panel* and it estimates the number of those living in poverty at the beginning of the new millennium to be at least 10 per cent of the German population. This return of poverty – even in its classic form of the labouring poor – is still news which the German public is very reluctant to accept, but is central to the social and political debate initiated by the so-called Hartz IV laws, passed in 2004.

Notes

1. See for example the exposition 'Armut. Perspektiven in Kunst und Gesellschaft' at Trier and Ulm in 2011 sponsored by the German Research fund (DFG): the catalogue: H. Uerlings, N. Trauth and L. Clemens (eds). 2011. *Armut. Perspektiven in Kunst und Gesellschaft*. Darmstadt: Primus.
2. H.G. Hockerts and W. Süß (eds). 2010. *Soziale Ungleichheit im Sozialstaat: Die Bundesrepublik Deutschland und Grossbritannien im Vergleich*. Munich: Oldenbourg; C. Kuller. 2004. *Familienpolitik im föderativen Sozialstaat. Die Formierung eines Politikfeldes in der Bundesrepublik Deutschland 1949–1975*, Munich: Oldenbourg; W. Rudloff. 1998. *Die Wohlfahrtsstadt. Kommunale Ernährungs-, Fürsorge- und Wohnungspolitik am Beispiel Münchens 1910–1933* Göttingen: Vandenhoek & Ruprecht; W. Süß. 2003. *Der 'Volkskörper' im Krieg: Gesundheitspolitik, Gesundheitsverhältnisse und Krankenmord im nationalsozialistischen Deutschland 1939–1945*. Munich: Oldenbourg; F. Wimmer. 2014. *Die völkische Ordnung von Armut: Kommunale Sozialpolitik im nationalsozialistischen München*. Göttingen: Wallstein.
3. Namely two research projects on urban and rural poverty in nineteenth- and twentieth-century Britain and Germany in the Collaborative Research Centre 600, 'Strangers and Poor People: Changing Patterns of Inclusion and Exclusion from Classical Antiquity to the Present Day', have been running from 2002 to 2014. For first results see: B. Althammer (ed.). 2007. *Bettler in der europäischen Stadt der Moderne: Zwischen Barmherzigkeit, Repression und Sozialreform*. Frankfurt/Main, New York: Lang; B. Althammer and C. Gerstenmayer (eds). 2013. *Bettler und Vaganten in der Neuzeit (1500–1933): Eine kommentierte Quellenedition*, Essen, Klartext; B. Althammer, A. Gestrich and J. Gründler (eds). 2014. *The Welfare State and the 'Deviant Poor' in Europe, 1870–1933*. Basingstoke: Palgrave Macmillan; A. Gestrich, S. King and L. Raphael (eds). 2006. *Being poor in modern Europe: Historical perspectives 1800–1940*. Oxford, Frankfurt//Main: Lang; K. Marx-Jaskulski. 2008. *Armut und Fürsorge auf dem Land. Vom Ende des 19. Jahrhunderts bis 1933*. Göttingen: Wallstein. For a full bibliography see http://www.fze.uni-trier.de/de/presse-und-service/gesamtbibliographie.
4. See H. Obinger P. Starke, J. Moser, C. Bogedan, E. Gindulis, and S. Leibfried. 2010. *Transformations of the Welfare State. Small States, Big Lessons*. Oxford: Oxford University Press; L. Leisering and S. Leibfried. 1999. *Time and Poverty in Western Welfare States. United Germany in Perspective*. Cambridge: Cambridge University Press; H. Obinger, S. Leibfried and F.G. Castles (eds). 2005. *Federalism and the Welfare State. New World and European Experiences*. Cambridge: Cambridge University Press.
5. S. Lessenich, I. Ostner (eds). 1998. *Welten des Wohlfahrtskapitalismus. Der Sozialstaat in vergleichender Perspektive*. Frankfurt/Main, New York: Campus; F.-X. Kaufmann, 2012b. *Variations of the Welfare State*. Heidelberg, New York, Dordrecht, London: Springer (German version: 2003. Varianten des Wohlfahrtsstasts, Frankfurt/Main: Suhrkamp); J. Schmid. 1996. *Wohlfahrtsstaaten im Vergleich. Soziale Sicherungssysteme in Europa: Organisation, Finanzierung, Leistungen und Probleme*. Opladen: Leske und Budrich.
6. G.A. Ritter. 1986. *Social Welfare in Germany and Britain: Origins and Development*. New York: Berg; E.P. Hennock. 1987. *British Social Reform and German Precedents: The Case of Social Insurance, 1880–1914*. Oxford: Clarendon Press. Id. 2007. *The Origin*

of the Welfare State in England and Germany, 1850–1914: Social Policies Compared. Cambridge: Cambridge University Press; H.G. Hockerts and W. Süß (eds). 2010. *Soziale Ungleichheit im Sozialstaat: Die Bundesrepublik Deutschland und Großbritannien im Vergleich.* Munich: Oldenbourg; C. Torp. 2015. *Gerechtigkeit im Wohlfahrtsstaat. Alter und Alterssicherung in Deutschland und Großbritannien von 1945 bis heute.* Göttingen: Vandenhoeck & Ruprecht.

7. C. Maurer. 2008. *Der Caritasverband zwischen Kaiserreich und Weimarer Republik.* Freiburg im Bresgau: Lambertus; J.-C. Kaiser. 1989. *Sozialer Protestantismus im 20. Jahrhundert. Beiträge zur Geschichte der inneren Mission 1914–1945,* Munich: Oldenbourg.

8. H.G. Hockerts. 2011. *Der deutsche Sozialstaat. Entfaltung und Gefährdung seit 1945,* Göttingen: Vandenhoek & Ruprecht; F.-X. Kaufmann. 2012a. *European Foundations of the Welfare State.* New York, Oxford: Berghahn; Kaufmann, *Variations;* id. 2013. *Thinking about Social Policy.* Heidelberg, New York, Dordrecht, London: Springer.

9. But see the systematic comparative approach for the period 1933 to 1990 in H.G. Hockerts (ed.). 1998. *Drei Wege deutscher Sozialstaatlichkeit.* Munich: Oldenbourg.

10. C. Sachße and F. Tennstedt. 1988–2012. *Geschichte der Armenfürsorge in Deutschland.* Stuttgart: Kohlhammer.

11. P. Brandmann. 1998. *Leipzig zwischen Klassenkampf und Sozialreform. Kommunale Wohlfahrtspolitik zwischen 1890 und 1929.* Cologne: Böhlau; H. Brüchert-Schunk. 1994. *Städtische Sozialpolitik vom Wilhelminischen Reich bis zur Weltwirtschaftskrise. Eine sozial- und kommunalhistorische Untersuchung am Beispiel der Stadt Mainz 1890– 1930,* Stuttgart: Steiner; G. Bußmann-Strelow. 1997. *Kommunale Politik im Sozialstaat. Nürnberger Wohlfahrtspflege in der Weimarer Republik.* Nuremberg: Stadtarchiv; D.F. Crew. 1998. *Germans on Welfare: From Weimar to Hitler,* Oxford, New York: Oxford University Press; Rudloff, *Wohlfahrtsstadt.*

12. Marx-Jaskulski, *Armut*; T. Stazic-Wendt. 2014. 'The 'New Morocco' Settlement between Trier and Euren, Germany: Drawing Boundaries and Constructing Deviance, 1925–1933', in Althammer, Gestrich and Gründler, *Welfare state and the 'deviant poor'*, pp. 78–102.

13. U. Lohalm. 2010. *Völkische Wohlfahrtsdiktatur. Öffentliche Wohlfahrtspolitik im nationalsozialistischen Hamburg* (Hamburg: Dölling und Galitz); Wimmer, *Ordnung;* Sachße/ Tennstedt, *Armenfürsorge,* vol. 3.

14. W. Gruner. 2002. *Öffentliche Wohlfahrt und Judenverfolgung. Wechselwirkungen lokaler und zentraler Politik im NS-Staat 1933–1942,* München: Oldenbourg; W. Süß. 2003. *Der "Volkskörper" im Krieg: Gesundheitspolitik, Gesundheitsverhältnisse und Krankenmord im nationalsozialistischen Deutschland 1939–1945,* München: Oldenbourg; M. Burleigh. 1994. *Death and Deliverance. 'Euthanasia' in Germany 1900–1945,* Cambridge. Cambridge University Press. M. Buggeln, M. Wildt (eds). 2014. *Arbeit im Nationalsozialismus,* München: Oldenbourg; M. Spoerer. 2001. *Zwangsarbeit unterm Hakenkreuz,* Stuttgart: DVA; D. Humann. 2011. *'Arbeitsschlacht'. Arbeitsbeschaffung und Propaganda in der NS-Zeit 1933–1939,* Göttingen: Wallstein.

15. M. Willing, 'Fürsorge', in G. Schulz (ed.). 2005. *Geschichte der Sozialpolitik in Deutschland seit 1945,* Bd. 3: *1949–1957.* Baden-Baden: Nomos, pp. 559–96; id. 'Sozialhilfe', in M.G. Schmidt (ed.), 2005b, *Geschichte der Sozialpolitik in Deutschland seit 1945,* vol. 7, *1982–1989, Finanzielle Konsolidierung und institutionelle Reform.* Baden-Baden: Nomos, pp. 479–516; id. 2008. *'Sozialistische Wohlfahrt': Die staatliche*

Sozialfürsorge in der Sowjetischen Besatzungszone und der DDR (1945–1990). Tübingen: Siebeck & Mohr; Bundesministerium für Arbeit und Sozialordnung (ed.). 2001–2008. *Geschichte der Sozialpolitik in Deutschland*, 11 vols. Baden-Baden: Nomos; F. Föcking. 2007. *Fürsorge im Wirtschaftsboom. Die Entstehung des Bundessozialhilfegesetzes von 1961*. Munich: Oldenbourg.

16. G. Room. 1995. *Beyond the Threshold: The Measurement and Analysis of Social Exclusion*. Bristol: Policy Press; D. Gallie and S. Paugam (eds). 2000. *Welfare Regimes and the Experience of Unemployment in Europe*. Oxford: Oxford University Press.

17. S. Schmidt. 2013. 'Inklusion/Exklusion. Neue Perspektiven für die historische Armutsforschung', in H. Uerlings and I.-K. Patrut (eds). *Inklusion/Exklusion und Kultur: Theoretische Perspektiven und Fallstudien von der Antike bis zur Gegenwart*. Cologne, Weimar, Vienna: Böhlau, pp. 123–42; L. Raphael. 2008. 'Figurationen von Armut und Fremdheit. Eine Zwischenbilanz interdisziplinärer Forschung', in L. Raphael and H. Uerlings (eds). 2008. *Zwischen Ausschluss und Solidarität: Modi der Inklusion/ Exklusion von Fremden und Armen in Europa seit der Spätantike*, vol. 6, *Inklusion/ Exklusion*. Frankfurt/Main: Lang, pp. 13–36; A. Hahn. 2008. 'Exklusion und die Konstruktion personaler Identitäten', in L. Raphael and H. Uerlings, *Zwischen Ausschluss und Solidarität*, pp. 65–96; Kaufmann, *European Foundations of the Welfare State*, pp. 146–179.

18. Althammer, Gestrich and Gründler, *The Welfare State and the 'Deviant Poor'*.

19. B. Althammer. 2007. 'Bettler in rheinischen Städten des 19. Jahrhunderts – Aachen und Düsseldorf', in B. Althammer (ed.). *Bettler in der europäischen Stadt der Moderne: Zwischen Barmherzigkeit, Repression und Sozialreform*. Frankfurt/Main, New York: Lang, pp. 151–92.

20. J. Tatarinov. 2015. *Kriminalisierung des ambulanten Gewerbes auf dem Land. Zigeuner- und Wandergewerbepolitik im späten Kaiserreich und in der Weimarer Republik*. Frankfurt/Main: Lang; M. Zimmermann (ed.). 2007. *Zwischen Erziehung und Vernichtung. Zigeunerpolitik und Zigeunerforschung im Europa des 20. Jahrhundert*, Stuttgart: Steiner.

21. Marx-Jaskulski, *Armut*.

22. R. Castel. 2003. *From Manual Workers to Wage Laborers: Transformation of the Social Question*. New Brunswick, NJ: Transaction Publishers.

23. P. Weingart, K. Bayertz and J. Kroll. 1988. *Rasse, Blut und Gene*. Frankfurt/Main: Suhrkamp; S. Kühl. 1997. *Die Internationale der Rassiste. Aufstieg und Niedergang der internationalen Bewegung für Eugenik und Rassenhygiene im 20. Jahrhundert*. Frankfurt/ Main: Campus; G. Broberg and N. Roll-Hansen (eds). 1996. *Eugenics and the Welfare State. Sterilization Policy in Denmark, Sweden, Norway, and Finland*. East Lansing: Michigan State University Press.

24. H.-W. Schmuhl. 2005. *Grenzüberschreitungen. Das Kaiser-Wilhelm-Institut für Anthropologie, menschliche Erblehre und Eugenik 1927–1945*. Göttingen: Wallstein; P. Weindling. 1989. *Health, Race and German Politics between National Unification and Nazism, 1870–1945*. Cambridge: Cambridge University Press; G. Bock. 1986. *Zwangssterilisation im Nationalsozialismus*. Opladen: Westdeutscher Verlag; M. Rotzoll et al. (eds). 2010. *Die nationalsozialistische 'Euthanasie'-Aktion 'T4' und ihre Opfer*. Paderborn, Munich, Vienna, Zurich: Schöningh.

25. B. Ziemann, K. Brückweh, F. Wetzell and D. Schumann. 2012. 'Introduction: The Scientization of the Social in Comparative Perspective', in K. Brückweh, F. Wetzell,

D. Schumann and B. Ziemann (eds), *Engineering Society: The Role of the Human and Social Sciences in Modern Societies, 1880–1980*. Houndmills, Basingstoke, Hampshire, New York: Palgrave, pp. 1–40, 2.

26. B. Althammer, 2014. 'Transnational Expert Discourse on Vagrancy around 1900', in Althammer, Gestrich and Gründler, *Welfare State and the 'Deviant Poor'*, pp. 103–25.

27. W. Rudloff. 2003. 'Das Wissen der kommunalen Sozialverwaltung in Deutschland', *Jahrbuch für europäische Verwaltungsgeschichte*, 15:59–88.

28. L. Leisering. 1993. 'Zwischen Verdrängung und Dramatisierung. Zur Wissenssoziologie der Armut in der bundesrepublikanischen Gesellschaft', *Soziale Welt* 44:486–511.

29. W. Süß. 2010. 'Vom Rand in die Mitte der Gesellschaft? Armut als Problem der deutschen Sozialgeschichte 1961–1999', in U. Becker, H.-G. Hockerts and K. Tenfelde (eds), *Sozialstaat Deutschland. Geschichte und Gegenwart*. Bonn: Dietz, pp. 123–40.

30. M. Steber and B. Gotto (eds). 2014. *Visions of Community in Nazi Germany. Social Engineering and Private Lives*. Oxford: Oxford University Press.

31. Kaufmann, *Thinking*.

Works Cited

Althammer, B. (ed.). 2007. *Bettler in der europäischen Stadt der Moderne: Zwischen Barmherzigkeit, Repression und Sozialreform*. Frankfurt/Main, New York: Lang.

———. 2014. 'Transnational Expert Discourse on Vagrancy around 1900', in B. Althammer, A. Gestrich and J. Gründler, *The Welfare State and the 'Deviant Poor' in Europe, 1870–1933*. Basingstoke: Palgrave Macmillan, pp. 103–25, 240–245.

Althammer, B., and C. Gerstenmayer (eds). 2013. *Bettler und Vaganten in der Neuzeit (1500–1933). Eine kommentierte Quellenedition*. Essen: Klartext.

Althammer, B., A. Gestrich and J. Gründler (eds). 2014. *The Welfare State and the 'Deviant Poor' in Europe, 1870–1933*. Basingstoke: Palgrave Macmillan.

Bock, G. 1986. *Zwangssterilisation im Nationalsozialismus*. Opladen: Westdeutscher Verlag.

Brandmann, P. 1998. *Leipzig zwischen Klassenkampf und Sozialreform. Kommunale Wohlfahrtspolitik zwischen 1890 und 1929*. Cologne: Böhlau.

Broberg, G., and N. Roll-Hansen (eds). 1996. *Eugenics and the Welfare State. Sterilization Policy in Denmark, Sweden, Norway, and Finland*. East Lansing: Michigan State University Press.

Brüchert-Schunk, H. 1994. *Städtische Sozialpolitik vom Wilhelminischen Reich bis zur Weltwirtschaftskrise. Eine sozial- und kommunalhistorische Untersuchung am Beispiel der Stadt Mainz 1890–1930*. Stuttgart: Steiner.

Buggeln, M., and M. Wildt (eds). 2014. *Arbeit im Nationalsozialismus*. Munich: Oldenbourg.

Bundesministerium für Arbeit und Sozialordnung (ed.). 2001–2008. *Geschichte der Sozialpolitik in Deutschland*, 11 vols. Baden-Baden: Nomos.

Burleigh, M. 1994. *Death and Deliverance. 'Euthanasia' in Germany 1900–1945.*
Cambridge: Cambridge University Press.

Bußmann-Strelow, G. 1997. *Kommunale Politik im Sozialstaat. Nürnberger Wohlfahrtspflege in der Weimarer Republik.* Nuremberg: Stadtarchiv.

Castel, R. 2003. *From Manual Workers to Wage Laborers: Transformation of the Social Question.* New Brunswick, NJ: Transaction Publishers.

Crew, D.F. 1998. *Germans on Welfare. From Weimar to Hitler.* New York, Oxford: Oxford University Press.

Föcking, F. 2007. *Fürsorge im Wirtschaftsboom: Die Entstehung des Bundessozialhilfegesetzes von 1961.* Munich: Oldenbourg.

Gallie, D., and S. Paugam (eds). 2000. *Welfare Regimes and the Experience of Unemployment in Europe.* Oxford: Oxford University Press.

Gestrich, A., S. King and L. Raphael (eds). 2006. *Being poor in modern Europe: Historical perspectives 1800–1940.* Oxford, Frankfurt/Main: Lang.

Gruner, W. 2002. *Öffentliche Wohlfahrt und Judenverfolgung. Wechselwirkungen lokaler und zentraler Politik im NS-Staat 1933–1942.* Munich: Oldenbourg.

Hahn, A. 2008. 'Exklusion und die Konstruktion personaler Identitäten', in L. Raphael and H. Uerlings, *Ausschluss und Solidarität: Modi der Inklusion/ Exklusion von Fremden und Armen in Europa seit der Spätantike,* vol. 6, *Inklusion/Exklusion,* Frankfurt/Main: Lang, pp.13–36, pp. 65–96.

Hennock, E.P. 1987. *British Social Reform and German Precedents: The Case of Social Insurance, 1880–1914.* Oxford: Clarendon Press.

———. 2007. *The Origin of the Welfare State in England and Germany, 1850– 1914. Social Policies Compared.* Cambridge: Cambridge University Press.

Hockerts, H.G. (ed.). 1998. *Drei Wege deutscher Sozialstaatlichkeit,* Munich: Oldenbourg.

———. 2011. *Der deutsche Sozialstaat. Entfaltung und Gefährdung seit 1945.* Göttingen: Vandenhoeck & Ruprecht.

Hockerts, H.G., and W. Süß, (eds). 2010. *Soziale Ungleichheit im Sozialstaat. Die Bundesrepublik Deutschland und Großbritannien im Vergleich.* Munich: Oldenbourg.

Humann, D. 2011. *'Arbeitsschlacht'. Arbeitsbeschaffung und Propaganda in der NS-Zeit 1933–1939.* Göttingen: Wallstein.

Kaiser, J.-C., 1989. *Sozialer Protestantismus im 20. Jahrhundert. Beiträge zur Geschichte der inneren Mission 1914–1945,* Munich: Oldenbourg.

Kaufmann, F.-X. 2002. *Sozialpolitik und Sozialstaat. Soziologische Analysen.* Opladen: VS Verlag für Sozialwissenschaften.

———. 2012a. *European Foundations of the Welfare State.* New York, Oxford: Berghahn Books.

———. 2012b. *Variations of the Welfare State.* Heidelberg, New York, Dordrecht, London: Springer.

Kühl, S. 1997. *Die Internationale der Rassisten. Aufstieg und Niedergang der internationalen Bewegung für Eugenik und Rassenhygiene im 20. Jahrhundert.* Frankfurt/Main: Campus.

Kuller, C. 2004. *Familienpolitik im föderativen Sozialstaat: Die Formierung eines Politikfeldes in der Bundesrepublik 1949–1975*. Munich: Oldenbourg.

Leisering, L. 1993. 'Zwischen Verdrängung und Dramatisierung. Zur Wissenssoziologie der Armut in der bundesrepublikanischen Gesellschaft', *Soziale Welt* 44:486–511.

Leisering. L., and L. Leibfried. 1999. *Time and Poverty in Western Welfare States: United Germany in Perspective*. Cambridge: Cambridge University Press.

Lessenich, L., and I. Ostner (eds). 1998. *Welten des Wohlfahrtskapitalismus. Der Sozialstaat in vergleichender Perspektive*. Frankfurt/Main, New York: Campus.

Lohalm, U. 2010. *Völkische Wohlfahrtsdiktatur. Öffentliche Wohlfahrtspolitik im nationalsozialistischen Hamburg*. Hamburg: Dölling und Galitz.

Marx-Jaskulski, K. 2008. *Armut und Fürsorge auf dem Land. Vom Ende des 19. Jahrhunderts bis 1933*. Göttingen: Wallstein.

Maurer, C. 2008. *Der Caritasverband zwischen Kaiserreich und Weimarer Republik. zur Sozial- und Mentalitätsgeschichte des caritativen Katholizismus in Deutschland*. Freiburg im Breisgau: Lambertus.

Obinger, H., S. Leibfried and F.G. Castles (eds). 2005. *Federalism and the Welfare State. New World and European Experiences*. Cambridge: Cambridge University Press.

Obinger, H., P. Starke, J. Moser, C. Bogedan, E. Gindulis and S. Leibfried. 2010. *Transformations of the Welfare State. Small States, Big Lessons*. Oxford: Oxford University Press.

Raphael, L. 2008. 'Figurationen von Armut und Fremdheit. Eine Zwischenbilanz interdisziplinärer Forschung', in L. Raphael and H. Uerlings. 2008. *Ausschluß und Solidarität: Modi der Inklusion/Exklusion von Fremden und Armen in Europa seit der Spätantike*, vol 6, *Inklusion/Exklusion*. Frankfurt/Main: Lang, pp.13–36.

Ritter G.A. 1986. *Social Welfare in Germany and Britain: Origins and Development*. New York: Berg.

Room, G. 1995. *Beyond the Threshold: The Measurement and Analysis of Social Exclusion*. Bristol: Policy Press.

Rotzoll, M. et al. (eds). 2010. *Die nationalsozialistische 'Euthanasie'-Aktion 'T4' und ihre Opfer*. Paderborn, Munich, Vienna, Zurich: Schöningh.

Rudloff, W. 1998. *Die Wohlfahrtsstadt. Kommunale Ernährungs-, Fürsorge- und Wohnungspolitik am Beispiel Münchens 1910–1933*, 2 vols. Munich: Vandenhoeck & Ruprecht.

———. 2003. 'Das Wissen der kommunalen Sozialverwaltung in Deutschland', in *Jahrbuch für europäische Verwaltungsgeschichte* 15:59–88.

Sachße Ch., and F. Tennstedt. 1980–2012. *Geschichte der Armenfürsorge in Deutschland*, 4 vols., Stuttgart: Kohlhammer.

Schmid, J. 1996. *Wohlfahrtsstaaten im Vergleich. Soziale Sicherungssysteme in Europa: Organisation, Finanzierung, Leistungen und Probleme*. Opladen: Leske und Budrich.

Schmidt, S. 2013. 'Inklusion/Exklusion. Neue Perspektiven für die historische Armutsforschung', in H. Uerlings and I.-K. Patrut (eds). *Inklusion/Exklusion und Kultur: Theoretische Perspektiven und Fallstudien von der Antike bis zur Gegenwart*. Cologne, Weimar, Vienna: Böhlau, pp.123–42.

Schmuhl, H.-W. 2005. *Grenzüberschreitungen. Das Kaiser-Wilhelm-Institut für Anthropologie, menschliche Erblehre und Eugenik 1927–1945*. Göttingen: Wallstein.

Spoerer, M. 2001. *Zwangsarbeit unterm Hakenkreuz*. Stuttgart: DVA.

Stazic-Wendt, T. 2014. 'The "New Morocco" Settlement between Trier and Euren, Germany: Drawing Boundaries and Constructing Deviance, 1925–1933', in B. Althammer, A. Gestrich and J. Gründler, *Welfare state and the 'deviant poor'*. Basingstoke: Palgrave Macmillan, pp. 78–102.

Steber, M., and B. Gotto (eds). 2014. *Visions of Community in Nazi Germany. Social Engineering and Private Lives*. Oxford: Oxford University Press, pp. 157–70.

Süß, W. 2003. *Der 'Volkskörper' im Krieg. Gesundheitspolitik, Gesundheitsverhältnisse und Krankenmord im nationalsozialistischen Deutschland 1939–1945*. Munich: Oldenbourg.

———. 2010. 'Vom Rand in die Mitte der Gesellschaft. Armut als Problem der deutschen Sozialgeschichte 1961–1989', in U. Becker, H.G. Hockerts and K. Tenfelde (eds): *Sozialstaat Deutschland. Geschichte und Gegenwart*. Bonn: Dietz, pp. 123–39.

Tatarinov, J. 2015. *Kriminalisierung des ambulanten Gewerbes auf dem Land. Zigeuner- und Wandergewerbepolitik im späten Kaiserreich und in der Weimarer Republik*. Frankfurt/Main: Lang.

Torp, C. 2015. *Gerechtigkeit im Wohlfahrtsstaat. Alter und Alterssicherung in Deutschland und Großbritannien von 1945 bis heute*. Göttingen: Vandenhoeck & Ruprecht.

Uerlings, H., N. Trauth and L. Clemens (eds). 2011. *Armut. Perspektiven in Kunst und Gesellschaft*. Katalog zur gleichnamigen Ausstellung, Stadtmuseum Simeonstift und Rheinisches Landesmuseum Trier, 10.04.2011–31.07.2011. Darmstadt: Primus.

Weindling, P. 1989. *Health, Race and German Politics between National Unification and Nazism, 1870–1945*. Cambridge: Cambridge University Press.

Weingart, P., K. Bayertz and J. Kroll. 1988. *Rasse, Blut und Gene*. Frankfurt/Main: Suhrkamp.

Willing, M. 2005a. 'Fürsorge', in G. Schulz (ed.), *Geschichte der Sozialpolitik in Deutschland seit 1945*, vol. 3, *1949–1957, Bewältigung der Kriegsfolgen, Rückkehr zur sozialpolitischen Normalität*. Baden-Baden: Nomos, pp. 559–596.

———. 2005b. 'Sozialhilfe', in M.G. Schmidt (ed.), *Geschichte der Sozialpolitik in Deutschland seit 1945*, vol. 7, *1982–1989, Finanzielle Konsolidierung und institutionelle Reform*. Baden-Baden: Nomos, pp. 479–516.

————. 2008. '*Sozialistische Wohlfahrt*': *Die staatliche Sozialfürsorge in der Sowjetischen Besatzungszone und der DDR (1945–1990)*. Tübingen: Siebeck & Mohr.

Wimmer, F. 2014. *Die völkische Ordnung von Armut. Kommunale Sozialpolitik im nationalsozialistischen.* Munich, Göttingen: Wallstein.

Ziemann, B., K. Brückweh, F. Wetzell and D. Schumann. 2012. 'Introduction: The Scientization of the Social in Comparative Perspective', in K. Brückweh, F. Wetzell, D. Schumann and B. Ziemann (eds), *Engineering Society: The Role of the Human and Social Sciences in Modern Societies, 1880–1980.* Houndmills, Basingstoke, Hampshire, New York: Palgrave, pp. 1–40.

Zimmermann, M. (ed.). 2007. *Zwischen Erziehung und Vernichtung. Zigeunerpolitik und Zigeunerforschung im Europa des 20. Jahrhundert.* Stuttgart: Steiner.

Lutz Raphael is Professor of Contemporary History at the University of Trier. His recent publications include: *Imperiale Gewalt und Mobilisierte Nation: Europa 1914–1945* (2011); 'Flexible Anpassungen und prekäre Sicherheiten. Industriearbeit(er) nach dem Boom', in M. Reitmayer and T. Schlemmer (eds), *Die Anfänge der Moderne. Umbrüche in Westeuropa nach dem Boom* (2014). He is co-editor of the books *Fremd und rechtlos? Zugehörigkeitsrechte Fremder von der Antike bis zur Gegenwart. Ein Handbuch* (2014); *Rescuing the Vulnerable: Poverty, Welfare and Social Ties in Modern Europe* (2016); and *Vorgeschichte der Gegenwart* (2016).

CHAPTER I

The Economy of Love

Welfare and Poor Relief in Catholic Territories of the Holy Roman Empire (1500 to 1800)

Sebastian Schmidt

Confessions and Welfare in Early Modern Historiography

Research on poverty, welfare provision and the lower social orders or outsiders in early modern Europe can be regarded as representing an established and independent branch of historiography.[1] At a very early stage, poor relief was interpreted by historians as a classic example of social disciplining.[2] These works primarily focused on urban developments in Central and Western Europe, where continuities in reform efforts can be traced between the medieval and early modern periods.[3] In general, these titles assign little importance to confessional affiliation and the Reformation's outcomes in shaping the development of welfare initiatives; they are instead interpreted as reflecting state building processes underway in both Catholic and Protestant territories and as reactions to the first manifestations of mass poverty since the late Middle Ages.[4]

Our understandings of the early modern poor, their lives and culture, have been advanced by the development of everyday and microhistory. Studies on England[5] have been especially prominent in this regard and have exerted a considerable influence on research concerning poor relief in the Holy Roman Empire.[6] If Martin Dinges' work on Bordeaux already investigated the potential existence of a particular 'poor mentality' in 1991, this topic was much more central to Helmut Bräuer's recent research on the poor in Upper Saxony.[7] By examining sources containing biographic information and affording qualitative perspectives, recent historiography has finally portrayed the poor as actors with agency and not merely the subjects of welfare institutions and their regulations.[8]

If recent years have therefore witnessed the emergence of a wide spectrum of research findings concerning individual aspects of poverty and its presence in various regions, other topics remain neglected. This fact certainly applies to the Christian confessions' roles in welfare provision, and especially trends within the Holy Roman Empire's Catholic municipalities. This gap in existing literature is all the more surprising as the potential roles played by the confessions in the field of poor relief and welfare represent a topic of central historiographical importance. Admittedly, Robert Jütte's pioneering 1984 work[9] on the authorities' provision of poor relief in Cologne and Frankfurt represented an early investigation into the potential influence of confessional difference on the formation of welfare policies. However, with regards to the Holy Roman Empire, the role of confessional factors in the emergence of specific welfare cultures can only be deemed well researched at the city level, not that of larger territorial states.[10] Recent works regarding confession's influence on the development of territorial poor relief, such as those of Hannes Ludyga and Tim Lorentzen, have come to completely different conclusions concerning the significance of confessional differences.[11]

For the Reich as a whole, confessional contexts and the specific characteristics of Catholic welfare provision have not yet attracted attention in a systematically comparative way. In a European perspective the Reich may be seen as a space where confessional differences known from West European countries of different confession, such as France, England or Scotland, coexisted for a long period. In her classic 1974 study of poverty in eighteenth-century France, Olwen Hufton demonstrated that no central system of municipal welfare provision was established, but that rather responsibility in this field had remained in the hands of ecclesiastical institutions in existence since the medieval period.[12] If this argument also applies to the Holy Roman Empire, it would mean that established historiographical portrayals of a comparable structural transformation of welfare provision in both Protestant and Catholic territories can no longer be presumed. Konrad Dussel's work has indeed revealed how fruitful it can be to devote greater attention to religious confession as a decisive influence in the formation of early modern welfare cultures. In his investigation of Speyer's poor policies, he documents a noticeably different pattern of development than in contemporary Protestant territories, distinguished by loyalty to traditional religious beliefs and patterns of behaviour.[13] On the contrary, the Elizabethan settlement of a general system of poor relief run by state authorities and funded by tax payers may seem the most advanced example of a Protestant solution to the problem. In the Reich similar approaches, such as that of Philipp of Hessen, the Duchy of Württemberg, or Frederik III, Elector Palatine of the Rhine, may be cited as support to an interpretation that underlines the impact of confessional culture and institutions.[14]

The extent to which confession-specific religious convictions influenced the formation of welfare legislation and the practices of charity within the Holy Roman Empire between the sixteenth and eighteenth centuries is a topic in need of further research. This chapter will analyse the changes that occurred within Catholic states' welfare discourses following the Reformation, and what impact these had on legislation concerning the poor and the institutional practices of welfare provision into the eighteenth century. It will use the Empire's electorates of Mainz and Trier as case studies to illuminate this last theme.

One must not forget that the confessional territorial states of the early modern period were largely taking up solutions developed in late medieval towns where the problems of poverty and destitution were concentrated and particularly urgent. Municipal welfare reforms were to be found across Western Europe at the beginning of the sixteenth century. These reforms were connected with various centralization efforts on the part of local authorities, attempts to bring welfare provision under secular control and efforts to differentiate the poor along the lines of 'deserving' and 'undeserving' individuals. The key category in making this distinction was an individual's readiness to work. This particular trend has frequently been seen in the historiography as heralding a decisive shift towards modernity. However, as a range of research projects have now demonstrated, this differentiation of the poor is hardly modern, but rather possesses an intellectual lineage stretching back to the classical world.[15] It can be found embedded as a normative value in a range of early and high medieval texts and theoretical discussions, such as Justinian's Code or Charlemagne's laws. Differentiating between the poor unable to work and those unwilling to do so therefore forms one of the most consistent historic tests that welfare authorities have used to decide who is deserving of help and who is not. In recognizing this fact, we are nevertheless confronted with the problem of explaining what caused these moral categories and semantics to be transformed into institutional practices at the beginning of the early modern period.

Many social historians answer this question purely with reference to socio-economic contexts and the so-called 'crisis of the late Middle Ages'. In the following pages, this chapter will argue in favour of an approach that takes into account the intellectual changes underway during the early modern period. For example, these decades witnessed a pronounced shift in the meanings of the terms 'love' and the 'economy of love'; concepts which had been systematically described by Thomas Aquinas in the thirteenth century. It seems wise to present Aquinas' concepts first, as his theory of welfare remained decisive in informing the activities of many Catholic institutions well into the early modern period. It must also be observed that contemporary Catholic theorists such as Juan Luis Vives (1493–1540) developed new concepts of welfare provision which were often held up as a model by Catholic rulers. In an instructive book, Andreas Keck has succeeded in comparing both of these welfare theories side by side.[16] Following his line of argument, this chapter proposes the theory that in the Holy Roman Empire's Catholic states, a particular type of welfare provision emerged which was above all shaped by the interaction of a wide spectrum of municipal political aspirations with local or decentralized institutional practices. Significant changes in the practices of welfare provision within Catholic states were only brought about in the eighteenth century by a stronger tendency on the part of governments to regulate various aspects of their populations' lives.

Intellectual Changes within Welfare Concepts: Thomas Aquinas' Welfare Theory and Its Aftermath

Acts of *caritas* – the provision of welfare and charitable giving – occupy a central position in Thomas Aquinas' conception of Christian ethics and understanding of how individual salvation is secured.[17] According to Aquinas, the devotion to one's neighbour is a habit which, when regulated by reason, can differentiate good from evil. An individual's inner decision to give charitably is followed by the resolution whether to act externally upon this decision. The success of this deed is of secondary importance for Aquinas in his estimation of what constitutes a Christian life. In his view, what really mattered was the correct decision; that is, the inner attitude of the individual before the action itself.[18] For Aquinas, it was this motivating attitude which decided how the charitable act of loving one's neighbour was to be judged.

Aquinas certainly postulated that all Christians are worthy of receiving charity. At the same time, however, he was aware of the practical problem and realised that in the context of limited resources, a hierarchy of welfare recipients must be established. He therefore asked when the divine commandment of giving is strictly compulsory for the Christian, and who is primarily to be considered one's neighbour. Aquinas always regarded the giving of alms as part of the *beneficientia*: a Christian duty if its recipients in a situation characterized by absolute need or deprivation.[19] In his estimation, those failing to provide alms in this situation had sinned. According to Aquinas, the giver of alms should be able to verify with his own eyes whether a donation was urgently necessary or not.[20] Thomas did not outline a duty of further investigation in these situations, nor did he discuss the importance of establishing the reasons as to why the recipient of charity was in this position. In Aquinas' view, personal contact between the giver and receiver was the only appropriate regulation of charitable activity.

In the triangular relationship established between the alms giver, receiver and God, according to Aquinas, the poor person's duty was to offer prayers to God on the giver's behalf. The poor thereby possessed a function in securing salvation, although this should rather be seen as an additional interest earned by the giver of charity on top of the capital gained initially by the charitable act itself, as through this act alone he or she could already be certain of God's benevolence. In most medieval artistic portrayals of charitable acts, it is therefore not the fortunate poor person, but rather the consciously Christian behaviour of the giver, which is portrayed as central. In these portrayals, the passive endurance of poverty represents a silent act of consent to the divine order. The giving of alms is portrayed as a conscious act delivered from a position of power, affirming and renewing society's Christian value system and hierarchical order. To a greater extent than the recipient of charity, in Aquinas' ethics of help the giver has a duty afforded by his or her agency to give selflessly and replicate divine love.

As a result, being poor, and the act of giving alms in particular, represented highly promising means of gaining eternal life within Aquinas' understanding of the salvation economy. These gains could, of course, only be cashed in eternity. The presence of poverty did not thereby contradict the existence of just government, as we can observe, for instance, in the Sienese fresco of the same name, in which a beggar is portrayed as a normal phenomenon in an everyday scene.[21] As a consequence, welfare policy did not form an obligatory responsibility of state authorities. Monasteries, the Hospitaller Order and monastic brotherhoods assumed responsibility for the poor and sick. Michel Pauly has shown how dense the Hospitallers' network was in the Rhein-Maas-Mosel area alone between the medieval and early modern periods.[22]

If we analyse understandings of welfare in terms of inclusion and exclusion, we can discern that in the medieval period the *caritas* concept possessed an all-embracing inclusive dimension, which in Aquinas' thought found its limits in the act of *benevolentia*, or benevolence. Welfare provision, as so-called *beneficentia,* was, by contrast, considerably limited. Underpinning these restrictions was the role of personal evaluations of what counts as a situation of 'extreme need' deserving of charitable relief, as well as the precondition that after giving alms, the donor must still possess the means necessary to live a life according to his or her station in the social order.[23] The inclusion of the poor thereby takes place only intermittently in the personal contact between giver and receiver. It extends only as far as providing the receiver with the necessities required to sustain life, and does not extend to improving his or her opportunities to participate in society. The giving of alms cannot therefore serve as a pre-emptive means of combating poverty.

Intellectual Changes in Welfare Concepts: the Theories of Geiler von Kaysersberg and Juan Luis Vives at the Onset of the Early Modern Period

How did these understandings of poverty and welfare change at the end of the Middle Ages? Reflecting humanism's increasing influence, elites ascribed more significance to practical behaviours as well as their consequences for the people in question. That is to say, it was expected that the giver of alms was not only a good Christian, as manifested by the act of giving itself, but also that he or she attempted to calculate which consequences his or her charity would have. As this task was often beyond the individual in question, other institutions were now supposed to assume the responsibility. For example, the Strasburg Cathedral preacher Geiler von Kaysersberg demanded of the city's secular authorities that they should separate the beggars capable of work from those incapable of it and introduce compulsory work duties for the former. In order to implement a precise categorization, he suggested a 'general police visitation of the beggars, in which their individual needs and possible ability to work would be ascertained'.[24]

Geiler von Kaysersberg saw the sin-removing strength of alms as endangered if they were distributed to those undeserving of them.[25] In order to free the alms giver of this doubt, Geiler deemed it a duty of the state authorities to ensure that he or she would only come into contact with members of the deserving poor. For Geiler, the personal contact between alms giver and receiver remained important. However, this no longer applied in the view of Juan Luis Vives, who, for a few years from 1523 onwards served as the Oxford tutor of the future Queen of England Mary I.[26] He became famous for his theoretical discussion of poor relief, *De subventione pauperum*, which he wrote for Bruges' city council and was published in 1526.[27]

By contrast to Thomas Aquinas and Geiler von Kaysersberg, Vives saw the advantages potentially conferred by a centralized control and distribution of benefits. In his view, this was a precondition for their purposeful use. According to Vives, only the individual possessing accurate knowledge of where genuine need exists can usefully give alms[28] ('... we must not give to everyone what he desires, but only what is expedient for him'.[29])

This is where the desire to control welfare provision and acquire relevant information concerning its use became so crucial in Vives' thought. It was not enough for him, as it had been for Thomas Aquinas, to ascertain poor individuals' need by visual means. Vives was less interested in the giver's motivations than in the situation and impact of charitable giving on the recipient. The donation's ultimate aim was to exert a pedagogic, ethical influence on its recipient.

This conception of alms giving also marked a clear departure from Aquinas' thinking. The purpose of the activity was no longer the duty to alleviate a life-threatening situation of deprivation, but rather to afford help to alleviate need in the widest sense, which should ideally be tackled as early as possible. Its key aim was to help individuals to help themselves.[30] Aid must not therefore wait for the meeting of a suitable giver with an appropriate receiver, but must rather be offered as speedily as possible. As Vives wrote: 'Quickly means before necessity presses upon the person, before it drives him to a crime or misdeed, before he blushes with shame in being constrained to beg '.[31]

Encouragement and compulsion, but also deterrence and even corporal punishment, were appropriate means in Vives' estimation to make virtuous citizens out of poor beggars. Welfare now meant teaching those members of the poor capable of work to do so continually and industriously. The most visible institutional change in welfare provision from the late sixteenth century onwards was indeed the almost universal appearance of workhouses and institutions of correction.

We thus have, in the sixteenth century, in one of the earliest theoretical treatments of welfare provision and its appropriate functions, a clear shift in focus from the alms giver to its recipient. This change can also be observed in contemporary art. If in the medieval world, the giver generally stands in the centre of representations of alms giving, in the early modern period the recipient is increasingly the focus of attention. Moreover, this portrayal no longer dwells solely on the poor as *pauperes Christi*, but also expresses stigmatizing perspectives on the poor as individuals lacking civic virtues. At the beginning of the early modern period, the image of the deceitful beggar had a wide circulation in pictures and literature. The most famous example is certainly the *Liber Vagatorum,* but Sebastian Brant's *Ship of Fools* also warned of such beggars.[32] Over the following decades, portrayals of civic institutions and their officials offering welfare provision and identifying the 'true', deserving poor became more widespread than the established image of the individual act of alms giving.[33]

The act of *caritas* continued to be seen in the early modern period as the highest theological virtue. Nevertheless, by interacting with humanist conceptions of society, above all those concerning upbringing and education, the motivation of the alms giver lost its sole centrality within social thought, whose focus was increasingly directed towards the success of welfare provision as well as recipients' potential for moral reformation.

Vives considerably expanded the concept of alms giving with his theories and demanded an ongoing effort to afford the poor better chances to improve their condition and participate in society. He envisaged this form of inclusion as being institutionally anchored, independent of the need for an individual alms giver and capable of being implemented by force. If medieval scholastic theologians' understandings of welfare had conceived of the poor as playing an important role in the securing of divine grace and salvation, Vives deemed welfare provision as a secular problem for the state authorities who should regulate and implement it efficiently. Responsibility for poor relief thereby shifted from sacred to secular spheres and became a constitutive part of the political system.

If the medieval conception of alms giving expected its reciprocation in the form of divine grace, in the early modern period, the gain associated with charity was made dependent on its worldly success. These pedagogic benefits would reveal themselves over the long term. What rapidly became obvious, however, was the financial burden of welfare provision on local communities. A badly designed system of alms giving was deemed a completely wasted investment. On the one hand, we thereby have the shift from a purely idealized demand for the poor's inclusion in society to institutionally based mechanisms of inclusion in which the zone of social exclusion is paradoxically more clearly defined. Henceforth, it was precisely those individuals among the poor who did not want to reciprocate the benefits they received from welfare provision who were to be made ready and able to work via a stay in a house of correction.

Moreover, with the transfer of welfare provision into the domain of secular politics, the boundaries of political community became increasingly significant for its administration. If the Strasbourg preacher Kaysersberg condemned the 'indigenous principle' (the idea that natives of a region stood at the top of a hierarchy of individuals entitled to receive aid), Vives by contrast emphasized it strongly. In his view, local authorities (*Kommune*) were responsible for the poor living in their areas. There thereby developed, in Vives' thinking, an institutional hierarchy in terms of the poor's inclusion in systems of welfare provision, which not only separated the 'deserving' from the 'undeserving' poor but also locals from outsiders. The 'deceitful' foreign vagrant became the deviant counterpart of the native, local 'ashamed' poor person. The provision of social security and welfare benefits for the 'deserving' poor therefore simultaneously entailed state repression, marginalization and exclusion of many other individuals in need. These ideas of Vives were outlined so extensively in order to demonstrate that certain welfare concepts favoured by Protestants were also esteemed in Catholic circles.

A common feature of welfare reforms around 1500 was that their authors no longer perceived their basis as lying in the act of alms giving as a ritualized means of gaining salvation, but rather in the imperative of acting in a purposeful and rational manner as well as a moral one by investigating the impact of welfare provision and help.[34] The idea that charity is a Christian duty did not disappear but it was purposefully defined, as henceforth not every form of support was considered legitimate charity before its tangible benefits were first examined.

Intellectual Changes in Welfare Concepts: the Economizaton of the Concept of the Commonweal and Welfare in the Eighteenth Century

At the beginning of the eighteenth century another important transformation process can be discerned in administrative documents concerning public welfare. The sixteenth century's welfare concepts still placed the individual at the centre of their aims concerning the 'economy of love'. For example, Vives' ideas focused on inculcating the poor with virtue in order to create a harmonious community. By contrast, the eighteenth century's conception of the commonweal was more strongly influenced by considerations of power politics. If the work to be performed by the poor had primarily been seen in previous centuries as a means of education, which possessed the positive side effect of helping local authorities' finances and needs, in the eighteenth century, it was explicitly designed to strengthen the state's economy and augment its power.

The question of economic utility became dominant in discussions of welfare relating to the 'deserving' and 'undeserving' poor in the late eighteenth century, denoting a clear difference from earlier thought. For example, the governments of the electorates of Mainz and Trier were of the opinion that the quantities of yarns spun in workhouses reflected the inmates' inner attitudes towards the state.[35] In this perspective, only those prepared to demonstrate a willingness to serve the state were counted as truly needy or deserving.

The abolition of poverty now began to be seen as an attainable aim of state policy. Beggars were correspondingly seen as symptoms of bad government. For the publishing jurist and statesman Justus Möser (1720–1794) every poor person on the street was an expression of state failure.[36] This idea's profound difference from the fourteenth century portrayal of 'good government' in Siena is evident.

Anti-utopian ideas gained increasing traction as the dark side of a rational, economically orientated welfare state became apparent in many European societies. In the early eighteenth century, for example, Jonathan Swift heavily criticized contemporary welfare concepts for their justification and legal legitimation of state intrusion into the spheres of the family and education, and for their primarily financial motivation. His 1729 essay, 'A Modest Proposal', satirically suggested that poor Irish babies should be sold as food to their wealthier compatriots in order to ensure that they would be 'beneficial to the public' rather than a 'burden'.[37]

In so doing, Swift drew attention to the inhumanity of concepts which had emerged under the labels of humanity and welfare. His satire also evokes the asymmetries of power between poor families and their rulers, with Swift speaking from the perspective of the rich, and satirically exaggerating the dependency of their well-being on the exploitation of poor children. In so doing, he broke with established literary conventions, particularly by advocating the implementation of exaggeratedly inhumane policies. His satire therefore represented a subversive resignification of what, in his view, represented inhumane attitudes concerning charity and welfare.

Political elites increasingly considered the integration of the poor into the functions of the economy as no longer a mere opportunity, but rather an incumbent duty to ensure their service of the state. Members of the poor who did not share this concern were characterized as deviant. In the electorate of Mainz, the archbishop named beggars capable of work as 'saboteurs of their own happiness' and individuals whose behaviours would ultimately be detrimental to the state.[38] In this respect, the 'pursuit of happiness' not only represented a core element of personal freedom, but also included the obligation on the part of government to create the preconditions for individuals to achieve this ideal.

With the criminalization of begging as well as the establishment of an interpretation of poverty as an individual problem of motivation, the eighteenth century paved the way for the ideas of the nineteenth and twentieth centuries, which conceived of poverty and begging as pathological problems to be combated by economic policy. The political discourses of the eighteenth century indeed particularly judged mendicant (begging) monks much more negatively than had previously been the case. Although these individuals lived according to religious and moral principles, they were now seen as damaging to the state. In contemporary encyclopaedias, it was indicated that monks did not earn enough with their penitential works to pay for their own clothes' cords, the nail for a farmer's plough or the maintenance of an army. These documents emphasized that the security and welfare of the state rested precisely on their subjects' work and labour.[39] The instrumentalization of welfare for the state's purposes was clearly expressed here.

It is extremely important to emphasize at this point that the intellectual developments outlined over previous pages were not uniformly turned into reality on the ground across the Holy Roman Empire's Catholic territories. For example, in many Catholic discourses on poor relief, the position continued to be maintained that the regulation of alms giving should only be done by looking at its recipients, as emphasized by Domingo de Soto.[40] An internal Church dispute nevertheless developed concerning whether giving in the case of doubt was ethically commanded or forbidden. Within the Roman Catholic Church, various answers were given to this question.

In many of the Empire's Catholic territories, both positions are discernible, reflecting a peculiar mixing of institutional welfare practices during the early modern period. This chapter accordingly argues that it is in precisely this fusion of approaches that a special kind of 'Catholic welfare culture' can be identified; a phenomenon which was itself characterized by a range of regional differences and nuances.

Welfare Legislation and Practices in the Catholic Territorial State: the Electorates of Trier and Mainz

How did this tension shape welfare cultures in the Empire's ecclesiastical electorates, and what influence did it have on efforts at including and excluding different groups among the poor? In the electorates of Trier and Mainz, the governmental authorities attempted to construct centralized systems of welfare provision. As early as 1533, following the examples of Nuremberg, Strasburg and Luxemburg, the relevant officials in Trier demanded that the needy be divided into categories of the 'deserving' and 'undeserving' and that the former be identified.[41] The electorate of Trier's Poor Order was indeed exceptional in that it was released at a very early stage in comparison to similar legislation in other Catholic states.[42] Most centrally established poor boxes in Protestant territories followed the Lutheran model embodied by the Leisnig Poor Order of 1523, whereas Catholic states generally orientated their welfare practices around the theories of Juan Luis Vives and the 'Ypres Model'.[43]

A survey of varying states' legislation concerning the poor clearly shows that the widespread assumption that begging was generally banned in Protestant municipalities, but continued to be permitted in Catholic ones, is inaccurate. Rather, states loyal to both confessions produced comparable legal codes. This is clearly revealed by the passing of repressive legislation against beggars and vagrants in Catholic territories. In the electorates of Mainz and Trier, this new perspective on the poor could be articulated in established semantics. The archbishop demanded the 'extermination' of foreign, 'deceitful' beggars, vagabonds and 'gypsies' (that is to say, those capable of work). At the electorates' borders metal sheets were posted, providing visual portrayals of the relevant punishments for disobeying these laws.[44]

The three most important welfare institutions for the poor in Trier were the city's alms office, which the Church had introduced as a central 'poor box' for the needy, St Jacob's Hospital and St Simeon's Hospital. For a long time, however, the alms office lacked sufficient resources (as were commonly provided in Protestant states) to really make a major difference. This situation only improved in the 1590s due to generous private donations. These monies stemmed from the wills of several influential Trier citizens who had been found guilty of witchcraft and executed.[45]

An important point with regards to the culture of Catholic poor relief was that monastic institutions often opposed the development of a centralized municipal system of welfare provision.[46] The Monastery of St Mathias is important to name in this context (the only apostle's burial site north of the Alps other than Santiago de Compostella), in addition to the even wealthier and more significant Monastery of St Maximin, which occasionally attempted to establish its independence within the Empire from the electorate of Trier. These monastic institutions did not in any respect follow Vives' welfare theories, and rather continued to orientate their charitable activities around Thomist concepts of *caritas*, the principles which Domingo de Soto had defended against Vives. According to these monks, beggars in need should immediately be given alms at the monastery's door without further investigation or regulation. If we examine the amounts of money given to charity in Trier during this period, we see that monastic giving considerably exceeded that from the city's alms office. Contemporary estimates in 1765 put the monasteries' charitable donations at around 2000 gulden.[47] By contrast, the average annual charitable expenditures of the city's central alms office merely totalled 250 gulden.[48]

The fact that wealthy monasteries were of great significance for the welfare provision of their immediately surrounding areas is further underlined by evidence from the electorate of Mainz's archives. Here, the authorities first attempted to create a central bank or box for poor relief in the early eighteenth century. Research on the Eberbach monastery near Mainz (made famous by the filming of *The Name of the Rose*) reveals that a majority of the poor from all surrounding villages visited the monastery on a daily basis.

From the perspective of the poor, monasteries had a secure place in the economy of welfare relief. Sources relating to the electorate of Mainz imply that it was especially families with a large number of children who availed themselves of these charitable donations, not only by sending their offspring to monasteries for their daily meals, but also by compelling them to collect wood on the way; 208 out of 533 recorded members of the poor from the Eltville office took their daily meals at a monastery.[49] The Abbess Dietz of the Gottesthal nunnery complained at the end of the eighteenth century that over 500 members of the poor visited her institution daily. Even if this number is potentially exaggerated, it must be presumed that the nunnery represented an important point of call for alms recipients from the surrounding villages.

If Gottesthal represented a small monastic institution, Eberbach was in a different league. This was reflected in the welfare provision it could offer. For example, a budgetary statement of 1566 reveals that within the abbey alone around 11,500 kg of rye flour (1,764 bushels) had been gathered to bake into bread, partly to distribute to the poor at the monastery's door.[50] As late as 1788, the secular Eltville authorities estimated that the monastery's annual charitable expenditure at 1,500 gulden and over 6,000 bushels of corn.[51] This represents over a third of the total value of alms payments made in the area that year.

The secular authorities regarded monastic institutions as attracting undeserving beggars and the so-called 'midwives of laziness', as the jurist Heinrich Gottlob von Justi termed them.[52] The rulers of the electorate of Mainz accordingly attempted to suppress monasteries' charitable giving. Although a complete secularization of the monasteries as implemented by Joseph II was not attempted within the electorate of Mainz, these governmental measures nevertheless exerted an enormous pressure on monastic institutions. Various measures implemented under the elector Emmerich Joseph (1763–1774) led to conflict between the archbishopric's chapter and the territory's secular government.[53] In 1770, the tax collector (*Amtskellner*) of Eltville sent a letter to the Abbot of Eberbach as well as the abbesses of the convents of Gottesthal and Tiefenthal, in which he demanded them to cease the practice of giving alms to the poor at their institutions' doors and instead to hand over the relevant monies to a central state-run poor box.[54]

The monasteries and nunneries decisively rejected this demand. The priors of the Dominicans, Augustinians and Carmelites emphasized that they would only support this rule if no beggars would henceforth be allowed to approach their doors. Doing so, the purpose of the rule became the precondition of their agreement, as an official himself observed.[55] Comparable confrontations had already taken place fifty years earlier in the electorate of Trier. The reactions of monastic institutions were similar to those described in the electorate of Mainz. Mendicant monks' freedoms were also restricted in these territories during the eighteenth century.[56]

The private donation of alms was completely forbidden in the electorates of Trier and Mainz during the eighteenth century. Breaking this law did not merely expose an individual to secular judicial punishments, but was also interpreted as a sin by the territories' archbishops.[57] On the ground, however, these regulations were frequently flouted. Various government decrees of 1721 contained the complaint that alms giving on the street was continuing.[58]

Conclusion

A particular type of Catholic welfare provision in the early modern empire can therefore be identified. The maintenance of traditional forms of *caritas* continued to shape the practice of welfare, rendering the construction of a centralized system of provision all but impossible. This did not, however, reflect a different, 'Catholic' view of poverty or the appropriate functions of state welfare. On the contrary, in Catholic as in Protestant states, governments attempted to assume control of the administration and provision of welfare and poor relief. They harshly disciplined institutions which opposed this aim. The governments of Catholic states were less successful than their Protestant counterparts in doing this due to the special legal statuses of various ecclesiastical institutions within their territories. Here, we are primarily dealing with the legal and economic independence of these institutions, rather than a different theological understanding of *caritas* (although this did exist). When discussing the prince bishoprics of the Holy Roman Empire, one cannot accordingly speak of a single Catholic Church's welfare system, but rather ones characterized by complexity and differentiation. Study of administrative reports does not substantiate the thesis that Catholic states' welfare provision was hereby rendered less efficient. It is indeed evident that poor people living near great monastic institutions such as Eberbach received more alms than their equivalents in Protestant territories received from central, government-controlled poor boxes.

From today's perspective, it seems less relevant to investigate whether a centralized or decentralized system of welfare provision proved more effective than the shifts in cultural attitudes towards the poor during the period covered by this chapter. It is indeed discernible in the present that an economization of welfare and social aid is increasingly shaping European governments' policies in this field, with early modern concepts concerning poverty also returning. Leading politicians are again talking about 'state-damaging parasites' and conversations are taking place as to whether it would be advantageous to replace a welfare model based on the reciprocal concepts of 'support and demand' with one of 'help and deterrence'. In Germany, the so-called 'heredity' of idleness is increasingly understood as reflecting an individual, rather than a societal, failure.

In a similar fashion, the early modern period witnessed the transformation of voluntary schemes addressing poverty into ones underpinned by compulsion, which frequently served the state's interests rather than those of the poor themselves. The exchange between an 'economy of love' and the state-favoured 'love of economy' often meant designing policies to reconcile the individual's happiness with the state's welfare, rather than setting the individual's freedoms centre stage. In this manner, the withdrawal of welfare support as well as its development could take on despotic traits. That this was irreconcilable with Christian concepts and natural law was well understood in the eighteenth century. A certain pluralism of welfare institutions, as we have observed in the prince bishoprics of Trier and Mainz, nevertheless ensured realities on the ground were more complex. The final episcopal ruler of Mainz, the Archbishop Karl Theodor von Dalberg, indeed expressed criticism of the workhouse concept. He demanded that in the process of compelling the poor to perform hard labour, care must be taken to ensure that their human dignity is not also taken from them.[59]

Notes

This chapter has been translated by Thomas Brodie.

1. For an overview of the historiography, see Th. Strohm and M. Klein (eds). 2004. *Die Entstehung einer sozialen Ordnung,*. Heidelberg: Winter, vol.1; W. von Hippel, 1995. *Armut, Unterschichten, Randgruppen in der frühen Neuzeit.* Munich: Oldenbourg; for review of research and work in this field published between 1993 and 1995 see: K. Härter. 1999. 'Soziale Disziplinierung durch Strafe? Intentionen frühneuzeitlicher Policeyordnungen und staatliche Sanktionspraxis', *Zeitschrift für historische Forschung* 26:365–79.

2. R. Jütte. 1981. 'Poor Relief and Social Discipline in Sixteenth Century Europe'. *European Studies Review* 11:25–52; see also W. Schulze. 1987. 'Gerhard Oestreichs Begriff "Sozialdisziplinierung in der Frühen Neuzeit"', *Zeitschrift für Historische Forschung* 14:265–302. This perspective was also simultaneously criticized: see M. Dinges. 1991. 'Frühneuzeitliche Armenfürsorge als Sozialdisziplinierung? Probleme mit einem Konzept'. *Geschichte und Gesellschaft* 17:5–29. For the debate regarding social disciplining see R. Jütte. 1991. 'Disziplin zu predigen ist eine Sache, sich ihr zu unterwerfen eine andere (Cervantes) – Prolegomena zu einer Sozialgeschichte der Armenfürsorge diesseits und jenseits des Fortschritts' *Geschichte und Gesellschaft* 17:92–101; Härter, 'Disziplinierung durch Strafe'; J. Richter. 2001. *Frühneuzeitliche Armenfürsorge als Disziplinierung – Zur sozialpädagogischen Bedeutung eines Perspektivenwechsels.* Frankfurt/Main: Lang; Ch. Sachße and F. Tennstedt (eds). 1986. *Soziale Sicherheit und soziale Disziplinierung. Beiträge zu einer historischen Theorie der Sozialpolitik.* Frankfurt/Main: Suhrkamp; U. Knefelkamp. 2001. 'Sozialdisziplinierung oder Armenfürsorge? Untersuchung normativer Quellen in Bamberg und Nürnberg vom 14. bis zum 17. Jahrhundert', in H. Bräuer and E. Schlenkrich (eds), *Die Stadt als Kommunikationsraum – Beiträge zur Stadtgeschichte vom Mittelalter bis ins 20. Jahrhundert, Festschrift für Karl Czok zum 75. Geburtstag.* Leipzig: Leipziger Universitätsverlag, pp. 515–33.

3. R. Jütte. 1994. *Poverty and Deviance in Early Modern Europe.* Cambridge: Cambridge University Press; W. Fischer. 1982. *Armut in der Geschichte. Erscheinungsformen und Lösungsversuche der 'Sozialen Frage' in Europa seit dem Mittelalter.* Göttingen: Vandenhoeck & Ruprecht; Th. Riis (ed.). 1981–1990. *Aspects of Poverty in Early Modern Europe*, 3 vols. Stuttgart: Klett-Cotta.

4. B. Geremek. 1991. *Geschichte der Armut. Elend und Barmherzigkeit in Europa.* Munich: Beck, p. 260.

5. See Th. Sokoll. 2000. 'Negotiating a Living: Essex Pauper Letters from London, 1800–1834'. *International Review of Social History* 45:19–46; W. Newman-Brown. 1984. 'The Receipt of Poor Relief and Family Situation: Aldenham, Hertfordshire 1630–90', in R.M. Smith (ed.), *Land, Kinship and Life-Cycle.* Cambridge: Cambridge University Press, pp. 405–422; Boulton, J. 2000. '"It Is Extreme Necessity That Makes Me Do This": Some "Survival Strategies" of Pauper Households in London's West End During the Early Eighteenth Century', *International Review of Social History* 45:47–69; L. Fontaine and J. Schlumbohm. 2000. *Household Strategies for Survival, 1600–2000: Fission, Faction, and Cooperation.* Cambridge: Cambridge University Press; R. Dyson. 2004. 'Who were the poor of Oxford in the late eighteenth and early nineteenth

centuries?', in A. Gestrich, S.A. King and L. Raphael (eds), *Being Poor in Modern Europe. Historical Perspectives 1800–1940.* Bern: Lang, pp. 43–68; S. King. 2000. *Poverty and Welfare in England, 1700–1850.* Manchester: Manchester University Press.

6. See here a selection of extensive and important recent studies on everyday life in the early modern period: G. Ammerer. 2003. *Heimat Straße. Vaganten im Österreich des Ancien Régime.* Vienna: Verlag für Geschichte und Politik; F. Hatje. 2002a. *'Gott zu Ehren, der Armut zum Besten'. Das Hospital zum Heiligen Geist und Marien-Magdalenen-Kloster in der Geschichte Hamburgs vom Mittelalter bis in die Gegenwart.* Hamburg: Convent; H. Bräuer. 1996. *'… und hat seithero gebetlet'. Bettler und Bettelwesen in Wien und Niederösterreich während der Zeit Kaiser Leopolds I.* Cologne: Böhlau; id. 1997. *Der Leipziger Rat und die Bettler. Quellen und Analysen zu Bettlern und Bettelwesen in der Messestadt bis ins 18. Jahrhundert.* Leipzig: Leipziger Universitätsverlag; M. Rheinheimer. 2000. *Arme, Bettler und Vaganten. Überleben in der Not 1450–1850.* Frankfurt/Main: Fischer Taschenbuch; E. Schubert. 2001. 'Erscheinungsformen der Armut in der spät-mittelalterlichen deutschen Stadt', in H. Bräuer and E. Schlenkrich (eds), *Die Stadt als Kommunikationsraum.* Leipzig: Leipziger Universitätsverlag, pp. 659–97. Using a range of sources, especially 'ego documents', supplications, visitation and court files and wills, scholars have begun to investigate the subjective dimensions of poverty. For petitions and supplications see H. Bräuer,. 2001. 'Persönliche Bittschriften als sozial- und mentalitätsgeschichtliche Quellen. Beobachtungen aus frühneuzeitlichen Städten Obersachsens', in G. Ammerer, C. Rohr and A.S. Weiss (eds), *Tradition und Wandel. Beiträge zur Kirchen-, Gesellschafts- und Kulturgeschichte.* Festschrift für Heinz Dopsch. Munich: Oldenbourg, pp. 294–304; M. Scheutz. 2008. 'Supplikationen an den ersamen Rat um Aufnahme ins Bürgerspital. Inklusions- und Exklusionsprozesse am Beispiel der Spitäler von Zwettl und Scheibbs', in S. Schmidt (ed.), *Arme und ihre Lebensperspektiven in der Frühen Neuzeit.* Frankfurt/Main: Lang, pp. 157–206. For the poor's wills, see K. Simon-Muscheid. 2003. 'Ein rebmesser hat sine frowe versetzt für 1 ß brotte. Armut in den oberrheinischen Städten des 15. und 16. Jahrhunderts', in H. Bräuer (ed.). 2003. *Arme – ohne Chance? Kommunale Armut und Armutsbekämpfung vom Spätmittelalter bis zur Gegenwart.* Leipzig: Leipziger Universitätsverlag, pp. 39–70. For the visitations of beggars, see M. Scheutz. 2003. *Ausgesperrt und gejagt, geduldet und versteckt. Bettlervisitationen im Niederösterreich des 18. Jahrhunderts.* St Pölten: Niederösterreichisches Institut für Landeskunde. For analysis of interrogation protocols see Ammerer, *Straße.* By contrast, the extraction of biographic details from directories of the poor and vagrants has only attracted in-depth study over the past decade. See S. Pichlkastner, *Das Wiener Stadtzeichnerbuch 1678–1685. Ein Bettlerverzeichnis aus einer frühneuzeitlichen Stadt.* Vienna (unpublished manuscript).

7. H. Bräuer. 2008. *Zur Mentalität armer Leute in Obersachsen, 1500 bis 1800.* Leipzig: Leipziger Universitätsverlag On this point see also M. Rheinheimer. 1998. Jakob Gülich. '"Trotzigkeit" und "ungebührliches Betragen" eines ländlichen Armen um 1850', in M. Rheinheimer (ed.), *Subjektive Welten. Wahrnehmung und Identität in der Neuzeit.* Neumünster: Wachholtz, pp. 223–52; F. Hatje. 2006. '"Dieser Stadt beste Maur vndt Wälle". Frühneuzeitliche Armenfürsorge und Sozialbeziehungen in der Stadtrepublik', in S. Schmidt and J. Aspelmeier (eds), *Norm und Praxis der Armenfürsorge in Spätmittelalter und früher Neuzeit.* Stuttgart: Steiner, pp. 203–17.

8. For example, see T. Wales. 1984. 'Poverty, Poor Relief and the Life-Cycle: Some Evidence from Seventeenth-Century Norfolk', in R.M. Smith (ed.), *Land, Kinship*

and Life-Cycle. Cambridge: Cambridge University Press, pp. 351–404; T. Hitchcock, P. Sharpe and P. King (eds). 1997. *Chronicling Poverty. The Voices and Strategies of the English Poor, 1640–1840*. New York: Palgrave Macmillan; Th. Sokoll (ed.). 2001. *Essex Pauper Letters*. Oxford: Oxford University Press; N. Schindler. 1994. 'Die Ramingsteiner Bettlerhochzeit 1688/89. Armut, Sexualität und Hexenpolitik in einem Salzburger Bergwerk des 17. Jahrhunderts', *Historische Anthropologie* 2:165–92. Bräuer, *Arme – ohne Chance?*; F. Hatje. 2002b. '"Wenn die bösen Tage kommen". Einige Bemerkungen zu Alter, Armut und ,'Selbstbehauptung' in der städtischen Gesellschaft des "langen" 18. Jahrhunderts', in A. Conrad et al. (eds), *Zeitenwenden. Herrschaft, Selbstbehauptung und Integration zwischen Reformation und Liberalismus*. Münster: LIT, pp. 481–505; Ulbricht, O. 1994. 'Die Welt eines Bettlers um 1775. Johann Gottfried Kästner'. *Historische Anthropologie* 2:371–98. For the poor in institutional care see: F. Bretschneider. 2008. *Gefangene Gesellschaft. Eine Geschichte der Einsperrung in Sachsen im 18. und 19. Jahrhundert*. Konstanz: UVK-Verlags-Gesellschaft; J. Gründler. 2013. *Armut und Wahnsinn. 'Arme Irre' und ihre Familien im Spannungsfeld von Psychiatrie und Armenfürsorge in Glasgow, 1875–1921*. Munich: Oldenbourg.

9. R. Jütte. 1984. *Obrigkeitliche Armenfürsorge in deutschen Reichsstädten der frühen Neuzeit. Städtisches Armenwesen in Frankfurt am Main und Köln*. Cologne: Böhlau.

10. For city welfare provision see: P. Friess. 2003. 'Poor Relief and Health Care Provision in South-German Catholic Cities during the Sixteenth Century', in Th. M. Safley (ed.), *The Reformation of Charity. The Secular and the Religious in Early Modern Poor Relief*. Boston/Leiden: Brill Academic Publishers, pp. 76–91; S. Kröger. 2006. *Armenfürsorge und Wohlfahrtspflege im frühneuzeitlichen Regensburg*. Regensburg: Pustet; A. Wagner. 2011. *'Gleicherweiß als wasser das feuer, also verlösche almuse die sünd'. Frühneuzeitliche Fürsorge- und Bettelgesetzgebung der geistlichen Kurfürstentümer Köln und Trier*. Berlin: Duncker & Humblot. Regarding confraternities and foundations, see: B. Schneider. 1989. *Bruderschaften im Trierer Land: ihre Geschichte und ihr Gottesdienst zwischen Tridentinum und Säkularisation*. Trier: Paulinus; A. Bräcker. 2011. 'Die Elendenbruderschaft Koblenz in der Frühen Neuzeit'. *Archiv für mittelrheinische Kirchengeschichte* 63:157–80; M. Escher-Apsner. 2003. 'Bauförderung, Seelsorge und Armenfürsorge. Die Münstermaifelder Bruderschaft St. Trinitas/St. Michael'. *Archiv für mittelrheinische Kirchengeschichte* 55:147–76; id 2004. *Stadt und Stift. Studien zur Geschichte Münstermaifelds im hohen und späteren Mittelalter*. Trier: Kliomedia. The Münster City Archive has been prominent in publishing material concerning charitable foundations. See: R. Klötzer. 1997. *Kleiden, Speisen, Beherbergen. Armenfürsorge und soziale Stiftungen in Münster im 16. Jahrhundert (1535–1588)*. Münster: Aschendorff; Th. Küster. 1995. *Alte Armut und neues Bürgertum. Öffentliche und private Fürsorge in Münster von der Ära Fürstenberg bis zum Ersten Weltkrieg (1756–1914)*. Münster: Aschendorff; F.-J. Jakobi et al. (ed.). 1996. *Stiftungen und Armenfürsorge in Münster vor 1800*. Münster: Aschendorff. Id. 2002. *Strukturwandel der Armenfürsorge und der Stiftungswirklichkeit in Münster im Laufe der Jahrhunderte*. Münster: Aschendorff; S. Rabeler. 2005. 'Karitatives Handeln, Stiftungswirklichkeiten und Personenbeziehungen – Überlegungen zu einer Sozialgeschichte der Armenfürsorge im mittelalterlichen Lübeck'. *Zeitschrift des Vereins für Lübeckische Geschichte und Altertumskunde* 85:11–24; id. 2007. 'Zur Sozialgeschichte der Armenfürsorge in den Städten des südlichen Ostseeraums (13.–16. Jahrhundert). Ein Forschungsprojekt'. *Hansische Geschichtsblätter* 125:187–98.

11. H. Ludyga. 2010. *Obrigkeitliche Armenfürsorge im deutschen Reich vom Beginn der Frühen Neuzeit bis zum Ende des Dreißigjährigen Krieges (1495–1648)*. Berlin: Duncker & Humblot, p. 365; T. Lorentzen. 2008. *Johannes Bugenhagen als Reformator der öffentlichen Fürsorge*. Tübingen: Mohr Siebeck, p. 124.

12. O.H. Hufton. 1974. *The Poor of Eighteenth-Century France, 1750–1789*. Oxford: Clarendon Press, p. 195; id. 1983. 'Social Conflict and the Grain Supply in 18th century France', *Journal of Interdisciplinary History* 14:303–331. See also S. Kahl. 2005. 'The Religious Roots of Modern Poverty Policy: Catholic, Lutheran, and Reformed Protestant Traditions Compared'. *European Journal of Sociology* 1:91–126, who presumes the existence of fundamental confessional differences, and claims there was a uniform tolerance of begging in prince bishoprics, in contrast to strict policing in Protestant states.

13. K. Dussel, 1995. 'Katholisches Ethos statt Sozialdisziplinierung? Die Armenpolitik des Hochstifts Speyer im 18. Jahrhundert'. *Zeitschrift für die Geschichte des Oberrheins* 143:221–44.

14. Strohm and Klein, *Entstehung einer sozialen Ordnung*, vol. 1, pp. 180–210; vol. 2, pp. 302–27.

15. M. Collinet (ed.). 2014. *Caritas – Barmherzigkeit – Diakonie. Studien zu Begriffen und Konzepten des Helfens in der Geschichte des Christentums vom Neuen Testament bis ins späte 20. Jahrhundert*. Berlin: LIT; Geremek, *Geschichte der Armut*, p. 87.

16. A. Keck. 2010. *Das philosophische Motiv der Fürsorge im Wandel. Vom Almosen bei Thomas von Aquin zu Juan Luis Vives' De subventione pauperum*. Würzburg: Echter.

17. For the scholastic theory of alms giving, see T. von Aquin. 1959. *Summa Theologica, Bd. 17: Die Liebe* (1. Teil): II–II. Frage 23–33. Graz: Styria. See question 32.

18. Keck, *Motiv der Fürsorge*, p. 63.

19. von Aquin, *Summa*, p. 272; Keck, *Motiv der Fürsorge*, p. 76; K. Dort. 2014. '"Caritas" und Fürsorge in mittelalterlichen Quellen', in M. Collinet, (ed.). 2014. *Caritas – Barmherzigkeit – Diakonie. Studien zu Begriffen und Konzepten des Helfens in der Geschichte des Christentums vom Neuen Testament bis ins späte 20. Jahrhundert*. Berlin: LIT, p. 73.

20. Keck, *Motiv der Fürsorge*, p. 82.

21. F. Dorn. 2001 'Gerechtigkeit, Kommune und Frieden in Ambrogio Lorenzettis Fresken in der Sala della Pace des Palazzo Pubblico von Siena', in F. Dorn and J. Schröder (eds), *Festschrift für Gerd Kleinheyer zum 70. Geburtstag*. Heidelberg: Müller, pp. 127–77.

22. M. Pauly. 2007. *Peregrinorum, pauperum ac aliorum transeuntium receptaculum. Hospitäler zwischen Maas und Rhein im Mittelalter*. Stuttgart: Steiner.

23. Dort, 'Caritas', p. 72.

24. R. Voltmer. 2005. *Wie der Wächter auf dem Turm. Ein Prediger und seine Stadt. Johannes Geiler von Kaysersberg (1445–1510) und Straßburg*. Trier: Porta-Alba.

25. Ibid, p. 560.

26. S. Zeller. 2006. *Juan Luis Vives (1492–1540). (Wieder)Entdeckung eines Europäers, Humanisten und Sozialreformers jüdischer Herkunft im Schatten der spanischen Inquisition*. Freiburg/Breisgau: Lambertus.

27. For a bilingual edition (original Latin and English translation) see J.L. Vives. 2002. *De subventione pauperum sive de humanis necessitatibus libri II*, introd., critical ed., transl. and notes ed. by Constantinus Matheeussen and Charles Fantazzi (eds). Leiden, Boston: Brill. See another English translation by P. Spicker. 2010. *The Origins of Modern Welfare: Juan Luis Vives, De Subventione Pauperum, and City of Ypres, Forma Subventionis Pauperum*. Oxford: Lang.

28. Keck, *Motiv der Fürsorge*, p. 153.
29. For the English translation see Vives, *De subventione*, p. 23; here also the Latin original (Vives, *De subventione*, p. 22): 'non enim dandum cuique est quod expetit, sed quod ei expedit'; for a German translation of 1533 see J.L. Vives. 1533. *Von Almusen geben Zwey buechlin Ludovici Vivis. Auff diß new xxxiij. Jar durch D. Casparn Hedion verteütscht und eim Ersamen Radt unnd frummer burgerschafft zu Straßburg zugeschriben. Allen Policeyen nutzlich zu lesen.* [Straßburg]: 'Dann nit einem yeden zugeben ist / das er erfordert / sonder das jm nützet'. See also Keck, *Motiv der Fürsorge*, p. 151.
30. Keck *Motiv der Fürsorge*, p. 165.
31. Vives, *De subventione*, p. 85.
32. S. Brant. 2004. *Das Narrenschiff.* Wiesbaden: Marix [Reprint Basel 1494]; B. Althammer and C. Gerstenmayer (eds). 2013. *Bettler und Vaganten in der Neuzeit (1500–1933). Eine kommentierte Quellenedition.* Essen: Klartext, pp. 30–41.
33. Ph. Helas. 2008. 'Repräsentation der Wohltätigkeit. Der Akt des Gebens und Nehmens im Bild zwischen dem 13.–20. Jahrhundert', in L. Raphael and H. Uerlings (eds), *Zwischen Ausschluss und Solidarität. Modi der Inklusion/Exklusion von Fremden und Armen in Europa seit der Spätantike.* Frankfurt/Main, pp. 37–64.
34. M. Weber. 1980. *Wirtschaft und Gesellschaft.* Tübingen: Mohr Siebeck, p. 31.
35. U. Eisenbach. 1994. *Zuchthäuser, Armenanstalten und Waisenhäuser in Nassau. Fürsorgewesen und Arbeitserziehung vom 17. bis zum Beginn des 19. Jahrhunderts.* Wiesbaden: Historische Kommission für Nassau, p. 39.
36. J. Möser. 1995. 'Etwas zur Verbesserung der Armenanstalten (1767)', in M. Rudersdorf, *'Das Glück der Bettler' – Justus Möser und die Welt der Armen. Mentalität und soziale Frage im Fürstbistum Osnabrück zwischen Aufklärung und Säkularisation.* Münster: Aschendorff, p. 336.
37. J. Swift. 1972. 'Bescheidener Vorschlag, wie man verhüten kann, dass die Kinder armer Leute in Irland ihren Eltern oder dem Lande zur Last fallen, und wie sie der Allgemeinheit nutzbar gemacht werden können (1729)', in G. Graustein (ed.), *Ausgewählte Werke in drei Bänden, 2: Politische Schriften.* Frankfurt/Main: Insel, p. 513f; (trans. J. Swift, 1729. *A Modest Proposal for preventing the Children of Poor People from Being a Burthen to their Parents, or The Country and for Making them Beneficial to the Publick.* Dublin).
38. Hessisches Hauptstaatsarchiv Wiesbaden, Abt. 108, Nr. 2665 (Poor Law Act of Elector Friedrich Karl Joseph von Erthal, dated 2 January 1787).
39. 'Kloster'. 1787. In J.G. Krünitz (ed.), *Oekonomische Encyklopädie, oder allgemeines System der Staats-, Stadt-, Haus, u. Landwirtschaft in alphabetischer Ordnung.* Berlin: Joachim Pauli, vol. 40, p. 728 (retrieved 5 November 2009 from http://www.kruenitz1.uni-trier.de/).
40. D. de Soto. 2004. 'Über die Regelung der Armenhilfe (1545). Mit einer Einleitung von Larissa C. Seelbach', in Strohm and Klein, *Entstehung einer sozialen Ordnung*, vol. 1, pp. 340–99.
41. Blattau, I. 1844–1849. *Statuta synodalia, ordinationes et mandata archidiocesis Treverensis*, vols 1–5. Trier: Lintz, vol. 2, pp. 81–86.
42. Wagner, *Gleicherweiß*, pp. 85–122.
43. U. Köpf (ed.). 2002. *Deutsche Geschichte in Quellen und Darstellung*, vol. 3, *Reformationszeit 1495–1555.* Stuttgart: Reclam, pp. 207–211; Strohm and Klein, *Entstehung einer sozialen Ordnung*, vol. 2, pp. 20–41.

44. H. Uerlings, N. Trauth and L. Clemens (eds). 2011. *Armut. Perspektiven in Kunst und Gesellschaft.* Katalog zur gleichnamigen Ausstellung, Stadtmuseum Simeonstift und Rheinisches Landesmuseum Trier, 10.04.2011–31.07.2011. Darmstadt: Primus. S. Schmidt. 2013. 'Zu Repräsentationen von Armut und sozialer Sicherheit sowie den institutionellen Fürsorgepraktiken im Kurfürstentum Trier', in Ch. Kampmann and U. Niggemann (eds), *Sicherheit in der Frühen Neuzeit. Norm – Praxis – Repräsentation.* Cologne: Böhlau, pp. 496–507.
45. M. Ackels. 1984. 'Das Trierer städtische Almosenamt im 16. und 17. Jahrhundert. Ein Beitrag zur Analyse sozialer Unterschichten'. *Kurtrierisches Jahrbuch* 24:75–103, here 79.
46. S. Schmidt. 2011b. 'Kloster-Karitas und staatliche Armenfürsorge in Kurmainz am Ende des Alten Reichs', in K. Krimm et al (eds), *Armut und Fürsorge in der frühen Neuzeit* (Oberrheinische Studien, 29). Ostfildern, pp. 223–35.
47. B. Resmini. 2002. 'Aufklärung und Säkularisation im Trierer Erzstift, vornehmlich bei den Klostergemeinschaften in der Eifel und in der Stadt Trier', in G. Mölich et al (eds), *Klosterkultur und Säkularisation im Rheinland.* Essen: Klartext, p. 87
48. Stadtarchiv Trier, Ta 2/1–6: Almosenei-Rechnungen 1591–1793.
49. S. Schmidt. 2004. 'Armenfürsorge in Stadt und Land. Maßnahmen gegen Armut und Bettelei in Mainz sowie im Rheingau im 17. und 18. Jahrhundert,' in H. Bräuer (ed.), *Arme – ohne Chance? Kommunale Armut und Armutsbekämpfung vom Spätmittelalter bis zur Gegenwart.* Leipzig: Leipziger Universitätsverlag, pp. 71–98.
50. G. Schnorrenberger. 1977. *Wirtschaftsverwaltung des Klosters Eberbach im Rheingau, 1423–1631.* Wiesbaden: Historische Kommission für Nassau, p. 79.
51. Hessisches Hauptstaatsarchiv Wiesbaden, Abt. 108, 2665 (Amtsschreiben from 12 February 1788).
52. J.H.G. von Justi. 1965. *Grundfeste zu der Macht und Glueckseligkeit der Staaten, oder ausfuehrliche Vorstellung der gesamten Policeywissenschaft 1.* Aalen: Scientia. [Reprint Koenigsberg/Leipzig 1760], p. 268.
53. K. Härter. 2005. *Policey und Strafjustiz in Kurmainz. Gesetzgebung, Normdurchsetzung und Sozialkontrolle im frühneuzeitlichen Territorialstaat.* Frankfurt/Main: Klostermann.
54. Hessisches Hauptstaatsarchiv Wiesbaden, Abt. 108, 2667.
55. Hessisches Hauptstaatsarchiv Wiesbaden, Abt. 101, 378.
56. Wagner, *Gleicherweiß*, pp. 207, 209–212
57. Poor Law Act of Elector Lothar Franz von Schönborn (dated 22 August 1710), Stadtarchiv Mainz, LVO.
58. See the Poor Law Acts (dated 20 and 21 August 1721), Stadtarchiv Mainz, LVO.
59. A. Freyh. 1978. *Karl Theodor von Dalberg. Ein Beitrag zum Verhältnis von politischer Theorie und Regierungspraxis in der Endphase des Aufgeklärten Absolutismus.* Frankfurt/Main: Lang, p. 129.

Works Cited

Ackels M. 1984. 'Das Trierer städtische Almosenamt im 16. und 17. Jahrhundert. Ein Beitrag zur Analyse sozialer Unterschichten'. *Kurtrierisches Jahrbuch* 24:75–103.

Althammer, B., and C. Gerstenmayer (eds). 2013. *Bettler und Vaganten in der Neuzeit (1500–1933). Eine kommentierte Quellenedition*. Essen: Klartext.

Ammerer, G. 2003. *Heimat Straße. Vaganten im Österreich des Ancien Régime*. Vienna: Verlag für Geschichte und Politik.

Aquin, T. v. 1959. *Summa Theologica, Bd. 17: Die Liebe* (1. Teil): II–II. Frage 23–33. Graz: Styria.

Blattau, I. 1844–1849. *Statuta synodalia, ordinationes et mandata archidiocesis Treverensis*, vols 1–5. Trier: Lintz.

Boulton, J. 2000. '"It Is Extreme Necessity That Makes Me Do This": Some "Survival Strategies" of Pauper Households in London's West End During the Early Eighteenth Century', *International Review of Social History* 45:47–69.

Bräcker, A. 2011. 'Die Elendenbruderschaft Koblenz in der Frühen Neuzeit', *Archiv für mittelrheinische Kirchengeschichte* 63:157–80.

Brant, S. 2004. *Das Narrenschiff*. Wiesbaden: Marix [Reprint Basel 1494].

Bräuer, H. 1996. '*… und hat seithero gebetlet'. Bettler und Bettelwesen in Wien und Niederösterreich während der Zeit Kaiser Leopolds I*. Cologne: Böhlau.

———. 1997. *Der Leipziger Rat und die Bettler. Quellen und Analysen zu Bettlern und Bettelwesen in der Messestadt bis ins 18. Jahrhundert*. Leipzig: Leipziger Universitätsverlag.

———. 2001. 'Persönliche Bittschriften als sozial- und mentalitätsgeschichtliche Quellen. Beobachtungen aus frühneuzeitlichen Städten Obersachsens', in G. Ammerer, C. Rohr and A.S. Weiss (eds), *Tradition und Wandel. Beiträge zur Kirchen-, Gesellschafts- und Kulturgeschichte. Festschrift für Heinz Dopsch*. Munich: Oldenbourg, pp. 294–304.

——— (ed.). 2003. *Arme – ohne Chance? Kommunale Armut und Armutsbekämpfung vom Spätmittelalter bis zur Gegenwart*. Leipzig: Leipziger Universitätsverlag.

———. 2008. *Zur Mentalität armer Leute in Obersachsen, 1500 bis 1800*. Leipzig: Leipziger Universitätsverlag.

Bretschneider, F. 2008. *Gefangene Gesellschaft. Eine Geschichte der Einsperrung in Sachsen im 18. und 19. Jahrhundert*. Konstanz: UVK-Verlags-Gesellschaft.

Bühren, R. v. 1998. *Die Werke der Barmherzigkeit in der Kunst des 12.–18. Jahrhunderts: zum Wandel eines Bildmotivs vor dem Hintergrund neuzeitlicher Rhetorikrezeption*. Hildesheim, Zürich, New York: Olms.

Collinet, M. (ed.). 2014. *Caritas – Barmherzigkeit – Diakonie. Studien zu Begriffen und Konzepten des Helfens in der Geschichte des Christentums vom Neuen Testament bis ins späte 20. Jahrhundert*. Berlin: LIT.

Dinges, M. 1991. 'Frühneuzeitliche Armenfürsorge als Sozialdisziplinierung? Probleme mit einem Konzept', *Geschichte und Gesellschaft* 17:5–29.

Dorn, F. 2001. 'Gerechtigkeit, Kommune und Frieden in Ambrogio Lorenzettis Fresken in der Sala della Pace des Palazzo Pubblico von Siena', in F. Dorn and J. Schröder (eds), *Festschrift für Gerd Kleinheyer zum 70. Geburtstag*. Heidelberg: Müller, pp. 127–177.

Dort, K. 2014. '"Caritas" und Fürsorge in mittelalterlichen Quellen', in Collinet, *Caritas* pp. 49–77.

Dussel, K. 1995. 'Katholisches Ethos statt Sozialdisziplinierung? Die Armenpolitik des Hochstifts Speyer im 18. Jahrhundert'. *Zeitschrift für die Geschichte des Oberrheins* 143: 221–44.

Dyson, R. 2004. 'Who were the poor of Oxford in the late eighteenth and early nineteenth centuries?', in A. Gestrich, S.A. King and L. Raphael (eds), *Being Poor in Modern Europe. Historical Perspectives 1800–1940*. Bern: Lang, pp. 43–68.

Eisenbach, U. 1994. *Zuchthäuser, Armenanstalten und Waisenhäuser in Nassau. Fürsorgewesen und Arbeitserziehung vom 17. bis zum Beginn des 19. Jahrhunderts*. Wiesbaden: Historische Kommission für Nassau.

Escher-Apsner, M. 2003. 'Bauförderung, Seelsorge und Armenfürsorge. Die Münstermaifelder Bruderschaft St. Trinitas/St. Michael'. *Archiv für mittelrheinische Kirchengeschichte* 55:147–176.

———. 2004. *Stadt und Stift. Studien zur Geschichte Münstermaifelds im hohen und späteren Mittelalter*. Trier: Kliomedia.

Fischer, W. 1982. *Armut in der Geschichte. Erscheinungsformen und Lösungsversuche der 'Sozialen Frage' in Europa seit dem Mittelalter*. Göttingen: Vandenhoeck & Ruprecht.

Fontaine, L., and J. Schlumbohm. 2000. *Household Strategies for Survival, 1600–2000: Fission, Faction, and Cooperation*. Cambridge: Cambridge University Press.

Freyh, A. 1978. *Karl Theodor von Dalberg. Ein Beitrag zum Verhältnis von politischer Theorie und Regierungspraxis in der Endphase des Aufgeklärten Absolutismus*. Frankfurt/Main: Lang.

Friess, P. 2003. 'Poor Relief and Health Care Provision in South-German Catholic Cities during the Sixteenth Century', in Th. M. Safley (ed.), *The Reformation of Charity. The Secular and the Religious in Early Modern Poor Relief*. Boston/Leiden: Brill Academic Publishers, pp. 76–91.

Geremek, B. 1991. *Geschichte der Armut. Elend und Barmherzigkeit in Europa*. Munich: Beck.

Gründler, J. 2013. *Armut und Wahnsinn. 'Arme Irre' und ihre Familien im Spannungsfeld von Psychiatrie und Armenfürsorge in Glasgow, 1875–1921*. Munich: Oldenbourg.

Härter, K. 1996. 'Bettler – Vaganten – Deviante. Ausgewählte Neuerscheinungen zu Armut, Randgruppen und Kriminalität im frühneuzeitlichen Europa', *Ius Commune* 23: 281–321.

———. 1999. 'Soziale Disziplinierung durch Strafe? Intentionen frühneuzeitlicher Policeyordnungen und staatliche Sanktionspraxis', *Zeitschrift für historische Forschung* 26, 365–79.

———. 2005. *Policey und Strafjustiz in Kurmainz. Gesetzgebung, Normdurchsetzung und Sozialkontrolle im frühneuzeitlichen Territorialstaat*. Frankfurt/Main: Klostermann.

Hatje, F. 2002a. '*Gott zu Ehren, der Armut zum Besten'. Das Hospital zum Heiligen Geist und Marien-Magdalenen-Kloster in der Geschichte Hamburgs vom Mittelalter bis in die Gegenwart.* Hamburg: Convent.

———. 2002b. '"Wenn die bösen Tage kommen". Einige Bemerkungen zu Alter, Armut und "Selbstbehauptung" in der städtischen Gesellschaft des „langen" 18. Jahrhunderts', in A. Conrad et al. (eds), *Zeitenwenden. Herrschaft, Selbstbehauptung und Integration zwischen Reformation und Liberalismus.* Münster: LIT, 481–505.

———. 2006. '"Dieser Stadt beste Maur vndt Wälle". Frühneuzeitliche Armenfürsorge und Sozialbeziehungen in der Stadtrepublik', in S. Schmidt and J. Aspelmeier (eds), *Norm und Praxis der Armenfürsorge in Spätmittelalter und früher Neuzeit.* Stuttgart: Steiner, pp. 203–17.

Helas, Ph. 2007. 'Darstellungen der Mantelspende des Heiligen Martin vom 12. bis zum 15. Jahrhundert als Indikator der Veränderung sozialer Praktiken'. *Archiv für Kulturgeschichte* 89(2):257–81.

———. 2008. 'Repräsentation der Wohltätigkeit. Der Akt des Gebens und Nehmens im Bild zwischen dem 13.–20. Jahrhundert', in L. Raphael and H. Uerlings (eds), *Zwischen Ausschluss und Solidarität. Modi der Inklusion/ Exklusion von Fremden und Armen in Europa seit der Spätantike.* Frankfurt/ Main: Lang, pp. 37–64.

Hippel, W. v. 1995. *Armut, Unterschichten, Randgruppen in der frühen Neuzeit.* Munich: Oldenbourg.

Hitchcock, T., P. Sharpe, and P. King (eds). 1997. *Chronicling Poverty. The Voices and Strategies of the English Poor, 1640–1840.* New York: Palgrave Macmillan.

Hufton, O.H. 1979. *The Poor of Eighteenth-Century France, 1750–1789.* Oxford: Clarendon Press.

———. 1983. 'Social Conflict and the Grain Supply in 18th century France', *Journal of Interdisciplinary History* 14:303–331.

Jakobi, F.-J. et al. (eds). 1996. *Stiftungen und Armenfürsorge in Münster vor 1800.* Münster: Aschendorff.

———(eds). 2002. *Strukturwandel der Armenfürsorge und der Stiftungswirklichkeit in Münster im Laufe der Jahrhunderte.* Münster: Aschendorff.

Justi, J.H.G. v. 1965. *Grundfeste zu der Macht und Glueckseligkeit der Staaten, oder ausfuehrliche Vorstellung der gesamten Policeywissenschaft 1.* Aalen: Scientia. [Reprint Koenigsberg/Leipzig 1760].

Jütte, R. 1981. 'Poor Relief and Social Discipline in Sixteenth Century Europe', *European Studies Review* 11:25–52.

———. 1984. *Obrigkeitliche Armenfürsorge in deutschen Reichsstädten der frühen Neuzeit. Städtisches Armenwesen in Frankfurt am Main und Köln.* Cologne: Böhlau.

———. 1991. 'Disziplin zu predigen ist eine Sache, sich ihr zu unterwerfen eine andere (Cervantes) – Prolegomena zu einer Sozialgeschichte der Armenfürsorge diesseits und jenseits des Fortschritts', *Geschichte und Gesellschaft* 17:92–101.

————. 1994. *Poverty and Deviance in Early Modern Europe*. Cambridge: Cambridge University Press.

Kahl, S. 2005. 'The Religious Roots of Modern Poverty Policy: Catholic, Lutheran, and Reformed Protestant Traditions Compared', *European Journal of Sociology* 1:91–126.

Keck, A. 2010. *Das philosophische Motiv der Fürsorge im Wandel. Vom Almosen bei Thomas von Aquin zu Juan Luis Vives' De subventione pauperum*. Würzburg: Echter.

King, S. 2000. *Poverty and Welfare in England, 1700–1850*. Manchester: Manchester University Press.

Klötzer, R. 1997. *Kleiden, Speisen, Beherbergen. Armenfürsorge und soziale Stiftungen in Münster im 16. Jahrhundert (1535–1588)*. Münster: Aschendorff.

Knefelkamp, U. 2001. 'Sozialdisziplinierung oder Armenfürsorge? Untersuchung normativer Quellen in Bamberg und Nürnberg vom 14. bis zum 17. Jahrhundert', in H. Bräuer and E. Schlenkrich (eds), *Die Stadt als Kommunikationsraum – Beiträge zur Stadtgeschichte vom Mittelalter bis ins 20. Jahrhundert, Festschrift für Karl Czok zum 75. Geburtstag*. Leipzig: Leipziger Universitätsverlag, pp. 515–33.

Köpf, U. (ed.). 2002. *Deutsche Geschichte in Quellen und Darstellung*, vol. 3, *Reformationszeit 1495–1555*. Stuttgart: Reclam.

Kröger, S. 2006. *Armenfürsorge und Wohlfahrtspflege im frühneuzeitlichen Regensburg*. Regensburg: Pustet.

Krünitz, J.G. (ed.), *Oekonomische Encyklopädie, oder allgemeines System der Staats-, Stadt-, Haus, u. Landwirtschaft in alphabetischer Ordnung*. Berlin, vol. 40, p. 728. Retrieved 5 November 2009 from http://www.kruenitz1.uni-trier.de/

Küster, Th. 1995. *Alte Armut und neues Bürgertum. Öffentliche und private Fürsorge in Münster von der Ära Fürstenberg bis zum Ersten Weltkrieg (1756–1914)*. Münster: Aschendorff.

Lorentzen, T. 2008. *Johannes Bugenhagen als Reformator der öffentlichen Fürsorge*. Tübingen: Mohr Siebeck.

Ludyga, H. 2010. *Obrigkeitliche Armenfürsorge im deutschen Reich vom Beginn der Frühen Neuzeit bis zum Ende des Dreißigjährigen Krieges (1495–1648)*. Berlin: Duncker & Humblot.

Möser, J. 1995. 'Etwas zur Verbesserung der Armenanstalten (1767)', in M. Rudersdorf, *'Das Glück der Bettler' – Justus Möser und die Welt der Armen. Mentalität und soziale Frage im Fürstbistum Osnabrück zwischen Aufklärung und Säkularisation*. Münster: Aschendorff, p. 336.

Newman-Brown, W. 1984. 'The Receipt of Poor Relief and Family Situation: Aldenham, Hertfordshire 1630–90', in R.M. Smith (ed.), *Land, Kinship and Life-Cycle*. Cambridge: Cambridge University Press, pp. 405–22.

Pauly, M. 2007. *Peregrinorum, pauperum ac aliorum transeuntium receptaculum. Hospitäler zwischen Maas und Rhein im Mittelalter*. Stuttgart: Steiner.

Pichlkastner, S. *Das Wiener Stadtzeichnerbuch 1678–1685. Ein Bettlerverzeichnis aus einer frühneuzeitlichen Stadt*. Vienna (unpublished manuscript).

Rabeler, S. 2005. 'Karitatives Handeln, Stiftungswirklichkeiten und Personenbeziehungen – Überlegungen zu einer Sozialgeschichte der Armenfürsorge im mittelalterlichen Lübeck', *Zeitschrift des Vereins für Lübeckische Geschichte und Altertumskunde* 85:11–24.

———. 2007. 'Zur Sozialgeschichte der Armenfürsorge in den Städten des südlichen Ostseeraums (13.–16. Jahrhundert). Ein Forschungsprojekt', *Hansische Geschichtsblätter* 125:187–98.

Resmini, B. 2002. 'Aufklärung und Säkularisation im Trierer Erzstift, vornehmlich bei den Klostergemeinschaften in der Eifel und in der Stadt Trier', in G. Mölich J. Oepen and W. Rosen (eds), *Klosterkultur und Säkularisation im Rheinland*. Essen: Klartext, pp. 81–104.

Rheinheimer, M. 1998. Jakob Gülich. '"Trotzigkeit" und "ungebührliches Betragen" eines ländlichen Armen um 1850', in M. Rheinheimer (ed.), *Subjektive Welten. Wahrnehmung und Identität in der Neuzeit*. Neumünster: Wachholtz, pp. 223–52.

———. 2000. *Arme, Bettler und Vaganten. Überleben in der Not 1450–1850*. Frankfurt/Main: Fischer Taschenbuch.

Richter, J. 2001. *Frühneuzeitliche Armenfürsorge als Disziplinierung – Zur sozialpädagogischen Bedeutung eines Perspektivenwechsels*. Frankfurt/Main: Lang.

Riis, Th. (ed.). 1981–1990. *Aspects of Poverty in Early Modern Europe*, 3 vols. Stuttgart: Klett-Cotta.

Sachße, Ch., and F. Tennstedt (eds). 1986. *Soziale Sicherheit und soziale Disziplinierung. Beiträge zu einer historischen Theorie der Sozialpolitik*. Frankfurt/Main: Suhrkamp.

Scheutz, M. 2003. *Ausgesperrt und gejagt, geduldet und versteckt. Bettlervisitationen im Niederösterreich des 18. Jahrhunderts*. St. Pölten: Niederösterreichisches Institut für Landeskunde.

Scheutz, M. 2008. 'Supplikationen an den ersamen Rat um Aufnahme ins Bürgerspital. Inklusions- und Exklusionsprozesse am Beispiel der Spitäler von Zwettl und Scheibbs', in S. Schmidt (ed.), *Arme und ihre Lebensperspektiven in der Frühen Neuzeit*. Frankfurt/Main: Lang, pp. 157–206.

Schindler, N. 1994. 'Die Ramingsteiner Bettlerhochzeit 1688/89. Armut, Sexualität und Hexenpolitik in einem Salzburger Bergwerk des 17. Jahrhunderts', *Historische Anthropologie* 2:165–92.

Schmidt, S. 2004. 'Armenfürsorge in Stadt und Land. Maßnahmen gegen Armut und Bettelei in Mainz sowie im Rheingau im 17. und 18. Jahrhundert', in Bräuer, *Arme – ohne Chance? Kommunale Armut und Armutsbekämpfung vom Spätmittelalter bis zur Gegenwart*. Leipzig: Leipziger Universitätsverlag, pp. 71–98.

———. 2011. 'Kloster-Karitas und staatliche Armenfürsorge in Kurmainz am Ende des Alten Reichs', in K. Krimm and R. Brüning (eds). *Armut und*

Fürsorge in der frühen Neuzeit (Oberrheinische Studien, 29). Ostfildern: Thorbecke, 223–235.

————. 2013. 'Zu Repräsentationen von Armut und sozialer Sicherheit sowie den institutionellen Fürsorgepraktiken im Kurfürstentum Trier', in Ch. Kampmann and U. Niggemann (eds), *Sicherheit in der Frühen Neuzeit. Norm – Praxis – Repräsentation.* Cologne: Böhlau, pp. 496–507.

Schneider, B. 1989. *Bruderschaften im Trierer Land: ihre Geschichte und ihr Gottesdienst zwischen Tridentinum und Säkularisation.* Trier: Paulinus.

Schnorrenberger, G. 1977. *Wirtschaftsverwaltung des Klosters Eberbach im Rheingau, 1423–1631.* Wiesbaden: Historische Kommission für Nassau.

Schubert, E. 2001. 'Erscheinungsformen der Armut in der spätmittelalterlichen deutschen Stadt', in H. Bräuer and E. Schlenkrich (eds), *Die Stadt als Kommunikationsraum.* Leipzig: Leipziger Universitätsverlag, pp. 659–97.

Schulze, W. 1987. 'Gerhard Oestreichs Begriff "ozialdisziplinierung in der Frühen Neuzeit"'. *Zeitschrift für Historische Forschung* 14:265–302.

Simon-Muscheid, K. 2003. 'Ein rebmesser hat sine frowe versetzt für 1 ß brotte. Armut in den oberrheinischen Städten des 15. und 16. Jahrhunderts', in Bräuer, *Arme – ohne Chance? Kommunale Armut und Armutsbekämpfung vom Spätmittelalter bis zur Gegenwart.* Leipzig: Leipziger Universitätsverlag, pp. 39–70.

Sokoll, Th. 2000. 'Negotiating a Living: Essex Pauper Letters from London, 1800–1834', *International Review of Social History* 45:19–46.

———— (ed.). 2001. *Essex Pauper Letters.* Oxford: Oxford University Press.

Soto, D. d. 2004. 'Über die Regelung der Armenhilfe (1545). Mit einer Einleitung von Larissa C. Seelbach', in Th. Strohm and M. Klein (eds), *Die Entstehung einer sozialen Ordnung Europas.* Heidelberg: Winter, vol. 1, pp. 340–99.

Spicker, P. 2010. *The Origins of Modern Welfare: Juan Luis Vives, De Subventione Pauperum, and City of Ypres, Forma Subventionis Pauperum.* Oxford: Lang.

Strohm, Th. and M. Klein (eds). 2004. *Die Entstehung einer sozialen Ordnung Europas,* 2 vols. Heidelberg: Winter.

Swift, J. 1972. 'Bescheidener Vorschlag, wie man verhüten kann, dass die Kinder armer Leute in Irland ihren Eltern oder dem Lande zur Last fallen, und wie sie der Allgemeinheit nutzbar gemacht werden können (1729)', in G. Graustein (ed.), *Ausgewählte Werke in drei Bänden, 2: Politische Schriften.* Frankfurt/Main: Insel, p. 513; (trans. J. Swift, 1729. *A Modest Proposal for preventing the Children of Poor People from Being a Burthen to their Parents, or the Country and for Making them Beneficial to the Publick.* Dublin).

Thomas von Aquin. 1959. *Summa Theologica,* vol. 17, *Die Liebe (1. Teil): II–II.* Frage 23–33. Graz: Styria.

Uerlings, H., N. Trauth and L. Clemens (eds). 2011. *Armut. Perspektiven in Kunst und Gesellschaft.* Katalog zur gleichnamigen Ausstellung, Stadtmuseum Simeonstift und Rheinisches Landesmuseum Trier, 10.04.2011–31.07.2011. Darmstadt: Primus.

Ulbricht, O. 1994. 'Die Welt eines Bettlers um 1775. Johann Gottfried Kästner', *Historische Anthropologie* 2:371–98.

Vives, J.L. 1533. *Von Almusen geben Zwey buechlin Ludovici Vivis. Auff diß new xxxiij. Jar durch D. Casparn Hedion verteütscht und eim Ersamen Radt unnd frummer burgerschafft zu Straßburg zugeschriben. Allen Policeyen nutzlich zu lesen.* [Strasbourg]

————. 2002. *De subventione pauperum sive de humanis necessitatibus libri II,* C. Matheeussen und Ch. Fantazzi (eds). Selected Works of J.L. Vives, 4. Leiden, Boston: Brill.

Voltmer, R. 2005. *Wie der Wächter auf dem Turm. Ein Prediger und seine Stadt. Johannes Geiler von Kaysersberg (1445–1510) und Straßburg.* Trier: Porta-Alba.

Wagner, A. 2011. 'Gleicherweiß als wasser das feuer, also verlösche almuse die sünd'. *Frühneuzeitliche Fürsorge- und Bettelgesetzgebung der geistlichen Kurfürstentümer Köln und Trier.* Berlin: Duncker & Humblot.

Wales, T. 1984. 'Poverty, Poor Relief and the Life-Cycle: Some Evidence from Seventeenth-Century Norfolk', in R.M. Smith (ed.), *Land, Kinship and Life-Cycle.* Cambridge: Cambridge University Press, pp. 351–404.

Weber, M. 1980. *Wirtschaft und Gesellschaft.* Tübingen: Mohr Siebeck.

Zeller, S. 2006. *Juan Luis Vives (1492–1540). (Wieder)Entdeckung eines Europäers, Humanisten und Sozialreformers jüdischer Herkunft im Schatten der spanischen Inquisition.* Freiburg/Breisgau: Lambertus.

Sebastian Schmidt is a former postdoctoral researcher at Trier University. His recent publications include: 'Inklusion/Exklusion. Neue Perspektiven für die historische Armutsforschung', in H. Uerlings and I.-K. Patrut (eds). *Inklusion/ Exklusion und Kultur: Theoretische Perspektiven und Fallstudien von der Antike bis zur Gegenwart.* (2013), pp.123–42; 'Zu Repräsentationen von Armut und sozialer Sicherheit sowie den institutionellen Fürsorgepraktiken im Kurfürstentum Trier', in Ch. Kampmann and U. Niggemann (eds), *Sicherheit in der Frühen Neuzeit. Norm – Praxis – Repräsentation.* (2013), pp. 496–507; 'Neue Formen der Armenfürsorge in den geistlichen Kurstaaten der Frühen Neuzeit', in L. Clemens, A. Haverkamp and R. Kunert (eds), *Formen der Armenfürsorge in hoch- und spätmittelalterlichen Zentren nördlich und südlich der Alpen.* (2011), pp. 309–31.

CHAPTER 2

German Pauper Letters and Petitions for Relief

New Perspectives on Nineteenth- and Twentieth-Century Poor Relief

Andreas Gestrich

This chapter revisits the well-researched field of nineteenth- and twentieth-century poor relief in Germany. It does so by concentrating on sources which have received surprisingly little attention from German historians of welfare so far, namely letters, petitions and the minutes of the oral depositions of the poor asking for relief. These documents provide not only a unique insight into the needs and cares of the poor themselves, but also into their understanding of how poor relief administrations worked and hierarchies functioned, into their wider view of society and their sense of entitlement to relief, and, in particular, into their linguistic strategies for dealing with the authorities. These letters and petitions allow us to observe poor relief administrations 'from below', and to look at the agency of the poor and how they interacted with the administration.

The value of these sources was discovered over a decade ago by Thomas Sokoll, who published a seminal edition of what he called 'pauper letters' from the British county of Essex.[1] Unlike in Britain, it was only very recently that this inspired equivalent research in German archives, where similar sources can be found. This chapter is based on the first large-scale attempt to retrieve, edit and analyse German pauper letters and petitions from various areas, and economic and social contexts from the late eighteenth to the early twentieth centuries.[2] The main difference between the British and the German sources is that whereas the Essex pauper letters edited by Thomas Sokoll are letters written by or on behalf of paupers who resided outside their parish of settlement, this type of letter from absent parishioners is very rare in Germany. Here, support for migrants tended to be negotiated by the officials of the respective parishes of residence and settlement, so that – unlike in England – any money would have been transferred through official channels only, and not sent to the absent pauper directly. German archives, however, hold many letters directed from within a parish, either to the local poor relief administration or to the mayor, the local nobility or even to the king himself, requesting various kinds of support.[3]

As a historical source, these letters are not without their pitfalls. One of the main problems concerns the authenticity of the voice we hear or read in them. Were they physically written by the poor themselves? If not, as was clearly often the case, is it still they who speak through a letter if it was written with the help of a scribe? Do we know whose help the poor employed both to write a letter physically and to compose its contents? In the first two sections this chapter looks at these questions by examining first the formal side of petitions and then the writing process itself. The third part analyses the language and the rhetorical strategies of these letters, and the final section considers what can be learned from them about the way paupers interacted with poor relief or welfare administrations.

Suppliken, Bittschriften, Eingaben: German Pauper Letters and Petitions

In Germany, as elsewhere, the normal procedure of applying for poor relief was to make an oral deposition with a member of the local board of poor relief.[4] However, relief records also contain large quantities of written applications sent by post or delivered by hand to the board. They came primarily from local residents and were addressed either directly to the relevant officials or, more frequently, to administrators at a higher level asking them to intercede with the local board on their behalf or to help them directly. In British terminology most of these written requests to superiors would be classified as petitions, the more informal ones as pauper letters.[5]

Partly depending on the subject matter, partly depending on the addressee, the term used by early modern and nineteenth-century German administrations for such letters or petitions tended to be *Suppliken* or *Supplikationen,* i.e. humble requests, or simply *Bittschriften,* the German term for an ordinary written request.[6] Frequently, administrations and archives applied *Suppliken* also as an umbrella term for all types of letter and petition.[7] Even though it is often difficult to differentiate exactly between the different source types, distinguishing between them is not trivial, as up to the middle of the nineteenth century requests directed to the higher echelons of city or state administrations needed not only to be submitted in writing, but also follow certain epistolary and rhetorical conventions. Applicants had to be, or otherwise use, experienced writers to compose a *Supplik.*

To submit a written request to local or government authorities was considered a right of every subject or citizen.[8] This is true not only for the early modern period, but also for the *Kaiserreich* as well as the Weimar Republic and, after the Second World War, East and West Germany. In the Weimar and Federal Republics the right to petition was guaranteed by the constitution.[9] During the Nazi period this right was not officially abandoned, but was in fact much restricted. Nevertheless, many people addressed letters directly to the Führer.[10] In East Germany submitting petitions was very much part of the political process, partly replacing the possibility of taking legal action against the government and its administrative bodies. In East Germany all petitions were termed *Eingaben,* and their treatment by officials was regulated in 1953 in a specific *Eingaben-Verordnung.* Even though this ruling was directed towards dealing with 'suggestions and complaints',[11] these *Eingaben* often merely requested help in particularly difficult circumstances.

Whereas it was the norm for ordinary requests for relief to be filed in person with the overseers of the poor, there were also various reasons for these applications to be sent or delivered as letters by paupers living within the parish. Some application letters were sent because the applicants were ill and could not leave the house. Requests for relief submitted to private charities, which often had no regular office hours, but occasional board meetings on demand, may also have required written applications. Frequently, however, these *Bittschriften* were written by the so-called shamefaced poor who consciously avoided open contact with the official bodies of poor relief and preferred to send their requests in writing.[12]

Formal *Suppliken* to the higher levels of administrations had to be submitted in writing. They could concern many different subject matters and eighteenth-century legal scholars introduced the potentially still valid systematic distinction between two separate groups, namely *Suppliken* in legal matters (*Suppliken in Rechtssachen*) and those asking for a special favour without any legal claim or entitlement to it (*Suppliken in Gnadensachen*). As there was no specific legal entitlement to relief let alone particular kinds of relief in Germany until the onset of the insurance-based modern welfare system in the late nineteenth and early twentieth centuries, poor relief administrations tended to consider requests for relief as *Gnadensachen.* However, the boundaries between these two types were often blurred, as requests for relief frequently employed legal as well as social or moral arguments.[13]

Suppliken could be submitted by an individual or collectively by several individuals or even by whole parishes.[14] Collective *Suppliken* tended to address political or administrative grievances (i.e. *Suppliken in Rechtssachen*) and have been the object of intensive international research over the past two decades.[15] Much less research, however, has been devoted to the *Suppliken* of individuals asking for material or administrative help in times of need.[16] This is also still true for the East German *Eingaben,* which were often addressed to the highest levels of state or party organization. Between 1949 and 1989, for example, more than 70,000 citizens took these queries to the head of state every year.[17] Wilhelm Pieck, the first president of the GDR, received over 200,000 letters in 1952, more than 80,000 of which were classified and filed as *Eingaben.* The issues they addressed were clearly not limited to questions of relief, but touched on all aspects of social, political and economic life in the GDR. However, they frequently also dealt with problems of economic hardship, of food supplies, the expense of provisions and the lack of adequate housing, and the failures of the GDR administration in these contexts.

Writing to the head of the city or even to the head of state was not usually the applicants' first approach, but was rather the result of a long prehistory of unsuccessful negotiations with the lower levels of the local welfare administrations.[18] *Suppliken*, therefore, very often follow a series of *Bittschriften*. As they often went to different parts of the administration or government, they were not always kept and archived together. Where they were kept together and collected in personal files which might sometimes stretch over many years, they give access to the needs of the poor, but also to their capacity to negotiate relief, to their hopes and strategies and also their moods and frustrations, if they were not able to reach their aims.

Whose Voice? *Suppliken, Bittschriften* and *Eingaben* as Ego Documents

In their ordinary *Bittschriften* or *Eingaben*, as well as in *Suppliken,* the applicants needed to establish their entitlement to relief. Whereas some paupers were very robust in stating their claims in short letters, it was seen by many of the applicants as a complex task which involved not only the detailed demonstration of their neediness, but also the proof that they were 'deserving poor', i.e. subjects or citizens who were also morally worthy of the support of the parish or the superior addressed for relief. This could result in detailed descriptions not only of their difficult economic circumstances, their illnesses, family bereavements and similar misfortunes, but also of how they positioned themselves in society. It was in this context that many applicants referred to, for example, shared social and moral values such as the need to be economically independent, while others portrayed themselves as respectable citizens of the parish or as faithful servants of the noble family they approached for help. It seems, therefore, that many of these *Suppliken* and *Bittschriften* provide us with something rare for this stratum of society, namely ego documents.

Ego documents, a term coined by the Dutch historian J. Presser in the 1950s, comprise a wide range of text genres (autobiographies, memoirs, diaries, letters, judicial depositions) in which authors explicitly write or give testimony about their own affairs, and their self-perception and reflections on their position in their social environment, such as with regard to family, parish, social class or nation.[19] However, is it really the poor themselves who speak in these documents? As indicated above, *Suppliken* and *Bittschriften* had to follow certain formal standards (proper addresses and salutations) and epistolary conventions otherwise they risked refusal. This suggests that many applicants needed help with their composition, and some even needed someone else to physically write it, by employing neighbours, friends or even professional scribes.

In his analysis of English pauper letters, Thomas Sokoll came to the (not uncontested) conclusion that pauper letters

> are highly credible first-hand narratives of the living conditions and experiences of the labouring poor of late eighteenth and early nineteenth century England. As any form of written evidence, they display rhetorical elements. But these rhetorical elements must not be regarded as in any way interfering with their 'true' substantive message.[20]

In fact, in Sokoll's opinion, many English pauper letters were similar to recordings of oral depositions and as a result he advised historians to read them aloud, 'since they record the "voices" of the poor'.[21]

In the case of German *Bittschriften* and *Suppliken*, and even partly of the East German *Eingaben*, things seem to have been more complicated. Formal petitions to the higher levels of administration and government were likely to require the help of professional scribes or advisors, simply as a result of their formal nature. However, in some territories, until the middle of the nineteenth century, even ordinary *Bittschriften* had to follow certain formal standards or, as in the case of Württemberg, were required to be written by trained scribes. It is not until the mid nineteenth century that in the course of the revolution of 1848/49 all such restrictions on all forms of petitions were abandoned. The question of who the authors of the petitions actually were becomes, therefore, even more pressing.

Many of the ordinary *Bittschriften* have a formal structure and a difference between the hand of the main letter and the signature can be clearly detected, both of which indicate that paupers employed help, very often professional help. Sometimes the name of the scribe is even noted on the letter. When, for example, the poor Jewish widower Wolf Massenbacher from the equally impoverished Württemberg village of Unterdeufstetten applied to the Superior Council of the Israelite Church in Württemberg (Israelitischer Oberkirchenrat) for relief, he signed the letter with three crosses. His signature was attested by the local teacher who added, 'Out of pity written for free by teacher M. Kling from this village'.[22]

The fact that letters were frequently written not by the paupers themselves poses the problem of the authenticity of the voice we hear in them and therefore also questions the validity of Sokoll's claim that they can be treated as ego documents. However, the fact that paupers needed the help of scribes is also interesting. It opens up a wide range of new questions concerning paupers' networks and the infrastructure of writing as well as the production of the actual content of the letters and the ways they were phrased.

In the case of poor Wolf Massenbacher we know that this elderly Jew was assisted by the Christian village teacher (but not by the local poor relief funds!). But it also seems as if the teacher had composed the entire argument and the wording of the letter. It is well written and resembles in parts the sample letters given for such requests in letter writing manuals. Passages such as the following are perhaps not even the 'voice' of a rural village teacher:

> Having been married here for 25 years I was initially able to provide honourably for my family, particularly at the side of a faithful spouse, and I felt happy as long as I was healthy and my trade went well. However, soon it should come differently as the pains and aches of old age set in early with me. Too early came to me the dreary days which displease the ordinary human ... It was only through the great diligence and parsimoniousness of my wife and the charitable noble character of fellow Jews that I was able to survive that long ...[23]

It is unlikely that this was the language of an illiterate elderly country Jew, who would probably have spoken Jiddish rather than High German. It seems clear that the whole phraseology and key terms used in this letter were not his own language, but came from his helper, the teacher, and probably from the letter writing manuals the latter would have possessed for teaching letter writing to his pupils.[24]

Apart from local teachers, who were the obvious writing experts in most localities, it has to be asked what other sources the social infrastructure provided when the paupers needed to have letters written in times before the 'emancipation of writing'.[25] Fortunately there are sources available to historians because governments frequently distrusted scribes, assuming that many of them also incited paupers to ask for relief or file complaints in form of *Suppliken*. In the 1820s the Prussian government, therefore, tried to enforce a closer supervision of scribes in all parts of the kingdom. Local administrations were asked to keep lists of names of scribes, information on the income they derived from their services and their general moral conduct.[26] In Trier, a provincial town in the Prussian Rheine Province, for example, twenty-one scribes tried to make a living in 1820 from offering their services to the less than 10,000 inhabitants. It can be presumed that several of them also wrote letters for the poor and that they were probably paid by them according to the success of their work.

Despite the formal requirements and the available presence of scribes, there are also many other examples of letters clearly written by the paupers themselves, where the voice of the pauper can be heard in the manner assumed for the English pauper letters by Thomas Sokoll. When, for example, Helena Dütz, a washerwoman from Deutz, whose husband was in prison, wrote to the Mayor, she used an eloquent opening sentence, but then continued in colloquial language without punctuation and many spelling mistakes:

> ... the reason for my request is the following As you know my husband is imprisoned and me Poor woman with the 5 children are in misery now Yes Mr Mayor the destitution forces me to turn to you, for there is no surviving in this situation was not, I do have the washing for the military but that is not enough to live off for this requires Healthy people whereas I now suffer often from chest and stomach pain Unfortunately it is impossible to manage like that on your own without help ...[27]

Letters like these from the late nineteenth century are clear examples that paupers could and did by then write their own letters to the overseers of the poor. The advance of compulsory schooling and the massive political petitioning in the context of the revolution of 1848 ended the disciplinary approach of governments as far as the requirements for formal petitions were concerned.[28] Individuals who were dissatisfied with the decisions made by the local relief boards seemed now to have less hesitation in turning to higher levels of the administration in order to request support. The source material analysed so far also demonstrates that from the second half of the nineteenth century onwards, petitions were increasingly written by the applicants themselves without the help of scribes.

It is interesting to note, however, that the practice of employing someone else to write on one's behalf did not stop completely. These may not always have been paid scribes, but neighbours and friends who helped formulate a letter or petition. In the GDR, for example, a high-ranking journalist and his wife specialized in writing successful *Eingaben* for neighbours, friends and often people who had simply heard about the success rate of their petitions. Apparently they did not do so for financial gain, but simply to help, and even continued the practice after 1989, assisting people grappling with the new administrative practices of the united Germany.[29] The memoirs of these East German journalists also serve as a reminder that writing petitions for someone else was a communicative process of listening to their stories, reading the previous exchanges with the administrations and deciding on the best strategies, which may have involved the physical presence of the applicants at a certain office or waiting for an opportunity to submit the letter in person to higher ranking officials.[30]

The German *Bittschriften* and *Suppliken* not only provide us with an insight into the advance of literacy in the course of the nineteenth century, but sometimes also into the complex social processes involved in the writing and submitting of such letters, as well as into the changing nature of written interaction between paupers and the administrators of poor relief. Later in the nineteenth and twentieth centuries many *Bittschriften* and *Suppliken* were physically written by the applicants themselves. Thus, unlike some of the earlier documents, they give much clearer access to the self-perceptions and identities of the poor (even if the applicants consulted with neighbours and friends about strategies of how best to phrase things).[31] In addition, as was shown here only in passing, these letters can serve as rich sources for the social history of poverty and the poor in general. They provide ample information on working conditions, unemployment, wages, living standards, housing and family and neighbourhood support networks in times of crisis.[32]

Language and Linguistic Strategies in Petitions for Poor Relief

Even though the minute books of some poor relief administrations recorded the depositions of the applicants in great detail and sometimes even as first-person narratives,[33] they rarely permit us to reconstruct exactly what happened when paupers applied for relief in person. The importance of petitions and the administrative procedures and responses they initiated, therefore, also lies in the fact that they provide us with an insight not only into the ways the paupers tried to negotiate relief, but also into the degrees to which poor relief administrations were open to such negotiations and, in particular, to intercessions from influential supporters. The purpose of *Bittschriften* and *Suppliken* was to gain support, and in attempting to achieve this purpose, employed particular rhetorical and linguistic strategies. From among the many recognized aspects of strategic writing, this chapter will address three: the strategy of deference and its limits, the strategy of appealing to a notion of justice by referring to customary rights or by comparing one's case to the support received by others, and that of self-integration into a moral community. This leaves aside other frequently used strategies such as referring to illness, old age, widowhood or the need to care for children.[34]

Deference and Its Limits

In early modern and early nineteenth-century Germany, *Suppliken* to superiors such as the king, the local nobility or the mayor of a town, were required to follow certain formats and, in particular, apply certain rules of correct courteous salutation and address. These requirements were part of the attempt to curb the flood of petitions, by forcing people to use expensive professional help. It was also intended to make the administrative processing of these petitions easier. Nineteenth-century letter writing manuals made these rules accessible so they could be increasingly applied to all levels of petitioning by individuals without the help of professional scribes. Within this framework of general courtesy, however, the degree of deferential language used in *Suppliken* could also be a strategic device designed to win the favour of the addressee. In this case deferential language was not restricted to the formulaic salutations, but was also included in other parts of the letter where it would not normally be expected, or at least not to such a degree.

Such over-deferential letters were particularly frequent in cases when the applicants turned either to the head of state or to the local nobility for help. Even on the eve of the First World War, in areas such as the small south German principality of Hohenlohe-Bartenstein, the language of petitions could be extremely deferential. In October 1913 Fritz H. from Bartenstein started a self-authored petition to the prince as follows:

> Most noble [*duchlauchtigster*] Prince and Master,
> Whoever is weary and burdened in our parishes takes his refuge to his protector whose benign grace has always been our consolation. .... In this time of need I turn to our most graceful Master and Prince and beg for favour and mercy [*Huld und Gnade*] for a person who has now ended his working life and become frail...[35]

This type of apparent humility, expressed in deferential language in a *Supplik*, was no exception in Hohenlohe in the years before (and possibly even after) the First World War. In the patriarchal environment of these petty principalities, asking for help, particularly for extraordinary help, implied acceptance of social hierarchy.

To a lesser extent this highly deferential mode of communication was also frequently applied when petitions were sent to important people, such as the *Regierungspräsident* in Potsdam to whom an unemployed carpenter, Otto T., turned for relief in the 1920s, addressing him as 'hochgeehrter' rather than as the ordinary 'sehr geehrter Herr Regierungspräsident'.[36] When petitions were addressed to the local administration, we find a wide variety of salutations, sometimes fairly deferential, but very often not exceeding the normal measure of courtesy. In Stralsund, however, where many paupers turned to the old guild foundations, which were still administered separately from the ordinary parish relief, most applicants continued to use very deferential language towards the aldermen (*Altermänner*) of these guilds and funds right through the nineteenth century, even though they were usually connected to them by their former profession.[37]

However, in other areas of Germany different and less deferential styles of letter writing and petitioning can also be observed. During the second half of the nineteenth century the paupers of the industrializing Cologne suburb of Deutz wrote surprisingly robust letters and seemed rarely to have used the strategy of deference to support their claims.[38] These letters from Deutz can be seen as early examples for a style of more self-confident petitioning which becomes more common in the twentieth century. It is interesting that during the Nazi period even letter writing manuals advise their readers to be more self-confident when submitting their claims to the authorities. In 1941, for example, a German letter writing manual advised its readers in the name of the new *Volksgemeinschaft* to stop the old practice of subaltern and sycophantic addresses when corresponding with state officials.[39] Another manual from 1937 gave similar advice, stressing that 'our new state is a state of the *Volksgemeinschaft*' and therefore 'the workman is just as important a member of the whole as the professor or minister'.[40] The term *Volksgemeinschaft* was a key term not only for concealing the authoritarian and bureaucratic nature of Nazi rule and presenting a tool for excluding and exterminating all those who were considered as not part of or beneficial to it. It was also accepted by many as an egalitarian and emancipatory concept defining their relationship to the state by turning it into 'our state'. This is reflected in the official advice provided to those writing to the authorities.

In post-war East and West Germany this more self-confident manner of approaching administrations continued, also in the case of *Eingaben*, or letters and petitions to welfare offices. In her comparative analysis of relief applications in the West German towns of Freiburg and Castrop-Rauxel and the East German town of Schwerin, Dorothee Lürbke found many examples of minimalistic applications merely stating 'applying herewith for …' without any courteous addresses and salutations.[41] Such short letters must, however, frequently be seen as part of an ongoing correspondence which might have commenced with more polite and extensive letters which may also have contained more deferential language.

Formulaic deferential salutations were by no means fixed, and the poor were able to play with differences. Otto T., for example, shifted from 'Hochgehrter Herr Regierungspräsident' to the less courteous 'Sehr geehrter Herr Regierungspräsident', when he became impatient with him and his administration. He followed this salutation with the opening sentence, 'For the last time I am writing to your Grace [*Hochwohlgeboren*]...' and ended it with quite strong words of criticism:

> If it is the case that your Grace [*Ew. Hochwohlgeb.*] lacks the power to give relief to a poor person in his miserable situation, then I beg you courteously to answer, but please do not remain silent, as remaining silent here is just as good as murdering someone. ... I had to do without food to pay for the stamps and paper [*musste ich mir am Munde absparen*]. You know perfectly well what this means. [42]

This inner dynamic, and particularly the shifts in deference in the course of longer correspondences, have been observed by Steven King, Thomas Sokoll and others in the case of English pauper letters.[43] It is also characteristic of German letters and petitions and is very revealing for the way paupers engaged with the authorities. It highlights their strong feelings of entitlement to being taken seriously, and the right to communicate not only with officials at the local level, but also with individuals further up the hierarchy.

Appealing to a Notion of Justice by Comparing

Modern debates on standards of relief acknowledge the fact that the recipients have a right to participate in 'ordinary social life' and that this comprises certain 'luxuries' beyond the mere provision of food and shelter.[44] In order to establish these social rights and define essentials for social integration, ways of life have to be compared.

Such notions of rights and social justice are not only applied by social scientists trying to define thresholds of poverty, but also by paupers themselves. Being denied these essentials for social integration (such as decent clothing) affects their notion of society treating them in a decent or exclusionary way.[45] However, paupers directed their comparisons not only towards the wealthier part of society. Comparison was also important in relation to what or how much other paupers in the parish received and could afford. In petitions for relief, such comparisons with other paupers may have been the outcome of a need for justice, but they were also employed strategically in order to support the claim to relief. Many petitions, therefore, hinted at cases of precedence which, in the eyes of the applicants, established something like an entitlement to receive the same support. This is a technique which can be found in these letters right into the twentieth century.

In the south German territory of the Princes of Hohenlohe, paupers used this technique quite openly and despite all deferential addresses, in order to increase pressure on the board to grant more relief. In 1846, for example, a widow wrote to the prince's chancellery that she was treated differently from other widows of former employees of the princely court, and felt that she had a right that this be redressed as she was 'the only widow of former servants of his Lordship without a flat provided by him'.[46] After the First World War a woman from Blomberg near Detmold complained to the regional government of the Lippe district that although her three sons had served in the armed forces, she had had to provide them with money during their time as prisoners of war, and after their return even had to pay for them to buy clothes so that they 'can let themselves be seen again in the streets like human beings'. She asked for a just distribution of certain available funds and claimed her share by stressing that 'distribution procedures have to be just'.[47] Other petitions contain the summary remark that they were just asking for 'what everybody else is getting'. [48] *Eingaben* from the GDR frequently claimed party officials and bureaucrats enjoyed certain privileges and easier access to scarce consumer goods. 'Do you bigwigs [*Bonzen*] think that an ordinary employee does not have the same appetite for a cigarette as you?' complained an anonymous writer in 1947 to one of the offices responsible for the distribution of consumables and goods.[49] Similar comparisons were made with regard to the allocation of living space or travel permits.[50] For Mühlberg the invocation of social justice, which was mostly based on comparisons with others, was one of the key strategic devices employed in the *Eingaben* of the GDR. However, even if the use of these comparisons represented a certain strategy, the psychological dimensions of equal treatment among the recipients of relief and their notion of fairness should not be underestimated, as they also touched on their perception of belonging and social inclusion or exclusion. Behind these strategies we can frequently detect a moral claim to entitlement not only to material good, but also to recognition.

Integration into a Moral Community

Across Europe, poor laws differentiated between the deserving and undeserving poor.[51] To establish deservedness was, however, a complicated process which went well beyond the proof of need. It was a communicative act through which the poor established their belonging to a community by showing that they shared its core values.[52] Being a Christian and showing some Christian knowledge was certainly an important part of this. Even in the twentieth century, the above-mentioned Otto T. added some religious poems to his letters to the Regierungspräsident in Potsdam, and Fritz H. from Neuenstein used religious language such as 'weary and burdened' (Matt.11: 28) in the course of his argument. Others attached supporting letters from local priests.[53] However, the strategic use of religious language should not obfuscate the fact that many of the poor were genuinely religious people and also had religious needs. This becomes particularly obvious in requests for support for a Christian individual burial. Elizabeth Hurren and Steven King have reminded us that, in the case of British pauper letters, the right to inclusion in the community was particularly frequently evoked in the case when paupers asked for support for a Christian burial for their deceased loved ones.[54] Such requests can also be found in German petitions.[55]

Other important means of stressing belonging were references to the shared value of work and the attempts to live frugally and to make do with the little resources at hand. These are well-known elements in English pauper letters and petitions, and they also appear frequently in the German ones. The above-mentioned Fritz H. from Neuenstein added to his deferential letter to the Prince of Hohenlohe an almost classic self-portrayal as a valuable member of society by stating that he had always been content [*zufrieden*] despite his meagre salary,

> because my ability to work upheld my self-esteem. However, now my ability to work is dwindling, and this misfortune, which only those can properly value who have this as their last bit of joy of life and property, turned me into a broken man who has to face the future full of sorrow.[56]

It is perhaps not surprising that in the GDR the reference to shared political and cultural norms was also a common feature of the *Eingaben,* and that the readiness to work hard and contribute to the new 'worker's state', (i.e. the proof of loyalty and good performance), was one of their features.

Other rhetorical tropes used by the applicants for linking themselves to the moral community of the parish or relief administrations were assertions such as that they had always looked after their parents or parents-in-law or that they had always been good citizens and paid their local taxes. Having looked after and cared for relatives implied that the applicants had not tried to pass the costs of the care for the elderly simply to the parish or the state, but had fulfilled their legal obligations to care for their closest relatives. Such acts of familial solidarity helped to establish ties and earn respect within the parish and thus to facilitate help. Such 'acts of kindness' were particularly noted by doctors and clergymen, who then often acted as important interlocutors on behalf of the applicants, when they could no longer bear the burden of care or were themselves in need of help.

This strong legal obligation between parents and children (but not between siblings!) to support close family members meant that paupers also had to justify at length if and why they could not provide help for their parents or children or why these were unable to contribute to the applicants' upkeep. A widow in Stralsund, for example, stressed in 1868 that she had worked day and night in order bring up her children so that they could now cater for themselves, but that 'fate determined that none of them, however hard they try, is in a position to pass any of their income on to me'.[57] Similarly, Elisabeth Julius, had to turn to the Merchants' Guild [*Kramer Zunft*] of her home town of Stralsund after her only brother had died in 1817 in Stockholm. She stated that with his death she had 'not only lost a brother, but also her only breadwinner" as she had only been able to survive with the help of his support. As the brother and his family were not legally bound to support her, and as the remains of his fortune went to his widow and their children, she would be without support at the age of seventy-four.

Elisabeth Julius established her claim by referring to the fact that her father had been a citizen of Stralsund and that her family had never before asked for any support. Established citizenship and the proof that one had always paid taxes was an important element of stating belonging and claiming entitlement to help in need. Such references to citizenship and loyal behaviour as a citizen are ubiquitous in German *Suppliken* and *Bittbriefen* throughout the nineteenth century, and still a regular feature of applications even after the Second World War.[58]

It is important to note, however, that such strategies could fail and were not always able to prevent marginalization and exclusion. Frequently parishes tried to rid themselves of the burden of costly paupers by forcing them to emigrate or at least to leave the parish. Some of the pauper petitions to the top of the administration in particular apparently came from people who were or felt entirely marginalized in their parish. The agricultural worker Andreas Link from Schmie, a small town north of Stuttgart, complained in a petition to the regional government in 1844 that he and his family were 'hated from all sides and suppressed', that the local authorities had cheated on him and his wife by helping his brother-in-law to disinherit his wife and children, that they had refused the family relief in times of extreme need, and that now that he was ill tried to put him into the worst possible accommodation.[59] Such marginalization did happen, and is difficult to see exactly from these letters how it originated. Some of the life histories revealed in these petitions show a long series of failures irrespective of how hard the individuals tried to integrate.

How weak or strong the social and kinship ties of the urban working classes were in the course of the nineteenth century has been a long debate in British social and family history. Several family historians have pointed out in recent years that their households were much more complex and the ties much stronger then formerly assumed. Steven King analysed English pauper letters and found urban paupers referring to their kinship much more frequently than rural ones, but also to their neighbourhood and other networks.[60]

In German pauper letters it is interesting to note that the importance of social embeddedness within a neighbourhood was not as often evoked or used as an argument to prove belonging as general references to good citizenship. The very term 'neighbour' is ubiquitous in English pauper letters, but rarely appears in the German samples. However, this does not mean that neighbourhoods did not work or matter. Next to parish priests or ministers it was neighbours who brought the needs of the poor, particularly the shamefaced poor, to the attention of magistrates. But as a strategic device in poor relief applications, social integration in the neighbourhood was not regularly evoked as a sign of good moral behaviour, and as far as the authorities were concerned, neighbours were not as important as they had no legal obligation to help.

Having Your Case Seen into: Welfare Administrations and the Power of *Suppliken*

After years of intensive research on the diverse origins and developments of European welfare states, recent historiography has increasingly turned to microstudies in order to analyse how welfare regimes functioned and how, within these larger frameworks, mechanisms of inclusion and exclusion of paupers were applied by local welfare bureaucracies.[61] It is in this context that pauper letters and petitions have also gradually come into focus as an important source.

Many *Suppliken* caused a review of bureaucratic decisions on a lower level. This frequently resulted in voluminous special files, often allowing historians to follow the entire case from the initial first request to the formal complaints or applications for relief submitted to the higher administrative levels, comprising correspondences which sometimes went on over many years.[62] For as much as *Suppliken* might have been regarded as a nuisance by the respective authorities, they still required a response and subsequent action.

When, for example, the above-mentioned Otto T. from Lankwitz was refused unemployment benefit in 1920 by the local magistrate, he turned to the Regierungspräsident in Potsdam and asked him to act on his behalf:

> I courteously ask Your Grace to make them pay me some unemployment money retrospectively, for my situation is painful and embarrassing as my clothing is worn out, so are my boots. And yet my situation would be so easily redressed if I could get some help, and I could earn my bread if only a friendly hand would intervene and therefore I am full of hope that Your Grace will be so kind as to order some help for me; I beg this for the sake of humanity, for I have to perish, if there is no help...[63]

By writing to superiors and asking for direct material help or support with a complaint against a decision by the inferior ranks of the administration, applicants could exercise considerable power. With this letter Otto T. was able to set the administrative machinery in motion and make the magistrates look into his case again and he exchanged letters with them and the Regierungspräsidium for several months. This demonstrates that, even in the early twentieth century, poor relief administrations and other social services were not always hierarchical modern bureaucracies which applicants could only access from the lowest level of local officials. They could, at least sometimes, also access it from the top or from the side, if they were able to convince and mobilize powerful 'allies' to intervene on their behalf.

As *Suppliken* were an effective instrument of interfering with bureaucratic procedures and decisions, it is hardly surprising that there were frequent attempts by administrations and governments to suppress at least excessive individual petitioning. As already seen, during the first decades of the nineteenth century, in many regions of Germany, there were attempts to identify and control unofficial scribes as part of a policy to restrict the number and content of petitions particularly to the king or local nobility, but also to the ordinary administrations of poor relief. In East Germany, too, administrations tried to limit the excessive use of *Eingaben* by introducing stricter procedures and rules for submitting them. However, even though administrations frequently tried to curb these possibilities of interfering with their decisions, requests and complaints to officials higher in the hierarchy continued to be made in the form of *Suppliken* and *Eingaben*, and relief administrations had to deal with them. In this respect the ability to write and bring forward their needs and complaints in written form empowered paupers to interact with administrations in a more confident way. The genre of *Bittschriften* and *Suppliken,* therefore, provides historians with a unique insight into the dynamics of the sometimes complex and extensive negotiation processes between paupers and poor relief administrations.

Conclusion

German petitions for relief shared many features with their English counterparts. However, there were also considerable differences. This chapter has demonstrated that the questions of text genres and writing processes require more careful analysis in the case of German *Bittschriften* and *Suppliken* than most scholars working on British pauper letters and petitions deem necessary. In Germany, until the middle of the nineteenth century, the help of scribes was obligatory in some territorial states for the submission of *Suppliken,* at least to the nobility and monarchs, but frequently also to the higher echelons of society. This changed after the revolution of 1848/49, when all such regulations were abandoned. However, as the case of the East German *Eingaben* shows, even in the twentieth century such documents were frequently the product not of an individual's efforts, but of cooperation between the applicants, their family and friends or better-educated helpers. Apart from their primary context of poverty and poor relief, German *Eingaben* and *Suppliken,* therefore, also provide particularly interesting sources for the history of literacy and writing in the lower classes – and what these skills enabled them to do.

This chapter has ended with a focus on this particular aspect of agency of the poor through literacy and the skill of writing and composing a letter to the relief administrations. The fact that they could and did complain about decisions made by the local relief boards, that they were able to question how the scarce resources of local poor relief funds were distributed, gave them considerable power. They could interfere, ask for more transparency and possibly for decisions to be revised. *Bittschriften* and *Suppliken* provide us with a perspective from below on the complex system of relief and they demonstrate how paupers positioned themselves not only as recipients of relief, but also as actors within this system.

These processes of revisiting a case similarly reveal an aspect which was not foregrounded in this chapter, but is also characteristic of establishing entitlement to relief, namely the extent to which decision-making processes were open to influences from outside. As a result, the people who spoke on behalf of the poor (the doctors, priests, neighbours or friends) could and should become an object of study that is just as interesting as the poor themselves. Such individuals who spoke on behalf of the poor reveal something about their social environment and networks. In the letters themselves, it is more the family, their contributions or inability to help which are emphasized by the applicants. The wider context of their case files, however, frequently reveals not only that – as is to be expected – their networks were larger, but also that establishing an entitlement to relief was rarely a clear case of legal rights. It was based on a complex process of proving one's status as a member of the deserving poor, which also relied on information provided by others.

In their *Bittschriften* and *Suppliken* the poor themselves, however, provided the basic information and established their own perspective on their entitlement to relief. This is what makes these letters so particularly interesting. Trying to establish their entitlement involved various levels of argument. It was not enough just to demonstrate one's material needs. This chapter has looked at three different strategies for making one's case and stating one's claim in writing: using deferential language; drawing comparisons with what other paupers received; and emphasizing integration into the social and moral community of the parish and society at large. In all three areas the letter writers applied these elements as rhetorical devices. However, in many letters one can also see that there is more behind certain formulations than just a strategy for obtaining relief. Deferential language could indicate clear expectations of the patriarchal obligations of the nobility or the monarch. The question of justice and equal treatment, in particular, was also a matter of being recognized as a person and member of the parish who had worked hard to survive and tried to be independent, but due to adverse circumstances or simply illness and old age was no longer able to do so.

Bittschriften and *Suppliken* can therefore open up a multiplicity of perspectives on the microstructures of early modern poor relief and of the modern welfare state as 'spaces of interaction' between applicants and administrations. They reveal the (slow) changes in these interactions through, for example, the spread of literacy. Applications to private or semi-public charities, such as the funds of the old guilds in towns like Stralsund, also provide an insight into the multi-layered structures even of modern welfare and the diverse economic sources of makeshift pauper economies. Collected on a larger national or international scale, such applications could reveal considerable regional differences in provision for the poor – a topic which has not been touched upon in this chapter. It is in need of further exploration, as these regional differences are rarely revealed in general overviews of the development of welfare states in national or international contexts.[64] Thus, even though *Bittschriften* and *Suppliken* are sources with their own caveats, they can cast new light on many new aspects of the mechanics of poor relief on a micro level and thereby help us to include the poor in the history of welfare.

Notes

1. T. Sokoll. 2001. *Essex Pauper Letters 1731–1837.* Oxford: Oxford University Press. See also Id. 2000. 'Negotiating a living: Essex pauper letters from London, 1800–1834' in L. Fontaine and J. Schlumbohm (eds), *Household Strategies for Survival 1600–2000.* Cambridge: Cambridge University Press, pp. 19–46; Id. 2006. 'Writing for relief: Rhetoric in English pauper letters 1800–1834', in A. Gestrich, S. King and L. Raphael (eds), *Being Poor in Modern Europe.* Bern: Lang, pp. 91–112. For collections of letters from other parts of Britain see also S.A. King and A. Levene (eds). 2006. *Voices of the Poor. Poor Law Depositions and Letters (Narratives of the Poor in Eighteenth-Century Britain 1).* London: Pickering & Chattoo.

2. The research project *Pauper Letters and Petitions for Poor Relief in Germany and Great Britain, 1770–1914 was* generously funded by the Deutsche Forschungsgemeinschaft and the Arts and Humanities Research Council. It is jointly directed by Steven King (Leicester) and the author of this paper. It will – along with others – result in a comparative online edition of German and British letters. For the project see http://www.ghil.ac.uk/research/solidarity_and_care/pauper_letters_and_petitions.html. A similar, albeit regionally restricted project (funded by the Fritz Thyssen Foundation) was conducted by Anke Sczesny and Rolf Kießling. It concentrated on the letters directed to the Augsburg Fugger Foundation. See A. Sczesny. 2012. *Der lange Weg in die Fuggerei. Augsburger Armenbriefe des 19. Jahrhunderts* (fugger-digital). Augsburg: Wißner; and A. Sczesny, R. Kießling and J. Burkhardt (eds). 2014. *Prekariat im 19. Jahrhundert. Armenfürsorge und Alltagsbewältigung in Stadt und Land.* Augsburg: Wißner. For an overview over European literature see A. Gestrich, E. Hurren and S.A. King. 2014. 'Narratives of Poverty and Sickness in Europe 1780 to 1938: Sources, Methods and Experiences', in id. (eds), *Poverty and Sickness in Modern Europe.* London: Bloomsbury, pp. 1–33.

3. For letters to the king see K. Tenfelde and H. Trischler (eds). 1986. *Bis vor die Stufen des Throns: Bittschriften und Beschwerden von Bergleuten im Zeitalter der Industrialisierung.* Munich: Beck or, similarly, for Belgium M. van Ginderachter. 2006. 'Public transcripts of Royalism: Pauper letters to the Belgian Royal Family (1880–1940)', in G. Deneckere and J. Deploige (eds), *Mystifying the Monarch: Studies on Discourse, Power and History.* Amsterdam. AmsterdamUniversity, pp. 223–34.

4. On the minutes of these oral depositions see A. Gestrich. 2014. 'Das Leben der Armen: "Ego-Dokumente" als Quellen zur Geschichte von Armut und Armenfürsorge im 19. Jahrhundert', in Sczesny, Kießling, Burkhardt (eds). *Prekariat*, pp. 39–60, here 42–44.

5. Sokoll, *Writing for Relief,* p. 99 categorizes his sources according to 'formal, linguistic and rhetorical characteristics' into 'standard letters', 'oral writings' and 'petitions'. For a critical engagement with these categories in the context of German documents see Sczesny, *Der lange Weg,* pp. 19–29. Sczesny divides the applications to the charitable foundation of the Fuggerei in Augsburg into very short letters with only minimum

information, clearly structured standard letters and very long and detailed depositions of needs, demands and circumstances.

6. Some legal scholars differentiate between *Supplikationen* as the continuation of a formal legal procedure which also required a certain format of writing, and a *Supplik* as an independent request without connection to an ongoing legal case and not requiring a certain format. In everyday administration, however, these terms were used interchangeably.

7. See, for the more formal character of a *Supplik*, also J. and W. Grimm. 1942. *Deutsches Wörterbuch*. Leipzig: Hirzel, vol. 20, p. 1251. In early modern German administrative language the term *Supplikation* seems predominant. It is only in the course of the nineteenth century that, due to the deferential connotations of the terms, *Supplik* or *Supplikation* were sometimes replaced by *Petition*. For a concise overview of the development and ambiguities of these terms in German legal and political contexts see for, example: A. Büttner. 2003. *Hoffnungen einer Minderheit: Suppliken jüdischer Einwohner an den Hamburger Senat im 19. Jahrhundert.* Münster: LIT, pp. 13–16.

8. See H. Neuhaus. 2000 '„Supplizieren und Wassertrinken sind jedem gestattet". Über den Zugang des Einzelnen zum frühneuzeitlichen Ständestaat', in D. Murswiek, et al. (eds). *Staat – Souveränität –Verfassung. FS Quaritsch.* Berlin: Duncker & Humblot.

9. Article 126 of the Weimar Constitution stipulated that 'every German has the right to turn to an office [*Behörde*] or the parliament in writing with a request or a complaint'. Article 17 of the West German constitution is more or less identical with the one in the Weimar constitution. See F. Mühlberg, 1999. *Informelle Konfliktbewältigung. Zur Geschichte der Eingabe in der DDR.* Chemnitz: unpublished Ph.D. dissertation, pp. 46–51.

10. For letters to Hitler see H. Eberle (ed.). 2007. *Briefe an Hitler. Ein Volk schreibt seinem Führer. Unbekannte Dokumente aus Moskauer Archiven – zum ersten Mal veröffentlicht.* Bergisch Gladbach: Verlagsgruppe Lübbe; for the legal and constitutional aspects of petitioning in the GDR see R. Schröder. 2008. *Zivilrechtskultur der DDR,* vol. 4, *Vom Inkasso- zum Feierabendprozess Der DDR Zivilprozess.* Berlin: Duncker & Humblot, pp. 104–24. For an overview of the constitutional right to petition in twentieth-century Germany see Mühlberg, *Konfliktbewältigung*, pp. 46–47.

11. See *Verordnung über die Prüfung von Vorschlägen und Beschwerden der Werktätigen*, 6 February 1953 in Mühlberg, *Konfliktbewältigung*, pp. 112–14.

12. Frequently, the overseer of the poor was also not available which was, for example the case with Carl Hader from the Cologne suburb of Deutz, who wrote: ' I dutifully tell your Grace that I have been to the office twice on Wednesday afternoon, but, due to your absence, was not able to state my case in person …', Historisches Archiv der Stadt Köln, Bestand 860, Stadtteil Deutz, Nr. 139, fol. 284.3, 7 September 1882.

13. For this differentiation see J.G. Krünitz. 1841. ‚Supplik', in *Oekonomische Encyklopädie oder allgemeines System der Staats-, Stadt- Haus- und Landwirthschaft in alphabetischer Ordnung*, 242 vols. Berlin: Joachim Pauli et al. 1773–1858, vol. 178, pp. 499–501, http://www.kruenitz1.uni-trier.de/ (retrieved 10 November 2015); also W. Hülle. 1973. 'Das Supplikenwesen in Rechtssachen. Anlageplan für eine Dissertation', in *Zeitschrift der Savigny-Stiftung für Rechtsgeschichte. Germanistische Abteilung* 90(1):194–212.

14. R. Fuhrmann, B. Kümin and A. Würgler. 'Supplizierende Gemeinden, Aspekte einer vergleichenden Quellenbetrachtung', in P. Blickle (ed.), *Gemeinde und Staat im alten Europa* (Historische Zeitschrift, Beihefte N.F., 25). Munich: Oldenbourg, pp. 267–324.

15. For a systematic overview over the typology of *Suppliken* and the latest research for early modern Europe see A. Würgler. 2001. 'Voices from the "Silent Masses": Humble Petitions and Social Conflicts in Early Modern Central Europe', in L. Heerma van Voss (ed.), *Petitions in Social History*. Cambridge: Cambridge University Press, pp. 11–34 and Id. 2005. 'Bitten und Begehren. Suppliken und Gravamina in der deutschsprachigen Frühneuzeitforschung', in C. Nubola and A. Würgler (eds), *Bittschriften und Gravamina. Politik, Verwaltung und Justiz in Europa (14.–18. Jahrhundert)*. Berlin: Duncker & Humblot, pp. 17–52.

16. The main exceptions are Chr. Hämmerle. 2003. 'Bitten – Klagen – Fordern. Erste Überlegungen zu Bittbriefen österreichischer Unterschichtsfrauen (1865–1918)', in *BIOS. Zeitschrift für Biographieforschung, Oral History und Lebensverlaufsanalysen* 16(1):87–110; and the contributions to Sczesny et al. (eds), *Prekariat*.

17. Mühlberg, *Konfliktbewältigung. Zur Geschichte der Eingabe in der DDR*. Chemnitz: unpublished Ph.D. dissertation; Id. 2004. *Bürger, Bitten und Behörden. Geschichte der Eingabe in der DDR*. Berlin: Karl Dietz, p. 7.

18. D. Lürbke. 2014. *Armut und Armutspolitik in der Stadt. Castrop-Rauxel, Freiburg und Schwerin im innerdeutschen Vergleich, 1955 bis 1975*. Freiburg: unpublished Ph.D. dissertation. There were, however, also regional differences. The Freiburg records contain many more letters with requests for support to higher officials outside the welfare administration than those in the other two cities.

19. On ego documents see R. Dekker. 2002. 'Jacques Presser's Heritage: Egodocuments in the Study of History', in *Memoria y Civilización* 5:13–37; W. Schulze (ed.). 1996. *Ego-Dokumente. Annäherungen an den Menschen in der Geschichte*. Berlin: Akademie; B. v. Krusenstjern. 1994. 'Was sind Selbstzeugnisse? Begriffskritische und quellenkundliche Überlegungen anhand von Beispielen aus dem 17. Jahrhundert', in *Historische Anthropologie. Kultur. Gesellschaft. Alltag* 2:462–71 as well as the website of the Centre for the Study of Egodocuments and History at the Huizinga Institute Amsterdam (http://www.egodocument.net/egodocument/egodocuments-1814.html); O. Ulbricht. 1996. 'Supplikationen als Ego-Dokumente. Bittschriften von Leibeigenen aus der ersten Hälfte des 17. Jahrhunderts als Beispiel', in W. Schulze (ed.), *Ego-Dokumente. Anäherungen an den Menschen in der Geschichte*. Berlin: Akademie, pp. 149–79.

20. Sokoll, *Writing*, p. 108.

21. Sokoll, *Writing*, p. 109.

22. 'Dessen Handzeichen beurkundet Lehrer Kling. Aus Mitleiden gratis verfaßt, von Lehrer M. Kling dahier'. Staatsarchiv Ludwigsburg StALb, E212 Israelitische Oberkirchenbehörde, Bü 416: Unterstützung von israelitischen Armen, 1837–1855; Wolf Massenbacher bittet die irsraelitische Oberkirchenbehörde um Unterstützung, 15 February 1854.

23. Ibid.: 'Seit 25 Jahren dahier verheirathet, war ich namentlich an der Seite einer treuen Lebensgefährtin (meiner Frau) anfangs im Stande, meine Familie mit Ehren durchzubringen und fühlte mich glücklich, so lange ich gesund war und meine Handels Unternehmungen guten Fortgang hatten. Bald aber sollte es anders werden, denn die Gebrechen des Alters und Kränklichkeiten aller Art stellten sich vor der Zeit bei mir ein; es kamen zu früh die trüben Tage, die dem natürlichen Menschen nicht gefallen; … Nur durch großen Fleiß und Sparsamkeit meiner Frau und durch den Wohlthätigkeitssinn edler Glaubensbrüder war es mir möglich, mein Leben so lange zu erhalten. Nun aber wurde mir meine Frau seit 3 Jahren durch den Tod entrissen, mein

Sohn in Amerika, von dem ich über 1½ Jahre nichts weiß und meine Tochter an der sächsischen Gränze mit geringem Lohn dienend, vermögen mich nicht zu unterstützen. 'So bin ich von aller Menschen Hülfe verlassen und muß bei meiner großen Noth die gegenwärtige theure Zeit doppelt schwer büßen, weßhalb ich mich sehne, bald einzugehen in eine bessere Heimath.

'Da ich aber nicht weiß, wann mich der Herr abruft und es Sünde wäre, mich dem Hungerstode hingeben zu wollen, so wage ich die submisse Bitte, eine Königliche israelitische Oberkirchens Behörde wolle mir, unter den erwähnten Umständen gnädigst zu einer Unterstützung behilflich seyn, damit nicht vollends mein überschuldetes Häuschen den Gläubigern zufällt und ich am Ende obdachlos unter freiem Himmel campieren müßte.

Zu jetziger theurer Zeit fängt der Wohltätigkeitssinn an, die notorisch arme Christengemeinde mit einer Suppenanstalt zu unterstützen; dagegen für mich armen Krüppel vermag die hiesige unbemittelte ... isr. filialgemeinde nichts, gar nichts beizutragen und so muß ich oft das liebe trockene Brod entbehren. Dieß aber ist nicht der Wille Einer Königlichen israelistischen Obers Kirchenbehörde, aus deren Hand auch so viele milde Gaben fließen.

Darum rufe ich zu Gott und guten Menschen um Hilfe in der Noth also um baldige gnädige Unterstützung, und sehe der Gewähr dieser meiner gedrungenen Bitte hoffnungsvoll entgegen, womit ich ehrerbietigst zeichne Einer Königlichen israelitischen Oberkirchen Behörde, unterthänigster Wolf Massenbacher'.

24. For German letter writing manuals see, for example: S. Ettl. 1984. *Anleitungen zu schriftlicher Kommunikation: Briefsteller von 1880 bis 1980*. Tübingen: Max Niemeyer; S. Grosse, M. Grimberg and T. Hölscher. 1989. *'Denn das Schreiben gehört nicht zu meiner Beschäftigung': Der Alltag kleiner Leute in Bittschriften, Briefen und Berichten aus dem 19. Jahrhundert. Ein Lesebuch.* Bonn: J.H.W. Dietz Nachf.

25. See I. McNeely. 2003. *The Emancipation of Writing. German Civil Society in the Making, 1790s–1820s.* Berkeley: University of California Press.

26. Landesarchiv Berlin (LAB) A Rep 003-01, Magistrat der Stadt Berlin, Armendirektion, Generalia, Findbuch, Bd.1, Nr. 84, 1) Bestimmungen über die Einreichung von Gesuchen und Beschwerden; 2) Die Bestrafung der unerlaubten Anfertigung von Bittschriften für andere gegen Bezahlung und die Abstellung der schriftlichen Bettelei.

27. Historisches Archiv der Stadt Köln, Bestand 860, Stadtteil Deutz, Nr. 137, fol. 454, 8 February 1873.

'Herrn Oberbergeister [sic!] dahier

Mit unterwürfigkeit lege ich Ihnen meine Bitte zu Füßen und stehe in erwartung das der Herr Porgemeister mir die selbige in Gnaden annehmen wird der Grund meiner Bitte ist folgend Es ist ja Ihnen bekannt wie das mein Mann verhaftet ist und ich Arme verlassene Frau jezt mit 5 Kinderin in den Elende stehen Ja Herr Porgemeister die Noth zwingt mich dazu Sie in anspruch zu nehmen, denn in dießer lage ist kein durchkommen war nicht, ich habe zware die Millihtär Wasche wo ich aber allein nicht mit durchkommen kann denn dieselbige fordert Gesunde Leuthe Dieweil ich aber nun häufig an Brust und Magenschmerzen Leite so ist es eine unmöglichkeit so alleine durchzu kommen Ohne das ich Hülfe haben, Insgesamt bin ich jezt 3½ Thaler Hausmiethe schuldich nebenbei ist auch eine Rechnung von Herrn Dockter Willems zur einsicht wovon soll ich aber ein solches hernehmen indem ich weder Hilfe noch Trost haben Ich würde nicht der Gemeinde zur last kommen noch weder in einer hinsicht belästigen, das wenn ich mein Mann wieder in der Mitte und zur Hilfe hätte, Nun möchte ich doch fußfällig den Herrn Porgemeister gebethen haben in dießer beziehung eine Hilfreiche Hand zu weisen und ein gutes Wort von mein Mann …, denn er ist ja doch soviel wie unschuldich in das Elende gestürtz denn ich sehe in der Meinung dass ja doch Rathsammer … ein gutes Wort war zulegen als der Gemeinde zu last zu fallen Wenn selbiges aber nicht geschehen kann so finde ich mich gegewärtig auf unterstützung einen antrag zu machen. Umgehend möchte ich nochmahls denn Herrn Porgemeister fußfällig gebethen mir in dießer lage behülflich zu sagen denn auf Sie alleine Stehet mein festes zutrauen das ich von Ihnen Hilfe erwarten

Achtungsvoll euer unterthänigste Bittstellerin

Helena Dütz

Polwerkstraße No. 4'

28. See J.H. Kumpf. 1983. *Petitionsrecht und öffentliche Meinung im Entstehungsprozeß der Paulskirchenverfassung 1848/49*. Frankfurt/Main, Bern, New York: Lang; C. Leys. 1955. 'Petitioning in the Nineteenth and Twentieth Centuries', *Political Studies*, 3:45–64.

29. Mühlberg, *Konfliktbewältigung*, pp. 308–16.

30. Mühlberg, *Konfliktbewältigung*, p. 316.

31. See also Hämmerle, 'Bitten – Klagen – Fordern' and C. Vanja. 2006. 'Patientenbiographien im Spiegel frühneuzeitlicher Bittschriften', *BIOS. Zeitschrift für Biographieforschung, Oral History und Lebensverlaufsanalysen* 19(1):26–35.

32. For this aspect see in particular H. Bräuer. 2001. 'Persönliche Bittschriften als sozial- und mentalitätsgeschichtliche Quellen. Beobachtungen aus frühneuzeitlichen Städten Obersachsens', in G. Ammerer, C. Rohr and A.S. Weiss (eds), *Tradition und Wandel. Beiträge zur Kirchen-, Gesellschafts- und Kulturgeschichte. FS Dopsch* Vienna, Munich: Oldenbourg, pp. 294–304; Id. and E. Schlenkrich. 2002. *Armut und Armutsbekämpfung. Schriftliche und bildliche Quellen bis um 1800 aus Chemnitz, Dresden, Freiberg, Leipzig und Zwickau. Ein sachthematisches Inventar*, 2 vols. Leipzig: Leipziger Universitätsverlag; Id. 2008, *Zur Mentalität armer Leute in Obersachsen 1500 bis 1800: Essays*. Leipzig: Leipziger Universitätsverlag.

33. Gestrich, 'Leben', p. 43.

34. See A. Gestrich and D. Heinisch. 2016. '"… They sit for days and have only their sorrow to eat". Old Age Poverty in German Pauper Narratives', in B. Althammer, L. Raphael and T. Stazic-Wendt (eds), *Rescuing the Vulnerable: Poverty, Welfare and Social Ties in Nineteenth- and Twentieth-Century Europe*. New York, Oxford: Berghahn; L. Gray. 2002. 'The experience of old age in the narratives of the rural poor in early modern Germany', in S. Ottaway, L. Bothelo and K. Kittridge (eds), *Power and Poverty: Old Age in the Pre-Industrial Past*, Westport: Greenwood Press, pp. 107–25; or T. Sokoll. 1997. 'Old Age in Poverty. The Record of Essex Pauper Letters, 1780–1824', in T. Hitchcock, P. King and P. Sharpe (eds), *Chronicling Poverty: The Voices and Strategies of the English Poor 1640–1840*. Baslngstoke: Palgrave, pp. 127–54.

35. Hohenlohisches Zentralarchiv Neuenstein HZAN, Ba 70, Öhringer Hospitalstiftung: Pfründenverzeichnisse der Hospitalverwaltung Öhringen; Bü 799: Bittgesuche um Pfründen und Verleihung von Pfründen, Bittgesuch des taubstummen Fritz H. um eine Pfründe, 'Bartenstein, 1. Oct. 1913: Durchlauchtigster Fürst und Herr! Wer in unserer Gemeinde mühselig und beladen ist, der flüchtet sich in der Not zu seinem Schirmherrn, dessen Güte von jeher unser Trost war. Der Unterzeichnete, Fritz Hofmann, befindet sich durch einen Unglücksfall in bedrängten Verhältnissen. Schon

als kleines Kind taubstum und durch große Opfer der Eltern zu einem tüchtigen Schreiner ausgebildet, war ich, trotzdem ich der Sprache u. des Gehörs beraubt war, immer hin trotz des geringen Verdienstes von 4 M. pro Woche zufrieden, da ich mir im Bewußtsein meiner Arbeitskraft mein Selbstbewußtsein aufrecht erhielt. Nun ist auch meine Arbeitskraft dahin und dieses Unglück, das nur der ermessen kann, der dies als letzte Summe von Daseins Freude und Besitz, hat mich zu einem gedrückten Menschen, der mit Sorgen in die Zukunft schauen muß, gemacht. In dieser Not komme ich zu unserem allergnädigsten Herrn und Fürsten und bitte um Huld und Gnade für einen, der nun so geruhsam aus dem werktätigen Leben ausgeschieden und so gebrechlich worden ist. Ich bitte Eure Durchlaucht ergebenst, mir eine erledigte Pfründe huldvollste zukommen zu lassen. Diese Bitte soll unterstützt werden durch heißes Gebetsstammeln eines Taubstummen für unser edles Fürstenhaus. Bartenstein, den 1. Oktober 1913. Fritz Hofmann.'

36. Brandenburgisches Landeshauptarchiv Potsdam (BLHA), Rep. 2A, I, SW, Nr. 807, Sonderakte betr. Erwerbslosenfürsorge, fol. 561 r., 12. July 1920.

37. See, for example, Stadtarchiv Stralsund (SAS), 4/9797 Gewandschneider-Kompanie, Anträge auf Unterstützung, 1855–1876, Antrag von Georgine Backhus, 26 September 1868: 'Die Wohllöblichen Altermänner des Gewandhauses bitte ich ganz gehorsamst '.… Ich lege daher meine herzliche Bitte den wohllöblichen Altermännern vertrauensvoll an das Herz und nenne mich Ihre gehorsamste Georgine Backhus geb. Laas'.

38. P. Hintzen. 2014. 'Was die Fürsorge leisten sollte – Gesuchsteller zwischen Notsituation und vorsichtiger Systemkritik', in A. Sczesny, R. Kießling and J. Burkhardt (eds), *Prekariat im 19. Jahrhundert. Armenfürsorge und Alltagsbewältigung in Stadt und Land.* Augsburg: Wißner, pp. 131–47, here 144–46.

39. A. Volkland. 1941. *So mußt Du Deine Briefe schreiben. Wegweiser und Muster für eindrucksvolle Briefe. Die Privatpost – Die Geschäftspost. Eingaben, Anträge und Gesuche.* Mühlhausen: Danner, p. 11 advised his readers in the name of the Volksgemeinschaft against 'Duckmäuserei, Speichelleckerei und kriecherische[r] Knechtseligkeit'. See also Ettl, *Anleitungen*, p. 177.

40. C. Elwenspoek. 1937. *Der rechte Brief – zur rechten Zeit. Eine Fibel des schriftlichen Verkehrs für jedermann.* Leipzig: Hesse & Becker, p. 33: 'Machen wir uns doch endlich klar, daß unser neuer Staat ein Staat der Volksgemeinschaft ist: Daß der Arbeiter heute als genauso wichtiges Glied des Ganzen gilt wie der Professor oder der Minister'. See also Ettl, *Anleitungen*, p. 177.

41. Lürbke, *Armut*, pp. 122–23. Lürbke explains this, however, as an adaptation to the style of bureaucratic forms rather than a specific expression of a new self-confident style of interacting with administrations.

42. BLHA Potsdam, Rep. 2A, I, SW, Nr. 807, Sonderakte betr. Erwerbslosenfürsorge, fol. 561 r., 12. July 1920.

43. Sokoll, *Writing*; S.A. King and A. Stringer. 2012. '"I have once more taken the Liberty to say as you well know": The development of rhetoric in the letters of the English, Welsh and Scottish sick and poor 1780s–1830s', in A. Gestrich, E. Hurren and S.A. King (eds), *Poverty and Sickness in Modern Europe: Narratives of the Sick Poor, 1780–1938.* London: Bloomsbury, pp. 69–92.

44. See, for example: the UNESCO concepts of poverty and their strategy for the eradication of poverty: http://www.unesco.org/ldc/strategy.htm (retrieved 29 July 2016).

45. On the importance of clothing in the context of English pauper letters see esp. S.A. King and C. Payne (eds). 2002. *The Dress of the Poor, 1700–1900*. Special edition *Textile History*; S.A. King. 2010. 'Kleidung und Würde. Über die Aushandlung der Armenunterstützung in England, 1800–40', in S. Hahn, N. Lobner and C. Sedmak (eds), *Armut in Europa 1500–2000*. Innsbruck, pp. 82–99. There is no parallel research so far on this topic in German poor relief applications.

46. HZAN, Ba 70, Domänenkanzlei II, Bü 800, Bittgesuche von Angehörigen der Rentamtsbezirke Bartenstein und Pfedelbach, 1846–1868, Erneutes Bittgesuch der Witwe Margarete Bachtler um freie Logis, 27 August 1846: 'Sollte aber dieses Local, hoher gnädigster Herrschaft nicht entbehrlich seyn, so bitte ich unterthänigst doch gnädigst einen Miethezins mir ertheilen zu wollen, … um gnädigste Entschädigung für die verfloßenen vielen Jahre, in welchen ich, als die einzige der fürstl. Dieners Wittwen ohne Herrschaftl. Wohnung zubrachte…'.

47. Landesarchiv Nordrhein-Westfalen, Abteilung Ostwestfalen-Lippe (Detmold), Kabinettsministerium, L 75 II 11, Nr. 7 Vol. II, Gesuch des Fabrikarbeiters Friedrich Reuter in Blomberg. Betrifft Bewilligung der Beschaffungsbeihilfe: 'Blomberg 28. Mai. 1920. Mit anliegendem Entscheid Lippischer Regierung betreffens der Beschaffungsbeihilfe kann ich mich unter keinen Umständen Einverstanden erklären, und bitte das Landespräsidium mir beizustehen, und die mir tatsächlich zustehende Beihülfe zu gewähren. Ich habe drei Söhne im Felde gehabt. davon ist fraglich vom Sebtember 1916 bis Sebt 1919 in Gefangenschaft gewesen, die Unterstützung die ich erhalten habe habe ich reichlich doppelt im Feindesland senden müssen. Ich verlange ja nur mein ausgelegtes Geld wieder welches ich habe bei der Rückker meines Sohnes aus der Gefangenschaft anwenden müssen um denselben die Gelegnheit zu geben sich als Mensch auf der Straße sehen lassen zu können. Auserdem behaubte ich erneut das die verteilung der bewilligten Summe nicht gerecht geschehen ist. War es nicht genug daß ich drei Söhne habe dem Vaterland stellen müssen, jetzt bürdet man mir auch noch auf, nach rückker dieselben als Menschen wieder einzukleiden und zu beköstigen, gerecht muß verfaren werden dem einen wie dem anderen und bitte daher um die erfüllung meiner Bitte. Ergebenst. Frau Reuter'.

48. See for example Stadtarchiv Eisenach, 10/1588: Bittgesuch der Wilhemina Böttger um eine Unterstützung, 13 March 1847: 'Ich ersterbe in der Hoffnung, wo ich auch hoffen kann das mir meine Bitte gewährt wirt in dem es doch so vielen zu theil wirt die es nicht zu nothwendig brauchen als ich …'.

49. Quoted from Mühlberg, *Konfliktbewältigung*, p. 276.

50. Ibid., pp. 277–80. For the role of *Wohnraum* in GDR *Eingaben* see also Lürbke, *Armut*, p. 143.

51. For a short introduction into the concept of 'deserving' and 'Würde' see L. Raphael. 2011. 'Würde der Armen', in H. Uerlings, N. Trauth and L. Clemens (eds), *Armut. Perspektiven in Kunst und Gesellschaft*. Darmstadt: Wissenschaftliche Buchgesellschaft, pp. 65–66.

52. See for Germany and concentrating on *Bittschriften* K. Marx-Jaruselski. 2014. 'Von der "Ökonomie des Notbehelfs" und "würdigen Armen" – Armenfürsorge und Ar mutsbewältigung im Spiegel von Antragsschreiben an die kommunale Verwaltung', in A. Sczesny, R. Kießling and J. Burkhardt (eds), *Prekariat im 19. Jahrhundert. Armenfürsorge und Alltagsbewältigung in Stadt und Land*. Augsburg: Wißner, pp. 179–90, here 187–90.

53. BLHA Potsdam, Rep. 2A, I, SW, Nr. 807, Sonderakte betr. Erwerbslosenfürsorge, fol. 552 r., 25 May 1920; Hohenlohisches Zentralarchiv Neuenstein, Ba 70, Öhringer Hospitalstiftung: Pfründenverzeichnisse der Hospitalverwaltung Öhringen; Bü 799: Bittgesuche um Pfründen und Verleihung von Pfründen, Bittgesuch des taubstummen Fritz H. um eine Pfründe, Bartenstein, 1 Oct. 1913.

54. E.T. Hurren and S.A. King. 2005. 'Begging for a Burial: Death and the Poor Law in Eighteenth and Nineteenth Century England', *Social History*, 30:321–41.

55. Frequently, relatives helped, but asked afterwards for a contribution to the burial costs. See, for example: SAS, 10/447 Kloster St Annen und Brigitten, Pastor Wüsthof bittet im Namen des Tagelöhners Scheel um Unterstützung zu den Beerdigungskosten seiner Schwiegermutter Kasper, 12 December 1876.

56. HZAN, Ba 70, Öhringer Hospitalstiftung: Pfründenverzeichnisse der Hospitalverwaltung Öhringen; Bü 799: Bittgesuche um Pfründen und Verleihung von Pfründen, Bittgesuch des taubstummen Fritz H. um eine Pfründe, 1 October 1913: 'immer hin trotz des geringen Verdienstes von 4 M. pro Woche zufrieden, da ich mir im Bewußtsein meiner Arbeitskraft mein Selbstbewußtsein aufrecht erhielt. Nun ist auch meine Arbeitskraft dahin und dieses Unglück, das nur der ermessen kann, der dies als letzte Summe von Daseins Freude und Besitz, hat mich zu einem gedruckten Menschen, der mit Sorgen in die Zukunft schauen muß, gemacht'.

57. SAS, Gewandschneider-Kompanie, Anträge auf Unterstützung, 1855–1876, Gesuch d. Witwe Stegelin, 5 Oct. 1868: 'Durch mühevolle Händearbeit, [indem?] ich durch Weißnätherei mich Tag und Nacht abgemüht habe, habe ich es dahin gebracht, da meine Kinder an[?]gelernt haben, und sich selbst jetzt ernähren können, das Geschick aber will es daß beim redlichsten Willen meiner Kinder, es denselben nicht möglich ist mir etwas mitzutheilen'.

58. See Lürbke, *Armut*, p. 125.

59. StALb, E 173, III: Kreisregierung Ludwigsburg, Spezialia, Bü 162: Arme, Oberamt Maulbronn, p. 4, 12 August 1844: '..., so erklärte ich demselben, daß ich durch elendes Versorgen, meiner, und meines Weibs Eltern, nicht Kreuzerswerth erbt habe, und hätte jedoch von Seiten meiner Schwiegereltern einen Antheil an einem Haus ererben sollen, worinnen ich meine Unterstüzung gefunden hätte, wenn meine Ortsbehörde Rücksicht, und Achtung auf meine arme, nothleidende Familie genommen hätten. Alwo sie meiner gedankenlosen und unverständigen Schwiegermutter, ein Testament für meine ledigen Schwager, helfen gemecht haben, und mein Weib und Kinder gänzlich enterbt, und von Aller Seiten gehaßt, und unterdrückt, so daß meine Ortsbehörden den Schluß gefaßt haben, mich mit meiner Familie, welche besteht in vier Kindern, in ein Stüblein von 8 Schuh breit, 11 bis 12 Schuh lang 8 1/2 Schuh hoch, und einerseits 2 Schuh tief im Erdreich sich befindet, von dem Armenstüblein abgetheilt, da jedoch ein Arrest für Verbrecher in besserer Ordnung sich befindet, so will man mich mit meiner Familie in einen solchen Biegel da hinein sperren; welcher noch ungesunder ist, als mein voriger Hauszins ...'.

60. For this discussion with reference to the English poor, see S.A. King. 2008. 'Friendship, Kinship and Belonging in the Letters of Urban Paupers 1800–1840', *Historical Social Research*, 33:249–77. There is still no German parallel to Keith Snell's magisterial account of the importance of community and belonging in Britain. See K. Snell. 2008. *Parish and Belonging: Community, Identity and Welfare in England and Wales, 1700–1950*. Cambridge: Cambridge University Press.

61. An early example of this approach for twentieth-century German welfare history is D. Crew. 1996. *Germans on Welfare. From Weimar to Hitler.* Oxford: Oxford University Press; see also P. Becker (ed.). 2011. *Sprachvollzug im Amt. Kommunikation und Verwaltung im Europa des 19. und 20. Jahrhunderts.* Bielefeld: transcript. This micro-perspective on welfare regimes and the processes of inclusion and exclusion was also the main focus of the Trier Collaborative Research Centre on 'Strangers and poor people. Changing Patterns of Inclusion and Exclusion from Classical Antiquity to the Present Day'. For some core results of this research programme see L. Raphael and H. Uerlings (eds). 2008. *Zwischen Ausschluss und Solidarität. Modi der Inklusion/Exklusion von Fremden und Armen in Europa seit der Spätantike.* Frankfurt/Main: Lang; for a full bibliography see http://www.fze.uni-trier.de/de/presse-und-service/gesamtbibliographie (retrieved 29 July 2016).

62. For a short overview and a fascinating set of examples of such *Eingaben* see Mühlberg, *Konfliktbewältigung*, pp. 355–86. It was particularly during the years after the war that the need for relief and the distribution of food seemed to have been frequent topics of such *Eingaben.*

63. BLHA Potsdam, Rep. 2A, I, SW, Nr. 807: Sonderakten betreffend Erwerbslosenfürsorge 1920, fol. 549r, 17 May 20:
    'Hochgeehrter Herr Regierungs-Präsident! Gestatten Ew. Hochwohlgeb. bitte folgende Zeilen, ich empfehle sie untertänigst Ihrer Güte: Ich bin seit längerer Zeit erwerbslos und habe noch keine Erwerbslosenunterstützung erhalten trotzdem ich hier in Lankwitz meine so sehr bedr[ückte] Lage dem Gemeinde-Vorstand angezeigt habe, mehrere Male und habe auch um Beschäftigung gebeten, doch alles war vergebens! [fol. 549v] Ich bin Tischler und 58 Jahr alt und war früher in einem Erziehungsheim tätig und besitze darüber ein gutes Zeugnis. Ich möchte Ew. Hochwohlgeb. Darum hiermit höfl. Gebeten haben, mir etwas an Erwerbslosenunterstützung gütigst nachzahlen zu laßen, denn meine Lage ist qualvoll und peinlich, da meine Kleidung reduziert ist, ebenso die Stiefel und doch wäre ich so leicht geholfen wenn eine Hilfe käme und ich könnte auch noch gut mein Brot verdienen wenn eine liebe Hand eingreifen wurde und darum hoffe ich zuversichtlich, indem Ew. Hochwohlgeb. so freundl. sein werden [fol. 550 r] und mir eine Hilfe erwirken laßen; ich bitte um der Menschlichkeit willen denn ich muß erliegen, wenn keine Hilfe kömmt! Mit vorzügl. Hochachtung Zeichnet ganz ergebenst Otto T. Lankwitz Mühlenstr. 28.'

64. See, however, S.A. King. 2011. 'Welfare regimes and welfare regions in Britain and Europe, c. 1750–1860', *Journal of Modern European History*, 9:42–66; L. Raphael. 2013. 'Grenzen von Inklusion und Exklusion. Sozialräumliche Regulierung von Armut und Fremdheit im Europa der Neuzeit', *Journal of Modern European History* 11:147–67.

Works Cited

Becker, P. (ed.). 2011. *Sprachvollzug im Amt: Kommunikation und Verwaltung im Europa des 19. und 20. Jahrhunderts.* Bielefeld: transcript.

Bräuer, H. 2001. 'Persönliche Bittschriften als sozial- und mentalitätsgeschichtliche Quellen: Beobachtungen aus frühneuzeitlichen Städten Obersachsens' , in G. Ammerer, C. Rohr and A.S. Weiss (eds), *Tradition und Wandel:*

Beiträge zur Kirchen-, Gesellschafts- und Kulturgeschichte. FS Dopsch. Vienna, Munich: Oldenbourg, pp. 294–304.

———. 2008. *Zur Mentalität armer Leute in Obersachsen 1500 bis 1800: Essays.* Leipzig: Leipziger Universitätsverlag.

——— and E. Schlenkrich. 2002. *Armut und Armutsbekämpfung: Schriftliche und bildliche Quellen bis um 1800 aus Chemnitz, Dresden, Freiberg, Leipzig und Zwickau. Ein sachthematisches Inventar,* 2 vols. Leipzig: Leipziger Universitätsverlag.

Büttner, A. 2003. *Hoffnungen einer Minderheit: Suppliken jüdischer Einwohner an den Hamburger Senat im 19. Jahrhundert.* Münster: LIT.

Crew, D. 1996. *Germans on Welfare: From Weimar to Hitler.* Oxford: Oxford University Press.

Dekker, R. 2002. 'Jacques Presser's Heritage: Egodocuments in the Study of History', *Memoria y Civilización* 5:13–37.

Eberle, H. (ed.). 2007. *Briefe an Hitler: Ein Volk schreibt seinem Führer: Unbekannte Dokumente aus Moskauer Archiven – zum ersten Mal veröffentlicht.* Bergisch Gladbach: Verlagsgruppe Lübbe.

Elwenspoek, C. 1937. *Der rechte Brief – zur rechten Zeit. Eine Fibel des schriftlichen Verkehrs für jedermann.* Leipzig: Hesse & Becker.

Ettl, S.1984. *Anleitungen zu schriftlicher Kommunikation: Briefsteller von 1880 bis 1980.* Tübingen: Max Niemeyer.

Fuhrmann, R., B. Kümin and A. Würgler.1998. 'Supplizierende Gemeinden: Aspekte einer vergleichenden Quellenbetrachtung', in P. Blickle (ed.), *Gemeinde und Staat im alten Europa.* Munich: Oldenbourg, pp. 267–324.

Gestrich, A. 2014. 'Das Leben der Armen: "Ego-Dokumente" als Quellen zur Geschichte von Armut und Armenfürsorge im 19. Jahrhundert', in A. Sczesny, R. Kießling and J. Burkhardt, (eds), *Prekariat im 19. Jahrhundert: Armenfürsorge und Alltagsbewältigung in Stadt und Land.* Augsburg: Wißner, pp. 39–60.

———, E. Hurren and S.A. King. 2012. 'Narratives of Poverty and Sickness in Europe 1780 to 1938: Sources, Methods and Experiences', in ibid. (eds), *Poverty and Sickness in Modern Europe.* London: Bloomsbury, pp. 1–33.

———, and D. Heinisch. 2016. '"… They sit for days and have only their sorrow to eat": Old Age Poverty in German Pauper Narratives', in: B. Althammer, L. Raphael and T. Stazic-Wendt (eds), *Rescuing the Vulnerable: Poverty, Welfare and Social Ties in Nineteenth- and Twentieth-Century Europe.* New York, Oxford: Berghahn, pp. 356–81.

Ginderachter, M. van. 2006. 'Public Transcripts of Royalism: Pauper Letters to the Belgian Royal Family (1880–1940)', in G. Deneckere and J. Deploige (eds), *Mystifying the Monarch: Studies on Discourse, Power and History.* Amsterdam: Amsterdam University Press, pp. 223–34.

Gray, L. 2002. 'The experience of old age in the narratives of the rural poor in early modern Germany', in S. Ottaway, L. Botelho and K. Kittridge (eds), *Power and Poverty: Old Age in the Pre-Industrial Past.* Westport: Greenwood Press, pp.107–25.

Grimm, J,. and W. 1942. *Deutsches Wörterbuch,* vol. 20. Leipzig: Hirzel.

Grosse, S., M. Grimberg and T. Hölscher. 1989. *'Denn das Schreiben gehört nicht zu meiner Beschäftigung': Der Alltag kleiner Leute in Bittschriften, Briefen und Berichten aus dem 19. Jahrhundert. Ein Lesebuch.* Bonn: J.H.W. Dietz Nachf.

Hämmerle, Chr. 2003. 'Bitten – Klagen – Fordern: Erste Überlegungen zu Bittbriefen österreichischer Unterschichtsfrauen (1865–1918)', *BIOS: Zeitschrift für Biographieforschung, Oral History und Lebensverlaufsanalysen* 16(1): 87–110.

Heerma van Voss, L. (ed.). 2001. *Petitions in Social History.* Cambridge: Cambridge University Press.

Hintzen, P. 2014. 'Was die Fürsorge leisten sollte – Gesuchsteller zwischen Notsituation und vorsichtiger Systemkritik', in A. Sczesny, R. Kießling and J. Burkhardt (eds), *Prekariat im 19. Jahrhundert. Armenfürsorge und Alltagsbewältigung in Stadt und Land.* Augsburg: Wißner, pp.131–47.

Hitchcock, T., P. King and P. Sharpe (eds).1997. *Chronicling Poverty: The Voices and Strategies of the English Poor 1640–1840.* Basingstoke: Palgrave.

Hurren, E.T., and S.A. King. 2005. 'Begging for a Burial: Death and the Poor Law in Eighteenth and Nineteenth Century England', *Social History*, 30:321–41.

Hülle, W. 1973. 'Das Supplikenwesen in Rechtssachen. Anlageplan für eine Dissertation', *Zeitschrift der Savigny-Stiftung für Rechtsgeschichte. Germanistische Abteilung,* 90(1):194–212.

King, S.A. 2008. 'Friendship, Kinship and Belonging in the Letters of Urban Paupers 1800–1840', *Historical Social Research* 33:249–77.

———. 2010. 'Kleidung und Würde. Über die Aushandlung der Armenunterstützung in England, 1800–40', in S. Hahn, N. Lobner and C. Sedmak (eds), *Armut in Europa 1500–2000.* Innsbruck, pp. 82–99.

———. 2011. 'Welfare regimes and welfare regions in Britain and Europe, c.1750–1860', *Journal of Modern European History,* 9.42–66.

———, and C. Payne (eds). 2002. *The Dress of the Poor, 1700–1900.* Special edition of the journal of *Textile History.*

———, and A. Levene (eds). 2006. *Voices of the Poor. Poor Law Depositions and Letters.* London: Pickering & Chattoo.

———, T. Nutt and A. Tomkins. 2006. *Narratives of the Poor in Eighteenth Century Britain.* London: Pickering & Chattoo.

———, and A. Stringer. 2012. '"I have once more taken the Liberty to say as you well know": The development of rhetoric in the letters of the English, Welsh and Scottish sick and poor 1780s–1830s', in A. Gestrich, E. Hurren and S.A. King (eds), *Poverty and Sickness in Modern Europe: Narratives of the Sick Poor, 1780–1938.* London: Bloomsbury, pp. 69–92.

Krünitz, J.G. 1841. 'Supplik', in *Oekonomische Encyklopädie oder allgemeines System der Staats-, Stadt- Haus- und Landwirthschaft in alphabetischer Ordnung,* 242 vols. Berlin: Joachim Pauli et al. 1773–1858, vol. 178, pp. 499–501, http://www.kruenitz1.uni-trier.de/. Retrieved 10 November 2015.

Krusenstjern, B. v. 1994. 'Was sind Selbstzeugnisse? Begriffskritische und quellenkundliche Überlegungen anhand von Beispielen aus dem 17. Jahrhundert', *Historische Anthropologie. Kultur. Gesellschaft. Alltag* 2:462–71.

Kumpf, J.H. 1983. *Petitionsrecht und öffentliche Meinung im Entstehungsprozeß der Paulskirchenverfassung 1848/49*. Frankfurt/Main, Bern, New York: Lang.

Lürbke, D. 2014. *Armut und Armutspolitik in der Stadt. Castrop-Rauxel, Freiburg und Schwerin im innerdeutschen Vergleich, 1955 bis 1975*. Freiburg: unpublished Ph.D. dissertation.

Leys, C. 1955. 'Petitioning in the Nineteenth and Twentieth Centuries', *Political Studies*, 3:45–64.

Marx-Jaskulski, K. 2014. 'Von der "Ökonomie des Notbehelfs" und "würdigen Armen" – Armenfürsorge und Armutsbewältigung im Spiegel von Antragsschreiben an die kommunale Verwaltung', in A. Sczesny, R. Kießling and J. Burkhardt (eds), *Prekariat im 19. Jahrhundert. Armenfürsorge und Alltagsbewältigung in Stadt und Land*. Augsburg: Wißner, pp. 179–90.

McNeely, I. 2003. *The Emancipation of Writing. German Civil Society in the Making, 1790s–1820s*. Berkeley: University of California Press 2003.

Mühlberg, F. 1999. *Informelle Konfliktbewältigung. Zur Geschichte der Eingabe in der DDR*. Chemnitz: unpublished Ph.D. dissertation. [http://www.qucosa.de/fileadmin/data/qucosa/documents/4337/data/dis.pdf].

———. 2004. *Bürger, Bitten und Behörden. Geschichte der Eingabe in der DDR*. Berlin: Karl Dietz.

Neuhaus, H. 2000. '"Supplizieren und Wassertrinken sind jedem gestattet". Über den Zugang des Einzelnen zum frühneuzeitlichen Ständestaat', in D. Murswiek, et al. (eds), *Staat – Souveränität –Verfassung. FS Quaritsch*. Berlin: Duncker & Humblot, pp. 475–92.

Nubola, C., and A. Würgler (eds). 2005. *Bittschriften und Gravamina: Petitionen, Gravamina und Suppliken in der frühen Neuzeit in Europa; Tagungen Trient, 25.–26. November 1999/Trient, 14.–16. Dezember 2000*. Berlin: Duncker & Humblot.

Raphael, L. 2011. 'Würde der Armen', in: H. Uerlings, N. Trauth and L. Clemens (eds). *Armut. Perspektiven in Kunst und Gesellschaft*. Darmstadt: Wissenschaftliche Buchgesellschaft, pp. 65–66.

———. 2013. 'Grenzen von Inklusion und Exklusion. Sozialräumliche Regulierung von Armut und Fremdheit im Europa der Neuzeit', *Journal of Modern European History* 11:147–67.

———, and H. Uerlings (eds). 2008. *Zwischen Ausschluss und Solidarität. Modi der Inklusion/Exklusion von Fremden und Armen in Europa seit der Spätantike*. Frankfurt/Main.: Lang.

Schröder, R. 2008. *Zivilrechtskultur der DDR, vol. 4: Vom Inkasso- zum Feierabendprozess Der DDR Zivilprozess*. Berlin: Duncker & Humblot.

Schulze, W. (ed.). 1996. *Ego-Dokumente. Annäherungen an den Menschen in der Geschichte*. Berlin: Akademie.

Sczesny, A. 2012. *Der lange Weg in die Fuggerei. Augsburger Armenbriefe des 19. Jahrhunderts* (fugger-digital). Augsburg: Wißner.

————, R. Kießling and J. Burkhardt (eds). 2014. *Prekariat im 19. Jahrhundert. Armenfürsorge und Alltagsbewältigung in Stadt und Land.* Augsburg: Wißner.

Snell, K. 2008. *Parish and Belonging: Community, Identity and Welfare in England and Wales, 1700–1950.* Cambridge: Cambridge University Press.

Sokoll, T. 1997. 'Old Age in Poverty. The Record of Essex Pauper Letters, 1780–1824', in T. Hitchcock, P. King and P. Sharpe (eds), *Chronicling Poverty: The Voices and Strategies of the English Poor 1640–1840.* Basingstoke: Palgrave, pp. 127–54.

————. 2000. 'Negotiating a living: Essex pauper letters from London, 1800–1834', in L. Fontaine and J. Schlumbohm (eds), *Household Strategies for Survival 1600–2000.* Cambridge: Cambridge University Press, pp. 19–46.

————. 2001. *Essex Pauper Letters 1731–1837.* Oxford: Oxford University Press.

————. 2006. 'Writing for relief: Rhetoric in English pauper letters 1800–1834', in A. Gestrich, S. King and L. Raphael (eds), *Being Poor in Modern Europe.* Bern: Lang, pp. 91–112.

Tenfelde, K., and H. Trischler (eds). 1989. *Bis vor die Stufen des Throns: Bittschriften und Beschwerden von Bergleuten im Zeitalter der Industrialisierung.* Munich: Beck.

Ulbricht, O. 1996. 'Supplikationen als Ego-Dokumente. Bittschriften von Leibeigenen aus der ersten Hälfte des 17. Jahrhunderts als Beispiel', in W. Schulze (ed.), *Ego-Dokumente. Anäherungen an den Menschen in der Geschichte.* Berlin: Akademie, pp. 149–79.

Vanja, C. 2006. 'Patientenbiographien im Spiegel frühneuzeitlicher Bittschriften', *BIOS. Zeitschrift für Biographieforschung, Oral History und Lebensverlaufsanalysen* 19(1):26–35.

Volkland, A. 1941. *So mußt Du Deine Briefe schreiben. Wegweiser und Muster für eindrucksvolle Briefe. Die Privatpost – Die Geschäftspost. Eingaben, Anträge und Gesuche.* Mühlhausen: Danner.

Würgler, A. 2001. 'Voices from the "Silent Masses": Humble Petitions and Social Conflicts in Early Modern Central Europe', in L. Heerma van Voss (ed.), *Petitions in Social History.* Cambridge: Cambridge University Press, pp. 11–34.

————. 2005. 'Bitten und Begehren. Suppliken und Gravamina in der deutschsprachigen Frühneuzeitforschung', in C. Nubola and A. Würgler (eds), *Bittschriften und Gravamina. Politik, Verwaltung und Justiz in Europa (14.–18. Jahrhundert).* Berlin: Duncker & Humblot, pp. 17–52.

Andreas Gestrich is Director of the German Historical Institute London. Recent publications include: *Being Poor in Modern Europe. Historical Perspectives 1800–1940* (co-edited with S.A. King and L. Raphael. (2006); 'Hungersnöte als Armutsfaktor', in S. Hahn et al. (eds), *Armut in Europa, 1500–2000* (2010); *The Welfare State and the 'Deviant Poor' in Europe 1870–1933* (co-edited with B. Althammer and J. Gründler, 2014).

CHAPTER 3

Vagabonds in the German Empire

Mobility, Unemployment and the Transformation of Social Policies (1870–1914)

Beate Althammer

Introduction

In 1910, the English government official William H. Dawson published a book on *The Vagrancy Problem* in which he deplored the 'national conservatism' of his compatriots when it came to fighting this social evil. On the European continent, he claimed, much more rational attitudes prevailed, namely in Belgium, Switzerland and Germany, to which large sections of his book are devoted: 'Alone of Western nations we still treat lightly and almost frivolously this excrescence of civilisation. Other countries have their tramps and loafers, but they regard and treat them as a public nuisance, and as such deny to them legal recognition; only here are they deliberately tolerated and to some extent fostered'.[1] Happily, he continued, things were finally changing. English public opinion was maturing, abandoning misguided soft-heartedness and exaggerated notions of personal liberty, and it was the object of his book to strengthen this 'healthy' development: 'The leading contention here advanced is that society is justified, in its own interest, in legislating the loafer out of existence'.[2] Repeated visits to continental detention colonies and labour houses had shown him how to achieve this goal: 'prolonged disciplinary treatment is the true remedy for the social parasite whose besetting vice is idleness'.[3] Britain, he asserted, urgently needed analogous institutions for the special treatment of beggars, vagabonds and loafers, not as a marginal supplement to the penal and welfare system but as a crucial missing link: 'Only when they cease to obstruct the path of the social reformer will it be possible to view in its true proportions and relationships the momentous question of society's obligation to the unemployed and the helpless poor'.[4]

Dawson's was not an isolated voice. Quite to the contrary: in the decades around 1900, the 'vagrancy problem' was a heatedly debated issue throughout Europe and the United States, and many scholars, officials, philanthropists and journalists who studied it referred to the countermeasures taken by other countries.[5] Notably among English reformers, it had become common to look across the channel for inspiration. Numerous articles, pamphlets and government reports described continental institutions for the 'reform' of vagrants as models from which something might be learnt, with Germany being one of the most frequently cited points of reference.[6] Dawson is a particularly illustrative example, however, because his career highlights how closely the 'vagrancy problem' was linked to the core themes of the emerging modern welfare state. Dawson was not really a specialist in vagrancy issues. He was, rather, one of the best-informed British experts on German social developments in general and above all on German social insurance, drawing on close professional and personal links to Germany.[7] From the 1880s onwards, he had propagated the favourable effects of German social policies in nearly a dozen books to a British public still very reluctant to embrace state interventions in the social realm, which seemed to endanger the classical liberal values of self-responsibility and individual autonomy. After the turn of the century, this reluctance subsided. In 1906, the new Liberal government recruited Dawson as a civil servant, and he was subsequently involved in preparing the social reform legislation of the pre-war years, particularly the National Insurance Act of 1911. It was no coincidence that Dawson wrote a book on the restraint of vagrancy at the very same time. As many other reformers, he was convinced that innovative, non-stigmatizing forms of assistance in favour of the respectable working classes demanded the elimination of 'social parasites' as an essential prerequisite. Interventionist social policies had two complementary sides, an enhancing and a suppressing one, and, in Dawson's view, Germany was clearly the more progressive nation than Britain in both respects.

But what did the German treatment of vagrancy actually look like? Was it as rational and efficient as Dawson suggested? Although the issue figured prominently on the social policy agenda of the time, it has received surprisingly little attention on the part of historians. As is true for early modern England, a considerable amount of research has been done on the beggars and vagabonds of the Holy Roman Empire.[8] But we know much less about the evolution of these social phenomena during the era of industrialization and their role in the conceptualization of modern welfare policies. Certainly, various aspects of the subject have been addressed both in regional case studies,[9] and in general works on nineteenth-century poverty and poor relief.[10] Yet more thorough analyses are still largely lacking.[11]

In this chapter I will sketch the outlines of such an analysis in four steps.[12] Firstly, I will describe the provisions of the criminal code regarding vagrancy offences and the practices of police and courts: who were the people prosecuted for begging and vagabondage, and how were they punished? Secondly,

I will address the foundation of the Wayfarers' Aid (*Wandererfürsorge*) as a new system of assistance aimed at monitoring 'honest' journeymen and work-seekers in order to prevent them from sliding into habitual vagrancy. Originally, this system found broad support, and it was also assessed positively by foreign observers such as Dawson. Enthusiasm among German social experts was, however, soon tempered, giving way to much more pessimistic perceptions of the wandering poor. This disillusionment encouraged the adoption of new 'scientific' explanations of the causes of vagrancy, to which I will turn in the third section. And, finally, I will return to a tentative comparison with Britain. I will argue that Dawson was right when he rated the German way of dealing with the problem as more advanced in some ways. But it was not more successful, and it resulted in a radicalization of opinions that resonated much less in 'conservative' Britain.

Criminal Prosecution

As in most European countries, begging and vagabondage were punishable offences in nineteenth-century Germany. While legal provisions had varied widely before national unification, the Imperial Penal Code of 1871 established uniform rules that remained largely unchanged up to 1933.[13] According to the code of 1871, begging, vagabondage and several related – but in practice far less important – transgressions, such as homelessness and work-shyness, were classified merely as petty offences, punishable with up to six weeks of arrest. In addition, however, culprits could be sent to a corrective workhouse for up to two years. As regards begging (*Betteln*), workhouse detention was only licit in the case of recidivism or aggravating circumstances such as uttering threats, while vagabonds (*Landstreicher*) could be committed after a first sentence. The penal code did not lay down definitions of these offences. Actually, they were notoriously difficult to define. Where was the limit to be drawn between acceptable and banned forms of asking for something? What distinguished forbidden vagabondage from simple travelling? Given the absence of unequivocal answers, the police and courts often proceeded inconsistently, even though legal commentaries, high court decisions and administrative instructions offered some guidelines.[14] Basically, punishable begging meant the act of demanding alms from a 'stranger' who had no specific responsibility for granting assistance, while the accusation of vagabondage targeted the state of wandering about without means of subsistence and with no verifiable efforts to find a legal livelihood.

Usually, prosecution remained sporadic. During the first half of the nineteenth century, begging had been an omnipresent reality that local authorities mostly tolerated with resignation. Large segments of the population did not consider it an offence at all: they continued to give alms to the local and wandering poor and rarely reported them to the police. Police forces were, moreover, thinly stretched, especially in rural regions, and often shunned the trouble of chasing after such destitute people. Then, from the late 1850s onwards, as the standard of living slowly began to rise with the take-off of German industrialization, it seemed as if the nuisance would gradually fade away. Arrests decreased notably, and workhouse populations shrank. But in the wake of the financial crisis of 1873, the trend reversed abruptly: like a 'ghost from past times', as one publicist wrote, the 'plague' of mendicancy and vagabondage dramatically reappeared.[15]

Around 1880, the resurgence of vagrancy greatly alarmed German society. Although it resembled a ghost from past times, contemporary observers were generally well aware of the fact that it was not the same phenomenon anymore as it had been in the early modern era. Instead, it was obviously linked somehow to the upheavals of industrialization, to the volatility of free capitalist markets and to the massive increase in labour migration, which was additionally boosted by unification. Now the citizens of all German states basically enjoyed the right of unrestricted movement and settlement within the entire territory of the 'Second' Empire – a freedom unheard of in the Holy Roman Empire of old and also in the German Confederation of 1815–1866. Against the backdrop of these new developments, the return of the old vagrancy problem appeared particularly disturbing, as it served to undermine optimistic beliefs in progress. Mobility was on the one hand an indicator of socioeconomic activity and national consolidation; but on the other hand it endangered conventional norms and ties, and this menacing side of the coin seemed to be becoming predominant when the economic boom of the early 1870s turned into a deep slump. Migrant workers were now quickly turning into jobless wanderers and presumably, as many observers predicted, into habitual vagrants. The evolving debate on the 'vagabond question' bundled together a whole range of worries about the disintegration of society in times of rapid change.[16]

In the wake of the economic crash, convictions for begging and vagabondage soared in most regions of the German Empire, peaking in the early 1880s. They nearly doubled in Prussia, by far the largest member state, and increased at even higher rates in many cities, such as in Düsseldorf, one of the administrative and commercial centres of the strongly industrialized Prussian Rhine Province. The striking rise in convictions reflects the impoverishing effects of widespread unemployment, but it was also due to a rekindled alertness on the part of governments: although perfectly aware of the economic nexuses, they repeatedly urged local authorities to prosecute vagrancy offences more strictly around 1880. That the German approach was comparatively rigorous is also demonstrated by the fact that conviction numbers were about seven- to eight-fold higher in Prussia than in England and Wales at the same time, as Table 3.1 shows, whereas the populations of both countries were of nearly identical size.[17]

Who were these thousands of people prosecuted for begging and vagabondage? Court files concerning petty offences have usually not been preserved, but some surviving court registers can give a general impression of their social composition. For the city of Düsseldorf, a register of all court hearings from October 1879 through mid November 1880 is available: it contains 899 cases, 309 tried for begging and 590 for vagabondage.[18] Since quite a few people were brought

Table 3.1 Convictions for Begging and/or Vagabondage 1877–1882

	German Empire	Prussia	Düsseldorf	England/Wales
1877	219,514	77,712	383	11,016
1878	280,518	92,685	432	12,901
1879	316,846	115,841	650	14,949
1880	320,548	119,269	947	17,559
1881	319,259	132,123	975	16,808
1882	278,040	118,245	655	17,983

Table 3.2 Persons Tried for Begging and Vagabondage in Düsseldorf, 1879/80

Age	Female	Male	Sum	Percent
15–19	8	65	73	9.7
20–29	32	209	241	32.1
30–39	7	189	196	26.1
40–49	5	113	118	15.7
50–59	1	82	83	11.1
60+	2	35	37	4.9
Unknown	0	3	3	0.4
Total Sums	**55**	**696**	**751**	**100.0**
Total Percentages	**7.3**	**92.7**	**100.0**	

to court more than once within this time period, 714 different individuals were involved: 198 because of begging, 479 because of vagabondage and 37 because of both offences. In Table 3.2 they are listed according to gender and age, with the 37 individuals appearing in both groups counted twice, to produce a total of 751. As the table shows, the defendants were overwhelmingly male and predominantly adults in their twenties and thirties, while women, teenagers and elderly people only made up a relatively small proportion. Those accused of begging were on average considerably older than those charged with vagabondage (9.8 per cent and 2.7 per cent respectively were aged sixty or over). But among them the female share was even smaller (4.7 per cent and 8.5 per cent respectively).

This gender and age structure shows a marked change when compared to earlier decades, when women, children and old people had usually dominated among the poor who came into conflict with the authorities for collecting alms. Among a sample of 107 beggars arrested in the city of Aachen in 1823, for instance, there were 61 women (57 per cent), 20 children under the age of 15 (18.7 per cent), and 12 elderly or disabled males (11.2 per cent), while only 14 (13.1 per cent) could be classified as able-bodied men.[19] Among a sample of 73 beggars seized by the police in the city of Trier in July 1843, there were 27 women (37 per cent), 22 children (30.1 per cent), and 24 males aged from 15 to 80 (32.9 per cent).[20] But also the structure of those prosecuted for vagabondage had differed markedly in earlier decades from the one displayed by the

Düsseldorf register of 1879/80. Among 220 people convicted for this offence by the district court of Koblenz in 1855, for example, there was a female share of 30.5 per cent (compared to only 8.5 per cent in Düsseldorf in 1879/80), while children from 8 to 14 accounted for 14.5 per cent (compared to 0 per cent) and youths from 15 to 19 for another 25.9 per cent (compared to 12.2 per cent).[21] By the late 1870s, both begging and vagabondage had developed into heavily gendered adult male offences – a historical novelty. Some of the men prosecuted in Düsseldorf were invalids, among them notorious local beggars who appeared in court again and again: the record holder was a 54-year-old casual labourer with an amputated arm, who was sentenced eight times within these thirteen months alone. But these were no longer typical cases. Rather, the vast majority were healthy men in their prime. Another marked change is observable with regard to individuals' places of origin. In the samples of 1823, 1843 and 1855, the bulk of the apprehended were resident poor people who lived in or near the locality where they had been caught, mostly from birth. In the Düsseldorf sample of 1879/80, however, the average defendant came from further afield: only 40 per cent of the beggars and 2 per cent of the vagabonds were residents of the city, while 56 per cent of the total originated from outside the administrative district (*Regierungsbezirk*) of Düsseldorf and 39 per cent from outside the Rhine Province. Finally, the sample of 1879/80 was, on average, professionally much better qualified than earlier ones had been. The most frequently listed single occupation was day labourer (143 individuals: 20.5 per cent of the males), but the skilled crafts clearly prevailed when added together. Metal workers (60: 8.6 per cent), joiners and carpenters (49: 7 per cent), shoemakers and tailors (46: 6.6 per cent), bakers and pastry cooks (30: 4.3 per cent) topped the list, and a wide range of other skilled or semiskilled professions followed. Itinerant trades such as hawkers were, by contrast, rarely mentioned.

Of course these local findings cannot be simply universalized, given the huge socioeconomic disparities within the German Empire. Yet other sources – for example lists of expelled foreigners or of workhouse inmates – point towards the same result: in late nineteenth-century Germany, it was primarily journeymen and fairly skilled migrant workers who were apprehended because of begging and vagabondage, whereas women, youths, old people and the local poor generally played a much diminished role. Legal reforms can account only for the disappearance of small children from the ranks of the prosecuted, as the age of criminal responsibility was raised to twelve years by the code of 1871. Other factors were just as important, among them the development of welfare provisions. Local families, particularly widowed or deserted mothers and children, together with old and infirm people, had always had the best chances to obtain public poor relief but, during the early decades of the nineteenth century, the amounts granted had been so sparse that asking for alms often remained an indispensable supplement. Despite continuing deficiencies, this was to some degree changing by the late nineteenth century. Moreover, a rapidly growing number of private and church charities also preferably assisted the same 'deserving' categories of the

Table 3.3 Sentences for Begging and Vagabondage in Düsseldorf 1879/80

	Begging	*Vagabondage*	*Sum*	*Percent*
Acquitted	0	4	4	0.5
1–6 days arrest	160	391	551	61.3
7–14 days arrest	87	154	241	26.8
3–6 weeks arrest	57	34	91	10.1
& committal to workhouse	5	7	12	1.3
Totals	**309**	**590**	**899**	

local poor. Able-bodied men, by contrast, could traditionally count on much less support, particularly when they were single and newcomers to a locality. By law, municipalities were required to provisionally assist every person in dire need, but this was a very theoretical obligation, and generally local relief agencies did not consider themselves responsible for assisting the unemployed, let alone jobless wanderers. It was the gap between improved provisions for the 'deserving' resident poor and the absence of social safety nets for the hugely increased number of highly mobile workers that reshaped the structure of apprehended beggars and vagabonds during the economic depression around 1880.

Judges seem to have realized that they were not, for the most part, dealing with 'social parasites' but rather with 'normal' men from the mobile working classes who had run into temporary trouble, and consequently passed lenient sentences. This was certainly true in Düsseldorf, as Table 3.3 shows. Virtually all the accused were found guilty, but over 60 per cent got away with less than one week of arrest, nearly 90 per cent with no more than two weeks. Just a little over 1 per cent were committed to the workhouse.

The predominance of short-term imprisonment was a common feature of the penalization of vagrancy in Germany and England, and indeed more generally of late nineteenth-century criminal justice. It was a feature under increasingly heavy attack from penal reformers. This kind of punishment, critics were sure, did not deter or improve anyone. It was a useless waste of effort and even likely to have counterproductive effects, especially on the morals of not yet hardened offenders, while old hands actually enjoyed short prison stays, as, among many others, the Bavarian interior minister contended in 1883:

> Since endeavours to improve our prisons have turned them into pleasant, well-ventilated, and in winter comfortably heated rooms, and the prisoners are served ample and tasty food, they have lost all horrors particularly for beggars and vagabonds; quite to the contrary: after wandering about for longer periods they offer a welcome place of rest, above all during the bad season, where vagrants can recuperate the necessary strength to proceed with their career and spend a worry-free time, mostly with companions, in sluggish idleness.[22]

Workhouse detention was designed as a remedy for such inadequacies of the prison system. Its original aim was to rehabilitate the vagrant poor by teaching them to earn a living honestly. Alternatively, it served as a deterrent and an instrument to force habitual idlers into productivity, keeping them under lock and key for longer than the ordinary scale of penal sanctions would have allowed. During the early nineteenth century, workhouse confinement had been a police measure that did not depend on a court ruling in most German states; in other states, notably in Prussia between 1843 and 1856, every criminal conviction for the relevant offences automatically led to a workhouse term. This changed with unification. Now a court ruling had to explicitly state whether the offender was to be referred to the competent police authority after having served his prison sentence, thus empowering the latter to take the final decision on committal to the workhouse. Practice, however, continued to be extremely disparate. Generally speaking, the number of punishments for begging and vagabondage per head of population was higher in southern Germany than in Prussia; but the percentage of committals to the workhouse was much lower. Even within Prussia there was nothing like a common approach. On average, Prussian courts referred about 15 to 20 per cent of convicted beggars and vagabonds to the district governments (that is, the competent police authority) during the early 1880s. The Düsseldorf court, however, did so in barely more than 1 per cent of cases, as shown in Table 3.3. There were many reasons for such disparities. Some judges were more leniently disposed than others, or did not believe in the expediency of workhouse detention; the capacity of disposable workhouses also mattered; and not least the eagerness of prosecutors to scrutinize the penal records of defendants varied. In the Düsseldorf register of 1879/80, the overwhelming majority was classified as having no or only trifling previous convictions – one main reason for their mild punishment. But when the Düsseldorf district government, unsatisfied with the rulings of the local court, instigated further investigations, it turned out that quite a few alleged first offenders had actually been to the workhouse before, some even several times.[23] Eventually, the district government succeeded in coaxing the court into a more rigorous approach, so that the number of referrals rose to sixty-four in 1881 and seventy-five in 1882.[24]

Nevertheless, court decisions remained highly heterogeneous, and this made them look arbitrary. In theory, they should have been based on a careful assessment of each individual case, but in reality it largely depended on mere luck whether culprits escaped with a few days in prison or ended up in the workhouse for a year or two. Many artful tramps were never caught at all, while others paid dearly for their clumsiness. On the other hand, the vagrant population also remained much more heterogeneous than statistical averages suggest. Three short individual stories may suffice to illustrate the wide range of fates which all formed part of the 'vagrancy problem' in Imperial Germany.

The first is a very typical story. It is about a young butcher journeyman from Bavaria, who was apprehended in the city of Essen (located within the administrative district of Düsseldorf) in January 1883, for allegedly having begged in a butcher's shop. Upon his arrest by the police, Aron Silbermann at first admitted the charge; but when brought to court the following day, he pleaded not guilty, declaring that he had only asked for work and was given the customary

'Master's Gift' (*Meistergeschenk*) instead, without having demanded it. He also declared that he had worked until recently in Frankfurt, departing from there with twenty-four Marks of travel money, and had never been punished before. The judge decided to adjourn the hearing in order to give the prosecutor the chance to summon witnesses. He did not remand the defendant in custody, however, but ordered him to be released for the time being because of a lack of prima facie evidence. Predictably, Silbermann could not be found later on, so the case had to be shelved without a verdict.[25] The local police were annoyed, and so was the Düsseldorf district government when informed about this and some similar occurrences, as they seemed to prove an overly lax attitude on the part of many judges, who naively believed the tales of defendants about their honest intentions. But what makes the story particularly interesting is the underlying dispute over the question as to what precisely constituted the offence of begging, and whether Silbermann's behaviour was to be qualified as such or not. Travelling journeymen had traditionally bridged periods out of work with asking for 'gifts', a makeshift economy not deemed shameful among artisans. The tolerance of authorities towards this 'abuse' of craft culture was, however, rapidly waning in the nineteenth century, and it was actually often denounced as one of the main roots of the German vagrancy problem. When journeymen approached normal citizens, this was usually equalled to outright begging, but things were more ambiguous when a master of one's own trade was approached: were journeymen entitled to request the Master's Gift, be it explicitly or implicitly through the ritual inquiry about 'work'? Jurists were divided over the issue. In 1890, the highest German court judged one such case, yet without establishing clarity: it ruled that asking for the Master's Gift was not illegal in places where it conformed to local custom.[26] This verdict only perpetuated the locally divergent practices of prosecution, and thus travelling journeymen continued to move in a legal grey area; just like Aron Silbermann, who had certainly visited scores of butcher's shops – and perhaps also other houses – on his way from Bavaria via Frankfurt and Cologne to Essen, and visited many more after he had dodged the Essen authorities.

While Silbermann had the demeanour of a basically honest young artisan on his traditional years of travel, the second story is about a man who fitted the conventional image of the 'habitual vagrant' almost perfectly. Not much more is known about him other than his criminal record, which is quite impressive.[27] Gustav Bernhard Eichhoven was born in Saxony, and he too was originally a journeyman, having learnt the carpentry trade. His early life seems to have been orderly; he was only once convicted in Leipzig for a small theft and for begging in 1866, at the age of twenty-eight. Then he emigrated to Holland, where he lived for about ten years. From the moment he came back to Germany in 1876, however, he collected a never-ending list of sentences for begging, vagabondage and resistance to authorities all across the Empire. After serving four short prison terms in towns of the Rhineland and Westphalia, he was committed to the Westphalian workhouse, Benninghausen, for three months. Shortly after his release, and a further prison sentence, he was again committed to the workhouse, this time to Moringen, in the Province of Hanover. After that he travelled through southern Germany, where he visited the prisons of Heilbronn (three times) and Mannheim (once), before being committed to the Hanoverian workhouse again. Then he was back in Mannheim and, as the result of two further convictions for begging, was expelled from the Grand Duchy of Baden. Another two sentences followed in the Bavarian city of Augsburg, then three in Stuttgart, as a consequence of which he was expelled from the Kingdom of Württemberg. After a further sentence in Heilbronn, he came to Altona in Schleswig-Holstein in 1879, where he was committed to the workhouse for twelve months. He seems to have been released early, because that same year he arrived in the Rhine Province once more (two sentences) and then in Wiesbaden, Province Hessen-Nassau (one sentence). Back in the Rhine Province, he served four more prison terms and two terms at the provincial workhouse Brauweiler, the second committal in December 1882 being the last entry in the surviving record. In sum, this man accumulated twenty-six prison sentences, six workhouse detentions and two expulsions from southern German states within the seven-year period from 1876 to 1882.

We do not know what drove Eichhoven into his restless travelling from arrest to arrest. Perhaps his long stay abroad, where he had even done his military service, played a role: it was questionable if he still had the status of a Saxon and German citizen upon his return to Germany, and this may have made it more difficult for him to settle down somewhere.[28] Moreover, he came back at a time of economic crisis, aged thirty-eight – not a young man anymore, although reportedly healthy. He was unmarried and seems not to have had any relatives he could turn to for support. There is no way of knowing if he tried to find stable employment or if he, at some point, reconciled himself to being a tramp. But what we do know for certain is that German vagrancy policies did nothing to stop his wanderings, let alone help him to reintegrate into society. Quite the opposite: like many other men of similar background he turned into a regular customer of the workhouse system, and with every committal his chances of ever becoming a respectable worker again were reduced a bit further.

In contrast to Silbermann's and Eichhoven's stories, which were both typical in their way, the third one is rather exceptional. It shows that an unfortunate series of events could bring even very unlikely candidates into the workhouse. Charlotte Ritter was a young woman from Württemberg, the daughter of small farmers. In 1893, she decided to join one of her brothers, a baker, who had emigrated to the United States. At first everything went well, but then she became ill and homesick, and so she travelled back to Europe as soon as she had earned enough to pay for the passage. On her way, she was cheated out of most of her belongings, and by the time she reached the Prussian border near Aachen in the summer of 1894, she was penniless. Picked up by the police, she was sentenced for homelessness to fourteen days imprisonment and committed to Brauweiler workhouse, originally for six months. Because of lazy and rebellious behaviour – she did not cope with her work task of peeling heaps of potatoes – the district government prolonged her term for another four months. When she was released, the train journey back to Württemberg again ended in disaster: she got lost and, being penniless once more, had to walk over a long distance. By the time she finally reached her parents' home, she was seriously ill and died shortly after. Her parents were upset, and they became even more upset when they received a letter from the workhouse director demanding that they pay for Charlotte's detention, as the family was not utterly poor: Charlotte had inherited a small sum from her deceased father. Her stepfather wrote petitions to the Prussian interior minister and even to the emperor, protesting about their daughter's harsh treatment and the bill, yet to no avail. The regional authorities who investigated the case found nothing irregular about it, and the parents were legally forced to pay.[29]

Charlotte certainly did not represent the average workhouse client. As various case studies on German workhouses have shown,[30] women constituted a minority among inmates, and by the late nineteenth century they were mostly committed for irregular prostitution. Their share among the detained beggars and vagabonds had become almost negligible, while 'homelessness' was a comparatively rare reason for workhouse confinement with regard to both men and women. Moreover, it seems quite extraordinary that this unfortunate girl was punished at all, instead of being helped to travel directly home to her parents from the Prussian border. By the 1890s, there were charities eager to assist vulnerable young women in most towns, but Charlotte had the bad luck of encountering officials who interpreted her mishaps as evidence of depravity and delivered her to the ordeal of 'correction'. It is unclear if the workhouse actually killed her, as her parents alleged, yet it was evidently an absurd and drastic measure in her case.

The workhouse detention of Charlotte Ritter seems all the more surprising as courts were generally becoming more and more reluctant to apply this measure. After their peak in the early 1880s, convictions for the relevant offences, as well as referrals to the competent police authority, decreased almost continuously, with workhouse inmates by tendency becoming older. As the director of Brauweiler workhouse complained in 1900, the average detainee population of his institution had dropped from nearly 1,600 in 1883 to only 785 during the previous year, a development that was, in his view, not solely due to the economic upswing, but mainly to misconceptions concerning the workhouse. Even judges, he lamented, frequently repeated the wrong assumption that 'whoever comes into a workhouse will not be improved but rather corrupted there'; because of this inaccurate understanding they would not refer young people anymore, but only completely run-down individuals with very long criminal records who were indeed mostly beyond improvement. Thus, in the director's view, the judges were themselves ruining the reformative potential of workhouse discipline; if they handed over offenders at an earlier stage of their deviant careers, much better results might be achieved: 'It is therefore to be deplored that the workhouses are not used in a manner that would be in the best interest of human society, and that so many false things are said about them out of ignorance'.[31]

By the turn of the twentieth century, such defences of the workhouse did not find much support anymore. Most German experts were in fact disenchanted with the achievements of this institution. Rates of recidivism had risen to extremely high levels; among the inmates of Brauweiler, for instance, about 60 per cent had been to a workhouse before at least once, and cases such as Eichhoven with six, eight or even ten committals, were no exception. When compared to the early 1880s, the vagrancy problem had once more changed its face. But in the perception of social and penal reformers it had by no means been resolved satisfactorily.

The Wayfarers' Aid

The economic crisis of the late 1870s not only boosted the number of convictions for begging and vagabondage to unprecedented levels; it also aroused concern among the more reflective members of Germany's elites that prosecution might hit the wrong individuals. Begging and vagabondage were particularly problematic offences as there always remained some doubt regarding how to distinguish a wilfully deviant lifestyle from transgressions out of necessity. Although virtually all penal and social experts basically shared the creed that these forms of behaviour must be suppressed because they endangered public order and undermined the work ethic, the legitimacy of punishment still seemed questionable in lots of cases. This was highlighted once more by the effects of the economic slump, when the interrelationship between the surge of vagrancy offences and massive unemployment became blatant.

Most German scholars and philanthropists who wrote about the vagrancy problem in the early 1880s were troubled by the fate of unemployed journeymen and workers. Many were highly critical of the defective system of public assistance, which frequently left laid-off men no other option than to abandon their places of residence in the uncertain hope of finding a new livelihood, and of the indiscriminate prosecution of penniless wayfarers. Alphons Thun, for instance, a young academic affiliated to the so-called Historical School of Economics, wrote in his study of industry on the Lower Rhine:

> They wander abroad with no aim and plan, not to make their fortune but to seek for work. But who gives them work? Nobody! So the poor man looking for work becomes a beggar; if he does not find a shelter, a homeless man; and when he has no legitimating documents, a vagabond.[32]

Similarly, the Düsseldorf prison chaplain, Pastor Stursberg, wrote in his influential book on the vagabond question:

> It is easy to say in times of general crisis: work, look for work! In such times this means nothing else than to say: you have to join the stream of the vagrant class without any chance of finding work! Thousands perish in this stream, and all too soon they lose the moral strength to pull themselves out of it again in better times.[33]

The second quotation, from the charity activist Stursberg, also points to the main worry that permeated the discourse on vagrancy in the early 1880s: social reformers were concerned about the material distress of the unemployed, but they were even more concerned about the moral dangers of life on the road. Bona fide work-seekers, they were convinced, would soon become demoralized by bad company, by humiliating arrests, by begging, drinking and sloth, and they would inevitably fall into the clutches of habitual vagabondage. This image of the morally endangered poor wanderer motivated the foundation of the Wayfarers' Aid (*Wandererfürsorge*).

The Wayfarers' Aid grew out of various roots in several German regions, but its most influential promoter soon became the well-known Lutheran pastor Friedrich von Bodelschwingh, head of the Bethel institutions in Bielefeld.[34] The philanthropic movement orchestrated by him planned to set up a nationwide network of relief stations where wandering work-seekers could find a meal and shelter for the night in return for a few hours of manual labour such as wood chopping or stone breaking. The basic idea thus resembled the English casual ward system, which had emerged after the enactment of the New Poor Law in 1834. In two respects, however, the German initiative differed fundamentally. Firstly, it was deliberately not associated with public poor relief. And secondly, it encompassed a much tighter supervision and moral guidance of its clientele. The aim was to rescue destitute but still honest wayfarers from the perils of the road, to separate them from the corrupting influence of habitual vagrants, and to channel them directly from one relief station to the next so that they would not go astray. A wayfarer pass was issued to clients in order to control their movements. The stations were preferably attached to Christian hostels, and they were also to serve as labour exchanges with a view to resettling clients into regular occupations. Partly, the Wayfarers' Aid movement sought to substitute the infrastructure of the by then largely defunct guilds, which had formerly assisted and supervised journeymen, yet its scope was wider. It addressed all wandering men – but only men – irrespective of their backgrounds and professions, as long as they were able and willing to work and proved this by performing the assigned labour task. Moreover, the relief stations were supplemented with charitable worker colonies, where run-down wanderers could stay for a longer period of time in order to recover under the salutary influence of steady labour and religious instruction. Bodelschwingh and his fellow campaigners did not aspire to save all vagrants: those who evaded the system of the Wayfarers' Aid, who continued to loaf and beg in spite of the assistance offered, were to be left to the police for punishment – and even heavier punishments than before. But they were convinced that a large portion could be saved, and that punishment was only justified if the bona fide work-seeker had a real alternative to violating the law.

Although the motivation of the initiators was thoroughly conservative, the Wayfarers' Aid was the first large-scale initiative to tackle the vagrancy problem by addressing it as a product of unemployment and of imbalances in the labour

market. Indeed, it was the first national initiative that tried to tackle the issue
of unemployment at all. As such, it was part of the social reform movement of
the 1880s that laid the foundations of the modern German welfare state. As is
well known, Germany pioneered the introduction of nationwide workers' insurance schemes against the risks of illness, occupational accidents, old age and
invalidity during this decade.[35] And as is equally well known, Chancellor Otto
von Bismarck promoted these schemes despite, or rather precisely because of,
his conservative, anti-socialist stance: they were a bid to integrate the working
classes into the Empire and to draw them away from left-wing agitators. For
a while, Bismarck also mused about the problem of unemployment. In 1884,
he even shocked his audience by stating in front of the Reichstag that workers
must not only be granted an entitlement to benefits when they lost their ability
to work, but a 'right to work' as long as they were healthy.[36] Bismarck's interest in the matter was short-lived, however, and a national unemployment and
labour market policy evolved only after the First World War. Nevertheless, the
economic crisis of the late 1870s, and the extensive debates about the workers'
insurance bills of the 1880s, gave rise to a new awareness of the structural risks
that endangered the working classes, among which the risk of redundancy figured prominently.[37]

The Wayfarers' Aid was the first attempt to construct something like a social
safety net for those who temporarily lacked a job as well as a home. Although
Bodelschwingh strictly rejected the revolutionary notion of a right to work and
stressed the purely charitable character of his scheme, he did want to give every
jobless wanderer the possibility to earn his living, thus preventing the unemployed from becoming vagabonds. That the vagrancy and the unemployment
issues were linked in such a manner shows how strongly the jobless were still
suspected of being potential loafers, and even outlaws. But it also reflects the
highly unstable situation of many workers, who actually took to the road in large
numbers whenever they saw better opportunities elsewhere or were forced to do
so after losing their income.

Originally, the Wayfarers' Aid movement was a great success. During the
1880s, about two dozen worker colonies and nearly 2,000 relief stations were
founded all over Germany. While the colonies were mostly run by Christian
societies on a denominational basis, the stations were operated partly by local
charities, partly by municipalities or counties, and public administrations
granted subsidies to both types of institution. In most Prussian provinces, provincial associations were launched to coordinate their activities, and also national
umbrella organizations came into being, which engaged in insistent lobbying.
State governments responded positively: at the same time that they pressed for
a rigorous prosecution of beggars and vagabonds, they also strongly encouraged
initiatives to assist and monitor the wandering poor. Bodelschwingh even succeeded in gaining the promotionally effective support of the imperial family.
Many observers were sure that the Wayfarers' Aid movement significantly contributed to a massive reduction in vagrancy offences, a reduction that apparently

persisted during the renewed economic slump of the early 1890s. The Berlin newspaper *Die Post*, for example, wrote in 1893 that the number of jobless wanderers on the roads had risen again to similar levels as in the early 1880s, but that the effects were now much less obnoxious:

> Then, the plague of vagrants was also a plague of beggars; in small troops they roamed about, advancing into the most remote regions, plundering the small village as well as the largest city, and extorting a vagrant tax from the population the amount of which is hard to imagine nowadays. Because today the vagrant stream is contained within a certain bed by the relief stations; one sees lots of them wandering along the main roads from station to station, but rarely does one see them off these station roads, and rarely does one see them entering houses in order to beg. This is the great achievement of the relief stations, despite their flaws and shortcomings: they have considerably reduced the plague of beggars and dammed back vagrancy to certain roads.[38]

Yet despite much original support and praise, the Wayfarers' Aid was confronted with severe difficulties. Actually, the same newspaper article spoke of a crisis that was threatening to dissolve the whole scheme. The reasons were manifold: most of the relief stations had never quite lived up to the high standards envisioned by Bodelschwingh and his allies, and they were interlinked to a coherent network only in small parts of Germany; many were overwhelmed by the new waves of wanderers triggered by the slump of the early 1890; local authorities withdrew financial support, forcing a large number to close down; in some regions, sectarian conflicts contributed to thwarting the movement; and the socialist workers' organizations appreciated neither relief stations nor worker colonies, denouncing them as patronizing and exploitative. Most important, however, was that an increasing number of social experts began to doubt if the system was really a viable solution to the issues it was trying to address. With regard to imbalances in the labour market, alternative instruments – primarily communal labour exchanges interlinked rather by telephone and railway than by station roads, but also experiments with unemployment insurance – were gaining ground. With regard to the vagrancy problem, on the other hand, the voluntary institutions of the Wayfarers' Aid were criticized for being too soft on their clientele. Suspicion arose that they attracted above all men who were unwilling or unable to integrate themselves into the labour market – indeed the same type of people who kept returning to the corrective workhouses. By making life easier for bums and loafers, critics claimed, the Wayfarers' Aid was actually perpetuating vagrancy instead of fighting it.

The Wayfarers' Aid survived these difficulties. Its umbrella organizations were, by the 1890s, firmly institutionalized, and their activism helps to explain why debates on the vagrancy problem continued to flourish in Germany right up to the Second World War. But the tone of the debate shifted markedly around the turn of the century. The initial optimism that the issue could be largely tackled simply by offering temporary assistance to work-seekers was in decline, even among the leaders of the movement.

New Scientific Interpretations

Up to the turn of the century, mainly officials, jurists and philanthropists had participated in the debate on the vagrancy issue, while the medical profession had played no substantial role. This changed when the psychiatrist Karl Bonhoeffer published an article in 1901 that made a lasting impact.[39] Bonhoeffer's contribution was based on a systematic survey of 400 recidivist beggars and homeless men who were arrested in the prison of Breslau. His starting point was, as he stated, the evident failure of both the criminal justice system and charitable endeavours to handle the problem, and his aim was to scientifically explain why they failed:

> The constant circulation of these individuals between freedom, prisons, and occasionally workhouses, the universally acknowledged deficiency of the measures so far undertaken to influence and combat them, urges us to explore the laws which underlie this behaviour. It is obvious that knowledge of these laws is the necessary precondition for all useful practical intervention.[40]

The results of his study were very clear-cut: they suggested that the behaviour of vagrants was rooted above all in mental defects. Of the 400 men examined, Bonhoeffer rated only 15 per cent as mentally more or less normal. The overwhelming majority did not suffer from insanity in the proper sense, but, according to his interpretation, from various states of mental abnormality which were more difficult to detect and usually due to adverse hereditary influences. The low quality or, literally, 'inferior value' (*Minderwertigkeit*) of their cerebral constitution had predisposed them for an 'antisocial' existence as habitual 'parasites'. This diagnosis implicated that it was extremely doubtful if efforts to rehabilitate such offenders could have any success at all. Bonhoeffer concluded that they ought to be taken out of the penal system and committed to convenient institutions of care instead, by force and indefinitely if necessary.

In the following years, several further psychiatric studies on beggars and vagabonds, mostly on workhouse inmates, were published. They all came to similar results: a large majority was judged to be mentally defective, suggesting that this was the main reason why vagrancy policies had shown such poor results so far. And some did not hesitate to generalize their findings far beyond the relatively small groups they had examined in person. Notably, Karl Wilmanns stressed that the wandering population at large suffered from analogous mental conditions: 'wide sections of our casual labourers, who live on theft and begging during parts of the year or exploit the support of worker colonies and relief stations, are on the same level as workhouse inmates with regard to their mental predispositions and their delinquency'.[41] Wilmanns, who dwelled upon the vagrancy issue like no other German psychiatrist, was also particularly explicit about the measures to take. He insisted that the 'antisocial elements' of 'inferior value' (*minderwertig*) who worked only sporadically or not at all, would necessarily have to be eliminated from public life on a permanent basis, if social progress in favour of the workers of 'full value' (*vollwertig*) was to be achieved: 'This cannot be avoided if the modern social institutions, especially unemployment insurance, are not to be constantly abused by those elements and the great plans not frustrated right from the start'.[42]

Wilmanns' dialectic of inclusion and exclusion resembles the one put forth by Dawson, quoted at the beginning of this chapter. But the reasoning was different. Dawson wanted to eliminate individuals who obstructed the path of social reform because of their wilful laziness, and he wanted to do so through correctional treatment in workhouses and labour colonies that was aimed at curing them from their vice. Wilmanns, on the other hand, wanted to eliminate individuals who obstructed the path of social reform because of an antisocial predisposition rooted in mental defects, and for him as well as other German psychiatrists it was already evident that a correctional treatment in workhouses and labour colonies – or, indeed, any treatment – was in most cases doomed to fail.

From the turn of the century, German penal and social experts, including many activists of the Wayfarers' Aid, quickly adopted this new medical explanation of vagrancy. This does not mean that older concepts were abandoned, but they were more or less mingled with the 'scientific' language and interpretations introduced by psychiatric surveys. Beggars and vagabonds were henceforth not perceived as simply destitute or badly brought up paupers as in the early nineteenth century. Nor were they primarily viewed as healthy strong men who were on the road of their own free will or because of temporary unemployment, as had been the case in the 1880s. Instead, the vagrancy problem was increasingly assessed in the light of medical notions that emphasized weakness and deficiency on the part of the individuals in question.

At the German National Congress on Poor Relief and Charity in 1908, for instance, one of the keynote speakers, Pastor Oskar Sell from Leipzig, declared 'that the so-called vagabonds and gift-asking journeymen consist to a large part of psychopaths …, that we are confronted with *ill* people and persons who have hit the road because of psychic-moral defects of some sort'.[43] In the same year, a Catholic pamphlet on the Wayfarers' Aid explained that 'a huge portion of the wandering poor is not fit for work in the normal sense because there are so many mentally and physically inferior men (*minderwertige Menschen*) among them'.[44] Shortly after, a Bavarian judge highlighted those among the multitudes of beggars and vagabonds 'who are, due to a pathological trait, so much possessed by an urge to roam (*Wandertrieb*) that they … are incapable of adapting themselves to a sedentary life'.[45] In 1911, the renowned Frankfurt professor of social work, Christian Klumker, lectured that:

> the bulk of vagrants are characterized, through their nature, by the inability to get along autonomously in the existing order of society; they are elements not adequate for society. They are people like, for example, the servant in Tolstoy's *Master and Man* who cannot stand on their own feet in our competitive struggle but who would be industrious under permanent proper direction or could have played an excellent role as serfs or slaves.[46]

A year later, the director of Brauweiler workhouse – the successor of the one mentioned above – reasoned that a large proportion of his inmates had to be viewed as 'physically and mentally inferior' and continued:

> I only mention the unfortunates who suffer from a debilitation of their mental health, whose condition does not justify their treatment in public asylums but who are still useless for society, further the countless people whose volition is so weak that they are dependent like children and cannot succeed in life, and finally the large host of alcoholics who are economically and morally ruined by their predisposition to drink, which they have not always acquired by their own fault.[47]

As a last example, a senior official of the Rhenish welfare administration may be quoted who contended in 1913 that the majority of wayfarers in Germany belonged to the physically and mentally defective 'scrap' of society which could not be integrated into the labour market even if they themselves desired it. Rhetorically he asked: 'How many are, as recent surveys have shown, mentally inferior down to complete idiots or lunatics? In how many is the urge to roam in particular something definitely pathological that the individual can hardly resist?' In view of these traits displayed by the average wayfarer, he concluded, it was absurd to facilitate their wanderings through relief stations. Rather, they should be compulsorily taken off the roads, regardless of whether they offended against the penal law or not: 'To let such people roam about freely is as unwarranted as it would be to let small children or lunatics wander along the highways. ... The respect for personal freedom is as inappropriate here as it is in the case of children and lunatics'.[48]

Conclusion

Although it is likely that the composition of the wayfarer population actually changed to a certain extent from the early years of the German Empire to the eve of the First World War, this 'real' change cannot sufficiently explain the fundamental shift in the way experts perceived and described the issue. In the 1880s, there was a marked willingness to see the vagrancy problem as closely linked to the economic phenomena of unemployment and labour migration, although it was also regarded as closely linked to the vices of idleness and crime. From the turn of the century, both associations faded. Instead, vagrancy was increasingly conceptualized as a result of mental predispositions that lay beyond the free will of the individual, and this interpretation was applied not only to multi-recidivist beggars and vagabonds but, more or less, to casual labourers, journeymen and poor wanderers in general. At the level of expert discourse, their rambling mode of mobility was considered as a dysfunctional and abnormal behaviour that did not fit into the modern industrial world. From a progressive point of view, it should not be regulated and thus assisted, as the Wayfarers' Aid had originally endeavoured, but abolished. For the 'full value' workers who became victims of the volatile labour market, new forms of support were designed, namely labour exchanges and unemployment insurance, although it took until after the First World War to establish them on a systematic basis. For the other parts of the fluctuating population, the inferior 'scrap', new measures were also called for. The instruments provided for by the nineteenth-century penal code were not regarded as sufficient anymore. One reason why the workhouse in its existing form had failed, many penal and social reformers now believed, was that the maximum term of two years was too inflexible: it did not make any sense to release detainees after this term who would almost certainly relapse into their former ways. What seemed to be necessary instead was another form of custody that took into account the mental state of the affected individuals.

Where this demand would ultimately lead, to a more therapeutic and caring approach or to pure and simple long-term confinement, was not clear yet. Both strategies as well as various combinations were proposed, and this ambivalence continued during the Weimar Republic. For in Germany, the First World War interrupted debates on the vagrancy problem, but by no means ended them: by the mid twenties, the issue was again high on the social policy agenda. Some experts rejected the use of compulsory measures; many others regarded their extension as imperative. In practice, no major legal reforms in the treatment of vagrancy were achieved before 1933. Yet overall there was a tangible radicalization in terminology and arguments. Whereas in the nineteenth century even the most wayward poor had always been conceived of as normal people and thus basically includable in society, this assumption was now questioned in a fundamental way. The new psychiatric findings seemed to scientifically prove that all attempts at inclusion were more or less doomed to fail. Even a moderate and liberal voice like Klumker, who hesitated to describe vagrants as such as pathological or defective, assessed them as inapt for normal societal life and in need of permanent direction: they could only find their place in a subaltern position like that of 'serfs or slaves'. Thus, the vagrancy problem worked as a catalyst through which notions of an insuperable human inequality diffused into social policy debates.

In Britain, the rise of the natural sciences certainly also made an impact on how poverty and deviance were perceived. Yet the reception of scientific explanations of social phenomena seems to have been generally more cautious, and at least with regard to the vagrancy problem it remained rather marginal in influence. Instead, the instruments that had long since been tested in Germany were still propagated as promising remedies. On the one hand, the concept of relief stations and voluntary rehabilitative colonies was widely discussed and experimented with; but it is particularly striking how strongly the idea of coercive labour institutions for the disciplining of loafers was supported by experts of nearly every political creed during the pre-war years. Larry Frohman has recently even claimed that such coercive institutions played a much more integral role in the visions of British social reformers than in those of their German counterparts.[49] This contention, however, ignores the fact that coercive workhouses already existed in Germany, while the British were still trying to set up a similar system. It also ignores the fact that the discussion had by this time moved on in Germany: German reformers had lost faith that drifters could be corrected through a limited period of disciplinary treatment in forced labour institutions; they were thinking about models of open-ended custody that would permanently seclude the inadaptable pathological elements from the normal spheres of society.[50]

Notes

1. William H. Dawson. 1910. *The Vagrancy Problem. The Case for Measures of Restraint for Tramps, Loafers, and Unemployables: with a Study of Continental Detention Colonies and Labour Houses.* London: P.S. King & Son, p. viii.

2. Ibid, p. ix.

3. Ibid, p. x.

4. Ibid, p. 249.

5. B. Althammer. 2014. 'Transnational Expert Discourse on Vagrancy around 1900', in B. Althammer, A. Gestrich and J. Gründler (eds), *The Welfare State and the 'Deviant Poor' in Europe, 1870–1933.* Basingstoke: Palgrave Macmillan, pp. 103–25, 240–45.

6. For example: C.J. Ribton-Turner. 1887. *A History of Vagrants and Vagrancy, and Beggars and Begging.* London: Chapman and Hall, pp. 507–75; *Reports on the Elberfeld Poor Law System and German Workmen's Colonies.* 1888. London: Parliamentary Papers C. 5341, pp. 45–50; [Reginald Brabazon] Earl of Meath. 1891. 'Labour Colonies in Germany', *The Nineteenth Century and After* 29(167), January, pp. 73–88; W. Carlile and V.W. Carlile. 1906. *The Continental Outcast: Land Colonies and Poor Law Relief.* London: T. Fisher Unwin; Vagrancy Committee. 1906. *Appendix to the Report of the Departmental Committee on Vagrancy.* London: Parliamentary Papers Cd. 2892, pp. 105–10, 120–28; Board of Trade. 1910. 'Labour Colonies on the Continent', in Royal Commission on the Poor Laws and Relief of Distress, *Appendix,* vol. IX, London: Parliamentary Papers Cd. 5068, pp. 768–99; Royal Commission on the Poor Laws and Relief of Distress. 1910. *Appendix,* vol. XXXII, *Reports on Visits Paid by the Labour Colonies Committee to Certain Institutions in Holland, Belgium, Germany, and Switzerland.* London: Parliamentary Papers Cd. 5199.

7. J. Filthaut. 1994. *Dawson und Deutschland. Das deutsche Vorbild und die Reformen im Bildungswesen, in der Stadtverwaltung und in der Sozialversicherung Großbritanniens 1880–1914.* Frankfurt: Lang; E.P. Hennock. 1987. *British Social Reform and German Precedents: the Case of Social Insurance, 1880–1914.* Oxford: Clarendon Press, pp. 33–36; G. Hollenberg. 1974. *Englisches Interesse am Kaiserreich: Die Attraktivität Preußen-Deutschlands für konservative und liberale Kreise in Großbritannien 1860–1914.* Wiesbaden: Steiner, pp. 230–42.

8. For example: C. Küther. 1983. *Menschen auf der Straße. Vagierende Unterschichten in Bayern, Franken und Schwaben in der zweiten Hälfte des 18. Jahrhunderts.* Göttingen: Vandenhoeck & Ruprecht; S. Kienitz. 1989. *Unterwegs – Frauen zwischen Not und Normen. Lebensweise und Mentalität vagierender Frauen um 1800 in Württemberg.* Tübingen: Tübinger Vereinigung für Volkskunde; E. Schubert. 1990. *Arme Leute, Bettler und Gauner im Franken des 18. Jahrhunderts,* 2nd edn. Neustadt/Aisch: Degener; R. Jütte. 1994. *Poverty and Deviance in Early Modern Europe.* Cambridge: Cambridge

University Press; M. Rheinheimer. 2000. *Arme, Bettler und Vaganten. Überleben in der Not 1450–1850.* Frankfurt: Fischer Taschenbuch; G. Ammerer. 2003. *Heimat Straße. Vaganten im Österreich des Ancien Régime.* Vienna: Verlag für Geschichte und Politik; H. Bräuer. 2010. *Kinderbettel und Bettelkinder Mitteleuropas zwischen 1500 und 1800. Beobachtungen, Thesen, Anregungen.* Leipzig: Leipziger Universitätsverlag.

9. For example: K. Meister. 1994. *Wanderbettelei im Großherzogtum Baden 1877–1913.* Mannheim: Institut für Landeskunde und Regionalforschung der Universität Mannheim.

10. C. Sachße and F. Tennstedt. 1998. *Geschichte der Armenfürsorge in Deutschland,* vol. 1, *Vom Spätmittelalter bis zum Ersten Weltkrieg,* 2nd edn. Stuttgart: Kohlhammer. While Sachße and Tennstedt refer to the persistence of vagrancy during the late nineteenth century in the first volume of their, by now, classic textbook on German poor law history, this subject is barely touched upon in the more recent overview by L. Frohman. 2008a. *Poor Relief and Welfare in Germany from the Reformation to World War I.* Cambridge: Cambridge University Press.

11. On neighbouring Austria, however, see S. Wadauer. 2011. 'Establishing Distinctions: Unemployment versus Vagrancy in Austria from the Late Nineteenth Century to 1938', *International Review of Social History* 56:31–70 and various other publications by the same author.

12. The chapter presents some results of a research project funded by the German Research Foundation (DFG) within the framework of the Collaborative Research Centre 600: 'Strangers and Poor People: Changing Patterns of Inclusion and Exclusion from Classical Antiquity to the Present Day' at the University of Trier from 2002 to 2012. A monograph is forthcoming.

13. Articles 361 and 362 of the Imperial Penal Code as well as many other relevant sources can be found in B. Althammer and C. Gerstenmayer (eds). 2013. *Bettler und Vaganten in der Neuzeit (1500–1933). Eine kommentierte Quellenedition.* Essen: Klartext.

14. For a summary of these definition problems, see, R. von Hippel. 1895. *Die strafrechtliche Bekämpfung von Bettel, Landstreicherei und Arbeitsscheu. Eine Darstellung des heutigen deutschen Rechtszustandes nebst Reformvorschlägen.* Berlin: Otto Liebmann, pp. 1–22.

15. A. Lammers. 1879. *Die Bettel-Plage.* Berlin: Leonhard Simion, p. 4.

16. For a more detailed analysis of contemporary perceptions of the 'new' vagrancy problem see B. Althammer. 2010. 'Der Vagabund. Zur diskursiven Konstruktion eines Gefahrenpotentials im späten 19. und frühen 20. Jahrhundert', in K. Härter, G. Sälter and E. Wiebel (eds), *Repräsentationen von Kriminalität und öffentlicher Sicherheit. Bilder, Vorstellungen und Diskurse vom 16. bis zum 20. Jahrhundert.* Frankfurt: Vittorio Klostermann, pp. 415–53.

17. The data in Table 3.1 for the German Empire and Prussia is taken from Bundesarchiv (BA), R1501, 101314; for Düsseldorf (here a few acquittals are included) from Hauptstaatsarchiv Düsseldorf (HStAD), RD, 8879, fol. 75–81. The numbers for England and Wales are taken from the yearly published volumes of *Judicial Statistics*; they refer to convictions for 'Begging' and 'Sleeping out' under the Vagrancy Act of 1824.

18. HStAD, RD, 8875, fol. 10–39: Register of proceedings against beggars, vagabonds and prostitutes by the local court (*Amtsgericht*) Düsseldorf from 1 October 1879 to 18 November 1880. The prostitution-cases (a further 143) are not considered here, although there is a small overlap with female beggars and vagabonds.

19. Stadtarchiv Aachen, AV, 3-6-1: Police reports on arrested beggars from March to September 1823.
20. Stadtarchiv Trier, Tb 15, 401: Police register of seized beggars from 20 to 29 July 1843.
21. Landeshauptarchiv Koblenz (LHAK), 441, 6655: Register of sentences passed by the district court (*Landgericht*) Koblenz in 1855.
22. BA, R1501, 101316, fol. 92–108: Report for the Imperial Interior Office, 6 February 1883. All translations of quotations from German sources are my own.
23. HStAD, RD, 8874: Instruction to the director of Brauweiler workhouse, 29 November 1880. The results of his investigations are noted in the above-mentioned court register, HStAD, RD, 8875, fol. 10–39.
24. HStAD, RD, 8879, fol. 75–81: Report from the mayor of Düsseldorf, 8 February 1883.
25. HStAD, RD, 8879, fol. 179–80: Police and court records on Aron Silbermann, 30 and 31 January 1883.
26. Reichsgericht. 1890. 'Was ist unter "Betteln" zu verstehen? Urteil vom 6. Juni 1890', *Entscheidungen des Reichsgerichts in Strafsachen* 20:434–36.
27. HStAD, RD 8879, fol. 57–59.
28. The Prussian administration discussed Eichhoven's citizenship in 1877 and again in 1883, but without coming to a definite conclusion. HStAD, RD, 8879, fol. 107–108: Report dated 24 February 1883. That he was expelled from Baden and Württemberg does not necessarily mean that he was qualified as a non-German foreigner there, because citizens of other German states who had repeatedly been convicted of begging or vagabondage could also be banished from the state territory. On the complicated issue of expulsion see B. Althammer. 2015. 'Grenzregime: Mobilität, Freizügigkeit und die Ausweisung von Fremden im 19. Jahrhundert', *Westfälische Forschungen* 65:17–35.
29. LHAK, 403, Nr. 10057, pp. 216–37, 304–12: Petition from Michael Bührle to the Prussian Ministry of the Interior, 20 June 1896, and subsequent correspondence on the case of Charlotte Ritter.
30. W. Ayaß. 1992. *Das Arbeitshaus Breitenau. Bettler, Landstreicher, Prostituierte, Zuhälter und Fürsorgeempfänger in der Korrektions- und Landarmenanstalt Breitenau (1874–1949)*. Kassel: Gesamthochschule Kassel; E. Elling-Ruhwinkel. 2005. *Sichern und Strafen. Das Arbeitshaus Benninghausen (1871–1945)*. Paderborn: Schöningh; B. Althammer. 2006. 'Functions and Developments of the *Arbeitshaus* in Germany: Brauweiler Workhouse in the Nineteenth and Early Twentieth Centuries', in A. Gestrich, S. King and L. Raphael (eds.), *Being Poor in Modern Europe: Historical Perspectives 1800–1940*. Oxford: Lang, pp. 273–97.
31. Archiv des Landschaftsverbands Rheinland, 8222, fol. 7–12: Report to the provincial administration, 15 August 1900.
32. A. Thun. 1879. *Die Industrie am Niederrhein und ihre Arbeiter. Erster Theil: Die links-rheinische Textilindustrie*. Leipzig: Duncker & Humblot, p. 52.
33. I I. Stursberg. 1882. *Die Vagabundenfrage,* 2nd edn. Düsseldorf: Rheinisch-Westfälische Gefängnis-Gesellschaft, p. 26.
34. E. Frie. 1997. 'Fürsorgepolitik zwischen Kirche und Staat. Wanderarmenhilfe in Preußen', in W. Loth and J.-C. Kaiser (eds), *Soziale Reform im Kaiserreich: Protestantismus, Katholizismus und Sozialpolitik*. Stuttgart: Kohlhammer, pp. 114–27; J. Scheffler. 2001. 'Die Anstalt Bethel und die "Brüder von der Landstraße". Anstaltsdiakonie und Wohlfahrtspflege am Beispiel der Wandererfürsorge', in M. Benad (ed.), *Bethels Mission. Beiträge zur Geschichte der v. Bodelschwinghschen Anstalten*, vol. 2, *Bethel im*

Spannungsfeld von Erweckungsfrömmigkeit und öffentlicher Fürsorge. Bielefeld: Luther, pp. 197–224.

35. E.P. Hennock. 2007. *The Origin of the Welfare State in England and Germany, 1850–1914: Social Policies Compared*. Cambridge: Cambridge University Press.

36. Reichstag. 1884. *Stenographische Berichte über die Verhandlungen des Reichstages*. Berlin, vol. 1884/1, 9 May, p. 481.

37. On the beginnings of German labour market policies, although with no or only brief mentions of the Wayfarers' Aid, see A. Faust. 1986. *Arbeitsmarktpolitik im deutschen Kaiserreich. Arbeitsvermittlung, Arbeitsbeschaffung und Arbeitslosenunterstützung 1890–1918*. Stuttgart: Steiner; K.C. Führer. 1990. *Arbeitslosigkeit und die Entstehung der Arbeitslosenversicherung in Deutschland, 1902–1927*. Berlin: Colloquium; B. Zimmermann. 2001. *La constitution du chômage en Allemagne: entre professions et territoires*. Paris: Maison des Sciences de l'Homme; H.-W. Schmuhl. 2003. *Arbeitsmarktpolitik und Arbeitsverwaltung in Deutschland 1871–2002: zwischen Fürsorge, Hoheit und Markt*. Nuremberg: Bundesanstalt für Arbeit; S. Münnich. 2010. *Interessen und Ideen: die Entstehung der Arbeitslosenversicherung in Deutschland und den USA*. Frankfurt: Campus.

38. *Die Post*, 12 March 1893.

39. K. Bonhoeffer. 1901. 'Ein Beitrag zur Kenntnis des großstädtischen Bettel- und Vagabondentums. Eine psychiatrische Untersuchung', *Zeitschrift für die gesamte Strafrechtswissenschaft* 21:1–65.

40. Ibid, p. 2. For a more detailed analysis of psychiatric interpretations of vagrancy see B. Althammer. 2013. 'Pathologische Vagabunden. Psychiatrische Grenzziehungen um 1900', *Geschichte und Gesellschaft* 39:306–337.

41. K. Wilmanns. 1911/12. 'Die praktische Durchführbarkeit der Bestimmungen über die verminderte Zurechnungsfähigkeit im Vorentwurfe', *Monatsschrift für Kriminalpsychologie und Strafrechtsreform* 8:138.

42. K. Wilmanns. 1904/05. 'Das Landstreichertum, seine Abhilfe und Bekämpfung', *Monatsschrift für Kriminalpsychologie und Strafrechtsreform* 1:605–6.

43. Deutscher Verein für Armenpflege und Wohltätigkeit. 1908. *Stenographischer Bericht über die Verhandlungen der 28. Jahresversammlung des deutschen Vereins für Armenpflege und Wohltätigkeit am 17. und 18. September 1908 in Hannover*. Leipzig: Duncker & Humblot, p. 80.

44. J. Weydmann. 1908. *Die Wanderarmenfürsorge in Deutschland*. Mönchengladbach: Volksverein für das katholische Deutschland, pp. 68–69.

45. E. Dosenheimer. 1908/9. 'Vorschläge zur Bekämpfung des Bettels und der Landstreicherei', *Monatsschrift für Kriminalpsychologie und Strafrechtsreform* 5:660–61.

46. Deutscher Verein für Armenpflege und Wohltätigkeit. 1912. *Stenographischer Bericht über die Verhandlungen der 31. Jahresversammlung des deutschen Vereins für Armenpflege und Wohltätigkeit am 20. und 21. September 1911 in Dresden*. Leipzig: Duncker & Humblot, p. 120.

47. H. von Jarotzky. 1912. *Die Bedeutung der Arbeitsanstalt Brauweiler für die Rheinprovinz. Vortrag gehalten vor dem Gefängnisverein zu Cöln am 27. November 1912*. Brauweiler, pp. 4, 8–9.

48. J. Horion. 1913. 'Die Wanderarbeitsstätten', *Zeitschrift für das Armenwesen* 14:119, 127–28.

49. L. Frohman. 2008b. 'The Break-up of the Poor Laws – German Style: Progressivism and the Origins of the Welfare State, 1900–1918', *Comparative Studies in Society and History* 50:998.
50. For a more elaborate comparative discussion see B. Althammer. 2016. 'Controlling Vagrancy: Germany, England and France, 1880–1914', in B. Althammer, L. Raphael and T. Stazic-Wendt (eds), *Rescuing the Vulnerable: Poverty, Welfare and Social Ties in Modern Europe*. New York: Berghahn, pp. 187–211.

Works Cited

Althammer, B. 2006. 'Functions and Developments of the *Arbeitshaus* in Germany: Brauweiler Workhouse in the Nineteenth and Early Twentieth Centuries', in A. Gestrich, S. King and L. Raphael (eds), *Being Poor in Modern Europe: Historical Perspectives 1800–1940*. Oxford: Lang, pp. 273–97.

———. 2010. 'Der Vagabund. Zur diskursiven Konstruktion eines Gefahrenpotentials im späten 19. und frühen 20. Jahrhundert', in K. Härter, G. Sälter and E. Wiebel (eds), *Repräsentationen von Kriminalität und öffentlicher Sicherheit. Bilder, Vorstellungen und Diskurse vom 16. bis zum 20. Jahrhundert*. Frankfurt: Vittorio Klostermann, pp. 415–53.

———. 2013. 'Pathologische Vagabunden. Psychiatrische Grenzziehungen um 1900', *Geschichte und Gesellschaft* 39:306–337.

———. 2014. 'Transnational Expert Discourse on Vagrancy around 1900', in B. Althammer, A. Gestrich and J. Gründler (eds), *The Welfare State and the 'Deviant Poor' in Europe, 1870–1933*. Basingstoke: Palgrave Macmillan, pp. 103–25, 240–45.

———. 2015. 'Grenzregime: Mobilität, Freizügigkeit und die Ausweisung von Fremden im 19. Jahrhundert', *Westfälische Forschungen*, 65:17–35.

———. 2016. 'Controlling Vagrancy: Germany, England and France, 1880–1914', in B. Althammer, L. Raphael and T. Stazic-Wendt (eds), *Rescuing the Vulnerable: Poverty, Welfare and Social Ties in Modern Europe*. New York: Berghahn, pp. 187–211.

———. and C. Gerstenmayer (eds). 2013. *Bettler und Vaganten in der Neuzeit (1500–1933). Eine kommentierte Quellenedition*. Essen: Klartext.

Ammerer, G. 2003. *Heimat Straße. Vaganten im Österreich des Ancien Régime*. Vienna: Verlag für Geschichte und Politik.

Ayaß, W. 1992. *Das Arbeitshaus Breitenau. Bettler, Landstreicher, Prostituierte, Zuhälter und Fürsorgeempfänger in der Korrektions- und Landarmenanstalt Breitenau (1874–1949)*. Kassel: Gesamthochschule Kassel.

Board of Trade. 1910. 'Labour Colonies on the Continent', in Royal Commission on the Poor Laws and Relief of Distress, *Appendix*, vol. IX. London: Parliamentary Papers Cd. 5068, pp. 768–99.

Bonhoeffer, K. 1901. 'Ein Beitrag zur Kenntnis des großstädtischen Bettel- und Vagabondentums. Eine psychiatrische Untersuchung', *Zeitschrift für die gesamte Strafrechtswissenschaft* 21:1–65.

Bräuer, H. 2010. *Kinderbettel und Bettelkinder Mitteleuropas zwischen 1500 und 1800. Beobachtungen, Thesen, Anregungen.* Leipzig: Leipziger Universitätsverlag.

Carlile, W., and V.W. Carlile. 1906. *The Continental Outcast: Land Colonies and Poor Law Relief.* London: T. Fisher Unwin.

Dawson, W.H. 1910. *The Vagrancy Problem. The Case for Measures of Restraint for Tramps, Loafers, and Unemployables: with a Study of Continental Detention Colonies and Labour Houses.* London: P.S. King & Son.

Deutscher Verein für Armenpflege und Wohltätigkeit. 1908. *Stenographischer Bericht über die Verhandlungen der 28. Jahresversammlung des deutschen Vereins für Armenpflege und Wohltätigkeit am 17. und 18. September 1908 in Hannover.* Leipzig: Duncker & Humblot.

———. 1912. *Stenographischer Bericht über die Verhandlungen der 31. Jahresversammlung des deutschen Vereins für Armenpflege und Wohltätigkeit am 20. und 21. September 1911 in Dresden.* Leipzig: Duncker & Humblot.

Dosenheimer, E. 1908/9. 'Vorschläge zur Bekämpfung des Bettels und der Landstreicherei', *Monatsschrift für Kriminalpsychologie und Strafrechtsreform* 5:657–71.

Elling-Ruhwinkel, E. 2005. *Sichern und Strafen. Das Arbeitshaus Benninghausen (1871–1945).* Paderborn: Schöningh.

Faust, A. 1986. *Arbeitsmarktpolitik im deutschen Kaiserreich. Arbeitsvermittlung, Arbeitsbeschaffung und Arbeitslosenunterstützung 1890–1918.* Stuttgart: Steiner.

Filthaut, J. 1994. *Dawson und Deutschland. Das deutsche Vorbild und die Reformen im Bildungswesen, in der Stadtverwaltung und in der Sozialversicherung Großbritanniens 1880–1914.* Frankfurt: Lang.

Frie, E. 1997. 'Fürsorgepolitik zwischen Kirche und Staat. Wanderarmenhilfe in Preußen', in W. Loth and J.-C. Kaiser (eds), *Soziale Reform im Kaiserreich: Protestantismus, Katholizismus und Sozialpolitik.* Stuttgart: Kohlhammer, pp. 114–27.

Frohman, L. 2008a. *Poor Relief and Welfare in Germany from the Reformation to World War I.* Cambridge: Cambridge University Press.

———. 2008b. 'The Break-up of the Poor Laws – German Style: Progressivism and the Origins of the Welfare State, 1900–1918', *Comparative Studies in Society and History* 50: 981–1009.

Führer, K.C. 1990. *Arbeitslosigkeit und die Entstehung der Arbeitslosenversicherung in Deutschland, 1902–1927.* Berlin: Colloquium.

Hennock, E.P. 1987. *British Social Reform and German Precedents: the Case of Social Insurance, 1880–1914.* Oxford: Clarendon Press.

———. 2007. *The Origin of the Welfare State in England and Germany, 1850–1914: Social Policies Compared.* Cambridge: Cambridge University Press.

Hippel, R. v. 1895. *Die strafrechtliche Bekämpfung von Bettel, Landstreicherei und Arbeitsscheu. Eine Darstellung des heutigen deutschen Rechtszustandes nebst Reformvorschlägen.* Berlin: Otto Liebmann.

Hollenberg, G. 1974. *Englisches Interesse am Kaiserreich: Die Attraktivität Preußen-Deutschlands für konservative und liberale Kreise in Großbritannien 1860–1914.* Wiesbaden: Steiner.

Horion, J. 1913. 'Die Wanderarbeitsstätten', *Zeitschrift für das Armenwesen* 14:117–131.

Jarotzky, H. v. 1912: *Die Bedeutung der Arbeitsanstalt Brauweiler für die Rheinprovinz. Vortrag gehalten vor dem Gefängnisverein zu Cöln am 27. November 1912.* Brauweiler.

Jütte, R. 1994. *Poverty and Deviance in Early Modern Europe.* Cambridge: Cambridge University Press.

Kienitz, S. 1989. *Unterwegs – Frauen zwischen Not und Normen. Lebensweise und Mentalität vagierender Frauen um 1800 in Württemberg.* Tübingen: Tübinger Vereinigung für Volkskunde.

Küther, C. 1983. *Menschen auf der Straße. Vagierende Unterschichten in Bayern, Franken und Schwaben in der zweiten Hälfte des 18. Jahrhunderts.* Göttingen: Vandenhoeck & Ruprecht.

Lammers, A. 1879. *Die Bettel-Plage.* Berlin: Leonhard Simion.

Meath, Earl of [Reginald Brabazon]. 1891. 'Labour Colonies in Germany', *The Nineteenth Century and After* 29(167), January, pp. 73–88.

Meister, K. 1994. *Wanderbettelei im Großherzogtum Baden 1877–1913.* Mannheim: Institut für Landeskunde und Regionalforschung der Universität Mannheim.

Münnich, S. 2010. *Interessen und Ideen: die Entstehung der Arbeitslosenversicherung in Deutschland und den USA.* Frankfurt: Campus.

Reichsgericht 1890. 'Was ist unter "Betteln" zu verstehen? Urteil vom 6. Juni 1890', *Entscheidungen des Reichsgerichts in Strafsachen* 20:434–36.

Reichstag. 1884. *Stenographische Berichte über die Verhandlungen des Reichstages,* vol. 1884/1. Berlin.

Reports on the Elberfeld Poor Law System and German Workmen's Colonies. 1888. London: Parliamentary Papers C. 5341.

Rheinheimer, M. 2000. *Arme, Bettler und Vaganten. Überleben in der Not 1450–1850.* Frankfurt: Fischer Taschenbuch.

Ribton-Turner, C.J. 1887. *A History of Vagrants and Vagrancy, and Beggars and Begging.* London: Chapman and Hall.

Royal Commission on the Poor Laws and Relief of Distress. 1910. *Appendix,* vol. XXXII, *Reports on Visits Paid by the Labour Colonies Committee to Certain Institutions in Holland, Belgium, Germany, and Switzerland.* London: Parliamentary Papers Cd. 5199.

Sachße, C., and F. Tennstedt. 1998. *Geschichte der Armenfürsorge in Deutschland,* vol. 1, *Vom Spätmittelalter bis zum Ersten Weltkrieg,* 2nd edn. Stuttgart: Kohlhammer.

Scheffler, J. 2001. 'Die Anstalt Bethel und die "Brüder von der Landstraße". Anstaltsdiakonie und Wohlfahrtspflege am Beispiel der Wandererfürsorge', in M. Benad (ed.), *Bethels Mission. Beiträge zur Geschichte der v. Bodelschwinghschen Anstalten*, vol. 2, *Bethel im Spannungsfeld von Erweckungsfrömmigkeit und öffentlicher Fürsorge*. Bielefeld: Luther, pp. 197–224.

Schmuhl, H.-W. 2003. *Arbeitsmarktpolitik und Arbeitsverwaltung in Deutschland 1871–2002: zwischen Fürsorge, Hoheit und Markt*. Nürnberg: Bundesanstalt für Arbeit.

Schubert, E. 1990. *Arme Leute, Bettler und Gauner im Franken des 18. Jahrhunderts*, 2nd edn. Neustadt/Aisch: Degener.

Stursberg, H. 1882. *Die Vagabundenfrage*, 2nd edn. Düsseldorf: Rheinisch-Westfälische Gefängnis-Gesellschaft.

Thun, A. 1879. *Die Industrie am Niederrhein und ihre Arbeiter. Erster Theil: Die linksrheinische Textilindustrie*. Leipzig: Duncker & Humblot.

Vagrancy Committee. 1906. *Appendix to the Report of the Departmental Committee on Vagrancy*. London: Parliamentary Papers Cd. 2892.

Wadauer, S. 2011. 'Establishing Distinctions: Unemployment versus Vagrancy in Austria from the Late Nineteenth Century to 1938', *International Review of Social History* 56:31–70.

Weydmann, J. 1908. *Die Wanderarmenfürsorge in Deutschland*. Mönchengladbach: Volksverein für das katholische Deutschland.

Wilmanns, K. 1904/05. 'Das Landstreichertum, seine Abhilfe und Bekämpfung', *Monatsschrift für Kriminalpsychologie und Strafrechtsreform* 1:605–20.

———. 1911/12. 'Die praktische Durchführbarkeit der Bestimmungen über die verminderte Zurechnungsfähigkeit im Vorentwurfe', *Monatsschrift für Kriminalpsychologie und Strafrechtsreform* 8:136–42.

Zimmermann, B. 2001. *La constitution du chômage en Allemagne: entre professions et territoires*. Paris: Maison des Sciences de l'Homme.

Beate Althammer is a postdoctoral researcher at the University of Trier and visiting lecturer at the University of Lüneburg. She is currently completing a monograph on vagrancy in nineteenth- and early twentieth-century Germany. She is author of *Das Bismarckreich 1871–1890* (2009) and co-editor of the volumes: *Bettler und Vaganten in der Neuzeit (1500–1933)* (2013); *The Welfare State and the 'Deviant Poor' in Europe, 1870–1933* (2014); and *Rescuing the Vulnerable: Poverty, Welfare and Social Ties in Modern Europe* (2016).

CHAPTER 4

The Welfare State and Poverty in the Weimar Republic

Wilfried Rudloff

At the Great Exhibition for Health, Social Welfare and Physical Exercise in Düsseldorf, which attracted seven and a half million visitors in 1926,[1] those interested could marvel at the visionary model of the architect and city planner Ludwig Hilberseimer, who compressed the diverse demands of modern urban planning into a topographic representation of a 'welfare city' (*Wohlfahrtsstadt*).[2] If, on the one hand, Hilberseimer's city model was intended to stand for the utopian moment of an avant garde urbanity,[3] on the other, visitors were simultaneously presented with a series of accurate insights into the contemporary state of health and welfare provision in German cities during the 1920s, in addition to plans for their improvement. The municipal welfare system, transcending and superseding the old poor relief, had become a vital element of municipal self-representation, demonstrating urban modernity and social progressiveness.

If one grasps, as intended, the concept of the 'welfare city', and uses it to make sense of German cities' welfare policies within the specific socio-economic and political conditions of the Weimar period, three topics primarily need to be addressed. Firstly, how the framework of welfare policy during these years extended far beyond the tasks and aims of the old poor relief – municipal welfare gained responsibility for a new and much wider spectrum of services. Secondly, how the 'welfare city' and 'welfare state' did not simply prove to be two different territorial layers for the uniform enforcement of the social state's tasks, but rather two distinct spheres for the provision of welfare, which followed diverse guiding and operational principles. Thirdly and finally, the enormous task load of local welfare policies shaped the fate of municipal politics as never before or after during the nineteenth and twentieth centuries. In no other period did

German cities carry the hallmark of the 'welfare city' so completely as during the Weimar years, and in no other period did the welfare policies of local authorities (*Kommunen*) attract so much public interest. The term 'welfare city' tries to mark these three basic developments. The term is not borrowed from contemporary discourse or technical terminology. The same is true for the terms 'social state' and 'welfare state', which were also not deeply rooted in Weimar's political vocabulary. If the latter was evoked at all, it was done so primarily pejoratively, and the phrase 'social state' only began its irresistible advance in Germany after 1945.[4]

By contrast, the juxtaposition and contrasting demarcation of the distinct systems of social policy (*Sozialpolitik*) and welfare (*Wohlfahrtspflege*) was well established among contemporary observers. At the heart of social policy stood social insurance and labour law; the roots of local welfare provision, lay, instead, in the traditions of poor relief. Contemporaries above all considered two distinctions to be decisive in this regard. Social policy was primarily concerned with tackling the living conditions of social classes and groups, whereas the starting point of welfare provision lay in alleviating the needs of destitute individuals.[5] On the one hand, social policies granted defined social rights based on concrete individual needs; on the other, welfare delivered aid 'according to the extent of individual need' without conceding clearly defined social and legal entitlements.[6] Ideally, while the interventions of social policies on the state level served to mitigate disparities between classes, the welfare policies of local authorities aimed at the correction of deficits ascribed to the individual personality of the claimants. In reality, of course, these boundaries were far less clearly drawn.

Mass Poverty and Reform Programmes in Local Authorities' Welfare Provision

For a long time, German research on the themes of poverty and welfare policy in the interwar period has been primarily interested in the institutional organization of welfare provision.[7] Cities' changing policies concerning the poor and the operational frameworks of local welfare bureaucracies have stood at the centre of historiographical focus.[8] By contrast, British research on the history of poverty during this period has devoted noticeably more attention to questions concerning the measurement, extent and structure of the phenomenon itself.[9] In so doing, it benefits from the elaborate surveys which were produced since the publication of the first volume of Charles Booth's 1889 *Life and Labour of the People in London*, by sociologists such as Seebohm Rowntree, Arthur Bowley, Hubert Llewelyn Smith or Herbert Tout. Comparable surveys, which (with the help of a previously agreed poverty line based on assessments of fundamental human needs) examine working class households or the general population of selected cities, do not exist for interwar Germany. In the tradition of Georg Simmel,[10] the poor are equated in the historiography of German welfare with welfare recipients. In short: whereas British historiography in this field presents itself primarily as research into poverty, its German equivalent has appeared far more frequently as work on welfare policies.

A clear aim pursued by British surveys of poverty during the interwar period was to find out whether the level of poverty had either risen or fallen in comparison to the prewar years. The assumption that it had generally been reduced, largely found confirmation in city surveys of London, York and Bristol. By contrast, contemporary observers in Germany were in no doubt whatsoever that poverty levels had increased enormously in comparison to the years prior to 1914. According to this perspective, Germany as a whole had to be considered an impoverished nation after the First World War. The semantics of poverty no longer solely served to illustrate positions of social and material marginality. 'Impoverishment' developed into a familiar term of societal self-description. Yet, poverty still became most visible where people gathered to apply for public assistance. Pictures of long queues in front of welfare offices, labour exchanges or public soup kitchens, thus served as central elements of Weimar's iconography of poverty.

If one turns to the statistics composed by German cities outlining the numbers of their welfare recipients (where a considerable number of the 'ashamed poor' are not included) due to a lack of other sources of empirical evidence, the indicators of a growth in poverty are obvious. The percentage of poor relief recipients in German cities had mostly oscillated between 2 and 4 per cent of the population in the decades prior to 1914.[11] After 1918, cities were forced to provide an unprecedentedly large proportion of their inhabitants with public welfare benefits. For example, in Frankfurt am Main, 9,909 persons were registered as recipients of poor relief in 1913. In 1926, the number was 69,500, some 12 per cent of the city's inhabitants and seven times higher than the period before the First World War.[12] In Bavaria in 1924, the first year after the end of hyperinflation, a statistical survey was conducted of the publicly supported poor, in which, by contrast to later surveys, the dependent family members of each individual were also counted. During 1924, the percentages of the population in permanent receipt of welfare payments were as follows: in Munich 7.9 percent; Nuremberg, 5.9 percent; and Augsburg 8.8 per cent. (By comparison, in the last decade prior to the outbreak of the First World War, only 2.8 per cent of Munich's population had relied on the receipt of ongoing poor relief). If one added the other recipients of short-term relief to these figures for the named Bavarian cities, the tallies oscillated between 17.3 per cent for Munich and 23.3 per cent for Augsburg. In rural localities, by contrast, the statistical levels of poverty had not changed considerably since the prewar period.[13] By 1929, in the major German cities for every 100 citizens, seven were recipients of welfare. This percentage would probably have to be doubled to provide an accurate picture of social conditions, as this survey did not include welfare recipients' dependent family members.[14] All in all, even in the Weimar Republic's more prosperous years, the proportion of city dwellers in receipt of welfare payments was at least twice as large as during the period prior to 1914, and often considerably higher than that.

One must also consider here a peculiarity of this welfare provision: with every heightening of the welfare rates (*Richtsätze*) agreed by cities, which served the welfare offices as poverty lines, not only the levels of paid support increased, but also the numbers of those qualifying for support, as wider strata of the less well-off now came to lie beyond that threshold. Rising figures in local authorities' poverty statistics did not result solely from an actual increase in poverty levels but could also have been caused by an adjustment of the parameters of welfare support (the opposite could also be the case, as with cuts to the base rate of welfare payment). The same did happen in England: although, as indicated, a decrease in poverty was diagnosed in Great Britain during the interwar period, the number of individuals receiving poor relief increased considerably during these years; from 412,000 on average in 1913, to 1,011,000 in 1926, if one takes the recipients of 'outdoor relief' as the key indicator. The combined tally of those receiving a form of poor relief in this period rose from 784,000 to 1,331,000.[15]

Already in the mid years of the Weimar Republic, the levels of poverty measured according to the numbers of the publicly supported poor, lay far higher than had generally been the case in Imperial Germany. Yet, an even larger proportion of the population saw itself forced to ask for welfare relief during the Republic's two periods of severe economic crisis, between 1918 and 1923 and between 1929 and 1933. Immediately following the hyperinflation of 1923, at the year's end in Frankfurt am Main, 39 per cent of the city's inhabitants were being supported by local welfare; in Nuremberg, 49 percent; and in Stettin, 56 percent.[16] Including the numbers of the supported unemployed, in December 1923 more than a quarter of the inhabitants of the large German cities was reliant on income support from public welfare.[17] Around a decade later, at the height of the Great Depression, between a quarter and a third of cities' populations were reliant on welfare payments in many localities. In Hamburg, 22 per cent of the population received some form of support in 1932; in May of that year, every fourth Berliner, and in Munich at the year's end between every fourth and fifth. In Cologne, in June 1932, no less than two-fifths of the city's inhabitants received public welfare support.[18]

What applied to the statistical extent of poverty also applied to the resulting welfare expenditures. In no other period of the twentieth century did the costs of welfare weigh so heavily on the shoulders of local authorities as in the years of the Weimar Republic. In comparison to the years prior to 1914, overall welfare payments formed a disproportionately large percentage of net municipal expenditures (*Zuschussbedarf*), a percentage which in general became all the higher the larger the city in question.[19] Even during the Weimar Republic's middle phase, which posed fewer social problems than the years of hyperinflation and the Great Depression, welfare bills continued to form around a third of local government expenditures (if one includes the expenditure for house building). For example, in the fiscal year 1925/26, welfare expenditures formed, on average, 38 per cent of local authorities' budgets.[20]

In a large city like Cologne, welfare's proportion of the city's total budget increased from around 18 per cent prior to the First World War to no less than 46 per cent in 1926.[21] During the economic crisis after 1929, when, other than debt servicing, almost all local government expenditures had to be drastically reduced, those for welfare services reached such heights that in many localities public finances were ruined.[22] According to the calculations of the statistical yearbook of German cities, the welfare expenditures of the ten largest cities (including the expenditure for youth welfare) formed 50.7 per cent of total local government expenditures.[23] In Duisburg, welfare expenditures devoured almost two-thirds of the city's total budget in 1932.[24] The ever increasing sums claimed by welfare budgets threatened to starve all other items of adequate funding. As the rapidly increasing costs of welfare were simultaneously accompanied by a dramatic collapse of local tax revenues, many local government parliaments saw themselves incapable of producing a balanced budget. In many cities, as a consequence, state regulators or commissars took over control of financial and budgetary matters.

The causes of this enormous financial strain were not difficult to recognize and are well researched. They need only be briefly summarized here. The responsibility for dealing with the consequences of war and hyperinflation lay primarily with cities and local government. Welfare policies in the postwar period were influenced less by endogenous reform impulses than by the severe social conditions they had to cope with. Two social groups heavily reliant on city welfare provision were characteristic of this tendency. Recipients of social insurance pensions (*Sozialrentner*) were in greater need of additional support from city welfare provision than before the war, as their pensions were no longer sufficient to secure the necessities of life.[25] Owners of small capital incomes, the so-called 'small rentiers' (*Kleinrentner*), who had not been included in the schemes of social insurance due to their occupation as independent craftsmen, small business owners, or as self-employed, had lost large proportions of their life savings through inflation and were now forced to turn to welfare offices. This manifested itself above all as a problem of elderly women and widowers among the middle classes. It was primarily wives and daughters from these circles who were affected by the 'new poverty'.[26] Without the dramatic devaluation of their financial assets, these individuals would have been able to cope by themselves, and would not have required recourse to public welfare. As victims of inflation, the 'social pensioners' and 'small rentiers' were provided higher welfare payments than other groups among the poor.

A third social group among the poor was no less emblematic of the mass distress of the Weimar Republic's population. Since the revolutionary government of November 1918 had established a specific branch of welfare provision for the unemployed, German cities had been involved, to varying degrees, in its implementation.[27] Unemployment benefits were financed jointly by the Reich government, federal states and local governmental authorities, and, from late 1923 onwards, mainly by contributions made by employers and workers. Until 1927, payments were dependent on passing a needs-based test (*Bedürftigkeitsprüfung*).[28] After unemployment benefits had been converted into a social insurance system in 1927, a residual group of the unemployed remained, who, due to inadequate employment periods, were not entitled to payments from insurance schemes, or whose claim periods had run out. Local welfare had to step in to provide for these individuals. During the Great Depression from 1929 onwards, and due to the massive increase of long-term unemployment, the number of these 'welfare unemployed' (*Wohlfahrtserwerbslose*) rose dramatically. In 1932, it exceeded by far the numbers of those unemployed who were still entitled to unemployment insurance payments. In December 1932, 54 per cent of all unemployed Germans supported by social insurance or welfare belonged to the category of the 'welfare unemployed', whereas the proportion of those in receipt of support from unemployment insurance had shrunk to 18 percent. (The others received an intermediate form of support, so-called 'crisis support' – *Krisenunterstützung*).[29]

The drastically increased costs of public welfare were exacerbated by factors other than the quantitative increase of poverty. Public providers of welfare had to close part of the gap which hyperinflation had torn in the substance and resources of private charity.[30] In the early 1920s, the balance between public and private welfare provision shifted markedly. Formerly, in a city like Frankfurt am Main, a rich culture of bourgeois philanthropy had ensured that the prewar welfare budget of 4 million marks was complemented by a sum of between 2.5 and 3 million marks derived from private charities and donations. After hyperinflation, in 1926, only 0.5 million marks derived from private sources, forming a mere 2.5 per cent of the public welfare expenditures.[31] For Hamburg, it has been calculated that the expenditures of public welfare and the revenues of charitable donations stood at a ratio of 2.5 to 1 in the years leading up to the First World War. At the end of the 1920s, the proportion was 100 to 1. Due to the inflationary devaluation of charitable associations' capital donations, their annual yields fell to a sixth of their prewar values, from almost 3 million marks to only 0.5 million in the early 1930s.[32] Inflation inflicted severe damage on the culture of municipal charities, by impoverishing considerable sections of the middle classes. After the war, the subsidy of charitable welfare associations by the Reich and local government acquired a previously unknown extent. In Munich, in 1927, the city placed 400,000 marks at the disposal of private welfare charities.[33] Private welfare institutions became yet more dependent on the nursing charges and reimbursements provided by the public purse for their services.[34]

Thus, one aspect of the welfare city's increasing significance was the considerably expanded scale and magnitude of the social problems for which municipal welfare bore responsibility. Another was that the welfare policies of the cities also played a considerable role in the qualitative extension of the Weimar welfare state.[35] It was of more than merely symbolic significance that the new revolutionary authorities, when releasing the suffrage law for the constitutional national parliament in November 1918, scrapped previous regulations which had denied the recipients of poor relief the right to vote.[36] Dependence on poor relief would no longer affect the status of an individual as a citizen. The odious term of *Armenpflege* (care of the poor) was replaced in legal terminology with *Fürsorge* (welfare). Within acutely difficult parameters, local authorities' welfare policies during the Weimar era reached out to new life situations among the citizenry, increasing the levels of services provided and expanding the range and quality of those on offer. Local authorities thereby generalized welfare policies which had already been discussed and developed in the decade prior to the First World War, but had not yet been widely implemented. The new legislative basis of welfare policies, the Reich Welfare Law of 1924/25 and the Reich Youth Welfare Law of 1924, centralized legislation in this field and served to unify the legal parameters of action. These laws also contained substantial improvements relative to the old legislative framework.[37] An ambitious youth welfare office, like that of Frankfurt am Main, expanded its service provision during the Weimar years partly by going beyond the requirements of the Reich law. In Frankfurt, the Youth Office adopted such tasks as recreational welfare programs (*Erholungsfürsorge*) for children with poor health, vocational counselling for adolescents, protective supervision (*Schutzaufsicht*) for children threatened by neglect (*Verwahrlosung*) and voluntary educational assistance (*freiwillige Erziehungshilfe*, an alternative to the more severe instrument of correctional education imposed by the courts).[38] Quantitatively, city youth offices' chief responsibilities lay in the tasks of legal guardianship (*Berufsvormundschaft*) and foster care. The municipal welfare offices spread their sphere of intervention further into the domain of 'incomplete' families. In certain large Rhineland cities, such as Düsseldorf, Cologne or Essen, youth offices were also involved in the construction of 'educational counselling centres', which were responsible for dealing with the psychiatric, psychological or therapeutic needs of 'difficult children'.[39] In terms of the provision of healthcare, the local health centres which had been founded in the last decades before the First World War in order to fight infant mortality, tuberculosis and venereal diseases, were now placed on a wider institutional footing and universalized.[40] The balance between the activities of the private associations and the municipal health initiatives shifted towards the latter. In 1908, there had been more tuberculosis welfare centres being run by private associations than by cities and rural districts (*Kreise*). Fifteen years later, by contrast, only 286 centres remained in the hands of private associations, whereas 1,133 belonged to cities or *Kreise*.[41] In most cities, the provision of healthcare in schools was also expanded, partly due to the alarming deterioration of children's health resulting from the First World War. In general, it was clear that local government's provision of healthcare was being considerably strengthened, not only due to the First World War's impact on the population's health, but also because of the increasing influence of bio-political and eugenic ideas. In a longer-term perspective, the 1920s were a golden age of local government health welfare (*Gesundheitsfürsorge*)[42]: alongside welfare for the poor and youth welfare, it formed a third arm of local authorities' welfare provision.

Newly founded sanatorium institutions also revealed raised standards and service. Modernized homes for the elderly, which, along with hospitals, aimed at a primarily bourgeois clientele, offered rooms with one or two beds instead of mass dormitories.[43] In terms of outdoor relief (*offene Armenpflege*), prior to 1914 there had been only few signs that the rates of support (*Richtsätze*) were based on a thoroughgoing assessment of the basic needs of the poor. During the Weimar years too, the standard rates of support fixed by local authorities were rarely based on a precise examination of the real subsistence needs of the poor. However, cities were at least now legally obliged to establish such standard rates of support, which were generally revised at more or less regular intervals by local government bodies.[44]

The local administration of welfare was also placed on a new footing.[45] At the Republic's onset, city welfare offices were established whose decentralized branches emerged in larger cities as the most important reference points concerning the topography of urban poverty. In Munich in 1891, seventeen civil servants and secretaries had been responsible for dealing with the ongoing tasks of poor relief. Four decades later, in the early 1930s, the number had increased to over 800. The municipal welfare administration of Hamburg was even employing 1,006.[46] Additionally, during the Weimar years, municipal youth and health offices (*Jugendämter* and *Gesundheitsämter*) were established, which were either independently organized or connected with the new welfare offices. Prior to the First World War, only a handful of these institutions had been in existence. In addition, in many places newly formed labour and housing offices (*Arbeitsämter* and *Wohnungsämter*) emerged as independent bodies. Urban welfare provision thereby gained not only a stronger bureaucratic character, but also became the training ground for a new class of professional welfare administrators. The voluntary guardians of the poor (*Armenpfleger*) who had provided the poor relief system with the core of its personnel prior to 1914 were increasingly marginalized by the rising number of fully employed female professionals. This new 'female' profession of the *Fürsorgerin* gave welfare a new face. During the Kaiserreich, by contrast, it had been necessary to overcome considerable resistance against even the voluntary participation of women in poor relief.[47] Involvement in public welfare now moved from being an honorary position to a profession; although it was never seriously considered possible to confront the mass deprivation of the Weimar Republic without the additional support of honorary helpers.[48] The welfare schools (*Soziale Frauenschulen*) attended by female trainees, which emerged as training centres for the new profession of public welfare provision, were, like the professional associations of individual welfare branches, prominently involved in the multiplication of the guiding principles and new ideals of public welfare. They thereby developed a professional ideology which aimed at the close pedagogic supervision of clients by trained female professionals, and deemed material support as a mere precondition for the true help offered, which consisted of changing individual behaviour and lifestyles.

Some of the most spectacular developments took place in municipal housing policy. Admittedly, housing initiatives by local authorities had already gathered momentum in large cities such as Frankfurt am Main and Düsseldorf prior to the First World War[49]; at the end of the war, however, the constellation of actors involved in the housing market changed fundamentally. Without local government involvement, the distribution of existing housing stock was all but impossible, let alone the construction of new apartments and houses. The dramatically increasing housing shortage since the war's end forced legislators to create new instruments of housing policy with primarily prohibitive and redistributive functions, infringing on the rights of private property owners in a manner which would have been unimaginable prior to 1914.[50] The regulation of rents was now a responsibility of municipal authorities. Dwellings could only be rented out with the consent of the relevant officials; local governments could also force property owners to accept the occupation of an empty flat or house. Cities' offices (*Mieteinigungsämter* and *Wohnungsämter*) were responsible for not only the regulation of rents but also the protection of tenants, and the distribution of available housing stock at the disposal of municipal housing offices. As a result of this transformation of private goods into public ones by city authorities, the inadequacies of housing distribution were now primarily attributed to the deficiencies of public administration. As rationing the shortage would not address the root of the problem, which lay instead in the insufficient amount of private housing construction, the main burden of municipal policy in this area shifted after 1924 to subsidizing the construction of new stock.[51] As governmental control of the housing sector increasingly relaxed after 1924, it was replaced by the onset of publicly subsidized projects to build new housing; 90 per cent of the new building activities in large and medium-sized cities between 1926/27 and 1932/33 were publicly funded.[52] To finance the grand municipal housing construction schemes of the mid Weimar years, local government authorities primarily availed themselves of the *Hauszinssteuer*, a tax introduced in 1924 whereby home owners (whose debts had been eliminated by inflation) would be required to make a contribution to the restoration of housing construction.[53]

Every city developed its own profile in terms of housing construction volume, financing techniques, the sponsored building companies employed, and also the architectural preferences and city planning concepts chosen. Those mainly involved in the building of housing stock were non-profit building societies, especially cooperative building associations (*Baugenossenschaften*). The construction of housing thereby became a characteristic of Weimar municipal policy, and the new residential areas, whether functional and modern in their design as in Frankfurt and Berlin, or moderately conservative as in Munich, became advertising shields of cities' self-representation.[54] The era of social housing construction had begun. It was above all local authorities who saw themselves confronted with the new tasks and were obliged to shoulder the accompanying financial commitments.

Differences, Specialities, Limitations: Welfare City and Welfare State

Local welfare policies were, on the one hand, a subsystem of the Weimar Welfare State, in whose overarching framework they fulfilled specific functions. On the other, via their special anchoring in local structures of local self-administration and municipal welfare culture, they followed their own regulatory logic, which differed from other parts of the welfare state. The characteristic features of this special municipal welfare system were (not without exaggeration) stressed time and again by the leading thinkers of the Weimar welfare system, and repeatedly brought to bear as points of reference against the divergent characteristics of social policy at the level of the central state.

Municipal welfare administration was supposed to distinguish itself by close, personal contact with the recipients of its aid. According to the ideals of the 'Elberfeld system', the most important organizational model of poor relief in the Kaiserreich, every honorary poor guardian had a very small number of cases to supervise in his locality, and this was supposed to be done in as continuous and intensive manner as possible.[55] These maxims of personal assistance and individual supervision by the guardians were also enshrined in the organizational concepts and ideals of the greatly professionalized and bureaucratized welfare system characteristic of the Weimar Republic. According to the operational principles of the new welfare system, the routines of social casework were supposed to rest on direct, ongoing and trusting contact between the welfare officials and recipients of aid. Regular house visits thereby formed a basic requirement of welfare assistance.[56] Such an understanding of welfare administration demanded a comparatively high level of knowledge formation. It was essential not merely to gain the necessary information about every entitlement to benefits, the welfare administration also aimed at creating a more complete picture of the behaviour of the poor.[57] Its ultimate aim was the rationalization of the lifestyles of the poor through individual persuasion.

In terms of its regulatory structure, public welfare further differed from social insurance due to the much wider scope of discretion conceded in the handling of the individual cases, which was exemplified by the system of individual means testing. In contrast to social insurance, with its stricter regulatory logic, municipal welfare administration followed the principles of the 'individualization' of welfare. Individualization meant that the public assistance had to be based on social diagnosis of each single case, tailored to the contingencies of the special needs of the individual in question. The leading thinkers of public welfare did not tire in their efforts to highlight this difference, which was portrayed as fundamental in order to stress the individual character of their service, and demarcate it from social insurance.[58] Alice Salomon wrote in 1921 in her 'Guiding Principles of Social Welfare', the best known textbook of the profession:

> Social policy is, according to its nature as a legislative measure of the state, restricted to those areas, where an equal regulation through inflexible rules is possible. Social welfare must go beyond this and provide for institutions which combat and prevent social grievances in a way that takes individual needs into consideration and is sensitive to the individual personality and character. Social welfare cannot operate according to a uniform system, but requires a lively engagement of people with one another.[59]

At the heart of social work's professional identity, therefore, stood an understanding of social assistance which was above all characterized by the ingredients of personal help, pedagogic mentoring and moral improvement of the poor. The deeper purpose of welfare was understood as lying not in the mere material support provided, but rather in ensuring the conformity of individual behaviour to the normative standards of the bourgeois way of life: orderly and healthy living, decent upbringing of children, resilient work ethic, thrift and personal responsibility. Where the welfare state, to paraphrase Gertrude Himmelfarb,[60] had dissociated moral from social policy, social welfare was meant to reunite them again. The wide-ranging arsenal of instruments at the disposal of cities' welfare administrations was therefore characterized by the interchange of service provision with invasive social disciplining.[61] By contrast to social insurance, public welfare rested not on the reciprocity of contribution and benefit, but rather on the interplay between promises of support and the fulfilment of moral duties. Social assistance was not to be understood as an end in itself, but had to serve higher aims: the restoration of individual economic independence, ('help to self-help': *Hilfe zur Selbsthilfe*), the moral improvement and social integration of clients, the reinvigoration of public health and national strength.

Public welfare thereby not only promised to guarantee a minimum standard of participation in precarious social goods, but also threatened to intrude into individuals' private spheres if certain expectations of behaviour were not fulfilled. Material support could be made dependent on involvement in compulsory work schemes in order to test recipients' willingness to work. 'Asocials' or persons who did not meet their maintenance obligations were threatened with the workhouse. David Crew emphasizes that youth welfare, with instruments such as protective supervision or correctional education, possessed the means to severely intervene in individuals' private lives:

> Compulsion and consent were inextricably combined in all the Youth Office's practices. Even the most 'voluntary' forms of child welfare opened the door to potential or actual coercion. Once the gaze of the Youth Office was fastened upon a family and its children, there could indeed be no guarantee that intervention would not escalate from the softer, more advisory forms to harder, more coercive ones.[62]

In terms of agency, the specifics of social welfare lay in its 'dual' organizational structure.[63] Public agencies were responsible for dealing with certain social problems, private ones for others. The actual distribution and demarcation of tasks on the ground was usually dependent on local infrastructures, resources, and the relationships between public and private actors. Overall responsibility lay with public welfare, which, according to the Reich Youth Welfare Law of 1924, was, however, obliged to support, consult and draw on private bodies and to respect their independence. The Reich Welfare Law of 1924 contained a clause whereby public welfare authorities would only be permitted to establish their own institutional facilities if suitable ones belonging to private agencies were not already available.

As public welfare often lacked its own facilities and was obliged to entrust its clients, in exchange for payment of a care allowance, into the hands of private, especially ecclesiastical institutions, many interdependencies emerged in the field of asylum care (*geschlossene Fürsorge*). While public officials were reliant on private infrastructures to accomplish their set tasks, private institutions were financially reliant on the reimbursements and allowances afforded by public bodies.[64] If charitable activity in the Kaiserreich had primarily represented a form of local associational culture, it now followed the organizational model first established by religious charities during the nineteenth century, and founded nationwide umbrella organizations. Membership of one of these bodies was a precondition to partake of the funds granted by the Reich government. At the city level, the local associations and institutions of private welfare functioned as front organizations of the social milieus they represented and embodied: the Catholic associations and institutions under the roof of the German Caritas Association (Deutscher Caritasverband), their Protestant equivalents within the Inner Mission (Innere Mission), the social democratic ones as part of the Workers' Welfare (*Arbeiterwohlfahrt*), the bourgeois organizations under the heading of the 'German Joint Welfare League' (Paritätischer Wohlfahrtsverband), and the Jewish ones within the framework of the 'Central Welfare Office of German Jews' (Zentralwohlfahrtsstelle der Deutschen Juden).[65]

However, it must be noted that the welfare profession's self-understanding cannot be taken at face value as an accurate portrayal of practice at the local level. The long periods of mass deprivation characteristic of the Weimar Republic prevented public welfare's guiding principles of a personal, individualized, and pedagogically orientated care of the poor from being effective. The Berlin welfare worker Justus Ehrhardt vividly illustrated this tendency during the economic crisis unleashed by the Wall Street Crash of 1929. In 1932, he described the depressed situation of municipal welfare provision with these words:

> Social pedagogy and individualized attempts at influencing clients' behaviour are not much esteemed anymore. Means testing, controls of possible undeclared employment, tightening of the welfare rates, and rejections of claims have become basic principles, whose immutability often destroys not only social work, but also the conscience and sense of responsibility among welfare workers.[66]

Weimar welfare suffered from the sheer preponderance of such forms of poverty, which ensured that mass provision rapidly became the norm. Overwhelmingly, individuals' plights did not stem from 'personal deficits', but were rather the consequences of economic crises which embraced German society as a whole, and could not be corrected by means of individual casework and supervision. In this sense, the 'welfare city' and the welfare state, or public welfare and social security, functioned not as separate spheres, but were characteristically interwoven, as will briefly be demonstrated here, in three contexts.[67]

Supplementing of Welfare State Income

To a far greater extent than prior to 1914, public welfare directly supplemented the services offered by social insurance. A great survey of social pension recipients conducted by the German Association for Public and Private Welfare (Deutscher Verein für öffentliche und private Fürsorge) in 1929 revealed that 30 per cent of these individuals were reliant on additional support from public welfare.[68] In a major city like Berlin, it was even as high as 40 per cent of the total number; three times as many as prior to the First World War. Apart from the cases of single male recipients of pensions, the average pension rate did not in general reach the level of the municipal welfare rates.[69] The difference in comparison to the pre-war period lay, moreover, not so much in the level of pensions, but rather in the decreased possibilities available to pensioners to earn additional incomes by means such as small jobs, family support or subletting accommodation.[70] In short, the opportunities to 'income package' had considerably declined since the First World War.[71] Municipal welfare therefore formed a kind of flexible reserve system within the welfare state. As the overburdened system of social security was repeatedly forced to enter a period of retrenchment, municipal welfare represented a supplement to social security, which had to be strongly extended. When an emergency decree by Reich Chancellor Franz von Papen of 1932 decisively cut old age and invalid pensions, the German Conference of Cities (Deutscher Städtetag) estimated that through this measure alone, extra costs of around 20 per cent would fall on municipal pensioner welfare programmes.[72]

The Last Net of the Welfare System

Simultaneously countless numbers of the unemployed, filtered out of unemployment insurance programmes by massive government cuts, were forced to turn to cities' welfare offices for help. Social insurance did not replace public welfare, but rather the reverse, with the latter replacing the former. The consequence was that whereas cities' finances were thrown into chaos, the Imperial Office for Unemployment Insurance and Labour Exchange's (Reichsanstalt für Arbeitslosenversicherung und Arbeitslosenvermittlung) budget for the fiscal year 1932/33 saw unemployment insurance acquire a surplus of no less than 53 per cent of its supporting expenditure.[73] The Reich government repaired the federal welfare state's budgets at the expense of the financial ruination of the 'welfare city'.

Model and Adaptation

Some actors in Weimar's public welfare system now made serious attempts to establish public welfare as a preferable alternative to the social security system of the state. The key characteristics of public welfare, especially the principle of individually tailored payment and service provision, and their dependency on a means test, were used to challenge the modes of regulation of social insurance. In a resolution of March 1931, the head of the German Association for Public and Private Welfare, the Reich's most influential umbrella organization in its field and the most important concentration of expertise, requested that the federal government not only create a united welfare system for all of the unemployed in place of existing unemployment insurance, but also demanded that its implementation would not be the responsibility of labour offices, but rather that of public welfare.[74] The German Association was not alone in making this request.[75] The means test as a marked characteristic of public welfare was indeed henceforth integrated into the regulatory structures of unemployment insurance. The Reich government used an emergency decree in June 1932 to ensure that payments from unemployment insurance would only continue to be made after the sixth week if recipients successfully demonstrated their need in a means test. Responsibility for implementing these tests lay with local public welfare. A similar measure had been introduced a year earlier for married women.[76] Unemployment insurance thereby qualitatively orientated itself around the practices of public welfare. This process exemplifies the tendency that the welfare state's periods of crisis and austerity are times of increased attractiveness for the guiding principles of public welfare.

Concluding Remarks: Political Profiles of the Welfare City

The historiography of public and private welfare systems in the Weimar Republic has clearly demonstrated that these fields became political battlegrounds to a much greater extent than they had been prior to the First World War. Before 1914, poor relief and its management had been the prerogative and domain of a restricted circle of administrative experts. The debates concerning poverty after 1918 were, by contrast, more politically charged and polarized. New actors became involved in this field. Important groups among the poor population, such as social pensioners, *Kleinrentner*, war victims and families with many children, managed to garner support from certain political interest groups to champion their needs. These groups attempted, with varying degrees of skill and success, to gain political sympathy for their constituency and became involved in the construction of contemporary images of poverty. The associations representing the 'new poverty' called assemblies, passed resolutions and protested against discrimination, thereby seeking to create a public space for the articulation of the poor's concerns; something that had traditionally been confined to the private sphere. Central to these groups' self-understanding was the belief that they did not represent humble applicants, but should rather be taken seriously as citizens entitled to make claims on the state.[77] In order to demonstrate their civic respectability, and to distinguish themselves from traditional groups among the poor, these new movements highlighted their backgrounds as workers who had paid tax and insurance contributions, as well as their identities as members of the middle class, war veterans or relatives of soldiers who had sacrificed their health and family life for the fatherland between 1914 and 1918.[78] The political parties made themselves the advocates of particular groups of clients, and charitable associations also became more heavily involved in political debates.

As the number of actors shaping public policy regarding poverty markedly expanded, the picture of the competing images and interpretations of poverty circulating in the arena of welfare policies acquired a decidedly heterogeneous character. In the Weimar Republic, the images and meanings of 'poverty' and 'poverty policy' could be directed towards social reform (the poor as possessors of social rights), towards social pedagogy (the poor as the recipients of pedagogic supervision), towards victim compensation[79] (the poor as victims of state failure), towards a traditional understanding of poverty (poverty being a reflection of personal failings), towards a bio-political understanding (poverty as a eugenic danger to the national racial body) or towards a Marxist interpretation (the poor as victims of capitalist exploitation). The heterogeneity of these influences and beliefs informed the 'compromise of contradictory forces',[80] which provided the basis of Weimar welfare legislation and policies.

These images of poverty were also evoked at the city level in various contexts; in the debates of city parliaments and in the discussions taking place within wider public spheres. According to Young-Sun Hong's interpretation of welfare state formation, there were fundamentally three main groups of actors who impressed their interpretations most forcefully on Weimar's welfare institutions: the bourgeois 'progressives', the social democrats and the 'Christian conservatives'.[81] Depending on local balances of political power they gained various levels of influence in localities across the Reich. The key force driving the expansion of modern social welfare was that of the 'progressives', who extended the welfare state's invasive capability further into the private spheres of the family and 'social reproduction', strengthened the preventative and therapeutic instruments at officials' disposal, and strove to increase the opportunities for individuals to participate in the labour market and to benefit from access to healthcare and education. Poverty and need were primarily understood as social phenomena and less the result of individual moral weakness. 'Progressives' saw expanded welfare benefits as one side of the coin; the other was that their beneficiaries owed strong recipro-cal duties and responsibilities to wider society.

Although they were the driving force behind the expansion of the Weimar welfare system, the 'progressives' were only able to implement their ideas in alliance with either conservative, confessional actors linked to the Christian Churches, or those affiliated with the SPD. With social democrats, 'progressives' shared the view that distress and deprivation were primarily caused by wide-ranging socio-economic factors, and that individuals had a right to participate in certain social goods. What divided 'progressives' from social democrats was their conception of the appropriate division of labour between public and private welfare providers. In contrast to progressives, social democrats wished to subor-dinate charitable organizations to public responsibility, and to facilitate a general shift in the balance of power from private to public sectors. In the eyes of confes-sional actors, by contrast, poverty was primarily a spiritual problem, whose roots lay in contemporary civilization's materialism, the decline of public morals, and the undermining of the family. Alongside preserving the independence of their own ecclesiastical welfare associations, these Catholic and Protestant actors' top priority was to ensure that the cities did not overextend itself, while limiting state officials' interventions in the familial private sphere.

Depending on economic and social circumstance, local balances of power, venerable traditions, path dependencies of local 'welfare culture'[82] and available resources, various models of city welfare provision could therefore emerge out of the interplay between influential welfare actors at the municipal level. As far as current research can discern, two contrasting modes of differentiation were salient in this context. The first mode concerned the intensity of social inter-vention exerted by the welfare cities. On the one hand, there emerged a politi-cally active 'welfare culture', offering comparatively high benefits, expansive and wide-ranging service provision, and characterized by a high degree of profes-sionalization and a tendency towards more active intervention. On the other was a more defensive, conservative type characterized by restraint in the aforemen-tioned categories. The first model was mostly the product of city administrations under social democratic or social liberal influence; the second typically reflected a stronger confessional-conservative imprint. Examples of the first type were Hamburg and Frankfurt am Main; Munich and Leipzig by contrast belonged to the second category. The second mode of differentiation often ran parallel to the first, and concerned the modes of cooperation and the division of labour between the public and private actors on the field of welfare. Here, one type of cities was striving to have the various tasks of welfare as much as possible fulfilled by public agencies. The other type, instead, was characterized by strong links and a high degree of interlocking between the public actors and the confessional associations working in this area, and also by a strong tendency of outsourcing public tasks to private actors.[83] Painting a more nuanced picture of German cities' welfare policies during the Weimar period must, however, remain the task of future research.

Notes

This chapter has been translated by Thomas Brodie.

1. P. Weindling. 1989. *Health, Race and German Politics between National Unification and Nazism, 1870–1945*. Cambridge: Cambridge University Press, pp. 413–14; compare with: G. Kall. 1926/27. 'Die Hauptabteilung "Soziale Fürsorge" auf der Gesolei', *Deutsche Zeitschrift für Wohlfahrtspflege* 2:296–99.

2. F. Gumpert. 1926. 'Eindrücke von der Gesolei', *Soziale Praxis* 35:716–17; F. Werner. 1926. 'Die Ausstellung der freien Wohlfahrtspflege in Düsseldorf', *Freie Wohlfahrtspflege* 1:123–24.

3. W. Nerdinger. 2003. 'Architekturutopie und Realität des Bauens zwischen Weimarer Republik und Drittem Reich', in W. Hardtwig (ed.), *Utopie und politische Herrschaft im Europa der Zwischenkriegszeit*, Munich: Oldenbourg, p. 277, (with a photograph of the model).

4. W. Abelshauser. 1987. 'Die Weimarer Republik – ein Wohlfahrtsstaat?' in W. Abelshauser (ed.), *Die Weimarer Republik als Wohlfahrtsstaat*. Stuttgart: Steiner, p. 10; K.P. Petersen and J.H. Petersen. 2013. 'Confusion and Divergence: Origins and Meanings of the Term "Welfare State" in Germany and Britain, 1840–1940', *Journal of European Social Policy* 23:37–51.

5. L. Heyde. 1931. *Abriß der Sozialpolitik*, 7th edn. Leipzig: Quelle und Meyer, p. 7; A. Weber. 1926. *Fürsorge und Wohlfahrtspflege. Eine Einführung in die soziale Hilfsarbeit*. Berlin, Leipzig: Gruyter, 25; S. Götze. 1933. *Grundlagen und Voraussetzungen der heutigen Wohlfahrtsarbeit*. Berlin: C. Heymann, p. 2.

6. *Deutsche Sozialpolitik 1918–1928*. 1929. Berlin: E.S. Mittler und Sohn, p. 236.

7. Exceptions to this rule are: K. Marx-Jaskulski. 2008. *Armut und Fürsorge auf dem Land: Vom Ende des 19. Jahrhunderts bis 1933*. Göttingen: Wallstein; and D.F. Crew. 1998. *Germans on Welfare. From Weimar to Hitler*. New York, Oxford: Oxford University Press; as a survey of research, compare W. Rudloff. 2002. 'Im Souterrain des Sozialstaates: Neuere Forschungen zur Geschichte von Fürsorge und Wohlfahrtspflege im 20. Jahrhundert', *Archiv für Sozialgeschichte* 42:474–520.

8. A considerable number of works dealing with local welfare policies during the Weimar Republic has been published in recent years. The most important starting points are: Ch. Sachße and F. Tennstedt. 1988–1992. *Geschichte der Armenfürsorge in Deutschland*, vols 2 and 3. Stuttgart: Kohlhammer; compare with: Y.-S. Hong. 1998. *Welfare, Modernity, and the Weimar State*, 1919–1933. Princeton: Princeton University Press; Crew, *Germans*; for local case studies compare with: H. Boettcher. 1988. *Fürsorge in Lübeck vor und nach dem Ersten Weltkrieg*. Lübeck: Schmidt-Römhild; H. Brüchert-Schunk. 1994. *Städtische Sozialpolitik vom Wilhelminischen Reich bis zur Weltwirtschaftskrise. Eine sozial- und kommunalhistorische Untersuchung am Beispiel der Stadt Mainz 1890–1930*. Stuttgart: Steiner; D. Marquardt. 1994. *Sozialpolitik und Sozialfürsorge der Stadt Hannover in der Weimarer Republik*. Hannover: Hahn; H.-P. Jans. 1994. *Sozialpolitik und Wohlfahrtspflege in Ulm 1870–1930. Stadt, Verbände und Parteien auf dem Weg zur modernen Sozialstaatlichkeit*. Stuttgart: Kohlhammer; G. Bußmann-Strelow. 1997. *Kommunale Politik im Sozialstaat. Nürnberger Wohlfahrtspflege in der Weimarer Republik*. Nuremberg: Stadtarchiv; P. Brandmann. 1998. *Leipzig zwischen Klassenkampf und Sozialreform. Kommunale Wohlfahrtspolitik zwischen 1890 und 1929*. Cologne, Vienna: Böhlau; J. Paulus. 1998. *Kommunale Wohlfahrtspolitik in Leipzig*

1930 bis 1945. Cologne, Vienna: Böhlau; W. Rudloff. 1998. *Die Wohlfahrtsstadt. Kommunale Ernährungs-, Fürsorge- und Wohnungspolitik am Beispiel Münchens 1910– 1933,* 2 vols. Göttingen: Vandenhoeck & Ruprecht; compare with: H.-U. Thamer and J.-Ch. Kaiser. 1995. 'Kommunale Wohlfahrtspolitik zwischen 1918 und 1933 im Vergleich (Frankfurt, Leipzig, Nürnberg)', in J. Reulecke (ed.), *Die Stadt als Dienstleistungszentrum. Beiträge zur Geschichte der 'Sozialstadt' in Deutschland im 19. und frühen 20. Jahrhundert.* St. Katharinen: Scripta-Mercaturae, pp.325–70; as a first introduction see: S. Hering and R. Münchmeier. 2000. *Geschichte der Sozialen Arbeit. Eine Einführung.*Weinheim, Munich: Juventa.

9. I. Gazeley. 2003. *Poverty in Britain, 1900–1965.* Houndmills, Basingstoke: Palgrave; E.P. Hennock. 1992. 'Concepts of Poverty in the British Social Surveys from Charles Booth to Arthur Bowley', in M. Bulmer, K. Bales and K. Kish Sklar (eds), *The Social Survey in Historical Perspective* (Cambridge: Cambridge University Press, pp. 189–216; T.J. Hatton and R.E. Bailey. 1998. 'Poverty and the Welfare State in Interwar London', *Oxford Economic Papers* 50:574–606; I. Gazeley and A. Newell. 2012. 'The End of Destitution: Evidence from Urban British Working Households 1904–37', *Oxford Economic Papers* 64:80–102; K. Laybourn. 1990. *Britain on the Breadline. A Social and Political History of Britain between the Wars.* Gloucester: Sutton, p. 43.

10. G. Simmel. 1908. 'Der Arme', in G. Simmel, *Soziologie. Untersuchungen über die Formen der Vergesellschaftung.* Leipzig: Duncker & Humblot, p. 489.

11. St. Steinbacher. 1921/22. 'Einige Ergebnisse großstädtischer Armenstatistik', *Allgemeines Statistisches Archiv* 13:276; compare with id. 1919. *Zahl und persönliche Verhältnisse der öffentlich Unterstützten in deutschen Großstädten.*Borna-Leipzig: Noske. According to the only official survey conducted on a national scale before 1914, the share of the population depending on poor relief in 1885 had been 3.4 percent: Kaiserliches Statistischen Amt (ed.). 1887. *Statistik der öffentlichen Armenpflege im Jahre 1885.* Berlin: Puttkammer & Mühlbrecht, p. 28.

12. M. Michel. 1926. *Städtischer Gemeindehaushalt und soziale Lasten vor und nach dem Kriege. Eine Untersuchung auf Gund der Haushaltspläne der Stadt Frankfurt a.M.* Frankfurt/Main: Deutscher Verein für öffentliche und private Fürsorge, pp. 16, 63.

13. H. Reiner. 1926. 'Das bayerische Fürsorgewesen auf Grund der Reichsverordnung über die Fürsorgepflicht im Rechnungsjahr 1924', *Zeitschrift des Bayerischen Statistischen Landesamtes* 58:171. Not included in these numbers were persons on unemployment relief schemes whose share of the total population had risen to 5.9 per cent in 1925.

14. E. Helbling. 1931. 'Die öffentliche Fürsorge. Ergebnisse der Reichsfürsorgestatistik für das Jahr 1929'. *Statistisches Jahrbuch Deutscher Städte* 26:329 (nintey-two cities were included in this survey).

15. K. Williams. 1981. *From Pauperism to Poverty.* London: Routledge Kegan Paul, pp. 156–66; M. Köhler. 1929. 'Reform der öffentlichen Armenpflege in England', *Deutsche Zeitschrift für Wohlfahrtspflege* 5:585–90.

16. 'Einfluß der Stabilisierung unserer Währung in der Wohlfahrtspfleg'. 1924. *Nachrichtendienst des Deutschen Vereins für öffentliche und private Fürsorge* 1924:439.

17. 'Soziale Unterstützungslasten in den Städten'. 1924. *Mitteilungen des Deutschen Städtetages* 1924:11.

18. For Hamburg see: Crew, *Germans,* p. 152; for Berlin see: D. Lehnert. 1991. *Kommunale Politik, Parteiensystem und Interessenkonflikte in Berlin und Wien. Wohnungs-, Verkehrs- und Finanzpolitik im Spannungsfeld von städtischer Selbstverwaltung und Verbandseinflüssen.*

Berlin: Haude und Sener, p. 497; for Munich see: Rudloff, *Wohlfahrtsstadt*, p. 902; F. Wimmer. 2014. *Die völkische Ordnung von Armut. Kommunale Sozialpolitik im nationalsozialistischen München*. Göttingen: Wallstein, p. 37; for Cologne see: F.-W. Henning. 1976. 'Finanzpolitische Vorstellungen und Maßnahmen Konrad Adenauers während seiner Kölner Zeit (1906 bis 1933)', in H. Stehkämper (ed.), *Konrad Adenauer. Oberbürgermeister von Köln*. Cologne: Rheinland, p. 49.

19. F. Saake. 1929. 'Strukturwandel der Finanzwirtschaft der Gemeinden und Gemeindeverbände', *Zeitschrift für Kommunalwirtschaft* 19:2–11, esp. 4.

20. Ibid. For the municipalities of Saxony the share was 56.3 per cent of the net expenditures. See H.G. Müller. 1933. *Die Ausgaben für Zwecke der Wohlfahrts- und Sozialpolitik in den Gemeinden und Gemeindeverbänden des Landes Sachsen in den Rechnungsjahren 1913, 1925 und 1926*. Lucka: Berger, p. 57.

21. Michel, *Städtischer Gemeindehaushalt*, p. 19. In Hannover the share was a quarter of the gross expenditures and 46 per cent of the net expenditures; M. Hansmann. 2000. *Kommunalfinanzen im 20. Jahrhundert. Zäsuren und Kontinuitäten: Das Beispiel Hannover*. Hannover: Hahn, p. 64.

22. L. Weiß. 1999. *Rheinische Großstädte während der Weltwirtschaftskrise (1929–1933). Kommunale Finanz- und Sozialpolitik im Vergleich*. Cologne: Böhlau; B. Zeppenfeld. 1999. *Handlungsspielräume städtischer Finanzpolitik. Staatliche Vorgaben und kommunales Interesse in Bochum und Münster 1913–1935*. Essen: Klartext; compare also more generally with: H. James. 1990. 'Municipal Finance in the Weimar Republic', in W.R. Lee and Eve Rosenhaft (eds), *The State and Social Change in Germany, 1880–1980*. New York, Oxford, Munich: Berg, pp. 228–53.

23. K. Seutemann. 1934. 'Finanzübersicht nach der Rechnung 1931', *Statistisches Jahrbuch Deutscher Städte* 29:229.

24. O. Schmeer. 1990. 'Sozialpolitik in Duisburg 1930–1933. Staatliche Sozialpolitik und kommunale Selbstverwaltung in der Krise der Weimarer Republik', *Duisburger Forschungen* 37:179–309.

25. K.Ch. Führer. 1990. '"Für das Wirtschaftsleben mehr oder weniger wertlose Personen". Zur Lage von Invaliden- und Kleinrentnern in den Inflationsjahren 1918–1924' *Archiv für Sozialgeschichte* 30:145–80; G. Eghigian. 1993. 'The Politics of Victimization: Social Pensioners and the German Social State in the Inflation of 1914–1924', *Central European History* 26:375–403; D.F. Crew. 1990. '"Wohlfahrtsbrot ist bitteres Brot". The Elderly, the Disabled and the Local Welfare Authorities in the Weimar Republic 1924–1933', *Archiv für Sozialgeschichte* 30:217–45.

26. R. Scholz. 1985. '"Heraus aus der unwürdigen Fürsorge". Zur Sozialpolitik und politischen Orientierung der Kleinrentner in der Weimarer Republik', in Ch. Conrad and Hans-Joachim von Kondratowitz (eds), *Gerontologie und Sozialgeschichte. Wege zu einer historischen Betrachtung des Alters*, 2nd edn. Berlin: Deutsches Zentrum für Altersfragen, pp. 319–50.

27. For municipal welfare schemes for the unemployed see, for example, Bußmann-Strelow, *Kommunale Politik*, pp. 267–329.

28. P. Lewek. 1992. *Arbeitslosigkeit und Arbeitslosenversicherung in der Weimarer Republik 1918–1927*. Stuttgart: Steiner.

29. W. Adamy and J. Steffen. 1982. '"Arbeitsmarktpolitik" in der Depression. Sanierungsstrategien in der Arbeitslosenversicherung 1927–1933', *Mitteilungen aus der Arbeitsmarkt- und Berufsforschung* 15:285; see also H. Homburg. 1984.

'Massenarbeitslosigkeit in Deutschland 1930–1933. Unterstützung und politische Verwaltung der Arbeitslosen'. *Sozialwissenschaftliche Informationen* 14:205–15; and ibid. 1985. 'Vom Arbeitslosen zum Zwangsarbeiter. Arbeitslosenpolitik und Fraktionierung der Arbeiterschaft in Deutschland 1930–1933 am Beispiel der Wohlfahrtserwerbslosen und der kommunalen Wohlfahrtshilfe', *Archiv für Sozialgeschichte* 25:251–98. H.-W. Schmuhl. 2003. *Arbeitsmarktpolitik und Arbeitsverwaltung in Deutschland von 1871 bis 2002. Zwischen Fürsorge, Hoheit und Markt.* Nuremberg: Institut für Arbeitsmarkt- und Berufsforschung der Bundesanstalt für Arbeit, p. 189.

30. W. Polligkeit. 1922. 'Der Einfluß der Finanznot auf die private Wohlfahrtspflege in den Städten', in *Bericht über die Verhandlungen des 37. Deutschen Fürsorgetages des Deutschen Vereins für öffentliche und private Fürsorge am 28. und 29. Oktober 1921 in Weimar.* Karlsruhe: G. Braun, pp. 44–54.

31. M. Michel. 1926/27. 'Städtepolitik und Soziales Aufgabengebiet'. *Deutsche Zeitschrift für Wohlfahrtspflege* 2:505.

32. M. Werner. 2011. *Stiftungsstadt und Bürgertum. Hamburgs Stiftungskultur vom Kaiserreich bis zum Nationalsozialismus.* Munich: Oldenbourg, p. 173.

33. Rudloff, *Wohlfahrtsstadt*, p. 491.

34. P. Hammerschmidt, 2003. *Finanzierung und Management von Wohlfahrtsanstalten 1920 bis 1936.* Stuttgart: Steiner, pp. 76, 126; Sachße and Tennstedt, *Geschichte der Armenfürsorge*, vol. 2, p. 170; Rudloff, *Wohlfahrtsstadt*, p. 488.

35. The classical study is: L. Preller. 1978. *Sozialpolitik in der Weimarer Republik*, new edn. Düsseldorf: Athenäum/Droste; as a short survey see: W. Rudloff. 2012. 'Ausbau und Krise – der deutsche Sozialstaat in der Weimarer Republik', in A. Kruke and M. Woyke (eds), *Deutsche Sozialdemokratie in Bewegung. 1848 – 1863 – 2013.* Bonn: Dietz, pp. 122–31.

36. S. Miller (ed). 1969. *Die Regierung der Volksbeauftragten 1918/19.* With an introduction by E. Matthias, 1. Teil. Düsseldorf: Droste, Dok. Nr. 35.

37. For Weimar welfare legislation see Sachße and Tennstedt, *Geschichte der Armenpflege*, vol. 2, pp. 99–104 and 142–52; Hong, *Welfare*, pp. 114–26.

38. K. Matron, 2012. *Kommunale Jugendfürsorge in Frankfurt am Main in der Weimarer Republik.* Frankfurt/Main: Henrich-Edition, pp. 129–78; for Weimar youth welfare, which is comparatively well researched, see also more generally D.J.K. Peukert. 1986. *Grenzen der Sozialdisziplinierung. Aufstieg und Krise der deutschen Jugendfürsorge von 1878 bis 1932.* Cologne: Bund; E. Harvey. 1993. *Youth and the Welfare State in Weimar Germany.* Oxford: Clarendon Press; M. Gräser. 1995. *Der blockierte Wohlfahrtsstaat. Unterschichtenjugend und Jugendfürsorge in der Weimarer Republik.* Göttingen: Vandenhoeck & Ruprecht; E.R. Dickinson. 1996. *The Politics of Child Welfare from the Empire to the Federal Republic.* Cambridge MA: Harvard University Press; M. Köster. 1996. *Jugend, Wohlfahrtsstaat und Gesellschaft im Wandel. Westfalen zwischen Kaiserreich und Bundesrepublik.* Paderborn: Schöningh; U. Uhlendorff. 2003. *Geschichte des Jugendamtes. Entwicklungslinien öffentlicher Jugendhilfe 1871 bis 1929.* Weinheim, Basel, Berlin: Beltz; S. Steinacker. 2007. *Der Staat als Erzieher. Jugendpolitik und Jugendfürsorge im Rheinland vom Kaiserreich bis zum Ende des Nazismus.* Stuttgart: Ibidem.

39. Steinacker, *Der Staat*, p. 155.

40. Weindling, *Health*, pp. 350–68; J. Vossen. 2001. *Gesundheitsämter im Nationalsozialismus. Rassenhygiene und offene Gesundheitsfürsorge in Westfalen 1900–1950.* Essen:

Klartext, pp. 173–201; M. Weyer-von Schoultz. 1994. *Stadt und Gesundheit im Ruhrgebiet 1850–1929. Verstädterung und kommunale Gesundheitspolitik am Beispiel der jungen Industriestadt Gelsenkirchen.* Essen: Klartext; as a contemporary survey see, W. Hagen. 1925. *Die Gesundheitsfürsorge einer Industriestadt. Erörtert am Beispiel der Stadt Höchst a.M.* Frankfurt/Main: Deutscher Verein für öffentliche und private Fürsorge; for infant care see S. Fehlemann. 2009. *Armutsrisiko Mutterschaft. Mütter- und Säuglingsfürsorge im rheinisch-westfälischen Industriegebiet 1890–1924.* Essen: Klartext; S. Stöckel. 1996. *Säuglingsfürsorge zwischen sozialer Hygiene und Eugenik. Das Beispiel Berlins im Kaiserreich und in der Weimarer Republik.* Berlin, New York: De Gruyter.

41. Sachße and Tennstedt, *Geschichte der Armenpflege,* vol. 2, p. 128.

42. A. Labisch and F. Tennstedt. 1985. *Der Weg zum 'Gesetz über die Vereinheitlichung des Gesundheitswesens' vom 3. Juli 1934. Entwicklungslinien und -momente des staatlichen und kommunalen Gesundheitswesens in Deutschland,* 2 vols. Düsseldorf: Akademie für öffentliches Gesundheitswesen, p. 70.

43. F. Goldmann. 1930. 'Siechenhäuser und Altersheime', in A. Gottstein (ed.), *Handbücherei für das gesamte Krankenhauswesen,.* Berlin: Julius Sprringer, vol. 3, pp. 235–318; see also K.H. Irmak. 2002. *Der Sieche. Alte Menschen und die stationäre Altenhilfe in Deutschland 1924–1961.* Essen: Klartext.

44. Sachße and Tennstedt, *Geschichte der Armenfürsorge,* vol. 2, p. 179.; S. Leibfried. 1985. 'Existenzminimum und Fürsorge-Richtsätze in der Weimarer Republik', in S. Leibfried, *Armutspolitik und die Entwicklung des Sozialstaats.* Bremen: Universität, pp. 186–240; (English version in: S. Leibfried. 1986. 'Welfare Guidelines in the 1920s: Regulating Weimar's Poor', in D.E. Ashford and E.W. Kelley (eds), *Nationalizing Social Security in Europe and America.* Greenwich, London: Jai Press, pp. 137–54.)

45. G. Roth. 1999. *Die Institutionen der kommunalen Selbstverwaltung. Die Entwicklung von Aufgaben, Organisation, Leitgedanken und Mythen von der Weimarer Republik bis Mitte der neunziger Jahre.* Berlin: Duncker & Humblot, pp. 41–129.

46. Rudloff, *Wohlfahrtsstadt,* p. 124; Crew, *Germans,* p. 152.

47. A. Bergler. 2011. *Von Armenpflegern und Fürsorgeschwestern. Kommunale Wohlfahrtspflege und Geschlechterpolitik in Berlin und Charlottenburg.* Stuttgart: Steiner, p. 164.

48. Ch. Sachße. 1986. *Mütterlichkeit als Beruf. Sozialarbeit, Sozialreform und Frauenbewegung 1871–1929.* Frankfurt/Main: Suhrkamp, pp. 250–96; (English version in Ch. Sachße. 1993. 'Social Mothers: The Bourgois Women's Movement and German Welfare-State Formation, 1890–1929', in S. Koven and S. Michel (eds). *Mothers of a New World. Maternalist Politics and the Origins of Welfare States.* New York, London: Routledge, pp. 136–58; S. Zeller. 1987. *Volksmütter. Frauen im Wohlfahrtswesen der 20er Jahre.* Düsseldorf: Schwann, p. 35; for the period before the war see also I. Schröder. 2001. *Arbeiten für eine bessere Welt. Frauenbewegung und Sozialreform 1890–1914.* Frankfurt/ Main, New York: Campus.

49. C. Zimmermann. 1991. *Von der Wohnungsfrage zur Wohnungspolitik. Die Reformbewegung in Deutschland 1845–1914.* Göttingen: Vandenhoeck & Ruprecht, p. 160; W. Krabbe. 1984. 'Die Anfänge des "sozialen Wohnungsbaus" vor dem Ersten Weltkrieg. Kommunalpolitische Bemühungen um eine Lösung des Wohnungsproblems', *Vierteljahrsschrift für Sozial- und Wirtschaftsgeschichte* 71:30 –58; W. Steitz and W. Krabbe. 1985. 'Kommunale Wohnungspolitik deutscher Großstädte 1871–1914', in H.J. Teuteberg (ed.), *Homo habitans. Zur Sozialgeschichte*

des ländlichen und städtischen Wohnens in der Neuzeit. Münster: Coppenrath und
Steiner, pp. 421–46.

50. K.Ch. Führer. 1995. *Mieter, Hausbesitzer, Staat und Wohnungsmarkt. Wohnungsmangel
und Wohnungszwangswirtschaft in Deutschland 1914–1960*. Stuttgart: Steiner; R. Bessel.
1993. *Germany after the First World War*. Oxford: Clarendon Press, pp. 166–94.

51. As a case study compare with G. Kuhn. 1998. *Wohnkultur und kommunale
Wohnungspolitik in Frankfurt am Main 1880 bis 1930. Auf dem Wege zu einer pluralen
Gesellschaft der Individuen*. Bonn: Dietz.

52. Wronski. 1934. 'Wohnungsbau und Kleinsiedlung' in *Statistisches Jahrbuch Deutscher
Städte*, pp. 295–323, 295.

53. M. Ruck. 1988. 'Die öffentliche Wohnungsbaufinanzierung in der Weimarer
Republik. Zielsetzung, Ergebnisse, Probleme', in A. Schildt and A. Sywottek (eds),
*Massenwohnung und Eigenheim. Wohnungsbau und Wohnen in der Großstadt seit der
Ersten Weltkrieg*. Frankfurt/Main, New York: Campus, pp. 150–221; ibid. 1987. 'Der
Wohnungsbau – Schnittpunkt der Sozial- und Wirtschaftspolitik. Probleme der öffent-
lichen Wohnungspolitik in der Hauszinsära 1924/25–1930/31', in W. Abelshauser, *Die
Weimarer Republik*, pp. 91–123.

54. G. Kähler. 1985. *Wohnung und Stadt. Hamburg, Frankfurt, Wien. Modelle sozialen
Wohnens in den zwanziger Jahren*. Braunschweig: Vieweg.

55. Sachße and Tennstedt, *Geschichte der Armenfürsorge*, vol. 1, p. 214; G. Berger. 1979.
*Die ehrenamtliche Tätigkeit in der Sozialarbeit. Motive, Tendenzen, Probleme. Dargestellt
am Beispiel des Elberfelder Systems*. Frankfurt/Main: Lang, p. 44.; Ch. Sachße. 1988.
'Ehrenamtlichkeit, Selbsthilfe und Professionalität. Eine historische Skizze', in
S. Müller and Th. Rauschenbach (eds). *Das soziale Ehrenamt. Nützliche Arbeit zum
Nulltarif.* Weinheim, Munich: Juventa, pp. 51–55.

56. 'Hausbesuch'. 1926. *Wohlfahrtsblätter der Stadt Köln* 1:4–5; 'Einige Grundregeln
zur Ausübung der Fürsorge'. 1927. *Blätter für die Leipziger Wohlfahrtspflege*
June 1927:59–60; for an interpretation of the instrument of the home visit
compare with: N. Ramsauer. 2000. 'Verwahrlost'. *Kindswegnahmen und die
Entstehung der Jugendfürsorge im schweizerischen Sozialstaat 1900–1945*. Zürich:
Chronos, p. 126.

57. W. Rudloff. 2003. 'Das Wissen der kommunalen Sozialverwaltung in Deutschland',
Jahrbuch für europäische Verwaltungsgeschichte, 15: 59–88. Alice Salomon mentioned
in her outline of the 'techniques of investigation' a number of sources of information useful for social workers, such as relatives, physicians, schools, former or present
employers, neighbours, landlords or other welfare institutions; see: A. Salomon. 1926.
Soziale Diagnose. Berlin: Heymann, p. 18; ibid. 1925/6. 'Zur Technik der Ermittlung',
Deutsche Zeitschrift für Wohlfahrtspflege 1:315–19.

58. R. Münchmeier. 1981. *Zugänge zur Geschichte der Sozialarbeit*. Munich: Juventa,
pp. 82–102; see Hong, *Welfare*, p. 171.

59. A. Salomon. 1921. *Leitfaden der Wohlfahrtspflege*. Leipzig, Berlin: Teubner, p. 20. All
translations from sources and works in German language are by Thomas Brodie.

60. G. Himmelfarb. 1991. *Poverty and Compassion. The Moral Imagination of the Late
Victorians*. New York: Knopf, p. 383.

61. Compare with. Rudloff, *Wohlfahrtsstadt*, p. 25.

62. Crew, *Germans*, p. 148; for an older interpretation of youth welfare in this sense see
also H. Schneider. 1964. *Die öffentliche Jugendhilfe zwischen Eingriff und Leistung. Eine*

juristisch-sozialpädagogische Analyse der Aufgaben des Jugendamtes und ihrer gesetzlichen Regelung. Berlin-Spandau/Neuwied am Rhein: Luchterhand.

63. Ch. Sachße. 1995. 'Verein, Verband und Wohlfahrtsstaat. Entstehung und Entwicklung der "dualen" Wohlfahrtspflege', in Th. Rauschenbach, Ch. Sachße and Th. Olk (eds), *Von der Wertgemeinschaft zum Dienstleistungsunternehmen. Jugend- und Wohlfahrtsverbände im Umbruch*. Frankfurt/Main: Suhrkamp, pp. 123–49.

64. See Hammerschmidt, *Finanzierung*.

65. J.-Ch. Kaiser. 1989. *Sozialer Protestantismus im 20. Jahrhundert. Beiträge zur Geschichte der Inneren Mission 1914–1945*. Munich: Oldenbourg; C. Maurer. 2008. *Der Caritasverband zwischen Kaiserreich und Weimarer Republik. Zur Sozial- und Mentalitätsgeschichte des caritativen Katholizismus in Deutschland*. Freiburg im Breisgau: Lambertus; Ch. Eifert. 1993. *Frauenpolitik und Wohlfahrtspflege. Zur Geschichte der sozialdemokratischen 'Arbeiterwohlfahrt'*. Frankfurt/Main, New York: Campus; for a local perspective see also W. Rudloff. 1997. 'Konkurrenz, Kooperation und Korporatismus. Wohlfahrtsvereine und Wohlfahrtsverbände in München 1900–1933', in A. Wollasch (ed.), *Wohlfahrtspflege in der Region. Westfalen-Lippe während des 19. und 20. Jahrhunderts im historischen Vergleich*. Paderborn: Schöningh, pp. 165–90. To the umbrella organizations mentioned above must further be added the Deutsche Rote Kreuz and the Zentralausschuß der Christlichen Arbeiterhilfe.

66. J. Ehrhardt. 1932/33. 'Gefahren der Jugendfürsorge', *Zentralblatt für Jugendrecht und Jugendwohlfahrt* 24:225–32, esp. p. 226.

67. For contemporary contributions to the discussion see: F. Wunderlich. 1932. *Versicherung, Fürsorge und Krisenrisiko*. Leipzig: Lühe & Co.; E. Schmidt. 1932. *Sozialversicherung und öffentliche Fürsorge. Die industriellen Grundlagen, das Beziehungsverhältnis und die Gegenwartsfragen*. Stuttgart: Kohlhammer; L. Schoenlank. 1933. *Das Versicherungsprinzip und das Fürsorgeprinzip in der Deutschen Sozialversicherung*. Berlin: Ebering.

68. W. Niemeyer, 1930. 'Die wirtschaftliche Lage der Sozialrentner in 92 deutschen Städten und 105 deutschen Landkreisen. Ergebnisse einer Erhebung vom März 1929', in *Sozialversicherung und öffentliche Fürsorge als Grundlagen der Alters- und Invalidenversorgung*. Karlsruhe: G. Braun, pp. 62, 64.

69. Krug v. Nidda, C.L. 1930. 'Bewertung der Ergebnisse der Erhebung', in *Sozialversicherung und öffentliche Fürsorge*, pp. 187–220, esp. p. 203.

70. Niemeyer, 'Die wirtschaftliche Lage', pp. 100–24.

71. See also: Ch. Conrad. 1996. 'Mixed Incomes for the Elderly Poor in Germany 1880–1930', in M. Katz and Ch. Sachße (eds), *The Mixed Economy of Social Welfare. Public/private relations in England, Germany and the United States, the 1870s to the 1930s*. Baden-Baden: Nomos, pp. 340–67; ibid. 1994. *Vom Kreis zum Rentner. Der Strukturwandel des Alters in Deutschland zwischen 1830 und 1930*. Göttingen: Vandenhoeck & Ruprecht, p. 309.

72. Rudloff, *Wohlfahrtsstadt*, p. 893.

73. Adamy and Steffen, '"Arbeitsmarktpolitik"', p. 287.

74. 'Entschließung des Vorstandes zur Arbeitslosenfrage'. 1931. *Nachrichtendienst des Deutschen Vereins für öffentliche und private Fürsorge* 12, p. 66.

75. For a broad analysis see: Ch. Berringer. 1999. *Sozialpolitik in der Weltwirtschaftskrise. Die Arbeitslosenversicherung in Deutschland und Großbritannien im Vergleich 1928–1934*. Berlin: Duncker & Humblot, p. 348; Schmidt, *Sozialversicherung*, p. 137.

76. H. Muthesius. 1932/33. 'Wirkungen der neuen Notverordnungen', *Deutsche Zeitschrift für Wohlfahrtspflege* 8:114–116, 'Entschließung des Vorstandes zur Arbeitslosenfrage'. 1931. *Nachrichtendienst des Deutschen Vereins für öffentliche und private Fürsorge* 12:114–16; see also Berringer, *Sozialpolitik*, p. 465.

77. Crew, '"Wohlfahrtsbrot"'; Rudloff, *Wohlfahrtsstadt*, pp. 851–70; Brandmann, *Leipzig*, pp. 279–91; Hong, *Welfare*, pp. 91–109.

78. Rudloff, *Wohlfahrtsstadt*, p. 854.

79. Compare with Eghigian, 'Politics'.

80. See the contemporary interpretation of K. Neundörfer, which has frequently been cited in recent literature: K. Neundörfer. 1925. 'Widerstreitende Mächte im Reichsgesetz für Jugendwohlfahrt', in J. Beeking (ed.), *Das Reichsgesetz für Jugendwohlfahrt und die Caritas*. Freiburg im Breisgau: Caritasverlag, pp. 47–77.

81. The following interpretation is based on Hong, *Welfare*.

82. Rudloff, *Wohlfahrtsstadt*, p. 33.

83. Compare with Thamer and Kaiser, 'Kommunale Wohlfahrtspolitik'.

Works Cited

Abelshauser, W. 1987. 'Die Weimarer Republik – ein Wohlfahrtsstaat?' in W. Abelshauser (ed.), *Die Weimarer Republik als Wohlfahrtsstaat*. Stuttgart: Steiner, pp. 9–31.

Adamy, W., and J. Steffen. 1982. '"Arbeitsmarktpolitik" in der Depression. Sanierungsstrategien in der Arbeitslosenversicherung 1927–1933', *Mitteilungen aus der Arbeitsmarkt- und Berufsforschung* 15:276–291.

Berger, G. 1979. *Die ehrenamtliche Tätigkeit in der Sozialarbeit. Motive, Tendenzen, Probleme. Dargestellt am Beispiel des Elberfelder Systems.* Frankfurt/Main: Lang.

Bergler, A. 2011. *Von Armenpflegern und Fürsorgeschwestern. Kommunale Wohlfahrtspflege und Geschlechterpolitik in Berlin und Charlottenburg.* Stuttgart: Steiner.

Berringer, Ch. 1999. *Sozialpolitik in der Weltwirtschaftskrise. Die Arbeitslosenversicherung in Deutschland und Großbritannien im Vergleich 1928–1934.* Berlin: Duncker & Humblot.

Bessel, R. 1993. *Germany after the First World War.* Oxford: Clarendon Press.

Boettcher, H. 1988. *Fürsorge in Lübeck vor und nach dem Ersten Weltkrieg.* Lübeck: Schmidt-Römhild.

Brandmann, P. 1998. *Leipzig zwischen Klassenkampf und Sozialreform. Kommunale Wohlfahrtspolitik zwischen 1890 und 1929.* Cologne, Vienna: Böhlau.

Brüchert-Schunk, H. 1994. *Städtische Sozialpolitik vom Wilhelminischen Reich bis zur Weltwirtschaftskrise. Eine sozial- und kommunalhistorische Untersuchung am Beispiel der Stadt Mainz 1890–1930.* Stuttgart: Steiner.

Bußmann-Strelow, G. 1997. *Kommunale Politik im Sozialstaat. Nürnberger Wohlfahrtspflege in der Weimarer Republik.* Nuremberg: Stadtarchiv.

Conrad, Ch. 1994. *Vom Kreis zum Rentner. Der Strukturwandel des Alters in Deutschland zwischen 1830 und 1930*. Göttingen: Vandenhoeck & Ruprecht.

———. 1996. 'Mixed Incomes for the Elderly Poor in Germany 1880–1930', in M. Katz and Ch. Sachße (eds), *The Mixed Economy of Social Welfare. Public/private relations in England, Germany and the United States, the 1870s to the 1930s*. Baden-Baden: Nomos, pp. 340–367.

Crew, D.F. 1990. '"Wohlfahrtsbrot ist bitteres Brot". The Elderly, the Disabled and the Local Welfare Authorities in the Weimar Republic 1924–1933', *Archiv für Sozialgeschichte* 30:217–45.

———. 1998. *Germans on Welfare. From Weimar to Hitler*. New York, Oxford: Oxford University Press.

Deutsche Sozialpolitik 1918–1928. 1929. Berlin: E.S. Mittler und Sohn.

Dickinson, E.R. 1996. *The Politics of Child Welfare from the Empire to the Federal Republic*. Cambridge/MA: Harvard University Press.

Eghigian, G. 1993. 'The Politics of Victimization: Social Pensioners and the German Social State in the Inflation of 1914–1924', *Central European History* 26:375–403.

Ehrhardt, J. 1932/33. 'Gefahren der Jugendfürsorge', *Zentralblatt für Jugendrecht und Jugendwohlfahrt* 24:225–232.

Eifert, Ch. 1993. *Frauenpolitik und Wohlfahrtspflege. Zur Geschichte der sozialdemokratischen 'Arbeiterwohlfahrt'*. Frankfurt/Main, New York: Campus.

'Einfluß der Stabilisierung unserer Währung in der Wohlfahrtspflege'. 1924, *Nachrichtendienst des Deutschen Vereins für öffentliche und private Fürsorge* 1924:439.

'Einige Grundregeln zur Ausübung der Fürsorge'. 1927, *Blätter für die Leipziger Wohlfahrtspflege* June 1927:59–60.

'Entschließung des Vorstandes zur Arbeitslosenfrage'. 1931, *Nachrichtendienst des Deutschen Vereins für öffentliche und private Fürsorge* 12:66.

Fehlemann, S. 2009. *Armutsrisiko Mutterschaft. Mütter- und Säuglingsfürsorge im rheinisch-westfälischen Industriegebiet 1890–1924*. Essen: Klartext.

Führer, K.Ch. 1990. '"Für das Wirtschaftsleben mehr oder weniger wertlose Personen". Zur Lage von Invaliden- und Kleinrentnern in den Inflationsjahren 1918–1924', *Archiv für Sozialgeschichte* 30:145–80.

———1995. *Mieter, Hausbesitzer, Staat und Wohnungsmarkt. Wohnungsmangel und Wohnungszwangswirtschaft in Deutschland 1914–1960*. Stuttgart: Steiner.

Gazeley, I. 2003. *Poverty in Britain, 1900–1965*. Houndmills, Basingstoke: Palgrave.

———, and A. Newell. 2012. 'The End of Destitution: Evidence from Urban British Working Households 1904–37', *Oxford Economic Papers* 64:80–102.

Goldmann, F. 1930. 'Siechenhäuser und Altersheime', in A. Gottstein (ed.), *Handbücherei für das gesamte Krankenhauswesen*. Berlin: Julius Springer, vol. 3, pp. 235–318.

Götze, S. 1933. *Grundlagen und Voraussetzungen der heutigen Wohlfahrtsarbeit.* Berlin: C. Heymann.

Gräser, M. 1995. *Der blockierte Wohlfahrtsstaat. Unterschichtenjugend und Jugendfürsorge in der Weimarer Republik.* Göttingen: Vandenhoeck & Ruprecht.

Gumpert, F. 1926. 'Eindrücke von der Gesolei', *Soziale Praxis* 35:716–17.

Hagen, W. 1925. *Die Gesundheitsfürsorge einer Industriestadt. Erörtert am Beispiel der Stadt Höchst a.M.* Frankfurt am Main: Deutscher Verein für öffentliche und private Fürsorge.

Hammerschmidt, P. 2003. *Finanzierung und Management von Wohlfahrtsanstalten 1920 bis 1936.* Stuttgart: Steiner.

Hansmann, M. 2000. *Kommunalfinanzen im 20. Jahrhundert. Zäsuren und Kontinuitäten: Das Beispiel Hannover.* Hannover: Hahn.

Harvey, E. 1993. *Youth and the Welfare State in Weimar Germany.* Oxford: Clarendon Press.

Hatton, T.J., and R.E. Bailey. 1998. 'Poverty and the Welfare State in Interwar London', *Oxford Economic Papers* 50:574–606.

'Hausbesuch'. 1926, *Wohlfahrtsblätter der Stadt Köln* 1:4–5.

Helbling, E. 1931. 'Die öffentliche Fürsorge. Ergebnisse der Reichsfürsorgestatistik für das Jahr 1929', *Statistisches Jahrbuch Deutscher Städte* 26:328–45

Henning, F.-W. 1976. 'Finanzpolitische Vorstellungen und Maßnahmen Konrad Adenauers während seiner Kölner Zeit (1906 bis 1933)', in H. Stehkämper (ed.), *Konrad Adenauer. Oberbürgermeister von Köln.* Cologne: Rheinland, pp. 123–53.

Hennock, E.P. 1992. 'Concepts of Poverty in the British Social Surveys from Charles Booth to Arthur Bowley', in M. Bulmer, K. Bales and K. Kish Sklar (eds), *The Social Survey in Historical Perspective.* Cambridge: Cambridge University Press, pp. 189–216.

Hering, S., and R. Münchmeier. 2000. *Geschichte der Sozialen Arbeit. Eine Einführung.* Weinheim, Munich: Juventa.

Heyde, L. 1931. *Abriß der Sozialpolitik*, 7th edn. Leipzig: Quelle und Meyer.

Himmelfarb, G. 1991. *Poverty and Compassion. The Moral Imagination of the Late Victorians.* New York: Knopf.

Homburg, H. 1984. 'Massenarbeitslosigkeit in Deutschland 1930–1933. Unterstützung und politische Verwaltung der Arbeitslosen', *Sozialwissenschaftliche Informationen* 14:205–15.

———. 1985. 'Vom Arbeitslosen zum Zwangsarbeiter. Arbeitslosenpolitik und Fraktionierung der Arbeiterschaft in Deutschland 1930–1933 am Beispiel der Wohlfahrtserwerbslosen und der kommunalen Wohlfahrtshilfe', *Archiv für Sozialgeschichte* 25:251–98.

Hong, Y.-S. 1998. *Welfare, Modernity, and the Weimar State, 1919–1933,* Princeton: Princeton University Press.

Irmak, K.H. 2002. *Der Sieche. Alte Menschen und die stationäre Altenhilfe in Deutschland 1924–1961.* Essen: Klartext.

James, H. 1990. 'Municipal Finance in the Weimar Republic', in W.R. Lee and Eve Rosenhaft (eds), *The State and Social Change in Germany, 1880–1980*. New York, Oxford, Munich: Berg, pp. 228–53.

Jans, H.-P. 1994. *Sozialpolitik und Wohlfahrtspflege in Ulm 1870–1930. Stadt, Verbände und Parteien auf dem Weg zur modernen Sozialstaatlichkeit*. Stuttgart: Kohlhammer.

Kähler, G. 1985. *Wohnung und Stadt. Hamburg, Frankfurt, Wien. Modelle sozialen Wohnens in den zwanziger Jahren*. Braunschweig: Vieweg.

Kaiser, J.-Ch. 1989. *Sozialer Protestantismus im 20. Jahrhundert. Beiträge zur Geschichte der Inneren Mission 1914–1945*. Munich: Oldenbourg.

Kaiserliches Statistischen Amt (ed.). 1887. *Statistik der öffentlichen Armenpflege im Jahre 1885*. Berlin: Puttkammer & Mühlbrecht.

Kall, G. 1926/27. 'Die Hauptabteilung "Soziale Fürsorge" auf der Gesolei', *Deutsche Zeitschrift für Wohlfahrtspflege* 2:296–99.

Köhler, M. 1929. 'Reform der öffentlichen Armenpflege in England', *Deutsche Zeitschrift für Wohlfahrtspflege* 5:585–90.

Köster, M. 1996. *Jugend, Wohlfahrtsstaat und Gesellschaft im Wandel. Westfalen zwischen Kaiserreich und Bundesrepublik*. Paderborn: Schöningh.

Krabbe, W. 1984. 'Die Anfänge des "sozialen Wohnungsbaus" vor dem Ersten Weltkrieg. Kommunalpolitische Bemühungen um eine Lösung des Wohnungsproblems', *Vierteljahresschrift für Sozial- und Wirtschaftsgeschichte* 71:30–58.

Krug v. Nidda, C.L. 1930. 'Bewertung der Ergebnisse der Erhebung', in *Sozialversicherung und öffentliche Fürsorge*, pp. 187–220.

Kuhn, G. 1998. *Wohnkultur und kommunale Wohnungspolitik in Frankfurt am Main 1880 bis 1930. Auf dem Wege zu einer pluralen Gesellschaft der Individuen*. Bonn: Dietz.

Labisch, A., and F. Tennstedt. 1985. *Der Weg zum 'Gesetz über die Vereinheitlichung des Gesundheitswesens' vom 3. Juli 1934. Entwicklungslinien und –momente des staatlichen und kommunalen Gesundheitswesens in Deutschland*, 2 vols. Düsseldorf: Akademie für öffentliches Gesundheitswesen.

Laybourn, K. 1990. *Britain on the Breadline. A Social and Political History of Britain between the Wars*. Gloucester: Sutton.

Lehnert, D. 1991. *Kommunale Politik, Parteiensystem und Interessenkonflikte in Berlin und Wien. Wohnungs-, Verkehrs- und Finanzpolitik im Spannungsfeld von städtischer Selbstverwaltung und Verbandseinflüssen*. Berlin: Haude und Sener.

Leibfried, S. 1985. 'Existenzminimum und Fürsorge-Richtsätze in der Weimarer Republik', in S. Leibfried, *Armutspolitik und die Entwicklung des Sozialstaats*. Bremen: Universität, pp. 186–240; (English version in: S. Leibfried. 1986. 'Welfare Guidelines in the 1920s: Regulating Weimar's Poor', in D.E. Ashford and E.W. Kelley (eds), *Nationalizing Social Security in Europe and America*. Greenwich, London. Jai Press, pp. 137–54.)

Lewek, P. 1992. *Arbeitslosigkeit und Arbeitslosenversicherung in der Weimarer Republik 1918–1927*. Stuttgart: Steiner.

Marquardt, D. 1994. *Sozialpolitik und Sozialfürsorge der Stadt Hannover in der Weimarer Republik*. Hannover: Hahn.

Marx-Jaskulski, K. 2008. *Armut und Fürsorge auf dem Land: Vom Ende des 19. Jahrhunderts bis 1933*. Göttingen: Wallstein.

Matron, K. 2012. *Kommunale Jugendfürsorge in Frankfurt am Main in der Weimarer Republik*. Frankfurt/Main: Henrich-Edition.

Maurer, C. 2008. *Der Caritasverband zwischen Kaiserreich und Weimarer Republik. Zur Sozial- und Mentalitätsgeschichte des caritativen Katholizismus in Deutschland*. Freiburg im Breisgau: Lambertus.

Michel, M. 1926. *Städtischer Gemeindehaushalt und soziale Lasten vor und nach dem Kriege. Eine Untersuchung auf Gund der Haushaltspläne der Stadt Frankfurt a.M.* Frankfurt/Main: Deutscher Verein für öffentliche und private Fürsorge

———. 1926/27. 'Städtepolitik und Soziales Aufgabengebiet'. *Deutsche Zeitschrift für Wohlfahrtspflege* 2:504–10.

Miller, S. (ed.). 1969. *Die Regierung der Volksbeauftragten 1918/19*. With an introduction by Erich Matthias, Part 1. Düsseldorf: Droste.

Müller, H.G. 1933. *Die Ausgaben für Zwecke der Wohlfahrts- und Sozialpolitik in den Gemeinden und Gemeindeverbänden des Landes Sachsen in den Rechnungsjahren 1913, 1925 und 1926*. Lucka: Berger.

Münchmeier, R. 1981. *Zugänge zur Geschichte der Sozialarbeit*. Munich: Juventa.

Nerdinger, W. 2003. 'Architekturutopie und Realität des Bauens zwischen Weimarer Republik und Drittem Reich', in W. Hardtwig (ed.), *Utopie und politische Herrschaft im Europa der Zwischenkriegszeit*, Munich: Oldenbourg, p. 269–286.

Muthesius, H. 1932/33. 'Wirkungen der neuen Notverordnungen', *Deutsche Zeitschrift für Wohlfahrtspflege* 8:114–116.

Neundörfer, K. 1925. 'Widerstreitende Mächte im Reichsgesetz für Jugendwohlfahrt', in J. Beeking (ed.), *Das Reichsgesetz für Jugendwohlfahrt und die Caritas*. Freiburg im Breisgau: Caritasverlag, pp. 47–77.

Niemeyer, W. 1930. 'Die wirtschaftliche Lage der Sozialrentner in 92 deutschen Städten und 105 deutschen Landkreisen. Ergebnisse einer Erhebung vom März 1929', in *Sozialversicherung und öffentliche Fürsorge als Grundlagen der Alters- und Invalidenversorgung*. Karlsruhe: G. Braun, pp. 35–186.

Paulus, J. 1998. *Kommunale Wohlfahrtspolitik in Leipzig 1930 bis 1945*. Cologne, Vienna: Böhlau.

Petersen, K.P., and J.H. Petersen. 2013. 'Confusion and Divergence: Origins and Meanings of the Term "Welfare State" in Germany and Britain, 1840–1940', *Journal of European Social Policy* 23:37–51.

Peukert, D.J.K. 1986. *Grenzen der Sozialdisziplinierung. Aufstieg und Krise der deutschen Jugendfürsorge von 1878 bis 1932*. Cologne: Bund.

Polligkeit, W. 1922. 'Der Einfluß der Finanznot auf die private Wohlfahrtspflege in den Städten', *Bericht über die Verhandlungen des 37. Deutschen*

Fürsorgetages des Deutschen Vereins für öffentliche und private Fürsorge am 28. und 29. Oktober 1921 in Weimar. Karlsruhe: G. Braun, pp. 44–54.

Preller, L. 1978. *Sozialpolitik in der Weimarer Republik*, new edn. Düsseldorf: Athenäum/Droste.

Ramsauer, N. 2000. *'Verwahrlost'. Kindswegnahmen und die Entstehung der Jugendfürsorge im schweizerischen Sozialstaat 1900–1945.* Zürich: Chronos.

Reiner, H. 1926. 'Das bayerische Fürsorgewesen auf Grund der Reichsverordnung über die Fürsorgepflicht im Rechnungsjahr 1924', *Zeitschrift des Bayerischen Statistischen Landesamtes* 58:168–193.

Roth, G. 1999. *Die Institutionen der kommunalen Selbstverwaltung. Die Entwicklung von Aufgaben, Organisation, Leitgedanken und Mythen von der Weimarer Republik bis Mitte der neunziger Jahre.* Berlin: Duncker & Humblot.

Ruck, M. 1987. 'Der Wohnungsbau – Schnittpunkt der Sozial- und Wirtschaftspolitik. Probleme der öffentlichen Wohnungspolitik in der Hauszinsära 1924/25–1930/31', in Abelshauser, *Weimarer Republik*, pp. 91–123.

———. 1988. 'Die öffentliche Wohnungsbaufinanzierung in der Weimarer Republik. Zielsetzung, Ergebnisse, Probleme', in A. Schildt and A. Sywottek (eds), *Massenwohnung und Eigenheim. Wohnungsbau und Wohnen in der Großstadt seit der Ersten Weltkrieg.* Frankfurt/Main, New York: Campus, pp. 150–221.

Rudloff, W. 1997. 'Konkurrenz, Kooperation und Korporatismus. Wohlfahrts vereine und Wohlfahrtsverbände in München 1900–1933', in A. Wollasch (ed.), *Wohlfahrtspflege in der Region. Westfalen-Lippe während des 19. und 20. Jahrhunderts im historischen Vergleich.* Paderborn: Schöningh, pp. 165–90.

———. 1998. *Die Wohlfahrtsstadt. Kommunale Ernährungs-, Fürsorge- und Wohnungspolitik am Beispiel Münchens 1910–1933*, 2 vols. Göttingen: Vandenhoeck & Ruprecht.

———. 2002. 'Im Souterrain des Sozialstaates: Neuere Forschungen zur Geschichte von Fürsorge und Wohlfahrtspflege im 20. Jahrhundert', *Archiv für Sozialgeschichte* 42:474–520.

———. 2003. 'Das Wissen der kommunalen Sozialverwaltung in Deutschland', *Jahrbuch für europäische Verwaltungsgeschichte,* 15: pp. 59–88.

———. 2012. 'Ausbau und Krise - der deutsche Sozialstaat in der Weimarer Republik', in A. Kruke and M. Woyke (eds), *Deutsche Sozialdemokratie in Bewegung. 1848 – 1863 – 2013.* Bonn: Dietz, pp. 122–31.

Saake, F. 1929. 'Strukturwandel der Finanzwirtschaft der Gemeinden und Gemeindeverbände', *Zeitschrift für Kommunalwirtschaft* 19:2–11.

Sachße, Ch. 1986. *Mütterlichkeit als Beruf. Sozialarbeit, Sozialreform und Frauenbewegung 1871–1929.* Frankfurt/Main: Suhrkamp; (abridged English version in Ch. Sachße. 1993. 'Social Mothers: The Bourgois Women's Movement and German Welfare-State Formation, 1890–1929', in S. Koven and S. Michel (eds). *Mothers of a New World. Maternalist Politics and the Origins of Welfare States.* New York, London: Routledge, pp. 136–58).

———. 1988. 'Ehrenamtlichkeit, Selbsthilfe und Professionalität. Eine historische Skizze', in S. Müller and Th. Rauschenbach (eds). *Das soziale Ehrenamt. Nützliche Arbeit zum Nulltarif.* Weinheim, Munich: Juventa, pp. 51–55.

———. 1995. 'Verein, Verband und Wohlfahrtsstaat. Entstehung und Entwicklung der 'dualen' Wohlfahrtspflege', in Th. Rauschenbach, Ch. Sachße and Th. Olk (eds), *Von der Wertgemeinschaft zum Dienstleistungsunternehmen. Jugend- und Wohlfahrtsverbände im Umbruch.* Frankfurt/Main: Suhrkamp, pp. 123–49.

——— and F. Tennstedt. 1988–1992. *Geschichte der Armenfürsorge in Deutschland*, vols 2 and 3. Stuttgart: Kohlhammer.

Salomon, A. 1921. *Leitfaden der Wohlfahrtspflege.* Leipzig, Berlin: Teubner.

———. 1925/6. 'Zur Technik der Ermittlung', *Deutsche Zeitschrift für Wohlfahrtspflege* 1:315–19.

———. 1926. *Soziale Diagnose.* Berlin: Heymann.

Schmeer, O. 1990. 'Sozialpolitik in Duisburg 1930–1933. Staatliche Sozialpolitik und kommunale Selbstverwaltung in der Krise der Weimarer Republik', *Duisburger Forschungen* 37:179–309.

Schmidt, E. 1932. *Sozialversicherung und öffentliche Fürsorge. Die industriellen Grundlagen, das Beziehungsverhältnis und die Gegenwartsfragen.* Stuttgart: Kohlhammer.

Schmuhl, H.-W. 2003. *Arbeitsmarktpolitik und Arbeitsverwaltung in Deutschland von 1871 bis 2002. Zwischen Fürsorge, Hoheit und Markt.* Nuremberg: Institut für Arbeitsmarkt- und Berufsforschung der Bundesanstalt für Arbeit.

Schneider, H. 1964. *Die öffentliche Jugendhilfe zwischen Eingriff und Leistung. Eine juristisch-sozialpädagogische Analyse der Aufgaben des Jugendamtes und ihrer gesetzlichen Regelung.* Berlin-Spandau/Neuwied am Rhein: Luchterhand.

Schoenlank, L. 1933. *Das Versicherungsprinzip und das Fürsorgeprinzip in der Deutschen Sozialversicherung.* Berlin: Ebering.

Scholz, R. 1985. '"Heraus aus der unwürdigen Fürsorge". Zur Sozialpolitik und politischen Orientierung der Kleinrentner in der Weimarer Republik', in Ch. Conrad and Hans-Joachim von Kondratowitz (eds), *Gerontologie und Sozialgeschichte. Wege zu einer historischen Betrachtung des Alters*, 2nd edn. Berlin: Deutsches Zentrum für Altersfragen, pp. 319–50.

Schröder, I. 2001. *Arbeiten für eine bessere Welt. Frauenbewegung und Sozialreform 1890–1914.* Frankfurt/Main, New York: Campus.

Seutemann, K. 1934. 'Finanzübersicht nach der Rechnung 1931', *Statistisches Jahrbuch Deutscher Städte* 29:211–48.

Simmel, G. 1908. 'Der Arme', in G. Simmel, *Soziologie. Untersuchungen über die Formen der Vergesellschaftung.* Leipzig: Duncker & Humblot, pp. 454–493.

'Soziale Unterstützungslasten in den Städten'. 1924, *Mitteilungen des Deutschen Städtetages* 1924:11.

Steinacker, S. 2007. *Der Staat als Erzieher. Jugendpolitik und Jugendfürsorge im Rheinland vom Kaiserreich bis zum Ende des Nazismus.* Stuttgart: Ibidem.

Steinbacher, St. 1919. *Zahl und persönliche Verhältnisse der öffentlich Unterstützten in deutschen Großstädten.* Borna-Leipzig: Noske.

———. 1921/22. 'Einige Ergebnisse großstädtischer Armenstatistik', *Allgemeines Statistisches Archiv* 13:276–307.

Steitz, W. and W. Krabbe. 1985. 'Kommunale Wohnungspolitik deutscher Großstädte 1871–1914', in H.J. Teuteberg (ed.), *Homo habitans. Zur Sozialgeschichte des ländlichen und städtischen Wohnens in der Neuzeit.* Münster: Coppenrath und Steiner, pp. 421–46.

Stöckel, S. 1996. *Säuglingsfürsorge zwischen sozialer Hygiene und Eugenik. Das Beispiel Berlins im Kaiserreich und in der Weimarer Republik.* Berlin, New York: De Gruyter.

Thamer, H.-U. and J.-Ch. Kaiser. 1995. 'Kommunale Wohlfahrtspolitik zwischen 1918 und 1933 im Vergleich (Frankfurt, Leipzig, Nuremberg)' in J. Reulecke (ed.), *Die Stadt als Dienstleistungszentrum. Beiträge zur Geschichte der 'Sozialstadt' in Deutschland im 19. und frühen 20. Jahrhundert.* St. Katharinen: Scripta-Mercaturae, pp. 325–70.

Uhlendorff, U. 2003. *Geschichte des Jugendamtes. Entwicklungslinien öffentlicher Jugendhilfe 1871 bis 1929.* Weinheim, Basel, Berlin: Beltz.

Vossen, J. 2001. *Gesundheitsämter im Nationalsozialismus. Rassenhygiene und offene Gesundheitsfürsorge in Westfalen 1900–1950.* Essen: Klartext.

Weber, A. 1926. *Fürsorge und Wohlfahrtspflege. Eine Einführung in die soziale Hilfsarbeit.* Berlin, Leipzig: Gruyter.

Weindling, P. 1989. *Health, Race and German Politics between National Unification and Nazism, 1870–1945.* Cambridge: Cambridge University Press.

Weiß, L. 1999. *Rheinische Großstädte während der Weltwirtschaftskrise (1929–1933). Kommunale Finanz- und Sozialpolitik im Vergleich.* Cologne: Böhlau.

Werner, F. 1926. 'Die Ausstellung der freien Wohlfahrtspflege in Düsseldorf', *Freie Wohlfahrtspflege* 1:123–24.

Werner, M. 2011. *Stiftungsstadt und Bürgertum. Hamburgs Stiftungskultur vom Kaiserreich bis zum Nationalsozialismus.* Munich: Oldenbourg.

Weyer-von Schoultz, M. 1994. *Stadt und Gesundheit im Ruhrgebiet 1850–1929. Verstädterung und kommunale Gesundheitspolitik am Beispiel der jungen Industriestadt Gelsenkirchen.* Essen: Klartext.

Williams, K. 1981. *From Pauperism to Poverty.* London: Routledge Kegan Paul.

Wimmer, F. 2014. *Die völkische Ordnung von Armut. Kommunale Sozialpolitik im nationalsozialistischen München.* Göttingen: Wallstein.

Wronski. 1934. 'Wohnungsbau und Kleinsiedlung', *Statistisches Jahrbuch Deutscher Städte*, pp. 295–323.

Wunderlich, F. 1932. *Versicherung, Fürsorge und Krisenrisiko.* Leipzig: Lühe & Co.

Zeller, S. 1987. *Volksmütter. Frauen im Wohlfahrtswesen der 20er Jahre.* Düsseldorf: Schwann.

Zeppenfeld, B. 1999. *Handlungsspielräume städtischer Finanzpolitik. Staatliche Vorgaben und kommunales Interesse in Bochum und Münster 1913–1935.* Essen: Klartext.

Zimmermann, C. 1991. *Von der Wohnungsfrage zur Wohnungspolitik. Die Reformbewegung in Deutschland 1845–1914.* Göttingen: Vandenhoeck & Ruprecht.

Wilfried Rudloff is a postdoctoral researcher in the project 'Quellen zur Geschichte der deutschen Sozialpolitik 1867–1914' at the Mainzer Akademie der Wissenschaften and Literatur. His recent publications include: *Quellensammlung zur Geschichte der deutschen Sozialpolitik 1867–1914*, vol. 7, *Kommunale Armenpflege* (2015); *Ausbau und Differenzierung der Sozialpolitik seit Beginn des neuen Kurses (1890–1904)*, vol. 4, *Arbeiterrecht* (2012).

CHAPTER 5

Welfare, Mobilization and the Nazi Society

Nicole Kramer

Social policy and the welfare state are themes which have provoked some con-troversies within the historiography of the Nazi Regime. When Martin Broszat argued, in the aftermath of the 1980s *Historikerstreit*, for the necessity of his-toricizing of the Nazi period, he used the blueprints for a comprehensive social insurance scheme outlined by the German Labour Front in 1940 as a case in point.[1] He stressed that these ideas have to be seen as part of long-term social policy developments and he pointed out some similarities with the Beveridge report published two years later. Those criticizing Broszat's approach warned that taking an isolated view of Nazi welfare measures would result in neglecting the racial-eugenic context in which they were formed.[2]

Quite recently, conflicting views on Nazi welfare became evident within the ongoing historiographical debate concerning the National Socialist concept of *Volksgemeinschaft*.[3] While some scholars think of it as merely propaganda con-struct, others use it as a yardstick to examine social and cultural change during the Third Reich. The latter understand *Volksgemeinschaft* as a key concept of Nazi rule which drove processes of inclusion and exclusion within society. Such a focus draws attention to welfare and social policy because they were vital tools used by state officials to distinguish *Volksgenossen* (Volk comrades') from *Gemeinschaftsfremde* (community aliens). Furthermore, it enabled the regime to interfere in people's private lives and to adjust the societal and political behav-iour of individuals. Research engaging with the concept of *Volksgemeinschaft* reveals both the exclusionary character of welfare programmes – which served to consolidate the persecution of racial outsiders – as well as their integrative roles within mainstream 'Aryan' society. First of all, Götz Aly's book, *Hitler's*

Beneficiaries. Plunder, Racial War, and the Nazi Welfare State, drew attention to welfare provisions and their alleged influence in maintaining the German population's loyalty to the regime during the Second World War.[4] Aly made the case that child benefits, family allowances for dependants of soldiers and a generous pension reform in 1941 bettered the lives of Germans, even workers. In so doing, the Nazi regime allegedly established a 'feel-good dictatorship' where offers of inclusion were welcomed by a majority of the German population.[5] Aly's conclusions were met with harsh criticism by historians. Many challenged his rather crude materialist explanation of human behaviour, especially the assumption that personal benefit led to enthusiastic and permanent support of Nazi politics. Moreover, he was accused of neglecting the regime's coercive structures as well as how much the standard of living of Germans decreased during the Third Reich. Describing the Nazi regime as a welfare state led by redistributive ideas anticipating some of the core welfare reforms the Federal Republic is known for, was strongly refuted by scholars who see exclusion and control as core principles of Nazi welfare.[6]

The chapter will explore how the German welfare regime was transformed under Nazi rule, during peacetime as well as during the Second World War. In doing so it relies on classic accounts like the seminal work of Christoph Sachße and Florian Tennstedt, whose study employs a long-term and encompassing perspective (social insurance, social assistance and social care).[7] However, the chapter aims to shed new light on Nazi welfare based on recent historiography focused on specific fields of welfare and the implementation of social policy at the local level. Moreover, insights into the day-to-day practice of social policy during the Second World War draw heavily on archival research.

This approach chimes with recent trends in the historiography of welfare regimes. Scholars interested in poverty and social assistance in particular, rely on microstudies, which are used to examine how the dialectics of inclusion and exclusion operate on the ground. Practices of welfare bodies are as important to this story as the client's experiences and attitudes.[8] For the Weimar period it is an especially well-established approach to rewrite the history of the welfare state by examining welfare's operation in a local context, as well as systematically including the dimension of the day-to-day practice of welfare agencies and the views of recipients.[9] In so doing these pieces of research give empirical evidence concerning how the interventionist state undermined rather than supported the legitimacy of the young republic. Moreover, they challenge the notion that overall welfare state development, especially the implementation of eugenic policies, can be explained with a top-down approach. They highlight the driving forces set free by the process of translating ideas into practice, causing conflicts and cleavages within the welfare triangle of reformers, social workers and recipients.

Meanwhile, recent studies have enriched the social history of Nazi welfare, too. We are therefore able to discuss the extent to which the examination of practices and interactions between welfare officers and their clients change our understanding of Nazi welfare. The chapter argues that a rather fine-grained analysis does challenge the polarized way of thinking about Nazi welfare based on the dyads of inclusion and exclusion as well as the individual and collective.

Finally, this chapter concludes by examining the Second World War and its catalytic effects on welfare provisions. Although in general the war is hardly considered to be a pacemaker of the German Welfare State (quite in contrast to the First World War)[10] it is, however, seen as the climax of the Nazi welfare system. Sachße and Tennstedt state that after 1938 'the authoritarian Nazi welfare state' turned into a *völkisch* welfare state.[11] Aly's notion of a 'feel-good dictatorship' also draws mainly on social trends and policy decisions during the war years. This chapter is mainly interested in the question of how the welfare regime responded to new social needs, such as the care of family members of men who were drafted for the Wehrmacht, survivors of 'fallen' soldiers and bombed-out people who had to be evacuated. Many of these wartime welfare programmes were mainly directed towards women.

Origins and Characteristics of Nazi Welfare

The emergence of a racial welfare state had already begun in the Weimar Republic. Since the 1980s, Detlev Peukert and others have pointed to the fact that the crisis of the welfare state at the end of the 1920s is key to understanding the shift from Weimar democracy towards Nazi dictatorship. His research focused on youth welfare, a field which was in the centre of social policy reform in the 1920s, pushed by a progressive pedagogical movement and thus bringing the contradictory nature of the Weimar welfare state to the fore. Peukert argued that the progressive individual approach failed, both because of the financial constraints during the Great Depression, and the general lack of understanding concerning the living situation of the 'target group'. Thus, many young workers rejected the way welfare officers tried to shape their lives according to middle-class cultural norms. This resistance prompted welfare authorities to gradually embrace practices of segregation and coercion which – according to Peukert's main line of argument – were already inherent in the concepts of progressivism.[12] The element of correctional education is a case in point.

However, Young-Sun Hong challenged this interpretation and showed that the road toward Nazi welfare state was far more twisted. Her close look at those public and voluntary welfare personalities who designed reformist projects raises doubts about continuities and the pathological potential of progressive pedagogical policies. She states that 'the crisis of the pedagogical movement culminated in a state of resignation and intellectual disarray' giving eugenic reformers a chance to realize their own ideas of selective racial welfare.[13]

Other historians also argued that the enormous increase of needy people nourished a debate on the limits of public welfare and the possibilities of re-privatizing social care. During the Great Depression, private voluntary welfare organizations had to step in because of the overload that authorities had to deal with. Their engagement though was not only seen as a temporary complement, but as an improvement of welfare services that the state could not realize otherwise: private action stands for a less bureaucratic and more personal way of providing welfare. Among those promoting this idea was the Nazi party, which promised to replace the 'socialist' welfare state through a caring *Volksgemeinschaft*.[14]

Although the criticism of Weimar welfare politics played an important role in Nazi propaganda, a clear blueprint of the Nazi version of welfare was missing. Therefore, the Nazi takeover in 1933 didn't mark an explicit break, but it accelerated the transformation process towards a racial welfare state. What were the key ideas of Nazi social policy? How was the caring *Volksgemeinschaft* imagined? In 1934, Ludwig Brucker and Walter Schuhmann, both belonging to Nazi social policy circles, outlined what the Third Reich's welfare state should look like. The 'primacy of community over the individual' marks the organizing idea and therefore the core of Nazi welfare. According to Brucker and Schuhmann, welfare policy didn't aim at improving the lives of individuals but was directed towards serving the interest of the *Volksgemeinschaft* and strengthening the entire racial community. This led to a system based on neither means tests nor entitlements. In fact the welfare regime turned into a 'performance-oriented community' (*Leistungsgemeinschaft*), a term originally used by Nazi leaders, but which has been picked up by historiography for discussing state and society during the Third Reich.[15] Benefits were restricted to clients who met the racial, eugenic and political criteria of the *Volksgemeinschaft*. However, even those who did had to earn to be cared for by the community.[16]

In general, social insurance seems less influenced by Nazi ideology than the field of social assistance.[17] Thus, the main principles of German social legislation, such as compulsory contributions and the social insurance system itself, remained untouched. However, self-governing bodies came under state control, which reflects the trend towards a more centralized bureaucracy – which had already started under the rule of the so-called 'presidential cabinets' at the end of the Weimar Republic. The Nazi government also held onto cuts dating back to the Great Depression but, as prices rose as a consequence of the economic upturn in the mid-1930s, it meant that average welfare benefits actually dropped. Critics of Aly's account emphasized such indications in order to challenge his notion that the majority of Germans profited from the Third Reich's redistributive policies.[18]

Nevertheless, the Nazi dictatorship also left some fingerprints of its own on the world of social insurance. In 1933, the focus lay primarily on the newest pillar of the German insurance system, which only had been introduced in 1927: unemployment insurance. The Nazi government's central aim was to reduce unemployment – and it succeeded, partly because of job-creation schemes, which were mainly financed through insurance contributions. Emergency public works (*Notstandsarbeiten*) proved a most effective measure to bring down unemployment rates. People were heavily pressured to take up these poorly paid as well as exhausting jobs which served to improve public infrastructure, such as building gas and electricity networks, as well as reclaiming floodplains.[19] Thus, unemployment insurance and labour placement administration wasn't about supporting those who had lost their jobs, but demonstrating that the new regime represented a turn for the better.

But even after unemployment rates dropped significantly in the second half the 1930s, labour administration held onto, and even expanded, dirigiste measures. As early as 1935, a compulsory employment record book (*Arbeitsbuch*) was introduced, enabling the state to control the labour market and contain job turnovers.[20] In 1938, the government introduced civil conscriptions by law, as well as the obligation for those graduating from school to notify the labour placement office (*Arbeitsamt*).[21] All in all, coercive measures became more important while the rights of employees were reduced. The labour administration turned into an agency allocating manpower according to the political and military purposes of the Nazi regime.[22]

Scholars interested in the Third Reich's labour policy have, however, commented on these developments in two ways. On the one hand, they stress the fact that changes towards a more interventionist and repressive labour market policy didn't result from interventions of Nazi organizations, but were rather implemented by the state bureaucracy itself. Hence, they challenge the notion of the duality between the 'normative state' and the 'prerogative state' once defined by Ernst Fraenkel as a core element of Nazi rule; the labour administration wasn't pushed from outside, but transformed on its own.[23] It was part of a new form of public state governance, aiming to establish a mobilized *Volksgemeinschaft*.[24] On the other hand, several studies have shown that Nazi policy towards workers wasn't based on repressive measures alone. In fact, the regime held out offers such as social benefits, as well as material and non-material rewards. The German Labour Front (Deutsche Arbeitsfront, DAF) may mostly have failed to replace the destroyed unions, but it did push some significant improvements regarding home-based work and safety at work, particularly concerning young people and women.[25]

Although pension insurance didn't change to the same extent as unemployment insurance, there were some significant reforms under Nazi rule. One of the more innovative decisions concerning social security legislation led to an expansion of groups covered by social insurance. From 1937 onwards, the possibility of a voluntary enrolment in the pension scheme was offered to all Germans under the age of forty years, including those living abroad. One year later, tradesmen had to enter the pension insurance. Such a policy of turning the industrial workers' insurance into a people's insurance was strongly supported by the German Labour Front.[26] This development brought in more members and more revenues and so the assets of the pension fund grew during the Third Reich. It resulted from reduced spending, too: during the war in particular, people of retirement age were dragged into the labour market, thereby reducing the number of pensioners.[27] The surplus, including the one generated by the social insurance schemes open since 1937, were used to finance war-related policies.

Furthermore, expanding the groups covered by pension insurance dove-tailed well with the ideological concept of a people's community. Germans of all occupations within, as well as beyond, the national border were offered the possibility of enrolment in the social insurance schemes. But what happened to those defined as 'community aliens' (*Gemeinschaftsfremde*)? And to what extent was the pension insurance shaped by racial ideology?[28] Since 1937, a paragraph introduced in the Reich Insurance Code in 1936 enabled the Ministry of the Interior, together with the Ministry of Labour, to withdraw pensions from persons who were accused of 'actions hostile to the state' (*staatsfeindliche Betätigung*) and therefore had to face persecution.[29] Moreover, emigrants had to worry about taking their pension with them. They had to apply in order to receive payments abroad. Even if such transfers were granted, due to currency regulation the pension was reduced to a small amount.[30]

When the possibility of a voluntary enrolment was introduced, in 1937, it had some implications for the position of women within the German welfare state. Since feminist approaches have established gender as a key criteria of welfare state analysis, it is common to focus on how social policy shapes gender relations.[31] Nonetheless, research hasn't centred much on the gendered nature and effects of Nazi welfare, at least not in terms of social insurance.[32] But from a gendered perspective it is worth mentioning that the reform of 1937 opened pension insurance to housewives, who for the first time had the chance to earn entitlements on their own.[33] As soon as family carers could enrol in pension insurance schemes, the German welfare state's basis on salaried labour was challenged. Clearly, the inclusion of housewives was not the lawmaker's intention, but a side effect of opening pension insurance to self-employed individuals.

By contrast, on other occasions the Nazi government quite explicitly strengthened the ideal of a male breadwinner model, thus ensuring the economic dependency of women.[34] This was the case when, in 1937, it reintroduced the opportunity for married women to opt out of the worker's pension system. This idea dated back to the early days of the pension insurance scheme in 1889. During the 1920s, this provision had been abolished due to the pressure exerted by feminist politicians, who pointed to the severe implications of opting out for the women concerned: women whose husband died at a young age, or who got divorced, were especially vulnerable to poverty in old age. When Nazi social-policy makers reintroduced this provision, they also changed it in a significant way: women who got married could opt out even without quitting their job. In 1937, the regime had no interest in luring married women away from the labour market, and they expected that the extra money would help newlyweds to start a family.[35] This policy was motivated by pronatalist ideas.

The regime's racial population policy also shaped the restructuring of social insurance in 1942, at least those parts addressing women. For the first time, female wage earners were granted the possibility of taking early retirement: those who gave birth to at least four children and whose husband was already dead could leave the working place by the age of fifty-five. Certainly the law was very selective, because only very few women met the strict criteria.[36] Nevertheless it created the option of early retirement for women in Germany – it can thus be seen as a stepping stone. Since 1957, when one of the most important pension reforms in the history of the German welfare state was affected,[37] the possibility of early retirement (by the age of sixty years) has applied to all women, regardless of the number of childbirths and marital status.

All in all, it might be true that the main principles of the German social insurance system remained untouched by Nazi rule. In fact, plans for a significant restructuring like the 'Robert Ley plan' which, in 1940, foresaw introducing a tax-financed model of pension insurance, failed.[38] However, as soon as one asks about the groups covered and the rules of eligibility it becomes clear that social insurances, too, served the idea of Nazi *Volksgemeinschaft*.

Compared to social security, the world of social care and social assistance was much more shaped according to ideas of Nazi welfare. The face-to-face contact with clients enabled local welfare officers and social workers to intervene in their lives.[39] Social assistance served as a major tool to achieve certain political goals: racial purification, population growth, preparation for war, and integration into a people's community.[40] It led to a differential practice of social care. Those who were considered valuable could expect to be cared for, even in a more extensive way than before. Benefits and services directed to this part of the population increased, covering much more than financial help in situations of acute need. The discussion about a shift from a welfare regime centred on poor relief towards a middle-class oriented welfare regime seemed highly justified. However, this kind of promoting care came with strings attached, exposing the welfare recipient to mobilization efforts by the regime and constant re-evaluation concerning his worthiness and eligibility according to racial and eugenic criteria, and also political behaviour.

Promoting the racial valuable, fit and loyal groups of society was foremost assigned to the National Socialist People's Welfare (Nationalsozialistische Volkswohlfahrt, NSV), a Nazi mass organization, which at the beginning of the Second World war counted about fifteen million members. Originally founded in Berlin in 1932, by a group of municipal welfare officers and social workers, whose aim was to influence welfare action in a National Socialist sense, the NSV became the centre of welfare action within the Nazi party next to the DAF.[41] It complemented rather than replaced the work of the welfare authorities, but it took over tasks from the private voluntary welfare organizations, especially the Workers' Welfare Association, which was shut down in 1933, but also from church agencies. The latter were able to continue their work, but they were incorporated in the German Association of Voluntary Public Welfare (Arbeitsgemeinschaft der Freien Wohlfahrtspflege Deutschlands), which was led by the NSV and controlled by the state, despite the misleading title. The NSV provided welfare that aimed to gain immediate access to potential recipients. Counselling, non-cash benefits, and services, for example, for expectant mothers or families, demanded face-to-face-consultation, which offered to NSV functionaries a supervising role and enabled them to interfere in the private lives of people. Besides the assistance for mother and child (Hilfswerk Mutter und Kind), the NSV was best known for the winter relief organization (Winterhilfswerk, WHW), which started out as only a temporary solution in 1933, when the regime needed higher welfare revenues without raising taxes. However, with sums of about 566 Million RM collected in 1938/39 it turned into a main pillar of the welfare system in financial terms. Street collections didn't bring in its main source of funding; this was charges on wages, which were de facto compulsory. This should be taken into account in discussions about tax burdens during the Third Reich.[42]

Given the large number of volunteers and paid staff working for the NSV and the WHW, these organizations proved an important tool, keeping members busy and mobilizing them, especially during war. But even before, they already served purposes different than carrying out welfare. In 1937, these widespread structures were used, for example, to issue gas masks as part of preparations for future air raids.[43]

The Nazi welfare, defined as *Volkspflege*, comprised both the inclusion of *Volksgenossen* and the exclusion of those seen as racially and eugenically inferior. However, while social and political integration had been a leading principle of welfare state building in Germany since the Bismarckian era, and deliberating acceptable levels of inequality is a main characteristic of social policy,[44] carrying out welfare to the point of drawing borders and enacting exclusion genuinely derives from Nazi concepts of society.[45]

The implementation of the racial and eugenic programmes relied heavily on the public health administration, which gathered the information necessary for discrimination and persecution. In 1934, via the Law for the Standardization of Health Care System (Gesetz zur Vereinheitlichung des Gesundheitswesens) the state took control of municipal public health offices.[46] This reform contributed to a centralization of the German welfare system and the harmonization of existing local and regional differences. 'Hereditary and racial care' (*Erb- und Rassenpflege*) became the most important task of the public health offices dominating health care for prioritized groups like infants and pregnant women or traditional health protection.[47] The latter, though, drew more attention as soon as the possibility of a new war emerged on the horizon in the late 1930s. The fear of venereal diseases and tuberculosis drove efforts to improve health conditions, especially through vaccinations. However, after these measures turned out to be successful in the 1930s, shortages of vaccine as a consequence of bad planning led to a major backlash resulting in high mortality rates during the Second World War.[48]

Ordered by the Law for the Protection of the Hereditary Health of the German People and the Law for the Prevention of Hereditarily Diseased Offspring, which came into effect in 1933 and 1935 respectively, public welfare offices served as survey agencies gathering a great deal of data on the social and medical conditions of the population. Their preoccupation with hereditary and racial care, and related measures such as sterilization and 'euthanasia', shows that health care policies were mainly concerned with maintaining the vitality of the *Volkskörper* instead of curing individual illness.

It should be stressed that exclusion in welfare terms during Nazism went beyond neglect and discrimination. In fact, welfare authorities and organizations actively took part in the persecution of clients, and the socio-biological logic of social policy also had a radicalizing influence, as research has shown.

Complexities of Welfare-State Practices

How far could the concepts of Nazi welfare be translated into practice? And which insights are offered by exploring the routines of welfare authorities and their interaction with clients? Studies on welfare politics at a local level revolve mainly around three key questions. Firstly, they examine the elbow room possessed by welfare officers and social workers, and in so doing contribute to challenging the historiographical model of the Nazi state as a centrally directed machine. Secondly, the interest lies in the welfare clients and the question: to what extent do local welfare case files give insights in their living situations as well as their agency when fighting for their interests? Finally, studies stress the different shades of exclusion and inclusion as well as the complex relationship between these two modes of belonging.

Wolf Gruner's work explored the role of communal and municipal welfare offices in developing a racialized welfare policy towards German Jews. He stressed how ideological and financial motives merged: welfare authorities felt overburdened when an increasing number of Jews asked for social benefits and assistance at a time many of them were impoverished by intensifying discrimination and segregation. As a consequence, from the mid-1930s onwards, benefits were cut back, recipients forced to take up compulsory work (*Pflichtarbeit*), and welfare authorities advocated the total exclusion of the Jewish poor. In 1939, Jewish welfare organizations directed by the Reich Association of the Jews in Germany (Reichsvereinigung der Juden in Deutschland) were obliged to take over the care for all Jewish welfare clients.[49]

Not only does Gruner's study present ample evidence that welfare services and payments were important instruments of the discrimination and persecution policy towards German Jews, but he also successfully makes his point about the interplay of local and central governance. Several local authorities were well ahead of the leading circles in Berlin in designing a comprehensive racialized welfare policy. The German Council of Municipalities (Deutscher Gemeindetag) enabled local authorities to coordinate their anti-Jewish measures. Moreover, it was a 'mediator between the local and national levels'.[50]

It is the same story when we turn to consider the Sinti and Roma. Local welfare officers had many possibilities to treat them differently long before Nazi government decided on a general policy to that end. Starting in 1934 their standard rates were reduced, extra payments or non-financial benefits were even refused and male recipients had to perform compulsory work.[51] After the Nazi seizure of power in January 1933, communal and municipal authorities promoted a welfare policy designed along racist lines.

Those studies contribute to a body of research re-evaluating the functioning of the Nazi state, especially the dynamics of the centre and periphery in policy making. In contrast to earlier studies, recent accounts stress the autonomy of local bureaucracies implementing Nazi policies. The polycratic nature of Nazi rule released competitive as well as synergetic forces. While older accounts state that the instalment of Nazi parties' authorities, such as the Gau – and Kreisleitungen of the NSDAP led to overlapping competencies, and therefore competitions between local governments, new scholarship underlines the cooperation and catalytic effects.[52]

If communal and municipal welfare offices had room to manoeuvre regarding discriminatory and racist policies, they were all the more autonomous when it came to favouring certain welfare recipients. In this context Florian Wimmer emphasized it might be misleading to concentrate on standard rates, which remained at the same low level they had dropped to during the depression. In his study of public welfare in Munich, he demonstrates that public welfare offices had other ways of favouring certain groups. First of all they made use of extra benefits, which also served propaganda purposes. For example, when the exhibition hall Haus der Deutschen Kunst opened in 1937, needy artists got one-off benefits of up to 100 RM. Christmas and Hitler's birthday also marked recurring occasions for extra payments.[53]

While such one-off payments probably had a limited impact on the recipients' living standards, the extent to which income from other transfers was considered made a bigger difference. The latter means a significant modification of the principle of subsidiarity, which strongly shaped the German welfare system. Nevertheless, as Wimmer outlined, as early as 1934, laws and acts adopted by the government favoured groups such as small capital pensioners (*Kleinrentner*), social pensioners (*Sozialrentner*), and victims of war, by raising the limits of personal allowances. Even more striking is the fact that benefits granted by the Nazi organization were not at all taken into account, and thus had the character of additional revenue, which increases their effects on the living standards of recipients. During the Weimar Republic it had been common practice to deal with financial allowances from church agencies in the same way. However, the benefits provided by NSV, WHW and DAF were of a wholly different dimension.[54]

These findings challenge the notion of the missing activity of Nazi government in the field of social assistance, which was repeatedly claimed in the case of the victims of war.[55] However, the regime established hierarchies among the recipients of social assistance, favouring certain groups and reflecting racial and eugenic criteria, but also political and welfare categories. This body of research also reveals the decisive role played by the individual welfare officers and social workers. So far, studies have concentrated mainly on female social workers and how they took part in disciplining and marshalling welfare recipients. Even more, they assisted the forced sterilization and 'euthanasia' programme of the Nazi government by reporting on people in their care. With the phrasing of their reports they influenced crucial decisions, such as whether a person was to be sterilized, and even worse judgements concerning who was defined as 'unworthy of life'. [56] Hence, the vocational group of female social workers shed some light on women as perpetrators within Nazi society. It is also an example of how social care can be seen as an extensively female part of enacting social engineering.

Primary sources documenting the day-to-day practice of welfare not only provide insights into the thinking and acting of social welfare workers but also concerning the attitudes of welfare recipients. Some of the clients protested against the decisions made by the authorities.[57] The majority of complaints were turned down, but some did succeed. The Genetic Health Court (Erbgesundheitsgericht) revised one third of the contested decisions it had under review.[58] Objecting to and complaining about the welfare state's decisions concerning themselves, gave clients the possibility to negotiate with the authorities, but in a very limited way. We have learned from research on the GDR that petitionary letters and protests kept up the communication between individuals and rulers, hence playing a role in preventing openly expressed criticism, which was difficult to do within a dictatorship.[59] Moreover, when examining the petitionary letters of people who had to face sterilization or other severely discriminatory measures, we can hardly speak of a chance to speak out, but a necessity of struggling for personal physical integrity and even life itself. Nevertheless, these documents reveal parts of the self-perception and individual interest of victims of Nazi persecution. Scholars interested in 'euthanasia' policies have put some effort into exploring this piece of history from the perspective of patients. In so doing they highlight the many ways in which people challenged the officials' narrative of their case by contrasting it with their own version. For example, coachman Karl Ahrendt had been placed into psychiatric care in 1907 because he had pretended to be a general, wearing a uniform, and seemed to be disoriented. His medical record held letters that show he tried to get discharged by proving his sanity. In 1936, he strongly criticized the newly adopted practice that patients able to work got different food and tobacco: the 82-year-old man pointed to the fact the he had worked enough during his lifetime and therefore deserved to be treated in the same way. His claims weren't successful; at least they didn't lead to a discharge. As a patient unable to perform work he was killed after thirty-four years of institutionalization.[60]

The documents of welfare recipients let us have a look at counter narratives and the ways people opposed discriminatory policies and repressive measures; they also shed light on the dissemination of Nazi ideology and propaganda among this group. Petitionary letters written by bereaved family members of killed soldiers during the Second World War tell a good deal about how individuals drew on concepts of Nazi ideology when promoting their own case, such as a widow did, whose husband was killed in action in 1941. She mentioned the 'heroic death' (*Heldentod*) of her husband three times in her letter in order to argue for benefits she expected to receive from the military welfare officer.[61] In another case, a soldier wrote on behalf of his aunt, complaining about how long it took to get the relevant paperwork taken care of. He spoke of her as a war widow, whose husband had fulfilled his duty to the fatherland. She and other war widows, he continued, should feel the 'solidarity of our fighting people'. Otherwise, he predicted, or almost threatened the addressee of his letter, that military morale and power would be undermined.[62] Even a female farmer used the 'right' phrasing when she demanded payments for her dead son's fiancée and child; because, in her opinion, in the case of the 'heroic death' of a soldier, the state was obliged to care for the bereaved.[63] All these examples indicate that individuals were well aware of how to communicate with officials and how to present themselves as being entitled to social policy benefits. Christoph Sachße und Florian Tennstedt stressed the fact that the Nazi officials used welfare benefits and services as a way of rewarding individuals and in so doing stripped them of stigmatized notions.[64] Indeed, those asking for social care had to prove their need and entitlement. Yet, regarding evidence of individual experiences, it is difficult to tell whether the Nazi era gave rise to a new type of self-confident welfare client.

Nevertheless, focusing on welfare recipients and their fight for their own interests gives reason to reconsider current interpretations about the characteristics of Nazi welfare. It might seem paradoxical that a welfare system, which claimed the primacy of the community, addressed the individuality of those in need. Quite recently, though, Moritz Föllmer has stressed that Nazi Germany was not all about the collective. He explores 'a Nazi version of cultivating individuality'[65] and finds evidence in the fields of consumption, the labour market, and eventually welfare. The director of the Berlin Welfare and Youth Office, interviewed by the *Völkische Beobachter* in 1937, praised the individual care provided to needy people. Ego documents regarding the everyday practice of social assistance, like the claims of welfare recipients, show us what they saw as their own rights and a more personal provision of care.[66]

Another argument why the primacy of the community drew attention to individual cases can be seen in the ubiquitous procedures of 'evaluating' people within Nazi society. First of all the Nazi party and its organizations carried out the task of investigating the backgrounds of individuals. When individuals applied for a position within the civil service, or soldiers got married, Nazi Party officials had to assess their political behaviour. Equally, welfare benefits like marriage loans (*Ehestandsdarlehen*) and child allowances, (the latter were introduced in 1936), required such assessments.[67] This bore striking similarities to the manner in which social workers became investigators, using home visits to gather information about daily routines, family lives and the household skills of people who asked for assistance. Every case had to be evaluated according to racial, eugenic and political criteria and the act of surveying drew attention to the individual situation of recipients and what shaped a highly differentiated practice of welfare.[68]

Indeed it is a correlation worth mentioning; Nazi society offered many situations where individual fulfilment was possible and individual initiative necessary. The importance of the 'common weal' highlighted by NSV slogans and in programmatic writings on welfare policy did not deny individuality when translated into practice. In contrast, in order to decide if potential recipients were worthy, their backgrounds had to be checked and they thereby became visible as individuals to the authorities.

Finally, the examination of welfare practices gives a more complex understanding of the interrelationships of inclusion and exclusion. It is well established that under Nazi rule inclusive politics were linked to exclusionary processes. However, the research on welfare and poverty has shown that these phenomena cannot be reduced to a binary dichotomy. In fact, welfare states generate politics of exclusion, which aim on inclusion at some points or under certain conditions.[69] Such cases can be observed when exploring the persecution of the so-called *Arbeitsscheue*, or 'work shy' people. This category was already in use during the Weimar Republic, but only after 1933 did work became a focal point in evaluating the population and emphasizing the character of the *Volksgemeinschaft* as a community centred on achievement.[70]

The treatment of unemployed individuals who refused a job offer, as well as workers leaving their workplace, changed rapidly after the Nazi takeover. Some of them could end up in workhouses (*Arbeitshäusern*) or even in concentration camps. However, their imprisonment could be a temporary measure aiming at imposing certain behaviour. Again, authorities focused on work performance as a criterion for deciding about a discharge.[71] Thus, exclusion could lead to inclusion, but reservations often remained. Those discharged from concentration camps or other detention facilities were still exposed to police surveillance.

A different kind of inclusive exclusion concerned the victims of sterilization. At the beginning of the Second World War, local Nazi offices as well as local health authorities founded marriage offices for the purpose of arranging marriages between persons who had been sterilized. This represented a partial offer of reintegration; as long as the new couples remained in a relationship with one another, not others.[72]

Furthermore, it could be stressed that individuals experienced alternating processes of inclusion und exclusion throughout their lives. Much research has emphasized the marginalization of the elderly during the Third Reich, as expressed by meagre improvements of pension rates.[73] Benjamin Möckel has argued that within an achievement-oriented community, the notion of retirement as a time in life when past efforts should be rewarded, was strongly contested by social policy officials and scholars interested in age and ageing. This policy line culminated in the mobilization of the elderly during the war: men aged sixty-five and over represented a valuable workforce as soon as younger men were drafted to serve in the Wehrmacht.[74] But there is also a different part of the story to be told. Local welfare offices put some effort into improving conditions in residential care. New homes were founded offering single and two bedrooms even for those elderly persons who depended on welfare benefits. These initiatives were driven by a discourse about granting a well-deserved old age on the one hand and pragmatic ideas on the other: the elderly should be attracted to move into residential care homes, leaving their larger dwellings for young families.[75]

When air-raid bombing aggravated the housing situation in German cities, the elderly were put under much more pressure. If their homes were destroyed and no family member was willing to care for them, some had to move into residential care facilities. Towards the end of the war, many experienced discrimination in the fields of medicine and medical care. Even worse, as Winfried Süß has shown, in some regions, frail elderly individuals were transferred to institutions which were involved in the 'euthanasia' program and were subsequently murdered; others died because of the systematic neglect in poorly equipped provisional homes.[76] Despite some attempts to improve the living conditions of the elderly during the 1930s, old age bore the potential of exclusion after a lifetime of social integration. This could be said about other periods as well, though the effects of age-related discrimination were not as lethal as in Germany during the Second World War.

War-Related Hardships and Emergency Welfare

To what extent did the Second World War change the German welfare regime? Recently the political scientist Hans Obinger and the historian Klaus Petersen called for a systematic re-evaluation of 'the relationship between war and the welfare state'.[77] They claim comprehensive accounts examining the full range of programmatic and institutional innovations are still lacking. On the one hand, new welfare programmes emerged and others expanded due to war-related hardships; on the other, there was 'a sharp trade-off between guns and butter', which stopped welfare state expansion or even caused financial cuts in social protection schemes.[78]

The failing of a general pension insurance reform in 1942 is a prominent example of the latter tendency. The Ministry of Labour was aiming to raise benefits and it partly succeeded in implementing some improvements for miners. However, the ministry's idea to increase benefits for all insured persons was vetoed by the Ministry of Finances, Lutz Graf Schwerin von Krosigk, who argued that in times of war he couldn't agree to such a rise in social spending.[79]

By contrast, other social groups were better cared for than ever before. Social-policy making during the Second World War concentrated to a considerable extent on the family members of soldiers. As during the First World War, they were able to apply for separation allowances and, compared to the situation twenty-five years earlier, these payments were generous. This welfare scheme was mainly motivated by the Nazi leaders' fear of a collapsing home front, which – according to them – had caused the defeat of November 1918. However, even if the separation allowance was created to ease the burden on wives and children at home, it was also directed towards the soldiers themselves, who should be assured that the state would care for their loved ones while they were risking their lives.[80]

Götz Aly draws on such material benefits, when he outlines his concept of a 'feel-good dictatorship'.[81] But did the extra money available for military wives maintain loyalty to the Nazi regime? Responding to Aly's argument, Birthe Kundrus points to the existence of an 'entitlement mentality' which resulted in emotions of gratitude as much as in feelings of disappointment.[82]

What happened to families when soldiers died? One of the most important sectors of Nazi welfare during the war, and one which was long neglected in later historical research, was care for the dependants of soldiers killed on active service. Unlike other welfare benefits and services, those involving the care of the bereaved were not cut back by the Nazi regime.

Some preliminary remarks need to be made about the structure of this welfare sector. Care for surviving family members of war casualties was assigned to the Wehrmacht administration by law in 1938.[83] The Wehrmacht High Command had asked for this assignment in order to control all areas that concerned soldiers, even those dealing with their relatives. The National Socialist War Victims' Charity (Nationalsozialistische Kriegsopferversorgung, NSKOV), too, had claimed, since the early 1930s, responsibility for transferring the care of veterans and the bereaved family members of dead soldiers to the army. In so doing, the victims of war should be clearly distinguished from other welfare clients. Actually this meant returning to the bureaucratic structures of the Kaiserreich.[84] The decision of 1938 did not last very long; at the war's end the administration of these matters reverted to the Ministry of Labour, which again handled all bereavement issues.[85] However, it was not only for the military to decide: in addition, the Nazi Party and its affiliated organizations, especially the NSKOV, offered non institutional services. In the case of the death of husbands or sons, bereaved women received help from more than one side. From the perspective of welfare recipients, this polycracy could be very useful.

The majority of adults receiving some form of welfare were women, and therefore welfare officers of the Wehrmacht and SS, as well as officials from the National Socialist War Victims' Charity, were all specifically advised on how to deal with women.[86] Benefits and services were enhanced during the war. Rates were increased and, more importantly, the group of recipients expanded. Parents who had been dependent on the income of sons who had died could receive a pension. Fiancées were entitled to pensions and other benefits if their betrothed had fallen in action and they could prove that a marriage had been planned.[87] The Nazi regime provided pensions and bereavement payments as well as non-material services such as helping with paperwork, finding new accommodation, making donations of furniture, and so on. Care measures began right from the moment when the notification of a soldier's death arrived. Nazi leaders were afraid that grieving women would lose faith in their political leadership, and so they tried very hard to control grief, not only at a symbolic level (especially through official grieving ceremonies) but also by ensuring that surviving relatives did not run into financial difficulties.[88]

While archival sources may provide a clear insight into the intentions of the Nazi regime, social reality involves much more complex considerations. Although the benefits and services eased the situation of many women, documents expressing gratitude towards the regime were rare. Because problems and criticisms are recorded much more often than acquiescence, the documents tell us a good deal about disappointment and anger within the population. It is worth taking a closer look at the reasons mentioned in these complains. Women criticized payment rates, but more often the process of applying for benefits and services and accessing them. This was an intrinsic problem caused by Nazi propaganda, which created an expectation of easy procedures. The Nazi leaders had promised to provide welfare in a non-bureaucratic manner, unlike the welfare administration of the Weimar Republic, which they accused of having forgotten the people's needs.[89] Even if this ideal did affect how welfare was managed in practice, provision was still carried out by bureaucratic institutions that had to go through the administrative process of reviewing and approving claims. Many conflicts concerning the so-called *Wehrdienstbeschädigung* were caused by welfare officers' obligation to determine that the death of a soldier was related to his military service in order to decide regarding relatives' entitlement to bereavement benefits.[90] For example, cases where the soldier in question had died because of a disease or had committed suicide did not normally qualify for the *Wehrdienstbeschädigung*. If provisions were denied because of these reasons, family members got very angry. In 1941, a war widow who lived near Coburg, and was the mother of three minor children, complained when she learned that these benefits had been denied her. Her husband had died of cancer and the physician in charge had stated that, in his opinion, this bore no relation to military service. Nevertheless, the widow challenged this decision by criticizing the authorities' bureaucratic manner and presenting herself as the only expert who was able to properly judge her deceased husband's state of health. She did not succeed, but many others did.[91]

Similarly to what can be observed when looking at separation allowances, the examination of documents related to the care for the bereaved tells different stories about welfare and mass loyalty. This corresponds with the findings of research on welfare in the late Weimar Republic, which have shown that gratitude and criticism were inextricably linked among welfare recipients. Furthermore, the reactions of those disappointed about services and benefits did not flow in one direction.[92] Returning to the Nazi period, it seems an oversimplification to point to the material self-interest of individuals as an explanation for the regime's stability during the war. However, even if the examination of everyday welfare practices may not explain the cohesion of wartime German society, it offers some insights into the roles of welfare recipients as well as the care of the bereaved.

Some women had to attract officials' attention before being awarded welfare provisions. Some unmarried women who had children by soldiers claimed for bereavement allowances, arguing that a wedding had already been planned. In their letters these women referred to population policy arguments, presenting themselves as favourable clients.[93] They accused the officials of ignoring this Nazi principle by insisting on legal marriage documents. In 1940, young unmarried mothers got the chance to apply for bereavement benefits. This became much easier when in 1941 the ex post marriage was affected by decree.[94] The example of unmarried women indicates that potential welfare recipients were proactive and even shaped the practices of the welfare state during the war.

Under Nazi rule, welfare was not only an instrument for integration, but also a means of disciplining and marshalling people. Apart from the demand for good political behaviour, the female population was pressurized when it came to issues of love and sexual relations outside marriage. The welfare administration was able to withdraw pensions and benefits if women were declared 'unworthy', as they were in cases of alleged adultery.[95] In order to formalize the process of withdrawal, a law was passed in March 1943 to make such action legal.[96]

Analysis of this particular piece of marital legislation shows that women were not just passive recipients. When it came to the withdrawal of benefits, the administration did not act without corroborating evidence. Welfare officers needed confirmation of their suspicions – perhaps a new-born child that could not be the offspring of the dead soldier. More often relatives, particularly the parents of the soldier, accused the widow of adultery and sued for an ex post divorce.[97] In so doing, parents had a better chance of securing entitlement to bereavement payments. An ex post divorce also affected questions regarding inheritance. Here, parental actions aiming at improving their own status contributed to the regime's exclusionary measures.

All in all, the care for widows and other bereaved relatives suggests that proactive behaviour was rewarded. Knowing how to communicate with welfare authorities became an important ability for individuals in order to improve their own living situations.

While the care for the bereaved was an already existing sector of welfare policy which expanded during the war, services for civilians, who were exposed to the effects of air raids, had to be built up from the ground. Air raids placed the populations of cities (where women were in the majority) right in the middle of a battlefield. Those who lost their homes or suffered injury needed help, and not everyone could count on family and friends when looking for food, drink, clothing and a place to stay. Local social workers and officials from local branches of Nazi organizations became aware of this problem and took action by establishing reception points.[98]

After air raids these reception points were much frequented, especially by people who were home based. In the meantime, factories and other places of work looked after their employees, and became important for organizing daily living under the conditions of war. It could be said that the reception points had the same function for non-workers. Bombed-out people received not only food and clothes, but replacements for documents such as identity cards and ration stamps. Furthermore, the NSV made evacuation arrangements for those who had no occupation within the city.[99] The examination of post air-raid relief measures shows that the number of people depending on welfare benefits and services – even it was only temporary – increased during the war. A study of the testimonies of people from Kassel, who experienced the major air raid of 22 March 1943, reveals that many had to make use of the Party's relief work in order to ensure their survival and that of their families. These testimonies were collected by a community office searching for missing people; some made their way to the archives and were later edited as survivors' accounts.[100] Even though they were produced for a different purpose, they clearly show the efforts made by women to get on after air raids, and to what extent they needed the assistance provided at the reception points.

In post air-raid relief work, however, by far the most challenging task was to manage evacuations. Official programmes were started in September 1940, sending children from Berlin, Hamburg and the Ruhr area to rural regions.[101] Children under the age of six had to be accompanied by their mothers, who accordingly had a chance to leave the bombed cities themselves. It was not until the bombing became especially severe, in 1942, that the Nazi leadership agreed to proceed with the evacuation of adults living in the cities. Women and the elderly with no work obligations had to go to 'non-threatened reception areas' where bombing was not yet a part of everyday life. When the numbers of damaged homes rose and the disruption to essential services (electricity, gas and water) increased, evacuation became not only a question of safety, but a necessity: there was overwhelming deprivation within the cities. In January 1945, the number of evacuees reached 9 million. According to official statistics, 1.8 million people arranged their own evacuation, but the majority joined the NSV's evacuation programme.[102]

A 53-year-old woman from Karlsruhe, interviewed by the United States Strategic Bombing Survey (USSBS), recalled how she and her daughters left the city after a big raid in 1944:

> The office of the local Nazi branch told us to leave Karlsruhe. Hundreds of people left. We had been put up in the vocational school for fourteen days. So we were sent to a small town, Demmingen near Effingen. It's about two hours by train. Everything was arranged for and paid for. We got a slip of paper and were told where to go and when to leave. We were put up in the house of a woman who had a big farm.[103]

Since there were plenty of women who had no family to go to when their own homes were destroyed, care for evacuees became one of the most important tasks undertaken by the NSV and other Nazi organizations. In spite of difficulties and confusions in the evacuation programme (especially towards the end of the war), the morale division of the USSBS, in its summarizing report, stated that 'the advantages had outweighed its disadvantages'.[104] When the USSBS interviewers asked about evacuation experiences, they were very surprised by the respondents' answers: they showed much less dissatisfaction than they had expected. The official German intelligence reports had pictured a high degree of discontent, but the morale division of the USSBS came to a different conclusion. In hindsight, we may suspect that the majority of evacuees valued their general reception and forgot about the attendant difficulties. Furthermore, even if women were unhappy with their circumstances away from home, this does not mean they condemned the whole Nazi system or questioned the legitimacy of the regime.

Unhappy or not, many evacuated women relied on the NSV or the NSF while travelling to their reception areas, and also when they arrived. Their needs, for furniture and a place to cook, and their troubles, perhaps friction with their hosts, gave them reasons to get in touch with the Nazi organizations, or else with the churches (which were also very concerned). A collection of letters written by Protestant evacuees of Wuppertal to their pastor gives an insight into how they settled in and where they could turn for help. In 1943, a woman with two children was looking for new accommodation since she could not stay with her relatives any longer, with whom she had initially moved in. Desperate for any help, she contacted the pastor but also applied to the NSV, which found a place for the family at a farm in northern Thuringia.[105]

Based on such letters and other primary sources, some observations may be made. The evacuees used any help available to solve the problems they faced while settling down and learning to get along in unfamiliar surroundings. The stories they told later about muddling through after the air raids testify not only to individual achievements, but also to a collective enterprise and a high degree of mutual support. With the ending of the Second World War air raids stopped, but providing emergency care still remained necessary. While the Allies at first suspended most items of social security legislation, social care provisions had to continue.[106]

Concluding Remarks

This chapter started off by outlining the new interest in welfare practices under Nazi rule, which is linked to the debate concerning the people's community (*Volksgemeinschaft*) and the levels of social and cultural cohesion within German society between 1933 and 1945. Such an approach may extend our understandings of the Nazi welfare state, which has thus far been seen as driven by racial and eugenic ideologies and the primacy of the community. What do we learn from this rather fine-grained analysis?

Two findings are of certain significance. Firstly, inclusion and exclusion, always part of state welfare policies, were stressed with overwhelming vigour during the Nazi era. By focusing on practices and perceptions of individuals it becomes evident that both aspects were intertwined. On the one hand, the temporary exclusion of German 'asocials' (*Asoziale*), who could potentially be reintegrated in the people's community, differed fundamentally from the treatment of those persecuted for reasons of race. On the other hand, individuals could gain access to welfare benefits by exposing others to discrimination and exclusion, as the example of care for bereaved women highlights.

Secondly, the programmatic statements of the regime aimed to place the community before the individual. And yet, the working out of these ideas and principles solicited individualistic rather than collectivistic practices. In order to decide on the worthiness of potential recipients, evaluating the individual case in hand became more important. Moreover, while collective protest was hardly possible under Nazi rule, people were able to use letters written to welfare authorities to express discontent.

While the First World War is seen as a 'turning point in the development of the welfare state' and a catalyst for its expansion, German historiography seems more hesitant when it comes to the influence of the conflict between 1939 and 1945.[107] The emergence of new poor demographics, such as war widows and veterans, provoked the rethinking of how clients were treated and the state discovered its interventionist power. Yet one question remains: what were the outcomes and legacies of the Third Reich and Second World War regarding the welfare regimes of post-war Germany? There are at least three places worth looking. Firstly, there are some thoroughly documented examples where Nazi legislation was partly confirmed after 1945. The maternity protection law is one prime example. Nazi leaders paid little attention to maternity protection legislation until 1942, at least not in legislative terms, but, in 1942, benefits were significantly increased: the law offered payments of full wages six weeks before and after childbirth.[108] However, the most striking aspect of the new act was the extension of coverage. Agricultural workers, domestic servants and so-called unpaid family workers (*helfende Familienangehörige*) were entitled to benefits, too. This provision significantly changed the way maternity protection was designed. For the first time, non-salaried labour was also recognized. Although the Maternity Protection Act existed only on paper and was not implemented due to the war, the wartime extensions concerning benefits and coverage were reasserted by the West German Parliament in 1952, whereas its racial and eugenic contents were stripped away.[109] What about other less familiar continuities? Are there patterns suggesting that changes implemented during the Nazi period were continued after 1945?

In order to get a fuller picture of these legacies, the post-war period has to be studied carefully by tracing arguments and decisions back to antecedents during the war years. This is the case when we look at the lowering of the mandatory retirement age for women in the pension reform of 1957. It was argued by politicians that female workers had to manage a double burden, because of their responsibility for the family and household and that they would therefore be exhausted earlier. This argument was not a new one. However, the hardships women had experienced during the war represented an important impetus to push early retirement for female workers.[110]

Secondly, referring to the Third Reich and its programmes was also a powerful argument to delegitimize reform proposals in the post-war period. This can be observed in 1946/47, when the Allies prepared a draft to introduce a social insurance model that would cover the entire population in a uniformly organized system. Those Germans opposing to these plans 'received ideological reinforcement from anti-Nazi arguments'.[111] The way the Allied draft aimed at centralization and collectivism within the social insurance system indeed resembled schemes favoured by the German Labour Front. Such arguments may have been used as a political strategy, while the material interests of private insurance companies and vocational groups motivated the opposition. Nevertheless, it can be seen as part of a discursive practice which shaped the social policy-making process.

Thirdly, it might be useful to consult British historiography, where it is fairly common to analyse the Second World War as a pacemaker for the post-war settlement.[112] Innovation induced by the effects of war did not only materialize in terms of new or modified provisions, but concerned institutional settings as well. There is a significant body of research exploring voluntary action and the third sector, arguing that the Second World War accelerated the establishing of new voluntary action schemes and organizations. In so doing, Matthew Hilton and others have challenged the older notion of a decline of voluntary action due to welfare state expansion in the second half of the twentieth century. On the contrary, the voluntary sector wasn't opposed to the state, but rather developed a very close relationship with its agencies. Hence, British historians are interested in the 'moving frontier' between the third sector and the state.[113]

Is this a promising perspective for the German case as well? Ewald Frie has shown by focusing on one of the major welfare associations, the Caritas, that the third sector participated in the 'golden era of welfare state expansion'. Furthermore he stresses the Nazi period's legacies when he claims that the Caritas had undergone major changes between 1933 and 1945. Its self-perception benefitted much from the idea that it had not been an adherent of the regime – strengthening its position and legitimacy after 1945. Another indicator as to what extent the war restructured the third sector can be found when looking at the Workers' Welfare Institution. It changed its appearance in the postwar era and became less recognizable as a socialist charity. 'Profiting from the distribution of NSV property, the organization greatly expanded the number of institutions it maintained (41 in 1930, 152 in 1949), thereby tacitly abandoning its hostility to private charitable activity'.[114]

Focusing systematically on the legacies and continuities concerning social insurance, as well as social assistance provision across the year 1945, ultimately contributes to a historicization of the 'golden era of welfare state expansion' during the 1950s and 1960s. If we look at these trends from the perspective of contemporary welfare clients, it becomes evident that many Germans, at least those who were seen as belonging to the *Volksgemeinschaft*, received some kind of welfare benefit and care during the war. Thus, there is some justification for seeing the Second World War as a starting point of the welfare expansion after 1945, but without neglecting the fact that ideologies of welfare changed significantly.

Notes

1. M. Broszat. 1987. 'Plädoyer für eine Historisierung des Nationalsozialismus', in H. Graml and K.-D. Henke (eds), *Nach Hitler. Der schwierige Umgang mit unserer Geschichte. Beiträge von Martin Broszat.* Munich: Oldenbourg, p. 171.

2. K.H. Roth. 1993. *Intelligenz und Sozialpolitik im "Dritten Reich": eine methodisch-historische Studie am Beispiel des Arbeitswissenschaftlichen Instituts der Deutschen Arbeitsfront.* Munich: Saur, p. 12.

3. For the whole range of current approaches, even critical ones, see: M. Steber and B. Gotto (eds). 2014. *Visions of Community in Nazi Germany. Social Engineering and Private Lives.* Oxford: Oxford University Press.

4. G. Aly. 2008. *Hitler's Beneficiaries. Plunder, Racial War, and the Nazi Welfare.*

5. See, for example: A. Tooze, 'Einfach verkalkuliert', in *taz Magazin*, 12 March 2005. www.taz.de/pt/2005/03/12/a0289.nf/text.ges,1 (retrieved 15 May 2016). See also the review panel of the online review journal *sehepunkte*: http://www.sehepunkte. de/2005/07/forum/goetz-aly-hitlers-volksstaat-raub-rassenkrieg-und-nationaler-sozialismus-frankfurt-am-2005-98/ (retrieved 15 May 2016).

6. See, especially W. Süß's review of G. Aly. 2005. *Hitlers Volksstaat. Raub, Rassenkrieg und nationaler Sozialismus* Frankfurt/Main: Fischer, in *sehepunkte* 5(2005): 7/8: http://www.sehepunkte.de/2005/07/7698.html (retrieved 16 May 2016).

7. Sachße, Ch. and F. Tennstedt. 1992. *Geschichte der Armenfürsorge in Deutschland*, vol. 3: *Der Wohlfahrtsstaat im Nationalsozialismus.* Stuttgart et.al.: Kohlhammer.

8. For the trends of recent research on welfare and poverty, see Lutz Raphael's introduction in this volume. Also, B. Althammer. 2014. 'Introduction: Poverty and Deviance in the Era of the Emerging Welfare State', in B. Althammer, A. Gestrich and J. Gründler (eds), *The Welfare State and the 'Deviant Poor' in Europe 1870–1933.* Basingstoke: Palgrave Macmillan, pp. 13–14.

9. W. Rudloff 1998. *Die Wohlfahrtsstadt. Kommunale Ernährungs-, Fürsorge- und Wohnungspolitik am Beispiel Münchens 1910–1933*, 2 vols. Göttingen: Vandenhoeck & Ruprecht; D. Crew. 1998. *Germans on Welfare. From Weimar to Hitler.* Oxford, New York: Oxford University Press; Y.-S. Hong. 1998. *Welfare, Modernity, and the Weimar State, 1919–1933.* Princeton: Princeton University Press.

10. For the interpretation of the First World War as a pacemaker of German social policy, see: M. Stolleis. 2013. *Origins of the German Welfare State. Social Policy to 1945.* Berlin, Heidelberg: Springer, p. 146.

11. Sachße and Tennstedt, *Geschichte der Armenfürsorge in Deutschland*, pp. 273–274.

12. D.J.K. Peukert. 1986.*Grenzen der Sozialdisziplinierung. Aufstieg und Krise der deutschen Jugendfürsorge 1878 bis 1932.* Cologne: Bund, p. 132.

13. Hong, *Welfare*, p. 240. Five years earlier, Elizabeth Harvey, who was exploring welfare politics related to young workers, was already arguing in the same direction. See E. Harvey. 1993. *Youth and the Welfare State in Weimar Germany.* Oxford: Clarendon Press, pp. 297–98.

14. Crew, *Germans*, pp. 208–11.

15. The term was first discussed by Timothy Mason, focusing on labour policy and the DAF; see: T. Mason. 1993. *Social Policy and the Third Reich. The Working Class and the 'National Community'.* Providence, Oxford: Berg Publishers, pp. 212, 219.

Also see H.U. Wehler. 2003. *Deutsche Gesellschaftsgeschichte: Vom Beginn des Ersten Weltkrieges bis zur Gründung der beiden deutschen Staaten 1914–1949.* Munich: Beck, vol. 4, p. 793.

16. B. Gotto and M. Steber, 'Introduction', in Steber and Gotto, *Visions of Community*.

17. Ch. Sachße and F. Tennstedt. 1992. 'Der Wohlfahrtsstaat im Nationalsozialismus', *Zeitschrift für Sozialreform* 38:131–32.

18. M. Spoerer and J. Streb. 2013. 'Guns and Butter – but not Margarine: The Impact of Nazi Economic Policies on German Food Consumption, 1933–1938', *Jahrbuch für Wirtschaftsgeschichte* 1:77. For empirical data on living standards in Germany during the 1930s, see: A. Wagner. 2007. 'Ein Human Development Index für Deutschland und die Entwicklung des Lebensstandards im "Dritten Reich", 1933–1939', *Vierteljahrschrift für Sozial- und Wirtschaftsgeschichte*, 94:309–32.

19. Recently, Detlev Humann has re-evaluated Nazi labour policy on a very broad empirical base. Among other things, he stresses the importance of the emergency public works for bringing down unemployment rates as well as for introducing repressive measures into the labour market. See D. Humann. 2011. *'Arbeitsschlacht'. Arbeitsbeschaffung und Propaganda in der NS-Zeit 1933.* Göttingen: Wallstein, pp. 241–89.

20. 'Gesetz über die Einführung eines Arbeitsbuches' from 26 February 1935, in RGBl. I, S., p. 311. The employment record books were completely issued in June 1938. These documents enabled the labour administration to produce statistical surveys. See S. Werner, H. Degner and M. Adamo. 2011. 'Hitlers gläserne Arbeitskräfte. Das Arbeitsbuch als Quelle von Mikrodaten für die historische Arbeitsmarktforschung', *Jahrbuch für Wirtschaftsgeschichte*, pp. 175–91.

21. D. Meskill. 2010. *Optimizing the German workforce from Bismarck to the Economic Miracle.* New York, Oxford: Berghahn Books, pp. 159–61; K. Linne. 2014. 'Von der Arbeitsvermittlung zum Arbeitseinsatz. Zum Wandel der Arbeitsverwaltung 1933–1945', in M. Wildt and M. Buggeln (eds), *Arbeit im Nationalsozialismus.* Munich: Oldenbourg, pp. 56–62.

22. This is stated by H.G. Hockerts. 2011. 'Das Gewicht der Tradition. Die deutsche Nachkriegssozialpolitik und der Beveridge-Plan', in H.G. Hockerts (ed.). *Der deutsche Sozialstaat. Entfaltung und Gefährdung seit 1945.* Göttingen: Vandenhoeck & Ruprecht, p. 51.

23. Linne, 'Arbeitsvermittlung', pp. 69–70.

24. For this new approach to state and governance during the Nazi period, see: R. Hachtmann. 2007. 'Neue Staatlichkeit: Überlegungen zu einer systematischen Theorie des NS-Herrschaftssystems und ihrer Anwendung auf die mittlere Ebene der Gaue' in J. John, H. Möller and T. Schaarschmidt (eds), *Die Gaue. Regionale Mittelinstanzen im zentralistischen Führerstaat.* Munich: Oldenbourg.

25. M. Schneider. 1999. *Unterm Hakenkreuz. Arbeiter und Arbeiterbewegung 1933 bis 1939.* Bonn: Dietz, pp. 238–40.

26. Sachße and Tennstedt, *Wohlfahrtsstaat*, pp. 61–62; Stolleis, *Origins of the German Welfare State*, p. 146.

27. B. Möckel. 2010. *'Nutzlose Volksgenossen'? – Der Arbeitseinsatz alter Menschen im Nationalsozialismus.* Berlin: Logos, p. 61–64.

28. L.-C. Schlegel-Voß. 2005. *Alter in der 'Volksgemeinschaft'. Zur Lebenslage der älteren Generation im Nationalsozialismus.* Berlin: Duncker & Humblot.

29. For further details, see: E. Reidegeld. 2006. *Staatliche Sozialpolitik in Deutschland,* vol 2: *Sozialpolitik in Demokratie und Diktatur 1919–1945.* Wiesbaden: VS Verlag für Sozialwissenschaften, p. 460.

30. P. Kirchberger. 1983. 'Die Stellung der Juden in der deutschen Rentenversicherung', in G. Aly, S. Heim and M. Karny (eds), *Sozialpolitik und Judenvernichtung. Gibt es eine Ökonomie der Endlösung?* Berlin: Rotbuch, pp. 116–17.

31. M. Daly and J. Lewis. 2000. 'The concept of social care and the analysis of contemporary welfare states', *British Journal of Sociology* 51:283–87.

32. Most of the studies interested in the articulation of gender through welfare benefits are focused on maternal and child welfare, such as marriage loans (*Ehestandsdarlehen*), for which newlyweds could apply, or relief schemed for mothers and children. See Humann, 'Arbeitsschlacht', pp. 118–35; and L. Pine. 1997. *Nazi Family Policy, 1933–1945.* New York, Oxford: Berg, pp. 88–116.

33. U. Haerendel. 2007. 'Geschlechterpolitik und Alterssicherung. Frauen in der gesetzlichen Rentenversicherung von den Anfängen bis zur Reform von 1957', *Deutsche Rentenversicherung,* 62(2/3):114.

34. The introduction of social insurance schemes by Bismarck already established the 'ideal of the male breadwinner earning a family wage': see K. Canning. 2006. *Gender History in Practice. Historical Perspectives on Bodies, Class, and Citizenship.* Ithaca, London: Cornell University Press, pp. 140–41.

35. For further detail on the history of opting out within the German social insurance scheme, see: D. Noll. 2010. *'...ohne Hoffnung im Alter jemals auch nur einen Pfennig Rente zu erhalten...'. Die Geschichte der weiblichen Erwerbsbiographien in der gesetzlichen Rentenversicherung.* Frankfurt/Main: Vittorio Klostermann, pp. 224–27.

36. For the debates on early retirement options for women in Germany and other German-speaking countries, see: U. Haerendel. 2010. 'Die Frauenaltersgrenze in der gesetzlichen Rentenversicherung: Geschichte, Funktion, Vergleiche mit dem Ausland', in S. Ruppert (ed.), *Lebensalter und Recht. Zur Segmentierung des menschlichen Lebenslaufs durch rechtliche Regelungen seit 1750.* Frankfurt/Main: Vittorio Klostermann, pp. 137–38.

37. The pension reform is well known for introducing the principle of 'dynamic adjustement' of pensions: see H.G. Hockerts. 2011. 'Wie die Rente steigen lernte: Die Rentenreform von 1957', in H.G. Hockerts, *Der deutsche Sozialstaat,* pp. 71–85.

38. See M.-L. Recker. 1985. *Nationalsozialistische Sozialpolitik im Zweiten Weltkrieg.* Munich: Oldenbourg, pp. 98–108.

39. Hong, *Welfare,* p. 273.

40. W. Schuhmann and L. Brucker. 1934. *Sozialpolitik im neuen Staat.* Berlin: Rink und Krause, pp. 15–16.

41. H. Vorländer. 1986. 'NS-Volkswohlfahrt und Winterhilfswerk des deutschen Volkes', *Vierteljahrshefte für Zeitgeschichte* 34:341–80, 344.

42. F. Tennstedt. 1987. 'Wohltat und Interesse. Das Winterhilfswerk des Deutschen Volkes: Die Weimarer Vorgeschichte und ihre Instrumentalisierung durch das NS-Regime', *Geschichte und Gesellschaft* 13:179–80.

43. A. Nolzen. 2007. '"Sozialismus der Tat": Die Nationalsozialistische Volkswohlfahrt (NSV) und der Luftkrieg gegen das Deutsche Reich', in D. Süß (ed.), *Deutschland im Luftkrieg. Geschichte und Erinnerung.* Munich: Oldenbourg, p. 59.

44. For the research on how welfare state provisions deliberate inequality, see: H.G. Hockerts and W. Süß (eds). 2010. *Soziale Ungleichheit im Sozialstaat. Die Bundesrepublik Deutschland und Großbritannien im Vergleich.* Munich: Oldenbourg.

45. Sachße and Tennstedt, *Wohlfahrtsstaat*, p. 138.

46. Law for the Standardization of the Health Care System, 3 July 1934, RGBl. 1933, I, p. 531.

47. See A. Christians. 2013. *Amtsgewalt und Volksgesundheit. Das öffentliche Gesundheitswesen im nationalsozialistischen München.* Göttingen: Wallstein. For the situation in Austria, see: H. Czech. 2007. 'From Welfare to Selection. Vienna's Public Health Office and the Implementation of Racial Hygiene Policies under the Nazi Regime', in M. Turda and P.J. Weindling (eds), *Blood and Homeland. Eugenics and Racial Nationalism in Central and Southeast Europe, 1900–1940.* Budapest, New York: CEU Press, pp. 322–23.

48. W. Süß. 2003. *Der 'Volkskörper' im Krieg. Gesundheitspolitik, Gesundheitsverhältnisse und Krankenmord im nationalsozialistischen Deutschland 1939–1945.* Munich: Oldenbourg, pp. 214–23.

49. W. Gruner. 2002. *Öffentliche Wohlfahrt und Judenverfolgung. Wechselwirkungen lokaler und zentraler Politik im NS-Staat 1933–1942.* Munich: Oldenbourg, pp. 314–17, 323–4.

50. Id. 1999. 'The German Council of Municipalities. (Deutscher Gemeindetag) and the Coordination of Anti-Jewish Local Politics in the Nazi State', *Holocaust Genocide Studies* 13:189.

51. U. Lohalm. 2010. *Völkische Wohlfahrtsdiktatur. Öffentliche Wohlfahrtspolitik im nationalsozialistischen Hamburg.* Hamburg: Dölling und Galitz, pp. 429–35.

52. W. Gruner. 2011. 'Die Kommunen im Nationalsozialismus: Innenpolitische Akteure und ihre wirkungsmächtige Vernetzung', in S. Reichardt and W. Seibel (eds), *Der prekäre Staat. Herrschen und Verwalten im Nationalsozialismus.* Frankfurt/Main: Campus; For approaches which highlight the efficacy of the polycratic nature of Nazi rule as well as the decisive role of communal and municipal authorities, see: B. Gotto. 2006. 'Polykratische Selbststilisierung. Mittel- und Unterinstanzen in der NS-Diktatur', in R. Hachtmann and W. Süß, *Hitlers Kommissare. Sondergewalten in der nationalsozialistischen Diktatur.* Göttingen: Wallstein; R. Hachtmann. 2011. 'Elastisch, dynamisch und von katastrophaler Effizienz – Anmerkungen zur Neuen Staatlichkeit des Nationalsozialismus', in Reichardt and Seibel, *Der prekäre Staat.*

53. F. Wimmer. 2014. *Die völkische Ordnung von Armut. Kommunale Sozialpolitik im nationalsozialistischen München.* Göttingen: Wallstein, pp. 245–47.

54. Ibid., pp. 237–38.

55. See, for example: D. Cohen. 2001. *The War Come Home. Disabled Veterans in Britain and Germany, 1914–1939.* Berkeley, Los Angeles, London: University of California Press, p. 170; N. Löffelbein, 2013. *Ehrenbürger der Nation. Die Kriegsbeschädigten des Ersten Weltkriegs in Politik und Propaganda des Nationalsozialismus.* Essen: Klartext, p. 253.

56. The role of female social workers was explored in detail by Esther Lehnert: see E. Lehnert. 2010. 'Fürsorge im Nationalsozialismus. Die Beteiligung von Fürsorgerinnen in einem ausmerzenden System', in C. Engelfried and C. Voigt-Kehlenbeck (eds). *Gendered Profession. Soziale Arbeit vor neuen Herausforderungen in der zweiten Moderne.* Berlin:

Springer, pp. 77–90; id. 2003. *Die Beteiligung von Fürsorgerinnen an der Bildung und Umsetzung der Kategorie 'minderwertig' im Nationalsozialismus. Öffentliche Fürsorgerinnen in Berlin und Hamburg im Spannungsfeld von Auslese und 'Ausmerze'.* Frankfurt/Main: Mabuse. For insights into primary sources such as the reports of female social workers and case files, see: A. Ebbinghaus (ed.). 1997. *Opfer und Täterinnen. Frauenbiographien des Nationalsozialismus.* Frankfurt/Main: Fischer.

57. For the situation in the Weimar Republic, consult Crew, *Germans*, p. 207. For examples during the Third Reich, see Lohalm, *Wohlfahrtsdiktatur,* pp. 297–98.

58. Christians, *Amtsgewalt*, pp. 157–58.

59. T. Lindenberger. 1999. 'Diktatur der Grenzen. Zur Einleitung', in T. Lindenberger (ed.), *Herrschaft und Eigen-Sinn in der Diktatur: Studien zur Gesellschaftsgeschichte der DDR.* Cologne: Böhlau, p. 32.

60. B. Brand-Clausen and M. Rotzoll. 2010. 'Schikaniert und schaponiert. Karl Ahrendt, Kutscher ohne Gnadenbrot', in M. Rotzoll et al. (eds), *Die nationalsozialistische 'Euthanasie'Aktion 'T4' und ihre Opfer. Geschichte und ethische Konsequenzen für die Gegenwart.* Paderborn: Ferdinand Schöningh, pp. 214–19. Fot a general consideration of documents reflecting the attitudes and perceptions of the victims of Nazi euthanasia, see: U. Müller and C. Wachsmann. 'Krankenakten als Lebensgeschichten', in Rotzoll, *'Euthanasie' Aktion 'T4'.*

61. Frieda L. to OKW, 12 July 1942, Bundesarchiv-Militärarchiv (BA-MA) Freiburg, RW 16/116.

62. Letter of sergeant H. to the military welfare officer, 2 April 1944 BA-MA Freiburg, RW 16/90. The original citation is: 'Die Art und Weise mit Kriegerwitwen zu verfahren, wird bei jedem Soldaten Empörung hervorrufen. Müssen wir doch alle damit rechnen, dass auch unsere Frauen und Kinder heute oder morgen in derselben Lage sind. Der Gedanke aber daran, dass auch ihnen in einer derart unerhörten Art und Weise begegnet werden kann, trägt bestimmt nicht zur Hebung der Wehrkraft und Wehrfreudigkeit bei. Er wird sich dagegen eher als Zersetzung derselben bemerkbar machen.'

63. Therese B. to Reichsregierung, 4 March 1940, BA-MA Freiburg, RW 16/90.

64. Sachße and Tennstedt, *Wohlfahrtsstaat*, p. 140.

65. S. Baranowski. 2004. *Strength through Joy. Consumerism and Mass Tourism in the Third Reich.* Cambridge: Cambridge University Press, p. 161.

66. M. Föllmer. 2010. 'Was Nazism Collectivistic? Redefining the Individual in Berlin, 1930–1945', *Journal for Modern History* 82(1):82–83.

67. Just recently, Kerstin Thieler has explored the assessment practice of Nazi party officials: see K. Thieler. 2014. *'Volksgemeinschaft' unter Vorbehalt. Gesinnungskontrolle und politische Mobilisierung in der Herrschaftspraxis der NSDAP-Kreisleitung Göttingen.* Göttingen: Wallstein, pp. 240–54.

68. Wimmer, *Ordnung*, pp. 206–07; Christians, *Amtsgewalt*, p. 107. The intrusive character of home visit routines was already significant during the Weimar Republic, but it deepened further since 1933. However, the beginning of the Second World War changed these circumstances: in Munich, for example, the number of social workers halved, causing a significant reduction of home visits as well.

69. L. Raphael. 2008. 'Figurationen von Armut und Fremdheit. Eine Zwischenbilanz interdisziplinärer Forschung', in L. Raphael and H. Uerlings (eds), *Zwischen Ausschluß und Solidarität. Modi der Inklusion/Exklusion von Fremden und Armen in Europa seit der Spätantike.* Frankfurt/Main: Peter Lang, pp. 21, 35.

70. W. Ayaß. 2012. '"Demnach ist zum Beispiel asozial …". Zur Sprache sozialer Ausgrenzung im Nationalsozialismus', in N. Kramer and A. Nolzen (eds), *Ungleichheiten im 'Dritten Reich'. Semantiken, Praktiken, Erfahrungen*. Göttingen: Wallstein, pp. 69–89, 71, 82–83; J. Hörath, (2014). '"Arbeitsscheue Volksgenossen"'. Leistungsbereitschaft als Kriterium der Inklusion und Exklusion, in Buggeln and Wildt, *Arbeit*, pp. 309–28.

71. See especially: Wimmer, *Ordnung*, pp. 300–3; Hörath, '"Arbeitsscheue Volksgenossen"'; D. Humann. 2012. 'Ordentliche Beschäftigungspolitik? Unterstützungssperren, Drohungen und weitere Zwangsmittel bei der "Arbeitsschlacht" der Nationalsozialisten', *Vierteljahrshefte für Zeitgeschichte*, pp. 61–65.

72. These examples are discussed in Christians, *Amtsgewalt*, pp. 158–59.

73. Schlegel-Voß, *Alter in der 'Volksgemeinschaft'*.

74. B. Möckel. 2011. '"Mit 70 Jahren hat kein Mensch das Recht, sich alt zu fühlen". – Altersdiskurse und Bilder des Alters in der NS-Sozialpolitik', *Österreichische Zeitschrift für Geschichtswissenschaft* 22(3):112–35; Möckel, 'Nutzlose Volksgenossen', pp. 52–70.

75. K.H. Irmak. 2002. *Der Sieche. Alte Menschen und die stationäre Altenhilfe in Deutschland 1924–1961*. Essen: Klartext Kettler, pp. 103–10; Wimmer, *Ordnung*, pp. 331–40.

76. Especially Süß, *Volkskörper*, pp. 308–10; Möckel, 'Nutzlose Volksgenossen', pp. 80–86.

77. Hans Obinger und Klaus Petersen argue towards a comparative approach and on a global scale, but the German case plays a prominent role in their considerations: see H. Obinger and K. Petersen. 2014. 'Mass Warfare and the Welfare State. Causal Mechanisms and Effects', ZeS-Working Paper no. 2, p. 8.

78. Ibid.

79. Recker, *Sozialpolitik*, pp. 296–304. Schwerin von Krosigk also pointed to the fact that raising the pension rates would increase the supply of money.

80. For the structures and practices of the separation allowances in the First and Second World War, see: B. Kundrus. 1995. *Kriegerfrauen. Familienpolitik und Geschlechterverhältnisse im Ersten und Zweiten Weltkrieg*. Hamburg: Hans Christians.

81. Aly, *Hitlers Volksstaat*.

82. B. Kundrus. 2014. 'Greasing the Palm of the Volksgemeinschaft? Consumption under National Socialism', in Gotto and Steber, *Visions of Community*, p. 167.

83. 'Fürsorge- und Versorgungsgesetz für die ehemaligen Angehörigen der Wehrmacht und ihre Hinterbliebenen (Wehrmachtfürsorge- und -versorgungsgesetz)' from 26 August 1938, RGBl. 1938, I. pp. 1077–79; 'Fürsorge- und Versorgungsgesetz für die ehemaligen Angehörigen der Wehrmacht bei besonderem Einsatz und ihre Hinterbliebenen (EWFVG)' from 6 July 1939, RGBl. 1939, I. pp. 1217–23. 'Aufzeichnung des Reichsarbeitsministeriums für eine Besprechung zwischen den Herrn Reichsministern Hess und Seldte, o.D.', in H. Heiber and P. Longerich (eds). 1983–92. Akten der Partei-Kanzlei der NSDAP. Rekonstruktion eines verlorengegangenen Bestandes. Sammlung der in anderen Provenienzen überlieferten Korrespondenzen, Niederschriften von Besprechungen usw. mit dem Stellvertreter des Führers und seinem Stab bzw. der Partei-Kanzlei, ihren Ämtern, Referaten und Unterabteilungen sowie mit Heß und Bormann persönlich. Munich: Saur, Regest 21034.

84. Löffelbein, *Ehrenbürger*, p. 85.

85. 'Erlass des Führers über die Wehrmachtsfürsorge und –versorgung' from 11 October 1943', in Heiber and Longerich, Akten der Partei-Kanzlei, Regest 14041. The SS was

in charge of its own men and had a separate welfare administration. Its structure, however, was quite similar to that of the army, only it had more manpower.

86. Talk by the Fürsorge- und Versorgungsabteilung des Wehrkreiskommandos VI, 6 May 1940, BA-MA Freiburg, RH 53-12/101.

87. Talk on 'Elternversorgung' (c.1941), BA-MA Freiburg, RW 16/228.

88. N. Kramer. 2011. *Volksgenossinnen an der Heimatfront. Mobilisierung, Verhalten und Erinnerung.* Göttingen: Vandenhoeck & Ruprecht, pp. 218–29.

89. Talk delivered by the chief of section 3 of the Wehrmachtsfürsorge- und -versorgungs-amtes Nuremberg, 6 January 1941, BA-MA Freiburg, RW 16/228; instruction no. 1 for the SS-Fürsorgeoffiziere, Fürsorge- und Versorgungsamt der Waffen-SS München, 1 June 1940, BA-MA Freiburg, RS 5/216.

90. Kramer, *Volksgenossinnen*, pp. 229–39.

91. Babette F. to Wehrmeldeamt Lichtenfels, 1 May 1941, (Staatsarchiv) StA Würzburg, Wehrmachtsfürsorge- und -versorgungsamt no. 56; Expertise of the military physician of the Wehrmachtsfürsorge- und -versorgungsamts Würzburg, 13 June 1941, ibid.; Babette F. to Wehrmachtsfürsorge- und -versorgungsamt Würzburg, 7 July 1941, ibid.

92. Crew, *Germans*.

93. See, for example, Maria N. to Wehrmachtsfürsorge- und -versorgungsamt Würzburg, 3 March 1943, StA Würzburg, Wehrmachtsfürsorge- und -versorgungsamt no. 54.

94. C. Essner and É. Conté. 1996., '"Fernehe", "Leichentrauung" und "Totenscheidung". Metamorphosen des Eherechts im Dritten Reich', *Vierteljahrshefte für Zeitgeschichte* 44:214.

95. In the same way, separation allowances were reduced or withdrawn: see Kundrus, *Kriegerfrauen*, pp. 391–92.

96. '5. Durchführungsverordnung zum Ehegesetz' from 18 March 1943, in RGBl. 1943, I. p. 145.

97. Mrs. H. to Partei-Kanzlei, 1 February 1943, Bundesarchiv (BA) Berlin, R 3001/466; minutes of the session of Zivilkammer 3 b, Landgericht München I, 19 January 1944, StA München, Landgerichte 10457; minutes of the session of Zivilkammer 3 b, Landgericht München I, 2 March 1944, StA München, Landgerichte 17381.

98. Minutes of meeting of the leading social workers in Hamburg, 22 May 1940, 4 July 1940, StA Hamburg, VG 25 November, vol. 2.

99. Report on 'Die kriegsbedingte Tätigkeit der NSV auf dem Gebiete der Evakuierung und Sofortmaßnahmen nach Luftangriffen' by Karl H., 19 May 1945, NARA RG 243/190/62/24/04, Entry 6, Box 562.

100. See the statement by Luise G., 29 March 1944, in 'Überlebensberichte: Der 22. Oktober 1943', Magistrat der Stadt Kassel (ed., Protokolle der Vermißtensuchstelle des Oberbürgermeisters der Stadt Kassel (Kassel, 1993, pp. 76–77; statement by Lotte G., 17 March 1944, ibid., pp. 66–67; statement by Auguste B., 12 April 1944, ibid., pp. 85–87.

101. Circular from Stabsleiter des Stellvertreters des Führers, Martin Bormann, to Reichs- und Parteistellen, 27 September 1940, in Gerhard Kock. 1997. 'Der Führer sorgt für unsere Kinder … ': Die Kinderlandverschickung im Zweiten Weltkrieg. Paderborn: Schöningh, pp. 353–58.

102. For the statistics, see M. Krause. 1997. *Flucht vor dem Bombenkrieg: 'Umquartierung' im Zweiten Weltkrieg und die Wiedereingliederung der Evakuierten in Deutschland 1943–1963.* Düsseldorf: Droste, p. 182.

103. Interview no. 45 with woman, fifty-three years old, housewife, Karlsruhe, Schedule A, 12 July 1945, NARA RG 243/190/62/24/04, Entry 6, Box 525. See also interview no. 17 with woman, nineteen years old, student, Hamburg, Schedule A, 9 June 1945, NARA RG 243/190/62/24/04, Entry 6, Box 518; letter from Luise W., 10 August 1987, Archiv des Deutschen Frauenrates Berlin, Frauenschicksale in Kriegs- und Nachkriegszeit. Most of the interview transcripts produced for the purpose of the United States Bombing Survey are written in English.

104. The United States Strategic Bombing Survey, p. 71.

105. Lotte Z. to Annemarie Mehrhoff, 21 July 1943, Archiv der Evangelischen Kirche im Rheinland, Düsseldorf, 7 NL 120/106; Lotte Zöller to Johannes Mehrhoff, 14 July 1943, ibid.; Lotte Zöller to Johannes Mehrhoff, 22 October 1943, ibid.

106. M. Boldorf, 2005. 'Zwischen Nothilfe und Professionalisierung. Ehrenamtliche soziale Arbeit in beiden Teilen Deutschlands nach 1945', *Westfälische Forschungen* 55:318–20.

107. Y.-S. Hong, 1992. 'The Contradictions of Modernization in the German Welfare State: Gender and the Politics of Welfare Reform in First World War Germany', *Social History* 17(2): 251.

108. 'Gesetz über den Schutz der erwerbstätigen Mutter' from 17 May 1942, RGBl. 1942, I., S., p. 321.

109. See C. König. 1988. *Die Frau im Recht des Nationalsozialismus. Eine Analyse ihrer familien-, erb- und arbeitsrechtlichen Stellung*. Frankfurt/Main: Peter Lang, pp. 210–13; R.G. Moeller. 1993. *Protecting Motherhood: Women and the Family in the Politics of Postwar West Germany*. Berkeley, Los Angeles, Oxford: University of California Press, pp. 156–57.

110. Haerendel, 'Geschlechterpolitik und Alterssicherung. Frauen in der gesetzlichen Rentenversicherung von den Anfängen bis zur Reform von 1957', p. 139.

111. H.G. Hockerts, 1981. 'German Post-war Social Policies against the Background of the Beveridge Plan. Some Observations Preparatory to a Comparison', in W. J. Mommsen, *The Emergence of the Welfare State in Britain and Germany, 1850–1950,*. London: Croom Helm, p. 317.

112. For the discussion about the effects of the Second World War on British welfare state developments, see H. Glennerster. 2006. *British social policy: 1945 to the present. Making Contemporary Britain*, 3rd edn. Oxford. Blackwell Publishing, pp. 18–64.

113. M. Hilton, J. McKay, N. Crowson and J.-F. Mouhot. 2013. *The Politics of Expertise: How NGOs Shaped Modern Britain*. Oxford: Oxford University Press.

114. E.R. Dickinson. 1996. *The Politics of German Child Welfare from the Empire to the Federal Republic*. Cambridge/MA, London: Harvard University Press, p. 247.

Works Cited

Althammer, B. 2014. 'Introduction: Poverty and Deviance in the Era of the Emerging Welfare State', in B. Althammer, A. Gestrich and J. Gründler (eds). *The Welfare State and the 'Deviant Poor' in Europe 1870–193*. Basingstoke: Palgrave Macmillan, pp. 1–17.

Aly, G. 2005. 2008. *Hitler's Beneficiaries. Plunder, Racial War, and the Nazi Welfare.* New York: Henry Holt and Company)

Ayaß, W. 2012. "'Demnach ist zum Beispiel asozial …'". Zur Sprache sozialer Ausgrenzung im Nationalsozialismus', in N. Kramer and A. Nolzen (eds), *Ungleichheiten im 'Dritten Reich'. Semantiken, Praktiken, Erfahrungen.* Göttingen: Wallstein, pp. 69–89.

Baranowski, S. 2004. *Strength through Joy. Consumerism and Mass Tourism in the Third Reich.* Cambridge: Cambridge University Press.

Boldorf, M. 2005. 'Zwischen Nothilfe und Professionalisierung. Ehrenamtliche soziale Arbeit in beiden Teilen Deutschlands nach 1945', *Westfälische Forschungen* 55:317–36.

Brand-Clausen, B., and M. Rotzoll. 2010. 'Schikaniert und schaponiert. Karl Ahrendt, Kutscher ohne Gnadenbrot', in Rotzoll et al., *Die nationalsozialistische 'Euthanasie' Aktion 'T4' und ihre Opfer. Geschichte und ethische Konsequenzen für die Gegenwart.* Paderborn: Schöningh, pp. 214–19.

Broszat, M. 1987. 'Plädoyer für eine Historisierung des Nationalsozialismus', in H. Graml and K.-D. Henke (eds), *Nach Hitler. Der schwierige Umgang mit unserer Geschichte. Beiträge von Martin Broszat.* Munich: Oldenbourg, pp. 166–73.

Canning, K. 2006. *Gender History in Practice. Historical Perspectives on Bodies, Class, and Citizenship.* Ithaca, London: Cornell University Press.

Christians, A. 2013. *Amtsgewalt und Volksgesundheit. Das öffentliche Gesundheitswesen im nationalsozialistischen München.* Göttingen: Wallstein.

Cohen, D. 2001. *The War Come Home. Disabled Veterans in Britain and Germany, 1914–1939,* Berkeley, Los Angeles, London: University of California Press.

Crew, D. 1998. *Germans on Welfare. From Weimar to Hitler.* New York, Oxford: Oxford University Press.

Czech, H. 2007. 'From Welfare to Selection. Vienna's Public Health Office and the Implementation of Racial Hygiene Policies under the Nazi Regime', in M. Turda and P.J. Weindling (eds), *Blood and Homeland. Eugenics and Racial Nationalism in Central and Southeast Europe, 1900–1940.* Budapest, New York: CEU Press, pp. 317–33.

Daly, M., and Lewis, J. 2000. 'The concept of social care and the analysis of contemporary welfare states', *British Journal of Sociology* 51:281–98.

Dickinson, E.R. 1996. *The Politics of German Child Welfare from the Empire to the Federal Republic.* Cambridge/MA, London: Harvard University Press.

Ebbinghaus A. (ed.). 1997. *Opfer und Täterinnen. Frauenbiographien des Nationalsozialismus.* Frankfurt/Main: Fischer.

Essner, C., and E. Conté. 1996. '"Fernehe", "Leichentrauung" und "Totenscheidung". Metamorphosen des Eherechts im Dritten Reich', *Vierteljahrshefte für Zeitgeschichte* 44:201–27.

Föllmer, M. 2010. 'Was Nazism Collectivistic? Redefining the Individual in Berlin, 1930–1945', *Journal for Modern History* 82(1):61–100.

Glennerster, H. 2006. *British social policy: 1945 to the present. Making Contemporary Britain*, 3rd edn. Oxford. Blackwell Publishing.

Gotto, B. 2006. 'Polykratische Selbststilisierung. Mittel- und Unterinstanzen in der NS-Diktatur', in R. Hachtmann and W. Süß, *Hitlers Kommissare. Sondergewalten in der nationalsozialistischen Diktatur*. Göttingen: Wallstein, pp. 28–50.

Gruner, W. 1999. 'The German Council of Municipalities (Deutscher Gemeindetag) and the Coordination of Anti-Jewish Local Politics in the Nazi State', *Holocaust Genocide Studies* 13:171–99.

———. 2002. *Öffentliche Wohlfahrt und Judenverfolgung. Wechselwirkungen lokaler und zentraler Politik im NS-Staat 1933–1942*. Munich: Oldenbourg.

———. 2011. 'Die Kommunen im Nationalsozialismus: Innenpolitische Akteure und ihre wirkungsmächtige Vernetzung', in S. Reichardt and W. Seibel (eds), *Der prekäre Staat. Herrschen und Verwalten im Nationalsozialismus*. Frankfurt/Main: Campus, pp. 167–211.

Hachtmann, R. 2007. 'Neue Staatlichkeit: Überlegungen zu einer systematischen Theorie des NS-Herrschaftssystems und ihrer Anwendung auf die mittlere Ebene der Gaue', in J. John, H. Möller and T. Schaarschmidt (eds), *Die Gaue. Regionale Mittelinstanzen im zentralistischen Führerstaat.*Munich: Oldenbourg, pp. 56–79.

———. 2011. 'Elastisch, dynamisch und von katastrophaler Effizienz – Anmerkungen zur Neuen Staatlichkeit des Nationalsozialismus', in S. Reichardt and W. Seibel (eds), *Der prekäre Staat. Herrschen und Verwalten im Nationalsozialismus*. Frankfurt/Main: Campus, pp. 29–73.

Haerendel, U. 2007. 'Geschlechterpolitik und Alterssicherung: Frauen in der gesetzlichen Rentenversicherung von den Anfängen bis zur Reform von 1957', *Deutsche Rentenversicherung* 62(2/3):99–124.

———. 2010. 'Die Frauenaltersgrenze in der gesetzlichen Rentenversicherung: Geschichte, Funktion, Vergleiche mit dem Ausland', in S. Ruppert (ed.), *Lebensalter und Recht. Zur Segmentierung des menschlichen Lebenslaufs durch rechtliche Regelungen seit 1750*. Frankfurt/Main: Vittorio Klostermann, pp. 127–50.

Harvey, E. 1993. *Youth and the Welfare State in Weimar Germany*. Oxford: Clarendon Press.

Heiber, H., and P. Longerich (eds). 1983–92. *Akten der Partei-Kanzlei der NSDAP. Rekonstruktion eines verlorengegangenen Bestandes*. Munich: Saur.

Hilton, M., J. McKay, N. Crowson and J.-F. Mouhot. 2013. *The Politics of Expertise: How NGOs Shaped Modern Britain*. Oxford: Oxford University Press.

Hockerts, H.G. 1981. 'German Post-war Social Policies against the Background of the Beveridge Plan. Some Observations Preparatory to a Comparison', in W.J. Mommsen, *The Emergence of the Welfare State in Britain and Germany, 1850–1950*. London: Croom Helm, pp. 315–39.

———(ed.). 2011. *Der deutsche Sozialstaat. Entfaltung und Gefährdung seit 1945*. Göttingen: Vandenhoeck & Ruprecht.

————. and W. Süß (eds). 2010. *Soziale Ungleichheit im Sozialstaat. Die Bundesrepublik Deutschland und Großbritannien im Vergleich*. Munich: Oldenbourg.

Hong, Y.-S. 1992. 'The Contradictions of Modernization in the German Welfare State: Gender and the Politics of Welfare Reform in First World War Germany', *Social History* 17(2):251–70.

————. 1998. *Welfare, Modernity, and the Weimar State, 1919–1933*. Princeton: Princeton University Press.

Hörath, J. 2014. '"Arbeitsscheue Volksgenossen". Leistungsbereitschaft als Kriterium der Inklusion und Exklusion', in M. Buggeln and M. Wildt (eds), *Arbeit im Nationalsozialismus*. Munich: Oldenbourg, pp. 309–28.

Humann, D. 2011. *'Arbeitsschlacht'. Arbeitsbeschaffung und Propaganda in der NS-Zeit 1933*. Göttingen: Wallstein.

————. 2012. 'Ordentliche Beschäftigungspolitik? Unterstützungssperren, Drohungen und weitere Zwangsmittel bei der "Arbeitsschlacht" der Nationalsozialisten', *Vierteljahrshefte für Zeitgeschichte* 60 (1): 33–67.

Irmak, K.H. 2002. *Der Sieche. Alte Menschen und die stationäre Altenhilfe in Deutschland 1924–1961*. Essen: Klartext Kettler.

Kirchberger, P. 1983. 'Die Stellung der Juden in der deutschen Rentenversicherung', in G. Aly, S. Heim and M. Karny (eds), *Sozialpolitik und Judenvernichtung. Gibt es eine Ökonomie der Endlösung?* Berlin: Rotbuch, pp. 11–132.

Kock, G. 1997. *'Der Führer sorgt für unsere Kinder …': Die Kinderlandverschickung im Zweiten Weltkrieg*. Paderborn: Schöningh.

König, C. 1988. *Die Frau im Recht des Nationalsozialismus. Eine Analyse ihrer familien-, erb- und arbeitsrechtlichen Stellung*. Frankfurt/Main: Peter Lang.

Kramer, N. 2011. *Volksgenossinnen an der Heimatfront. Mobilisierung, Verhalten und Erinnerung*. Göttingen: Vandenhoeck & Ruprecht.

Krause, M. 1997. *Flucht vor dem Bombenkrieg: 'Umquartierung' im Zweiten Weltkrieg und die Wiedereingliederung der Evakuierten in Deutschland 1943–1963*. Düsseldorf: Droste.

Kundrus, B. 1995. *Kriegerfrauen. Familienpolitik und Geschlechterverhältnisse im Ersten und Zweiten Weltkrieg*. Hamburg: Hans Christians.

————. 2014. 'Greasing the Palm of the Volksgemeinschaft? Consumption under National Socialism', in M. Steber and B. Gotto (eds), *Visions of Community in Nazi Germany. Social Engineering and Private Lives*. Oxford: Oxford University Press, pp. 157–70.

Lehnert, E. 2003. *Die Beteiligung von Fürsorgerinnen an der Bildung und Umsetzung der Kategorie 'minderwertig' im Nationalsozialismus. Öffentliche Fürsorgerinnen in Berlin und Hamburg im Spannungsfeld von Auslese und 'Ausmerze'*. Frankfurt/Main: Mabuse.

————. 2010. 'Fürsorge im Nationalsozialismus. Die Beteiligung von Fürsorgerinnen in einem ausmerzenden System', in C. Engelfried and C. Voigt-Kehlenbeck (eds), *Gendered Profession. Soziale Arbeit vor neuen Herausforderungen in der zweiten Moderne*. Berlin: Springer, pp. 77–90.

Lindenberger, T. 1999. 'Diktatur der Grenzen. Zur Einleitung', in T. Lindenberger (ed.), *Herrschaft und Eigen-Sinn in der Diktatur: Studien zur Gesellschaftsgeschichte der DDR*. Cologne: Böhlau, pp. 13–44.

Linne, K. 2014. 'Von der Arbeitsvermittlung zum Arbeitseinsatz. Zum Wandel der Arbeitsverwaltung 1933–1945', in M. Buggeln and M. Wildt (eds), *Arbeit im Nationalsozialismus*. Munich: Oldenbourg, pp. 53–70.

Löffelbein, N. 2013. *Ehrenbürger der Nation. Die Kriegsbeschädigten des Ersten Weltkriegs in Politik und Propaganda des Nationalsozialismus*. Essen: Klartext.

Lohalm, U. 2010. *Völkische Wohlfahrtsdiktatur. Öffentliche Wohlfahrtspolitik im nationalsozialistischen Hamburg*. Hamburg: Dölling und Galitz.

Mason, T. 1993. *Social Policy and the Third Reich. The Working Class and the 'National Community'*. Providence, Oxford: Berg Publishers.

Meskill, D. 2010. *Optimizing the German workforce from Bismarck to the Economic Miracle*. New York, Oxford: Berghahn Books.

Möckel, B. 2010. *'Nutzlose Volksgenossen'? – Der Arbeitseinsatz alter Menschen im Nationalsozialismus*. Berlin: Logos.

———. 2011. '"Mit 70 Jahren hat kein Mensch das Recht, sich alt zu fühlen" – Altersdiskurse und Bilder des Alters in der NS-Sozialpolitik', *Österreichische Zeitschrift für Geschichtswissenschaft* 22(3):112–35.

Moeller, R.G. 1993. *Protecting Motherhood: Women and the Family in the Politics of Postwar West Germany*. Berkeley, Los Angeles, Oxford: University of California Press (German version: 1997. *Geschützte Mütter: Frauen und Familien in der westdeutschen Nachkriegspolitik*. Munich: Deutsche Taschenbuch).

Müller, U. and Wachsmann, C. 2010. 'Krankenakten als Lebensgeschichten', in Rotzoll et al., *Die nationalsozialistische 'Euthanasie' Aktion 'T4' und ihre Opfer. Geschichte und ethische Konsequenzen für die Gegenwart*. Paderborn: Ferdinand Schöningh, pp. 191–99.

Noll, D. 2010. *'…ohne Hoffnung im Alter jemals auch nur einen Pfennig Rente zu erhalten…'. Die Geschichte der weiblichen Erwerbsbiographien in der gesetzlichen Rentenversicherung*. Frankfurt/Main: Vittorio Klostermann.

Nolzen, A. 2007. '"Sozialismus der Tat": Die Nationalsozialistische Volkswohlfahrt (NSV) und der Luftkrieg gegen das Deutsche Reich', in D. Süß (ed.), *Deutschland im Luftkrieg. Geschichte und Erinnerung*. Munich: Oldenbourg, pp. 57–69.

Obinger, H. and K. Petersen. 2014. 'Mass Warfare and the Welfare State. Causal Mechanisms and Effects', *ZeS-Working Paper* no. 2.

Peukert, D.J.K. 1986. *Grenzen der Sozialdisziplinierung. Aufstieg und Krise der deutschen Jugendfürsorge von 1878 bis 1932*. Cologne: Bund.

Pine, L. 1997. *Nazi Family Policy, 1933–1945*. New York, Oxford: Berg.

Raphael, L. 2008. 'Figurationen von Armut und Fremdheit. Eine Zwischenbilanz interdisziplinärer Forschung', in L. Raphael and H. Uerlings (eds), *Zwischen Ausschluß und Solidarität. Modi der Inklusion/Exklusion von Fremden und Armen in Europa seit der Spätantike*. Frankfurt/Main: Peter Lang, pp. 13–36.

Recker, M.-L. 1985. *Nationalsozialistische Sozialpolitik im Zweiten Weltkrieg*. Munich: Oldenbourg.

Reidegeld, E. 2006. *Staatliche Sozialpolitik in Deutschland, vol II: Sozialpolitik in Demokratie und Diktatur 1919–1945*. Wiesbaden: VS Verlag für Sozialwissenschaften.

Roth, K.H. 1993. *Intelligenz und Sozialpolitik im 'Dritten Reich': eine methodisch-historische Studie am Beispiel des Arbeitswissenschaftlichen Instituts der Deutschen Arbeitsfront*. Munich: Saur.

Rotzoll, M. et al. (eds). 2010. *Die nationalsozialistische 'Euthanasie'-Aktion 'T4' und ihre Opfer*. Paderborn, Munich, Vienna, Zürich: Schöningh.

Rudloff, W. 1998. *Die Wohlfahrtsstadt. Kommunale Ernährungs-, Fürsorge- und Wohnungspolitik am Beispiel Münchens 1910–1933*, 2 vols. Göttingen: Vandenhoeck & Ruprecht.

Sachße, Ch. and F. Tennstedt. 1992. *Geschichte der Armenfürsorge in Deutschland*, vol. 3: *Der Wohlfahrtsstaat im Nationalsozialismus*. Stuttgart et al.: Kohlhammer.

———. 1992. 'Der Wohlfahrtsstaat im Nationalsozialismus', *Zeitschrift für Sozialreform* 38:129–48.

Schlegel-Voß, L.-C. 2005. *Alter in der 'Volksgemeinschaft'. Zur Lebenslage der älteren Generation im Nationalsozialismus*. Berlin: Duncker & Humblot.

Schneider, M. 1999. *Unterm Hakenkreuz. Arbeiter und Arbeiterbewegung 1933 bis 1939*. Bonn: Dietz.

Schuhmann, W. and L. Brucker. 1934. *Sozialpolitik im neuen Staat*. Berlin: Rink und Krause.

Spoerer, M. and J. Streb. 2013. 'Guns and Butter – but not Margarine: The Impact of Nazi Economic Policies on German Food Consumption, 1933–1938', *Jahrbuch für Wirtschaftsgeschichte* 1:75–88.

Steber M. and B. Gotto (eds). 2014. *Visions of Community in Nazi Germany. Social Engineering and Private Lives*. Oxford: Oxford University Press.

Stolleis, M. 2013. *Origins of the German Welfare State. Social Policy to 1945*. Berlin, Heidelberg: Springer.

Süß, W. 2003. *Der 'Volkskörper' im Krieg. Gesundheitspolitik, Gesundheitsverhältnisse und Krankenmord im nationalsozialistischen Deutschland 1939–1945*. Munich: Oldenbourg.

Tennstedt, F. 1987. 'Wohltat und Interesse. Das Winterhilfswerk des Deutschen Volkes: Die Weimarer Vorgeschichte und ihre Instrumentalisierung durch das NS-Regime', *Geschichte und Gesellschaft* 13:157–80.

Thieler, K. 2014. *'Volksgemeinschaft' unter Vorbehalt. Gesinnungskontrolle und politische Mobilisierung in der Herrschaftspraxis der NSDAP-Kreisleitung Göttingen*. Göttingen: Wallstein.

Vorländer, H. 1986. 'NS-Volkswohlfahrt und Winterhilfswerk des deutschen Volkes', *Vierteljahrshefte für Zeitgeschichte* 34:341–80.

Wagner, A. 2007. 'Ein Human Development Index für Deutschland und die Entwicklung des Lebensstandards im "Dritten Reich", *1933–1939*', *Vierteljahrschrift für Sozial- und Wirtschaftsgeschichte* 94:309–32.

Wehler, H.U. 2003. *Deutsche Gesellschaftsgeschichte*, vol. 4: *Vom Beginn des Ersten Weltkrieges bis zur Gründung der beiden deutschen Staaten 1914–1949*. Munich: Beck.

Werner, S., H. Degner, H. and M. Adamo. 2011. 'Hitlers gläserne Arbeitskräfte. Das Arbeitsbuch als Quelle von Mikrodaten für die historische Arbeitsmarktforschung', *Jahrbuch für Wirtschaftsgeschichte*, pp. 175–91.

Wimmer, F. 2014. *Die völkische Ordnung von Armut. Kommunale Sozialpolitik im nationalsozialistischen München*. Göttingen: Wallstein.

Nicole Kramer is a postdoctoral researcher at Frankfurt University. Her recent publications include: *'Volksgenossinnen' an der 'Heimatfront'. Mobilisierung, Verhalten, Erinnerung*, (2011); *Ungleichheiten im 'Dritten Reich'. Semantiken, Praktiken, Erfahrungen*, (2012) (co-edited with A. Nolzen); 'Volksgenossinnen on the German Home Front: An Insight into Wartime Nazi Society', in B. Gotto and M. Steber (eds), *Visions of Community in Nazi Germany. Social Engineering and Private Lives*. (2014), pp. 171–186.

CHAPTER 6

Who Cares?

Gender, Poverty and Welfare in West Germany

Christiane Kuller

'… a man away from poverty' – Relationships between Gender Regimes, Poverty and the Welfare State

Writing in the encyclopaedia for social work under the category of 'female poverty', Monika Simmel-Joachim observed in 1993 that 'As long as a woman's material security in marriage and old age are dependent on her husband's income and pension … women are a man away from poverty'.[1] With this sentence, the sociologist summarized feminist criticism of the interactions between gender and social security in the German welfare state. What Simmel-Joachim characterized over twenty years ago as a systematic poverty risk for women is now no longer deemed as applying to women alone, according to the federal government's poverty report for 2013, but rather, to any person engaged in housework and the upbringing of children.[2] However, it must be recognized that the fundamental parameters shaping the division of labour in industrial societies since the nineteenth century, and the social insurance schemes introduced in Germany for workers in the 1880s, have survived relatively unchanged to this day. Individuals engaged in household work and the upbringing of children generally have limited opportunities to participate in the labour market. Those responsible for the family's domestic sphere, for whom the term 'care worker' has established itself internationally, frequently cannot seek salaried employment due to the 'double burden' of family work and 'normal' working conditions and the inadequacy of childcare facilities and provision, which is especially pronounced in Germany.

This dilemma continues in the Federal Republic's social security system. As such insurance systems in Germany have traditionally been linked to salaried employment, individuals engaged in domestic care work not only lack a salary, but also the associated social security coverage. Especially in old age, social benefits are tied strongly to previous employment. The risks the German social insurance system guards against are, moreover, ones closely associated with salaried employment (old age, invalidity caused by work accidents, sickness and need for care, unemployment). The risks associated with care work, by contrast, were for a long time not taken into consideration.

In the years after 1945, household and care work didn't remain blind spots in West Germany's social order.[3] Care work occupied a central place within the traditional image, dominant well into the 1960s, of a nuclear family consisting of a married heterosexual couple and their children. The wife and mother was responsible for caring for this unit, and in return she had the right to expect financial provision from her husband, who through his labour gained income and social security for all family members. As long as the husband lived, his wife benefited from his income – the so-called 'family wage' – and after his death she had the right to a widow's pension. As Robert Moeller has demonstrated, women in this situation did not have access to social insurance independently through their own contract of employment, but rather via a marital one.[4]

The widow's pension remained one of the most long-lasting relics of men and women's explicitly unequal treatment in West German social policy. Since 1912/13, pensions for surviving widows and children were paid from men's contributions. Men were not entitled to claim a 'widower's pension'. This situation was first changed in 1985 by the Law for Surviving Family Members and Periods of Child Raising (Hinterbliebenenrenten- und Erziehungszeiten-Gesetz).[5] Since then, men have also been entitled to claim 'widower's pensions'. The situation prior to 1985 has frequently been interpreted as one that privileged women. However, one can also read it as implying that a man's contributions were 'worth more' than those of a woman, as only they opened up surviving family members' entitlements to pensions in the event of the husband's death, even when his salary was no higher than that of his wife.[6]

This dual gender arrangement, which was also firmly anchored in the institutions of the Federal Republic's welfare state, only functions well when stable marriage and family structures are present. As long as durable relationships between couples exist, the significant risk to those persons engaged in household work remains concealed. When a relationship ends or if no judicially regulated partnership exists, the problems of this model of social insurance rapidly reveal themselves. As soon as the private regime of maintenance fails, those individuals engaged in the home are threatened with poverty, as they generally cannot provide for themselves by salaried labour, and, according to the gender norms dominant until the late 1960s, they should not do so. Simultaneously, they fall through the gaps in the social security net. A second working assumption embodied within the German social insurance system is that careers and employment afford opportunities for promotion. This does not always apply to female career trajectories.[7]

What remains if all these preconditions are missing is often merely the social assistance *(Sozialhilfe)* as the lowest rung of the welfare system. Its benefits are based on different principles than that of the social insurance system, as they do not refer to salaried employment and earlier contributions, but rather offer assistance based on need and are linked to means tests. As a result, single parents and women of retirement age formed, from the very beginning, the core clientele of the Federal Republic's poverty policies. For persons engaged in domestic care work, social assistance was a replacement for failed family networks and gaps in the social security system. In this sense, one can read West Germany's poverty debates as discussions about the foundational principles of the welfare state in the area of household care, whose problems became especially visible from the 1970s onwards due to changing gender roles and relations.

In the second half of the twentieth century, which stands at the heart of the following reflections, events and processes repeatedly shook traditional conceptions of the relationship between gender order and the social security system. The immediate post-war period was already a time of heightened female poverty. With so many men having been killed in the war or finding themselves in Allied captivity, the most visual images of want and deprivation in German society featured women, who bore responsibility for providing for their families with the essentials of life. Even after the desperate conditions of this early post-war period had been overcome, the widow with children for many years formed a symbolic figure of the poverty caused by the war. Although connections between gender-specific life situations, constructional principles of social insurance, and poverty had become visible and problematic since May 1945, a wide public and political discussion about female poverty and its roots in gender hierarchies only emerged in the 1970s.[8] The spectrum of those contributing to these debates extended from prominent conservative thinkers such as Heiner Geißler to left-wing feminists who developed totally different solutions to the problem. This chapter asks why the debate concerning the poverty risk accompanying care work initially barely gained any traction whatsoever, and which factors were the driving forces behind the topic's increasing influence during the 1970s and 1980s. It also considers in which contexts the topic was politicized during these decades, particularly with regards to the debates concerning the 'new social question' and 'new poverty' *(Neue Armut)*.

'I can't afford to go to work; I have to feed my family.' Gender Roles and Poverty in the Early Post-war Period

At the end of the Second World War, mass deprivation characterized German society. Crises of food provision, a lack of available housing, and shortages of supply in various fields affected great sections of the population, leaving millions impoverished, particularly the German refugees and expellees from the east and victims of Nazi persecution and war, in addition to those who had lost their homes and possessions due to Allied bombing. Poverty's image was that of a wide, all-encompassing emergency, which did not respect distinctions of social class or standing.[9] Contemporary sociological studies of poverty made reference to hunger, cold, lack of housing and homelessness as visible representations of the phenomenon. There was a lack of the necessities of everyday life, such as food, accommodation, heating materials and clothing. These shortages were understood as 'absolute poverty'; an existence-threatening, physical state of emergency, and it appeared ubiquitous and incapable of systematic limitation. Crucially, as a considerable proportion of German men had either been killed, or was missing, post-war poverty was to a considerable extent visible as a phenomenon affecting women, who commonly bore responsibility for their families' provision.

Although the mass deprivation of the early post-war period manifested itself as female poverty, at this time no debate developed regarding the phenomenon or placing traditional conceptions of gender order into question. This surprising fact can be explained with reference to the specific historical context. A first reason why the specific plight of women provoked little contemporary debate concerning appropriate gender roles can be discerned in a glance at the structures of poverty and the means by which they were overcome. The deprivation of the post-war period and the strategies used to combat it were closely linked with female gender roles, and barely connected to salaried employment. The quality of a family's material provision depended less on whether an adequate income linked to work could be established, but rather on whether material goods and produce such as food and heating materials could be acquired. Not only money was necessary for this, but also time and access to such resources. Women in Frankfurt who had been ordered to find some form of employment, neatly summed up this situation with the sentence: 'I can't afford to go to work; I have to feed my family.'[10] This means of overcoming need incentivized women to prioritize care work and home economics. Despite women's increased range of responsibilities in German society, rather than being eroded, traditional gender roles were paradoxically consolidated by the conditions of the early post-war period.[11] As salaried employment played only a small part in contemporary strategies aimed at overcoming poverty and occupied a marginal place in understandings of the phenomenon, there were few starting points for a critical discussion regarding traditional visions of social-political order. Furthermore, the social insurance system had also come to a complete standstill at the war's end.

A second factor contributing to this tendency was the contemporary belief that the post-war period's problems were not the results of inherent deficiencies in the social order, but rather caused by external factors: above all, Germany's defeat in the Second World War. The conviction predominated that post-war deprivation did not stem from fundamental malfunctions of the social order, but rather represented a temporary and exceptional situation that could be overcome with limited special measures. After the restoration of 'normality', traditional approaches to dealing with poverty would again function adequately.[12]

Among the victims of war were its widows who had to care for children. They formed a large group of single parents, who enjoyed high levels of political attention.[13] The services and benefits provided by public welfare, and later the Law on Compensation and Assistance for War Victims (*Kriegsopferversorgung*) initially afforded the war widow a life precariously close to the breadline, and she was accordingly a central figure in post-war debates about poverty in West Germany. The question of whether and how much, war widows with children should work, was particularly contested. The regulations of this law aimed at restoring the traditional family unit with the state replacing the male 'breadwinner' and ensuring that mothers would be kept from engaging in paid work; indeed, payments would be reduced if a mother took on work outside the home. Economic impulses were therefore designed to encourage war widows to adopt a traditional motherly role. Paradoxically, this contradicted the reintegration of war victims into the labour market, which this legislation in general envisaged. If war widows were not employed, and did not therefore pay social insurance contributions, a lifelong dependency on state benefits threatened. Schnädelbach emphasizes that women themselves played an important role in this context. Their behaviour was by no means merely passive, but rather represented, to paraphrase 'doing gender', 'doing widow'; that is to say, women played an important role in the construction of the societal public image of the war widow and her roles.[14]

This dilemma was characteristic of early post-war debates addressing the specific poverty of women with children, and continued to inspire a range of divergent guiding principles in policy making over the following years. The question of how to provide for war widows indeed represented an exceptional case, as the state bore primary responsibility for bringing about their precarious life situations. For it was the war, not private decisions or the peacetime death of husbands, which ensured that war widows were obliged to care for their children on their own. The state, which had sent these soldiers to war, assumed a duty of care and the role of provider for those single-parent families, whose fathers and husbands had died in the conflict.

The statistics of the first post-war years reveal that there were also other groups of single-parent families.[15] A key factor here was the short-term increase of illegitimate births. In 1946, around 120,000 live births out of a total of 733,000 in the Western occupation zones were born out of wedlock.[16] The number of divorces also increased sharply in the early post-war period, with the divorce rate only returning to low levels from 1950 onwards. In these divorces, women, with exceptional frequency, were declared guilty of having participated in extra-marital affairs during the long years of separation from their husbands.[17] These women typically had no work experience and, through the divorce, they lost their entitlement to benefits via their husband. The consequence was a high risk of poverty, as reflected in the welfare statistics of the 1950s. Other than inability to work, it was mainly separation and divorce as well as inadequate pensions which led to individuals relying on social assistance during this period.[18]

In 1948, a proposal to introduce the 'mother family' (*Mutterfamilie*) as a social unit equal to the 'full family' (*Vollfamilie*) reached the Parliamentary Council. According to the paper's author, Dorothea Klaje, single mothers should count as a 'family'; in her view, a family comes into being when a woman gives birth to her first child, and ends with the children reaching adulthood, regardless of whether the mother lives in a marriage or not. In her estimation, 'mother families' without husbands deserved to be incorporated within the social system as 'normal occurrences'. Klaje's proposal, however, received little by way of positive support. The constituent assembly instead decided that single parents who had never been married did not represent a family in the eyes of the law.[19]

The attention devoted to divorced mothers and mothers of illegitimate children on the part of politics and civil society was short lived. The boundaries between various groups of single parents soon deepened, ensuring that it made a big difference whether a single mother had been widowed (and was accordingly entitled to receive a pension), if she was divorced, or had given birth to an illegitimate child as a single woman.[20]

'Giving Mothers Back to the Family'. Family Wage and the Dual Gender Model as a Cornerstone of Social Policy in the 1950s

During the 1950s the picture of poverty changed in the Federal Republic of Germany. The numbers of those receiving social assistance more than halved in the space of a few years.[21] This above all reflected the fact that in this decade, large numbers of existing welfare recipients were moved into different systems of benefit provision. Among these individuals were a great number of war widows with children, who were incorporated in 1950 into the federal law for compensation and assistance for war victims (*Kriegsopferversorgung*). Recipients of this new entitlement were no longer forced to rely on social assistance, where demonstrable individual need was a key determinant of the levels of support offered, but rather had the legal right to a war victim's pension.[22] The specific reference to the consequences of war made these new provisions an exceptional policy instrument, which applied to a specific social group and was generationally bound to it.

The outsourcing of social problems resulting from the war considerably reduced the number of people relying on social assistance. By the end of the 1950s at the very latest, traditional income poverty also seemed to have been overcome by the economic miracle's achievements. During this period, unemployment levels went down and living standards increased for wide sections of the population. Policies specifically designed to tackle poverty only seemed necessary to address certain exceptional life situations. During the 1950s, social assistance became a marginal phenomenon in West German society.

Simultaneously, the image of poverty changed. Due to rising living standards, poverty was no longer tied to existential need, but rather revealed itself as a failure to keep pace with consumption levels in society as a whole. In this sense, poverty continued to be present in the Federal Republic. The standard rate for social assistance was implemented as a contemporary measure for the problem. From that point on, an individual was classed as poor if he or she had the right to receive social benefits or lived at the level of somebody in that situation.[23]

In hindsight, this definition has been subjected to considerable criticism, as in certain respects it merely reproduced the contemporary categorizations employed by the welfare authorities. Only those groups came into view who were explicitly entitled to poor relief. By contrast, 'hidden' poverty, which was not represented in official statistics and mainly affected women, remained invisible.[24] Even if welfare recipients' demographic composition in the 1950s cannot be precisely measured, it is apparent that heads of families and single persons in receipt of support were most commonly women – above all widows, female pensioners, and single mothers.[25]

If one searches for contemporary debates about the poverty risks associated with care work in the 1950s and 1960s, one will encounter them in discussions concerning divorce law and the reform of social assistance. The topic of care work was indirectly discussed, for example, when addressing help for carers or support to maintain a household. The Federal Law on Social Assistance (Bundessozialhilfegesetz) envisaged providing support in the event of families losing the care provided by a housewife and mother.[26] In 1961, divorce law was tightened up in the Federal Republic. This reform removed the 'breakdown principle', which, since the Third Reich, had offered the possibility of dissolving a failed marriage without the allocation of legal guilt or responsibility. The new divorce law, by contrast, aimed to improve the position of the 'innocent' marital partner and to afford him or her the possibility of preventing a divorce from taking place.[27] The background to this reform, which both Catholic and Protestant members of the CDU and CSU advocated in ecumenical unity, was, on the one hand, the Catholic understanding of marriage as indissoluble; on the other, rendering divorce more difficult was also understood as a protective measure for women, which prevented them from being 'driven' innocently from the materially secure status of 'wife'.[28]

During the 1960s, however, legal practice in this field developed in a different direction. Although a divorce without allocation of guilt was no longer formally possible after the law of 1961, in practice, many couples simply divorced for invented reasons which they had designed together in advance. Shortly before the reform of marriage in 1976, the proportion of such 'conventional divorces' lay around 90 per cent.[29] Already in the 1960s, the new regulations of divorce law were the subject of renewed debate, which centred on the necessity and financial practicality of an independent social insurance for non-working housewives.[30] The new law, passed in 1976, distanced itself completely from the viewpoint that questions of guilt were central to divorces and broke their link with former partners' levels of obligation to pay maintenance (Unterhaltspflicht); both spouses' maintenance claims now depended far more on their own financial and social situations. Of great importance in this context was the settlement of pension entitlements (*Versorgungsausgleich*) as both divorced spouses now possessed equal entitlement to invalidity and old age pensions earned during the marriage.[31] This change brought about a marked improvement in the living standards of divorced women.

Passed in 1961, the Federal Law on Social Assistance, which redesigned the lowest rungs of the West German welfare system, also reconsidered the question of poverty risk with regards to single parents.[32] Although a fundamental goal of social assistance was the incorporation of its recipients into the labour market, clients who had children of preschool age were, according to the law, not supposed to be working: household work formed a recognized alternative to paid employment. Single parents in receipt of social assistance were thereby released from the obligation to seek paid work until the children reached school age, and even thereafter part-time employment was deemed 'appropriate'.

However, no material equality between salaried employment and family work was incorporated into this law; single parents in this period could not earn pension entitlements. So the disadvantaging of 'unemployed' care workers vis-a-vis those engaged in salaried employment with regards to old age pensions was also reflected in social assistance, and was, as female feminist critics retrospectively emphasized in the 1980s, even achieved with force. Since the welfare authorities controlled the household budgeting and child raising of welfare recipients with children, feminist critics interpreted this as the welfare state's officials requiring single parents to do without a salary and the attached social insurance provisions. The regulations enshrined in the Federal Law on Social Assistance (Bundessozialhilfegesetz) were formulated in gender neutral terms. In practice, however, they disproportionately affected women.[33]

The problem of single parents disappeared from women's magazines and journals as well as sociological literature and political debate in the 1950s, resulting in the topic being marginalized for a long time.[34] The governmental Enquete Commission investigating the 'Situation of Women in Employment, Family Life and Society' only devoted one page out of six hundred to unmarried mothers in its report of 1966.[35] The first family report produced by the federal government in 1968 did, admittedly, deal in a brief section with the economic situation of 'incomplete' families. It did not, however, relate these findings to specific poverty risks.[36]

Whereas the individual poverty risks of persons engaged in care work were marginalized, there developed simultaneously a wide discussion about family poverty, which addressed very different concerns. For example, a memorandum produced by the Federal Family Ministry in 1959 proved that a considerable number of families were to be counted amongst the losers of the economic miracle.[37] In this report, the statistician Helga Schmucker calculated that in West Germany a quarter of families with two children had a lifestyle comparable to welfare recipients of social assistance and therefore lived at the poverty level.

Of the families with three children, one-third possessed this low standard of living; of the families with four children, two-thirds.

The debate concerning the poverty risk of families did not refer specifically to the situation of women or their individual poverty risk. Rather, this report labelled as scandalous the precarious situation of 'full families' as a social unit. Its findings orientated themselves around a normative 'complete' family with traditional divisions of labour among the parents, with mothers bearing responsibility for the household and upbringing of children. This memorandum indeed sought to stabilize traditional gender roles. It aimed to raise a working father's wage by means such as child benefit (*Kindergeld*) and other state subsidies according to individual family situations, so that his salary gained the character of a 'family wage'. It emphasized that these extra payments should allow mothers to devote themselves entirely to their families and households, thereby removing their need to participate in the labour market.[38]

It was indeed characteristic of West German family policy well into the 1960s that the debate concerning the individual poverty risk run by wives and mothers was obscured and overshadowed by state attempts to stabilize their indirect insurance via their husbands. Government policy's key aim was the strengthening of the traditional family as an institution, in which fathers and mothers played different roles. Child benefits (*Kindergeld*) and income tax-free allowances (*Steuerfreibeträge*) for families with children were designed to secure an adequate 'family wage' for the father as the family's 'breadwinner'. The 'family wage' debates of the 1950s and 1960s, which revolved around the question of how many children should be regarded as 'normal' and how generously social benefits had to be set, did not include a discussion concerning the problems of the 'male breadwinner – housewife' model, but rather assumed the existence of an ongoing heterosexual relationship between parents with unequal roles.[39] In this debate, as in others during the 1950s and 1960s, the specific poverty risk run by individuals engaged in care work received no consideration.

The dominance of the 'male breadwinner – housewife' model, with its two distinct gender-based roles, was clearly reflected also in the debates surrounding pension reform in the 1950s. In conjunction with preparations for this reform, which represented the most important tool of poverty policy in the early Federal Republic, there were proposals for a three-generation contract, which would organize an economic compensation (*Ausgleich*) between children, the employed and pensioners.[40] This model was notable in terms of gender politics by virtue of the fact that it would have remunerated housewives and mothers for their upbringing of children. Care work would thereby have become part of a contract between generations. Although this plan was supported by prominent academics and lobbyists, the federal government ultimately rejected the proposal and instead decided in 1957 to introduce a pension reform which only incorporated two generations: the employed and pensioners.[41]

Care work thereby continued to lack an autonomous place within the federal pension system. The government was actually more eager than before to encourage wives to remove themselves from pension insurance and to even withdraw their former payments. Many women gladly took advantage of this opportunity, which was later interpreted as an important cause of female poverty in old age. In a volume of feminist criticism directed at the welfare state in the 1980s, Annelies Kohleiss critically recalls that:

> The fateful development whereby women were permitted to withdraw their pension savings due to marriage can only be explained with reference to contemporary legislators' belief in the irreconcilability of marriage and career, and the legislative expectation and conviction that this state of affairs was not a specific of the present, but would rather continue long into the future.[42]

The pension reform of 1957 represents the greatest social reform of the 'old' Federal Republic, whose effects profoundly shaped the subsequent history of the West German welfare state. It ensured that millions of pensioners were protected from the threat of poverty in old age.[43] The new system of the 'dynamic' pension, whose payments kept pace with actual salary levels, enabled considerable increases in annuity rates. By contrast, women, who, for the good of their families, had given up employment and not paid in pension contributions during this period, continued to have access only to smaller pensions.[44] Of course, wives profited from their husbands' increased pensions, but the 'dynamic pension' did not afford most women the means to support an independent existence in old age. In 1960, the pensions of 97 per cent of all women who had previously been engaged in some form of blue collar work, and 68 per cent of women who had been white collar workers, afforded their recipients a living standard below the poverty line.[45]

Part-time work, which by international standards was incorporated into the Federal Republic's social insurance system at an early stage, played an ambivalent role in this context. Between 1962 and 1965, the federal government placed part-time employment at the same level as full time work within social insurance programmes.[46] Persons with part-time employment now had entitlements to unemployment support as well as old age and health insurance, benefits which they had previously been denied. Crucially, this opened up for wives and mothers, for the first time, the possibility of participating in social insurance schemes without having to take on a fulltime job, thereby offering them access to the labour-orientated mainstay of the West German welfare state.

This new regulation for part-time workers did not create an autonomous social insurance for wives and mothers, who engaged in part-time work in growing numbers during the 1960s. Part-time work naturally only represented a partial emancipation from the established model, which generally did not extend far enough to form an independent social insurance provision. This change can be described as a shift from the 'male breadwinner – housewife' model to a 'male breadwinner – supplementary earner' model. The characterization of the wife as an additional earner nevertheless differentiated her markedly from a 'normal working person'. The regulation of part-time work also failed to bring about a transformation of conceptions of gender roles. On the contrary, critics even saw this legislation's comparatively early establishment in the Federal Republic as a force stabilizing traditional gender roles in families, and one that hindered later reform attempts by 'denying' the difficulties of mothers who attempted to combine career and family life.[47] Caring for the family remained the task of women; until 1977 this was even explicitly written in the Family Code (*Familiengesetzbuch*).

In conclusion, two key points can be made. In family, pension and part-time employment policy, one clearly sees the government's overarching goal of maintaining traditional gender roles expressed in the social-political reforms of the 1950s and early 1960s. The welfare state's benefits were generally based on the ideal image of a 'complete family' and could often only be offered if a married couple based its partnership on the 'male breadwinner – housewife' model or the 'male breadwinner – supplementary earner' model and claimed entitlements collectively. Mothers only partook of many services when they were married to a 'breadwinner'; for example, in the case of old age pensions. Fathers could only take advantage of all available benefits if they had a so-called 'housewife' or 'extra supplemental earner' at their sides. For instance, this applied to income tax arrangements for married couples (*Ehegattensplitting*). By these means, both parents were assigned different roles. Economic dependency was clearly higher for mothers than for fathers, as, due to their employment, the latter possessed the primary access to income and social benefits.

This picture is completed if one incorporates contemporary marriage and family law into the equation. After marriage, wives had recourse to provision through their husbands, and were to a certain extent insured in this manner – as long as the marriage lasted. Apart from social policy, a veritable bundle of regulations upheld this regime of gender relations in the fields of tax, labour, family and marriage law. A range of factors other than the welfare state's functions also constructed and upheld this gender order. Above all, societal conceptions, norms and values contributed to sustaining the dominance of the 'male breadwinner – housewife' model during this period.[48]

On the other hand, since the introduction of the 'dynamic pension' in 1957, there developed in West German social policy a systematic dichotomy along the boundaries of gender identity. The regulations for employed individuals followed the fundamental principles of status-linked benefits. Receiving them was not supposed to lead to downward social mobility. Benefits' generosity was connected to the amount of income the individual had earned. By contrast, in welfare provision for families, which dealt with the care-giver side of things, benefits aimed to afford sufficient means to secure the minimum of human needs. The consequence was a worsening of a family's position if a parent ceased to be employed and became reliant on social security. This loss could only partially be made up for if two partners married, established a clear division of labour between care work and salaried employment, and thus pooled their entitlements. The difference between status-linked benefit payments for those engaged in the labour market and need-based provision for those at home was maintained. The following years brought less a revocation of traditional role allocations, but rather a transformation from gender specific to supposedly gender neutral formulations of the dependencies between parents.[49]

Married and Provided for? New Focus on an Old Topic

If the question of mothers' poverty risks had been increasingly marginalized during the 1950s due to the re-establishment of the traditional family model in West German society, certain social developments in the 1960s returned the topic to the political agenda. As early as the mid-1960s, statistics show an increase in the number of divorces. Simultaneously, the number of marriages decreased from 1962 onwards. Even if these developments could at least partly be explained with reference to demographic trends, these statistics nevertheless indicate that the institution of marriage was increasingly eroding as a foundation of the dual gender regime. In addition, the later 1960s also witnessed a massive decrease in the number of births.[50] The so-called '*Pillenknick*' appeared as an alarming development to many contemporaries, who saw it, along with a rise in illegitimate births and an increasing number of working mothers, as heralding the end of the 'golden age of the family'. These changes crucially undermined the West German welfare state's previous operational structures.

In 1976, the social policy minister of Rheinland-Pfalz, Heiner Geißler, published a report entitled 'The New Social Question'.[51] In a skilful manner, this report drew upon sociological and feminist debates as well as contemporary criticisms of the Federal Republic's welfare state.[52] Proceeding on the basis of the highly controversial thesis that in 1974 in West Germany, there were around 5.8 million people whose living standard lay below the level provided by social assistance, Geißler came to the conclusion that these poor individuals were above all 'underprivileged' because they did not belong to the category of 'producers', were not participating in the labour market, and could not organize themselves into trade unions. 'Female gender, old age and lots of children', were, according to Geißler's diagnosis, the key characteristics displayed by these victims of the 'new poverty'.[53] This phenomenon, unlike the 'old social question', did not relate to the conflict between labour and capital, but rather, in Geißler's opinion, stemmed from generational and gender conflicts.

In the course of his investigation, Geißler addressed the 'situation of women'. He stated:

> If women are only engaged in household and family tasks, then they are fundamentally disadvantaged vis-a-vis men and women in employment with regards to social security … The deficiencies of independent security for women are often hidden within intact marriages. In the event of divorce or of the husband's death, however, they openly reveal themselves.[54]

He went on to argue:

Contemporary social security provisions for non-working women contradict the fact that these individuals perform with their work in the family and household, especially with regards to the upbringing of children, not only crucial functions for the survival of the family, but also a significant service to wider society. The one-sided orientation of social insurance around the (generally employed) husband especially ignores the fact that his wife, by taking care of the children, is responsible for ensuring that he is able to devote himself fully to a career. The man's pensions entitlements are regularly 'jointly earned' by the non-working wife.[55]

If Geißler's portrayal up to this point had been inspired by feminist literature from the pens of Simone de Beauvoir, Renate Hellwig, Renate Meyer-Harter, Helge Pross, Alva Myrdal and Viola Klein,[56] the Christian Democratic social expert nevertheless came to conclusions which placed him in sharp opposition to many feminists. Fundamentally, there appeared to be two plausible ways of providing housewives and mothers with social insurance. One conceivable possibility was that mothers should concentrate primarily on caring for the household and childrearing, and should be encouraged to have several children. Their family work should then be remunerated by social policy measures such as the payment of a child-raising allowance (*Erziehungsgeld*) as well as the provision of an independent social security entitlement on the basis of the amount of time women spent raising children.

The other possible solution consisted of alleviating the tension confronting mothers between work and family life by providing such an extensive system of public childcare that they could engage in fulltime employment. Geißler advocated a clear position in his book, namely that the upbringing of children should remain in the family.[57] Geißler's suggestions did not aim to help mothers participate in the labour market; rather he wanted to strengthen household work, and above all the upbringing of children, as the 'essential cultural function of the woman'. His proposed solution therefore consisted of the payment of a child-raising allowance (*Erziehungsgeld*) to women who stayed home in the first years of their child's life.[58]

Geißler's arguments kicked off a lively debate. In particular, his criticisms of social policy, which, in his view, missed poverty's core through its fixation on the 'old social question', raised fundamental questions about the West German welfare state.[59] His theses also proved inflammatory regarding questions of gender equality. However, his suggestions concerning the social security of women were at this point nothing new. Rather, they were formed in the context of ongoing discussions since the 1960s about the introduction of a so-called motherly, parental or childcare wage.[60] These policies were proposed from diverse positions on the political spectrum: since the late 1960s, the German Trade Unions Association (Deutscher Gewerkschaftsbund) had demanded the introduction of parental leave and financial compensation for employed parents engaged in childcare; and in 1974, the CDU/CSU had proposed a 'parental allowance' (*Elterngeld*) to the Bundestag, a subsidy which, regardless of gender, would be paid to the parent who was responsible for staying at home and caring for children, regardless of whether that individual had previously worked or not. The Christian-Democratic parties advocated 'parental allowance' as a better alternative to the expansion of childcare institutions and the model project 'Day Mothers' (*Tagesmütter*) which the SPD government was implementing at this time. In 1974, this proposal failed to be implemented at the federal level due to its high costs. Nevertheless, federal states governed by the CDU/CSU, such as Lower Saxony, introduced a child-raising allowance (Landeserziehungsgeld).[61]

After the change of government at the federal level, in 1982, the CDU-led coalition decided in 1985 to introduce parental leave and the child-raising allowance across West Germany. This measure applied equally to mothers and fathers and was not tied to previous employment.[62] In the same year, the Kohl government also resolved to introduce a 'child year' into pension insurance. For the first time in the Federal Republic's history, care work was individually honoured in social insurance by affording mothers a year's pension payments per child.[63]

These reforms represented a marked symbolic step away from the 'male breadwinner – supplementary earner' model. For the first time, the upbringing of children was placed on the same level as salaried employment within the social security system. Individuals caring for children were now entitled to their own independent social security provision. This development was the expression of a new form of social policy, focused much less on the family as a whole, and much more on the individual. This new focus was part of a European-wide transformation process, whereby the relationships between individual, familial and societal solidarities and responsibilities fundamentally changed.[64] The reform of marriage law also played a part in these transformations, with the Federal Republic shifting its definitions in this field in the 1970s towards an equal partnership with greater individual responsibility, and a more just division of property. Characteristic of these changes were also the gender neutral formulations of the relevant legal documents.[65]

If one analyses these reforms in terms of their economic effects, it is nevertheless apparent that the new regulations continued to assign two unequal roles within a relationship. The child-raising allowance (*Erziehungsgeld*) of 1985 was so modest that it did not provide the basis for the existence of an independent household: the parent in receipt of these payments continued to be financially dependent on a 'breadwinner'.[66] For single parents, the child-raising allowance (*Erziehungsgeld*) as well as the 'baby year' in the pension system represented an insufficient basis to maintain an independent existence. It is hardly surprising that single parents furthermore formed a central group in the debates of the 1980s concerning the 'new poverty'.[67]

Quantitatively, the largest group among the Federal Republic's poor population in the 1980s was, however, older, single women.[68] At the start of the decade, around 8 per cent of women over sixty-five claimed social assistance, with a similar number estimated as failing to avail themselves of this entitlement due to shame or ignorance of their entitlement to it.[69] Many of these women had their own pensions and frequently also widow's pensions, the combination of which was nevertheless inadequate to meet their living costs.[70] The old age poverty of women in the 1980s brought biographies into the focus which had partly begun during the First World War; wars, economic crises and waves of unemployment had shaped these women's work biographies as much as normative gender expectations and social policies. Their poverty during the 1980s was the consequence of social frameworks and individual decisions which reached back over decades. These women's lives, which had been orientated around their roles as housewives and mothers, and prioritized their husbands as wage earners, found expression in their poverty during the 1980s. Contemporary observers moreover deemed the cause of this poverty to be gender discrimination in the labour market. Not only the many historic interruptions of employment, but also the low wages and precarious working conditions, were seen as the chief reasons why many women's pensions were so low.[71]

The reasons behind the poverty risks of single parents, by contrast, lay in the present. In 1982, in West Germany, there were around 1,658,000 single parents with unmarried children, of whom 84 per cent were women. This group, which had grown rapidly over the previous decade, formed in the 1980s one of the groups most at risk of poverty in the Federal Republic and reflected increasing numbers of divorces and illegitimate births.[72]

The life course of single parents did not necessarily lead to poverty: but they were at disproportionately high risk of it. In 1982, around 144,000 single women received social assistance and the great majority of them received no maintenance payments from their children's fathers. At the same time, single parents possessed limited employment possibilities as long as their children were young.[73] The poverty risk of single parents was also alarming as it frequently failed to respect distinctions of class. For example, among single mothers, there were especially large numbers with a high quality school diploma.[74] However, this poverty was also frequently temporally limited, with many single parents finding their way out of it within a few years.[75]

This poverty risk thereby highlighted with all the more clarity the inadequacy of a welfare regime that was predicated upon an outmoded gender regime. The poverty of women acquired specific factors through the interaction of gender roles with social policy, which could not be subsumed within the general term of 'new poverty'.[76] The topic was not 'new', but it was further overtaken by discussions concerning the 'new poverty' during the 1980s. The poverty risk of women, similar to that of the unemployed, nevertheless drew attention to a shared problem: namely, social security's orientation around the cornerstone of salaried work in West Germany. Heiner Geißler had also demonstrated this, but had come to traditional, conservative conclusions, and his proposed solutions were based on the restoration of traditional gender roles.

The Green Party's rise during the 1980s signalled the arrival of a political voice which cast fundamental doubt over the central place of employment in the Federal Republic's welfare state. In light of the 'crisis of working society' *(Krise der Arbeitsgesellschaft)*, the system seemed to be losing its foundations; in its unequal treatment of both genders, it was moreover morally indefensible in the eyes of many Greens. Their criticism of the welfare state was therefore much more fundamental than the preceding disputes concerning Heiner Geißler's arguments.[77]

The increasing importance attached to questions concerning care work in the 1970s and 1980s was linked to changing social conditions. If poverty policy can be taken as an indicator of the gaps in the welfare state's security net, then these holes appeared obvious from the 1970s onwards, as private welfare nets became increasingly fragile. It would nevertheless be reductionist to interpret developments in social policy as mere reactions to changing external conditions. They must simultaneously be located within longer-term discussions concerning categories of justice in the welfare state. If one understands the welfare state as an institution designed to balance out social inequalities which are not socially acceptable, then gender inequality advanced from the late 1960s onwards from being an acceptable (and supported) form of social inequality to one which was unacceptable.[78]

Apart from debates concerning poverty, from the 1970s onwards, the 'male breadwinner – supplementary earner' model was increasingly questioned as a basis of the West German welfare state. No fundamental political decisions, however, stemmed from this criticism in the 'old' Federal Republic. Indeed, due to changed social and cultural contexts, one can discern an increased appreciation for the significance of care work. But the model of a couple relationship has remained the social security system's guiding principle. Reforms – whether in integrating care workers into employment, or providing independent social security for care work – remained half-hearted in the 'old' Federal Republic.[79] The effects were clearly revealed in the development of poverty; the expanding group of single parents and elderly women had a significantly heightened poverty risk compared to the wider West German population. A state of affairs remained whereby only those domestic care workers who were married enjoyed financial security.

Notes

This chapter has been translated by Thomas Brodie.

1. M. Simmel-Joachim. 1993. '"Frauenarmut", in Deutscher Verein für öffentliche und private Fürsorge' (ed.), *Fachlexikon der sozialen Arbeit*. 3rd edn. Frankfurt/Main: Deutscher Verein für Öffentliche und Private Fürsorge, p. 353.
2. Bundesministerium für Arbeit und Soziales. 2013. *Lebenslagen in Deutschland: Der vierte Armuts- und Reichtumsbericht der Bundesregierung*. Berlin, pp. 6–15. The gender

neutral formulation of the poverty risks associated with care work in the present German poverty report have received some criticism, for it is overwhelmingly women who continue to be responsible for household work and the upbringing of children. A further reason for this criticism is that, partly due to their family commitments, but also independently of these, women occupy less desirable positions in the labour market. They disproportionately work in lower-paid fields and precarious employment conditions. For the criticism of gender neutral formulations, see also the statements of Sabrina Klaus-Schelletter and Ingo Kolf of the German Trade Unions Association (Deutscher Gewerkschaftsbund): S. Klaus-Schelletter, and I. Kolf. 2013. 'Analyse des Vierten Armuts- und Reichtumsberichts der Bundesregierung', *Sozialmagazin* 38(3–4):6–15.

3. This is rather a problem of the last twenty years, in which under the slogan of an 'adult worker model', activities outside the sphere of employment are marginalized. For criticism of this model, see: J. Lewis. 2006. 'Gender and Welfare in Modern Europe', *Past and Present, Supplement* 1:39–54.

4. R.G. Moeller. 1997. *Geschützte Mütter: Frauen und Familien in der westdeutschen Nachkriegspolitik*. Munich: Deutsche Taschenbuch, p. 214.

5. *Bürgerliches Gesetzbuch*: BGBl. 1985, I, pp. 1450–1471.

6. See A. Kohleiss. 1987. 'Frauenrechte in der gesetzlichen Rentenversicherung', in U. Gerhard, A. Schwarzer and V. Slupik (eds), *Auf Kosten der Frauen: Frauenrechte im Sozialstaat*. Weinheim/Basel: Beltz, p. 120.

7. B. Riedmüller. 1985. 'Armutspolitik und Familienpolitik: Die Armut der Familie ist die Armut der Frau', in S. Leibfried and F. Tennstedt (eds), *Politik der Armut und die Spaltung des Sozialstaats*. Frankfurt/Main: Suhrkamp, pp. 311–35.

8. Sommeruniversität für Frauen (ed.). 1977. *Frauen und Wissenschaft: Beiträge zur Berliner Sommeruniversität für Frauen: Juli 1976*. Berlin: Courage; id 1978. *Frauen als bezahlte und unbezahlte Arbeitskräfte: Beiträge zur 2. Berliner Sommeruniversität für Frauen: Oktober 1977*. Berlin: self-published; id. 1979. *Frauen und Mütter. Beiträge zur 3. Sommeruniversität von und für Frauen 1978*. Berlin: self-published.

9. B. Schäfers. 1992. 'Zum öffentlichen Stellenwert von Armut im sozialen Wandel der Bundesrepublik Deutschland', in S. Leibfried and W. Voges (eds), *Armut im modernen Wohlfahrtsstaat*. Opladen: Westdeutsche Verlag, pp. 104–23; C. Lorke. 2015. *Armut im geteilten Deutschland. Die Wahrnehmung sozialer Randlagen in der Bundesrepublik und der DDR*. Frankfurt, New York: Campus, pp. 48–51.

10. H. Thurnwald. 1948. *Gegenwartsprobleme Berliner Familien: Eine soziologische Untersuchung an 498 Familien*. Berlin: Weidmann, p. 18.

11. B. Willenbacher. 1988. 'Zerrüttung und Bewährung der Nachkriegsfamilie', in M. Broszat, K.-D. Henke and H. Woller (eds), *Von Stalingrad zur Währungsreform: Zur Sozialgeschichte des Umbruchs in Deutschland*. Munich: Oldenbourg, pp. 595–618.

12. C. Kuller. 2007. 'Soziale Sicherung von Frauen – ein ungelöstes Strukturproblem im männlichen Wohlfahrtsstaat: Die Bundesrepublik im europäischen Vergleich', *Archiv für Sozialgeschichte* 47: 209.

13. A. Schnädelbach. 2009. *Kriegerwitwen: Lebensbewältigung zwischen Arbeit und Familie in Westdeutschland nach 1945*. Frankfurt/Main: Campus.

14. Schnädelbach, *Kriegerwitwen*, pp. 44–46.

15. M. Kuhnhenne. 2005. *Frauenleitbilder und Bildung in der westdeutschen Nachkriegszeit. Analyse am Beispiel der Region Bremen*. Wiesbaden: VS Verlag für Sozialwissenschaften.

16. S. Buske. 2004. *Fräulein Mutter und ihr Bastard: Eine Geschichte der Unehelichkeit in Deutschland 1900–1970*. Göttingen: Wallstein, p. 196.

17. C. Kuller. 2004. *Familienpolitik im föderativen Sozialstaat: Die Formierung eines Politikfeldes in der Bundesrepublik 1949–1975*. Munich: Oldenbourg, p. 49.

18. M. Willing. 2005a. 'Fürsorge', in G. Schulz (ed.), *Geschichte der Sozialpolitik in Deutschland seit 1945*, vol. 3, *1949–1957: Bewältigung der Kriegsfolgen, Rückkehr zur sozialpolitischen Normalität*. Baden-Baden: Nomos, p. 591.

19. E. Heinemann. 1996. 'Complete Families, Half Families and No Families at All: Female Headed Households and the Reconstruction of the Family in the Early Federal Republic', *Central European History* 29:24; Moeller, *Geschützte Mütter*, pp. 126–29.

20. E. Heinemann. 1999. *What Difference Does a Husband Make? Women and Marital Status in Nazi and Postwar Germany*. Berkeley: University of California Press.

21. Willing, 'Fürsorge', p. 591.

22. H.G. Hockerts. 1986. 'Integration der Gesellschaft: Gründungskrise und Sozialpolitik in der frühen Bundesrepublik', *Zeitschrift für Sozialreform* 32:25–41.

23. Willing, 'Fürsorge', p. 591.

24. H. Hartmann. 1981. *Sozialhilfebedürftigkeit und 'Dunkelziffer der Armut': Bericht über das Forschungsprojekt zur Lage potentiell Sozialhilfebedürftiger*. Stuttgart et al.: Kohlhammer.

25. The parameters of categorization were repeatedly changed and the recipients of welfare social assistance did not represent a stable group, but rather a fluctuating one. F. Föcking. 2007. *Fürsorge im Wirtschaftsboom: Die Entstehung des Bundessozialhilfegesetzes von 1961*. Munich: Oldenbourg, pp. 71–84.

26. See ibid., pp. 298–308.

27. Kuller, *Familienpolitik*, p. 52.

28. U. Münch. 2007. 'Familien-, Jugend- und Altenpolitik', in M. Ruck and M. Boldorf (eds), *Geschichte der Sozialpolitik in Deutschland seit 1945*, vol. 4, *1957–1966: Sozialpolitik im Zeichen des erreichten Wohlstands*. Baden-Baden: Nomos, p. 566.

29. D.V. Simon. 1981. 'Die neuen Leitbilder im Ehe- und Familienrecht und ihre Konsequenzen für die Familie', in R. von Schweitzer (ed.), *Leitbilder für Familie und Familienpolitik*. Berlin: Duncker & Humblot, p. 30.

30. W. Schubert 2007 (ed.). 2007. *Die Reform des Ehescheidungsrechts von 1976: Quellen zum Ersten Gesetz vom 14.6.1976 zur Reform des Ehe- und Familienrechts*. Frankfurt/Main: Peter Lang; U. Münch. 2006. 'Familien-, Jugend- und Altenpolitik', in H.G. Hockerts (ed.), *Geschichte der Sozialpolitik in Deutschland seit 1945*, vol 5, *1966–1974: Eine Zeit vielfältigen Aufbruchs*. Baden-Baden: Nomos, p. 647.

31. Münch 2007, 'Familienpolitik', p. 649.

32. Föcking, *Fürsorge*.

33. B. Riedmüller. 1984. 'Frauen haben keine Rechte: Zur Stellung der Frauen im System sozialer Sicherheit', in I. Kickbusch and B. Riedmüller (eds), *Die armen Frauen: Frauen und Sozialpolitik*. Frankfurt/Main: Suhrkamp, pp. 52–58.

34. Moeller, *Geschützte Mütter*, p. 128.

35. Bundesregierung. 1966. 'Bericht der Bundesregierung über die Situation der Frauen in Beruf, Familie und Gesellschaft vom 14.9.1966: Bundestags-Drucksache 5/909'. Berlin.

36. Bundesregierung. 1968. 'Bericht der Bundesregierung über die Lage der Familien in der Bundesrepublik Deutschland, 25.1.1968: Bundestags-Drucksache V/2532'. Berlin.

37. Bundesministerium für Familien- und Jugendfragen. 1959. 'Die wirtschaftliche Situation der Familien in der Bundesrepublik: Denkschrift des Familienministeriums'. Bonn. Archived at the Bundesarchiv Koblenz, B 191/109.

38. As demonstrated by ministerial files, the core of this political conflict was the question of whether a market wage was sufficient to provide for a 'full' family with two children, or whether additional support was already necessary after with the birth of the second child. This report's political aim was the introduction of a 'second child payment allowance' (*Zweitkindergeld*) for 'family providers' with a low income. This was introduced in 1961. (Kuller, *Famienpolitik*, pp. 176–86.)

39. Kuller, *Familienpolitik*.

40. W. Schreiber. 1955. *Existenzsicherheit in der industriellen Gesellschaft: Vorschläge zur 'Sozialreform'*. Cologne: Bachem; H. Achinger. et al. (eds). 1955. *Neuordnung der sozialen Leistungen: Denkschrift auf Anregung des Herrn Bundeskanzlers*. Cologne: Greven.

41. H.G. Hockerts. 1980. *Sozialpolitische Entscheidungen im Nachkriegsdeutschland: Alliierte und deutsche Sozialversicherungspolitik 1945 bis 1957*. Stuttgart: Klett-Cotta; Kuller, *Familienpolitik*, pp. 171–73.

42. Kohleiss, *Frauenrechte*, p. 128. Translated by Thomas Brodie.

43. C. Torp. 2015. *Gerechtigkeit im Wohlfahrtsstaat. Alter und Alterssicherung in Deutschland und Großbritannien von 1945 bis heute*. Göttingen: Vandenhoeck & Ruprecht, pp. 67–108; D. Hilpert. 2012. *Wohlfahrtsstaat der Mittelschichten? Sozialpolitik und gesellschaftlicher Wandel in der Bundesrepublik Deutschland (1949–1975)*. Göttingen: Vandenhoeck & Ruprecht, pp. 133–37; U. Haerendel. 2007. 'Geschlechterpolitik und Alterssicherung: Frauen in der gesetzlichen Rentenversicherung von den Anfängen bis zur Reform 1957', *Deutsche Rentenversicherung* 62(2/3):118–21.

44. This problem was exacerbated by the salary gap between men and women.

45. Moeller, *Geschützte Mütter*, p. 210; H.G. Hockerts. 1992. 'Vom Nutzen und Nachteil der Parteienkonkurrenz: Die Rentenreform 1972 – ein Lehrstück', in K.D. Bracher et al. (eds), *Staat und Parteien: Festschrift für Rudolf Morsey zum 65. Geburtstag*. Berlin: Duncker & Humblot, pp. 903–34.

46. C. von Oertzen. 1999. *Teilzeitarbeit und die Lust am Zuverdienen: Geschlechterpolitik und gesellschaftlicher Wandel in Westdeutschland 1948–1969*. Göttingen: Vandenhoeck & Ruprecht.

47. The emergence of part-time work was accompanied by the creation of a segregated labour market for women characterized by markedly worse promotion and remunerative opportunities, thus deepening the 'gender gap': A. Myrdal and V. Klein. 1960. *Die Doppelrolle der Frau in Familie und Beruf*. Cologne: Kiepenhoeuer & Witsch, p. 210.

48. B. Pfau-Effinger. 1998. 'Gender cultures and the gender arrangement – a theoretical framework for cross-national comparisons on gender', *British Journal of Social Sciences* 11:147–66.

49. L. Luckhaus. 2008. 'Die Rolle der Abhängigkeit im britischen Sozialleistungsrecht. Auf der Suche nach einem neuen rechtlichen Bezugsrahmen', in *Dokumentation der Tagung 'Eigenverantwortung, private und öffentliche Solidarität – Rollenleitbilder im Familien- und Sozialrecht im europäischen Vergleich'*. Baden-Baden: Nomos, p. 265.

50. It is especially apparent today that it is the 'baby boom' of the early postwar period, far more than the drop in birth numbers after 1968, which must be interpreted as a deviation from long-term demographic trends.

51. H. Geißler. 1976. *Die Neue Soziale Frage*. Freiburg/Breisgau: Herder.

52. W. Süß. 2011. 'Umbau am "Modell Deutschland": Sozialer Wandel, ökonomische Krise und wohlfahrtsstaatliche Reformpolitik in der Bundesrepublik "nach dem Boom"', *Journal of Modern European History* 9:224–27; Lorke, *Armut*, pp. 237–41.

53. Geißler, *Soziale Frage*, p. 28.

54. Ibid. Text translated by Thomas Brodie.

55. Ibid. Text translated by Thomas Brodie.

56. Ibid, p. 23.

57. M. Wingen. 1978. 'Bevölkerungs- und familienpolitische Aspekte der sozialen Frage in entwickelten Industriegesellschaften', in H.P. Widmaier (ed.), *Zur Neuen Sozialen Frage*. Berlin: Duncker & Humblot, pp. 172–75.

58. Geißler, *Soziale Frage*, pp. 25, 40.

59. See especially Chapter 7, by Winfried Süß, in this volume.

60. W. Kolbe. 2002. *Elternschaft im Wohlfahrtsstaat: Schweden und die Bundesrepublik im Vergleich 1945–2000*. Frankfurt/Main: Campus; U. Münch and W. Hornstein. 2008. 'Familien-, Jugend- und Altenpolitik', in M.H. Geyer (ed.), *Geschichte der Sozialpolitik in Deutschland seit 1945*, vol. 6, *1974–1982: Neue Herausforderungen, wachsende Unsicherheiten*. Baden-Baden: Nomos, pp. 637–92.

61. Münch and Hornstein, 'Familienpolitik', p. 655.

62. Until the mid 1980s, there only existed the maternity leave introduced for employed women in 1979 prior to and after birth. Bleses and Seeleib-Kaiser interpreted this regulation as a late offshoot of earlier political projects, which, with their close reference to previous employment history and in their limitation of women, barely found any resonance in the contemporary debates of the late 1970s: P. Bleses and M. Seeleib-Kaiser. 2004. *The Dual Transformation of the German Welfare State*. Basingstoke: Palgrave Macmillan, p. 81.

63. Kuller, 'Sicherung von Frauen', p. 217.

64. E. Eichenhofer. 2008. 'Schlussfolgerungen aus Sicht des Sozialrechtsvergleichs. 20 Themen – 20 Thesen', in Bundesministerium für Familie, *Dokumentation der Tagung "Eigenverantwortung, private und öffentliche Solidarität – Rollenleitbilder im Familien- und Sozialrecht im europäischen Vergleich"*. Baden-Baden: Nomos, pp. 459–473, 459.

65. K. Scheiwe. 2005. 'Soziale Sicherungsmodelle zwischen Individualisierung und Abhängigkeiten – verliert das traditionelle "Ernährermodell" im Sozialversicherungsrecht an Bedeutung?', *Kritische Justiz* 38:127–151, 134.

66. Kolbe, *Elternschaft*, 412.

67. M. Willing. 2005b. 'Sozialhilfe', in M.G. Schmidt (ed.). *Geschichte der Sozialpolitik in Deutschland seit 1945*: Bd. 7: *1982–1989: Finanzielle Konsolidierung und institutionelle Reform*. Baden-Baden: Nomos, pp. 479–516. 511.

68. Lorke. *Armut*, p. 302 f.

69. S. Koeppinghoff. 1984. 'Endstation Sozialhilfe: Defizite der Einkommenssicherung von Frauen im Alter', in I. Kickbusch and B. Riedmüller (eds). *Die armen Frauen: Frauen und Sozialpolitik*. Frankfurt/Main: Suhrkamp, pp. 252–265, 252.

70. Riedmüller, 'Frauen', p. 315.

71. A. Pfaff. 1979. *Einzelgutachten für die Sachverständigenkommission für die soziale Sicherung der Frauen und der Hinterbliebenen*. Bonn: Bundesministerium für Arbeit und Soziales; Riedmüller, 'Frauen'; J. Allmendinger. 1994. *Lebensverlauf und Sozialpolitik: Die Ungleichheit zwischen Mann und Frau und ihr öffentlicher Ertrag*. Frankfurt/New York: Campus.

72. Riedmüller, 'Frauen', p. 317.
73. P. Schallhöfer. 1987. 'Frauen als Sozialhilfeempfängerinnen', in U. Gerhard, A. Schwarzer and V. Slupnik (eds), *Auf Kosten der Frauen: Frauenrechte im Sozialstaat.* Weinheim/Basel: Beltz, p. 270.
74. G. Gutschmidt. 1989. 'Armut in Einelternfamilien: Die "typisch weibliche Erwerbsbiographie" ist die zentrale Ursache für Einkommensarmut alleinerziehender Mütter', *Blätter der Wohlfahrtspflege* 136(11–12):335.
75. N. Ott et al. 2012. *Dynamik der Lebensform 'alleinerziehend': Gutachten für das BMAS, Forschungsbericht 421.* Bonn: Bundesministerium für Arbeit und Soziales.
76. A. Reichelt. 1989. 'Exkurs: Armut und Frauen', *Blätter der Wohlfahrtspflege* 136(11–12):341.
77. M.S. Graf. 2015. *Die Inszenierung der Neuen Armut im sozialpolitischen Repertoire von SPD und Grünen 1983–1987.* Frankfurt/Main: Peter Lang, pp. 112–115. For other approaches to the 'new poverty', such as that of the German Trade Unions Association (*Deutscher Gewerkschaftsbund*), which above all focused on the unemployed, see Chapter 8 in this volume.
78. C. Kuller. 2010. 'Ungleichheit der Geschlechter', in: H.G. Hockerts and W. Süß (eds). *Soziale Ungleichheit im Sozialstaat: Die Bundesrepublik Deutschland und Großbritannien im Vergleich.* München: Oldenbourg Verl., pp. 65–88, 83.
79. H.F. Zacher. 2001. 'Grundlagen der Sozialpolitik in der Bundesrepublik Deutschland', in Bundesministerium für Arbeit und Sozialordnung (ed.), *Geschichte der Sozialpolitik in Deutschland seit 1945*: Vol. 1, *Grundlagen der Sozialpolitik.* Baden-Baden: Nomos, p. 572.

Works Cited

Achinger, H. et al. (eds). 1955. *Neuordnung der sozialen Leistungen: Denkschrift auf Anregung des Herrn Bundeskanzlers.* Cologne: Greven.

Allmendinger, J. 1994. *Lebensverlauf und Sozialpolitik: Die Ungleichheit zwischen Mann und Frau und ihr öffentlicher Ertrag.* Frankfurt/Main, New York: Campus.

Bleses, P., and M. Seeleib-Kaiser. 2004. *The Dual Transformation of the German Welfare State,* Basingstoke: Palgrave Macmillan.

Bundesministerium für Arbeit und Soziales. 2013. *Lebenslagen in Deutschland: Der vierte Armuts- und Reichtumsbericht der Bundesregierung.* Berlin.

Bundesministerium für Familien- und Jugendfragen. 1959. 'Die wirtschaftliche Situation der Familien in der Bundesrepublik: Denkschrift des Familienministerium'. Bonn. Archived at the Bundesarchiv Koblenz, B 191/109.

Bundesregierung. 1966. 'Bericht der Bundesregierung über die Situation der Frauen in Beruf, Familie und Gesellschaft vom 14.9.1966: Bundestags-Drucksache 5/909'. Berlin.

———. 1968. 'Bericht der Bundesregierung über die Lage der Familien in der Bundesrepublik Deutschland, 25.1.1968: Bundestags-Drucksache V/2532'. Berlin.

Buske, S. 2004. *Fräulein Mutter und ihr Bastard: Eine Geschichte der Unehelichkeit in Deutschland 1900–1970*. Göttingen: Wallstein.

Eichenhofer, E. 2008. 'Schlussfolgerungen aus Sicht des Sozialrechtsvergleichs. 20 Themen – 20 Thesen', in Bundesministerium für Familien, *Dokumentation der Tagung 'Eigenverantwortung, private und öffentliche Solidarität – Rollenleitbilder im Familien- und Sozialrecht im europäischen Vergleich'*. Baden-Baden: Nomos, pp. 459–73.

Föcking, F. 2007. *Fürsorge im Wirtschaftsboom: Die Entstehung des Bundessozialhilfegesetzes von 1961*. Munich: Oldenbourg.

Geißler, H. 1976. *Die Neue Soziale Frage*. Freiburg/Breisgau: Herder.

Graf, M.S. 2015. *Die Inszenierung der Neuen Armut im sozialpolitischen Repertoire von SPD und Grünen 1983–1987*. Frankfurt/Main: Peter Lang.

Gutschmidt, G. 1989. 'Armut in Einelternfamilien: Die "typisch weibliche Erwerbsbiographie" ist die zentrale Ursache für Einkommensarmut alleinerziehender Mütter', *Blätter der Wohlfahrtspflege* 136 (11–12):335–338.

Haerendel, U. 2007. 'Geschlechterpolitik und Alterssicherung: Frauen in der gesetzlichen Rentenversicherung von den Anfängen bis zur Reform 1957', *Deutsche Rentenversicherung* 62(2/3):, 99–124.

Hartmann, H. 1981. *Sozialhilfebedürftigkeit und 'Dunkelziffer der Armut': Bericht über das Forschungsprojekt zur Lage potentiell Sozialhilfebedürftiger*. Stuttgart et al.: Kohlhammer.

Heinemann, E. 1996. 'Complete Families, Half Families and No Families at All: Female Headed Households and the Reconstruction of the Family in the Early Federal Republic', *Central European History* 29:19–60.

———— 1999. *What Difference Does a Husband Make? Women and Marital Status in Nazi and Postwar Germany*. Berkeley: University of California Press.

Hilpert, D. 2012. *Wohlfahrtsstaat der Mittelschichten? Sozialpolitik und gesellschaftlicher Wandel in der Bundesrepublik Deutschland (1949–1975)*. Göttingen: Vandenhoeck & Ruprecht.

Hockerts, H.G. 1980. *Sozialpolitische Entscheidungen im Nachkriegsdeutschland: Alliierte und deutsche Sozialversicherungspolitik 1945 bis 1957*. Stuttgart: Klett-Cotta.

————. 1986. 'Integration der Gesellschaft: Gründungskrise und Sozialpolitik in der frühen Bundesrepublik', *Zeitschrift für Sozialreform* 32:25–41.

————. 1992. 'Vom Nutzen und Nachteil der Parteienkonkurrenz: Die Rentenreform 1972 – ein Lehrstück', in K.D. Bracher et al. (eds), *Staat und Parteien: Festschrift für Rudolf Morsey zum 65. Geburtstag*. Berlin: Duncker & Humblot, pp. 903–34.

Klaus-Schelletter, S., and I. Kolf. 2013. 'Analyse des Vierten Armuts- und Reichtumsberichts der Bundesregierung', *Sozialmagazin* 38(3–4):6–15.

Koeppinghoff, S. 1984. 'Endstation Sozialhilfe: Defizite der Einkommenssicherung von Frauen im Alter', in I. Kickbusch and B. Riedmüller (eds), *Die armen Frauen: Frauen und Sozialpolitik*. Frankfurt/Main: Suhrkamp, pp. 252–65.

Kohleiss, A. 1987. 'Frauenrechte in der gesetzlichen Rentenversicherung', in U. Gerhard, A. Schwarzer and V. Slupik (eds), *Auf Kosten der Frauen: Frauenrechte im Sozialstaat*. Weinheim/Basel: Beltz, pp. 117–73.

Kolbe, W. 2002. *Elternschaft im Wohlfahrtsstaat: Schweden und die Bundesrepublik im Vergleich 1945–2000*. Frankfurt/Main: Campus.

Kuhnhenne, M. 2005. *Frauenleitbilder und Bildung in der westdeutschen Nachkriegszeit. Analyse am Beispiel der Region Bremen*. Wiesbaden: VS Verlag für Sozialwissenschaften.

Kuller, C. 2004. *Familienpolitik im föderativen Sozialstaat: Die Formierung eines Politikfeldes in der Bundesrepublik 1949–1975*. Munich: Oldenbourg.

———. 2007. 'Soziale Sicherung von Frauen – ein ungelöstes Strukturproblem im männlichen Wohlfahrtsstaat: Die Bundesrepublik im europäischen Vergleich', *Archiv für Sozialgeschichte* 47:199–236.

———. 2010. 'Ungleichheit der Geschlechter', in H.G. Hockerts and W. Süß (eds), *Soziale Ungleichheit im Sozialstaat: Die Bundesrepublik Deutschland und Großbritannien im Vergleich*. Munich: Oldenbourg, pp. 65–88.

Lewis, J. 2006. 'Gender and Welfare in Modern Europe', *Past and Present, Supplement* 1:39–54.

Lorke, C. 2015. *Armut im geteilten Deutschland. Die Wahrnehmung sozialer Randlagen in der Bundesrepublik und der DDR*. Frankfurt, New York: Campus.

Luckhaus, L. 2008. 'Die Rolle der Abhängigkeit im britischen Sozialleistungsrecht. Auf der Suche nach einem neuen rechtlichen Bezugsrahmen', in *Dokumentation der Tagung 'Eigenverantwortung, private und öffentliche Solidarität – Rollenleitbilder im Familien- und Sozialrecht im europäischen Vergleich'*. Baden-Baden: Nomos, pp. 260–80.

Moeller, R.G. 1997. *Geschützte Mütter: Frauen und Familien in der westdeutschen Nachkriegspolitik*. Munich: Deutscher Taschenbuch-Verlag.

Münch, U. 2006. 'Familien-, Jugend- und Altenpolitik', in H.G. Hockerts (ed.), *Geschichte der Sozialpolitik in Deutschland seit 1945*, vol. 5, *1966–1974: Eine Zeit vielfältigen Aufbruchs*. Baden-Baden: Nomos, pp. 633–708.

———. 2007. 'Familien-, Jugend- und Altenpolitik', in M. Ruck and M. Boldorf (eds), *Geschichte der Sozialpolitik in Deutschland seit 1945*, vol. 4, *1957–1966: Sozialpolitik im Zeichen des erreichten Wohlstands*. Baden-Baden: Nomos, pp. 549–610.

——— and W. Hornstein. 2008. 'Familien-, Jugend- und Altenpolitik', in M.H. Geyer (ed.), *Geschichte der Sozialpolitik in Deutschland seit 1945*, vol. 6, *1974–1982: Neue Herausforderungen, wachsende Unsicherheiten*. Baden-Baden: Nomos, pp. 637–92.

Myrdal, A., and V. Klein. 1960. *Die Doppelrolle der Frau in Familie und Beruf*. Cologne: Kiepenheuer & Witsch.

Oertzen, C. v. 1999. *Teilzeitarbeit und die Lust am Zuverdienen: Geschlechterpolitik und gesellschaftlicher Wandel in Westdeutschland 1948–1969*. Göttingen: Vandenhoeck & Ruprecht.

Ott, N., M. Hancioglu and B. Hartmann 2012. *Dynamik der Lebensform 'alleinerziehend': Gutachten für das BMAS, Forschungsbericht 421*. Bonn: Bundesministerium für Arbeit und Soziales.

Pfaff, A. 1979. *Einzelgutachten für die Sachverständigenkommission für die soziale Sicherung der Frauen und der Hinterbliebenen*. Bonn: Bundesministerium für Arbeit und Soziales.

Pfau-Effinger, B. 1998. 'Gender cultures and the gender arrangement – a theoretical framework for cross-national comparisons on gender', *British Journal of Social Sciences* 11:147–66.

Reichelt, A. 1989. 'Exkurs: Armut und Frauen', *Blätter der Wohlfahrtspflege* 136(11–12):339–41.

Riedmüller, B. 1984. 'Frauen haben keine Rechte: Zur Stellung der Frauen im System sozialer Sicherheit', in I. Kickbusch and B. Riedmüller (eds), *Die armen Frauen: Frauen und Sozialpolitik*. Frankfurt/Main: Suhrkamp, pp. 46–72.

———. 1985. 'Armutspolitik und Familienpolitik: Die Armut der Familie ist die Armut der Frau', in S. Leibfried and F. Tennstedt (eds), *Politik der Armut und die Spaltung des Sozialstaats*. Frankfurt/Main: Suhrkamp, pp. 311–35.

Schäfers, B. 1992. 'Zum öffentlichen Stellenwert von Armut im sozialen Wandel der Bundesrepublik Deutschland', in S. Leibfried and W. Voges (eds), *Armut im modernen Wohlfahrtsstaat*. Opladen: Westdeutsche Verlag, pp. 104–23.

Schallhöfer, P. 1987. 'Frauen als Sozialhilfeempfängerinnen', in U. Gerhard, A. Schwarzer and V. Slupik (eds), *Auf Kosten der Frauen: Frauenrechte im Sozialstaat*. Weinheim/Basel: Beltz, pp. 231–77.

Scheiwe, K. 2005. 'Soziale Sicherungsmodelle zwischen Individualisierung und Abhängigkeiten – verliert das traditionelle "Ernährermodell" im Sozialversicherungsrecht an Bedeutung?', *Kritische Justiz* 38:127–51.

Schnädelbach, A. 2009. *Kriegerwitwen: Lebensbewältigung zwischen Arbeit und Familie in Westdeutschland nach 1945*. Frankfurt/Main: Campus.

Schreiber, W. 1955. *Existenzsicherheit in der industriellen Gesellschaft: Vorschläge zur 'Sozialreform'*. Cologne: Bachem.

Schubert, W. (ed.). 2007. *Die Reform des Ehescheidungsrechts von 1976: Quellen zum Ersten Gesetz vom 14.6.1976 zur Reform des Ehe- und Familienrechts*. Frankfurt/Main: Peter Lang.

Simmel-Joachim, M. 1993. '"Frauenarmut"', in Deutscher Verein für öffentliche und private Fürsorge' (ed.), *Fachlexikon der sozialen Arbeit*, 3rd edn. Frankfurt/Main: Deutscher Verein für Öffentliche und Private Fürsorge, pp. 352–353.

Simon, D.V. 1981. ''Die neuen Leitbilder im Ehe- und Familienrecht und ihre Konsequenzen für die Familie', in R. von Schweitzer (ed.), *Leitbilder für Familie und Familienpolitik*. Berlin: Duncker & Humblot, pp. 27–39.

Sommeruniversität für Frauen (ed.). 1977. *Frauen und Wissenschaft: Beiträge zur Berliner Sommeruniversität für Frauen: Juli 1976*. Berlin: Courage.

————. 1978. *Frauen als bezahlte und unbezahlte Arbeitskräfte: Beiträge zur 2. Berliner Sommeruniversität für Frauen: Oktober 1977*. Berlin: self-published.

————. 1979. *Frauen und Mütter. Beiträge zur 3. Sommeruniversität von und für Frauen 1978*. Berlin: self-published.

Süß, W. 2011. 'Umbau am "Modell Deutschland": Sozialer Wandel, ökonomische Krise und wohlfahrtsstaatliche Reformpolitik in der Bundesrepublik "nach dem Boom"', *Journal of Modern European History* 9:215–40.

Thurnwald, H. 1948. *Gegenwartsprobleme Berliner Familien: Eine soziologische Untersuchung an 498 Familien*. Berlin: Weidmann.

Torp, C. 2015. *Gerechtigkeit im Wohlfahrtsstaat. Alter und Alterssicherung in Deutschland und Großbritannien von 1945 bis heute*. Göttingen: Vandenhoeck & Ruprecht.

Willenbacher, B. 1988. 'Zerrüttung und Bewährung der Nachkriegsfamilie', in M. Broszat, K.-D. Henke and H. Woller (eds), *Von Stalingrad zur Währungsreform: Zur Sozialgeschichte des Umbruchs in Deutschland*. Munich: Oldenbourg, pp. 595–618.

Willing, M. 2005a. 'Fürsorge', in G. Schulz (ed.), *Geschichte der Sozialpolitik in Deutschland seit 1945*, vol 3, *1949–1957: Bewältigung der Kriegsfolgen, Rückkehr zur sozialpolitischen Normalität*. Baden-Baden: Nomos, pp. 559–96.

————. 2005b. 'Sozialhilfe', in M.G. Schmidt (ed.), *Geschichte der Sozialpolitik in Deutschland seit 1945*, vol. 7, *1982–1989: Finanzielle Konsolidierung und institutionelle Reform*. Baden-Baden: Nomos, pp. 479–516.

Wingen, M. 1978. 'Bevölkerungs- und familienpolitische Aspekte der sozialen Frage in entwickelten Industriegesellschaften', in H.P. Widmaier (ed.), *Zur Neuen Sozialen Frage*. Berlin: Duncker & Humblot, pp. 149–185.

Zacher, H.F. 2001. 'Grundlagen der Sozialpolitik in der Bundesrepublik Deutschland', in Bundesministerium für Arbeit und Sozialordnung (ed.), *Geschichte der Sozialpolitik in Deutschland seit 1945:* vol 1: *Grundlagen der Sozialpolitik*. Baden-Baden: Nomos, pp. 333–684.

Christiane Kuller is Professor of Contemporary History at the University of Erfurt. Her recent publications include: 'Ungleichheit der Geschlechter', in: H.G. Hockerts and W. Süß (eds), *Soziale Ungleichheit im Sozialstaat. Die Bundesrepublik Deutschland und Großbritannien im Vergleich*, (2010), pp. 65–88; *Bürokratie und Verbrechen. Antisemitische Finanzpolitik und Verwaltungspraxis im nationalsozialistischen Deutschland* (2013); 'Drei-Generationen-Solidarität', in: B. Emunds and H.G. Hockerts (eds), *Den Kapitalismus bändigen. Oswald von Nell-Breunings Impulse für die Sozialpolitik*, (2015), pp. 195–210.

CHAPTER 7

A 'New Social Question'?

Politics, Social Sciences and the Rediscovery of Poverty in Post-boom Western Germany

Winfried Süß

Introduction

The German welfare state is a quantifiable object. Laws determine the size of current social security benefits and these provisions mostly stand in a fixed relation to previous social contributions. A lot of money is moved around in these processes: between the sick and the healthy; the employed and the unemployed; and a little, too, between the poor and the wealthy; but above all, between generations. The sums of money in circulation are enormous. In 1975, more than a third of West Germany's Gross National Product (GNP) was invested in social services. The major part of this capital – some 13 per cent of GNP – benefited retirees.[1]

Politicians have made much of these statistics. For a long time, they did so in the triumphalist language of faith in ongoing economic growth, which described the welfare state's development with metaphors of 'faster, higher and further'. Above all, in the early 1970s, verbs of movement with regards to the future shaped political communication concerning the welfare state. For instance, the then governing social-democratic–liberal coalition proudly calculated that the social budget already exceeded that of the military, and would continue to grow in the future.[2]

Since the oil price shocks of the 1970s, the growth of the welfare state has, by contrast, increasingly been discussed in terms of crisis. Debates concerning the 'cost explosion' in the health service (since 1975) and the financial crisis of the pension system (since autumn 1976) established a dominant narrative within West German socio-political discussion, stressing the need for fiscal retrenchment. Whereas previously the Federal Republic's political culture had deemed the expansion of the social expenditure ratio to be the proof of successful social policy, since the mid 1970s, 'success' was linked to the restriction of the welfare state's growth has occupied this role. In the context of shrinking possibilities of redistributive politics, the question now became central as to whether, and under what circumstances, the maintenance of the existing welfare system was possible and desirable.

This transformation was clearly expressed in a pronounced semantic shift. In the phase of welfare state expansion during the economic boom following the Second World War, the term 'social security' was above all used to refer to individual groups of recipients of benefits, in order to highlight a need for socio-political action. Since the mid-1970s, by contrast, the term has described the institutional framework of social insurance, and the need to preserve its long-term stability amidst changed economic circumstances.[3] For example, in 1979, the social democratic minister of labour, Herbert Ehrenberg, summarized the federal government's policies in these terms:

> Firstly, we have ... adjusted the system of social benefits to reflect changed economic parameters, without having placed this burden on the shoulders of the poor. Secondly, we have ensured the system of social insurance is embedded in our overall stabilization of the economic and political situation.[4]

It is therefore safe to assume that West German politicians working in the field of social policy had quite an exact understanding of the direction in which the welfare state was directing capital flows, and what these funds were supposed to achieve in society.

This assumption appears all the more plausible because the federal government introduced a statistical reporting system as early as 1968, which was closely related to the politics of domestic reform (*Innere Reformen*).[5] The Federal Ministry of Labour's 'social report' (*Sozialbericht*) and its 'social budget' (*Sozialbudget*) provided a differentiated and panoramic view of the social security system, which combined analysis of the status quo with a prognosis of future developments in the field.[6] This new form of socio-political knowledge was designed to help deploy statistical information more effectively as a policy tool by coordinating the various parts of the system of social security, and facilitating long-term social policy planning. The hope was that providing a better statistical basis for policy making, and incorporating the advice of academic experts, would defuse social conflicts concerning the distribution of wealth. This principle of 'rational social politics'[7] was a child of the Keynesian faith in modernization, which accorded the state an influential role in the mediation of different social interests.

A memorandum from the head office of the Federal Ministry of Labour from November 1975 nevertheless reveals that this assumption had to be reconsidered with regards to an important field of social policy. When, in order to respond to an opposition campaign, the ministry's leadership required up-to-date statistics concerning the extent of poverty in the Federal Republic, it was surprised to discover that the ministry only possessed information regarding the amounts of social assistance (*Sozialhilfe*) payments made to recipients. Relevant information detailing the distribution of income was also lacking. The relevant official in the Labour Ministry was forced to concede that it was impossible based on current data to determine the number of households whose income lay below the basic rate of supplementary benefit payments. If one defined poverty in relative terms as the distance from the population's average income, then the exact tally of poor individuals in the Federal Republic was neither known nor currently ascertainable. One had to be content with the estimates of the German Institute for Economic Research, whose findings the opposition had already abundantly cited.[8] In other words: with regards to one of its central tasks, the prevention of poverty, the West German welfare state was operating with restricted vision.[9] Government officials were reduced to the politically unconvincing tactic of searching for statistical errors in their opponents' criticisms.

This realization was profoundly discomforting for the social-democratic–liberal federal government. For it was during the parliamentary session of autumn 1975 that Heiner Geißler, the Christian Democratic minister of social affairs in Rheinland-Pfalz, set the 'new social question' on the political agenda at the very moment the federal government was attempting to implement the first major budgetary reduction of welfare provision since 1945.[10] He spectacularly claimed that over six million citizens were threatened by poverty.[11] His explanation for this was that, whereas the West German welfare state provided generously for employees, (the subjects of the so-called 'old social question'), the socio-political interests of those outside the labour market, (the elderly, women and families with children), received far less consideration, as they were not represented by a powerful lobby organization and had no opportunity to engage in collective bargaining. Geißler accordingly argued that the focus of welfare provision should be directed to this 'new social question' of the late twentieth century.

Geißler's provocative reference to the fragility of West German living standards contained considerable potential to irritate the federal government, as the latter's nervous reactions revealed.[12] It is therefore hardly surprising that his statistical evidence was highly contested. It is not necessary here to determine its levels of accuracy, although civil servants from the labour ministry were quickly able to demonstrate clear inconsistencies in Geißler's evidence.[13] Rather, this minor episode from the ministry's offices speaks to this chapter's central topic: namely, the production of knowledge concerning the impact of social policy, and the politicization of this information in the years 'after the boom'.[14] I argue that debates and arguments concerning poverty and anti-poverty policy acquired a particular importance within this context. During the 1970s and 1980s, fundamental debates concerning the identity of West German society as one shaped by the welfare state were primarily conducted as discussions about poverty.

This chapter focuses on three interconnected problems. Firstly, it investigates changes in the position of poverty within contemporaries' perceptions of the challenges confronting the West German welfare state. Secondly, it analyses transformations in the relationship between social science and social policy formation, and changes in related political processes. Thirdly, this chapter examines changes in the constellation of policy makers dealing with poverty. It argues that in all three fields, far-reaching changes were initiated in the late 1970s, which were closely connected to the politicization of academic scholarship concerning anti-poverty policy. Questions about poverty moved from the margins to the centre of West German political debates concerning welfare provision. Simultaneously, the field of actors dealing with poverty expanded extensively, via the increasing importance of social-scientific experts, new actors in civil society, and a changed position of welfare organizations.

Poverty in the Post-war West German Welfare State: Perceptions and Reality

The history of poverty in the 'Bonn Republic' was characterized by a 'varied, often highly contradictory coexistence of taboo and scandal.'[15] As a consequence, the perceived value of poverty policy changed repeatedly.[16] During the 'foundational social crisis' of the Federal Republic in the years immediately following 1945,[17] when overcoming the immediate consequences of war and dictatorship dominated the agenda of social policy, the poor relief as the 'lowest net of the welfare state' entailed assuming responsibility for the clients of existing social insurance programs. As a result, alleviating poverty represented a key priority and value of early West German social policy. However, following the economic miracle of the 1950s and the attendant expansion of the welfare state, policies aiming at alleviating poverty lost their central position within the realm of social policy.

Following the alleviation of post-war hardship, poverty became a phenomenon which overwhelmingly affected the elderly. To counter this situation, the pension reform of 1957 was introduced, forming one of the foundational reforms of West German social policy whose influence is still felt today. The 'dynamic pension' significantly increased the levels of old age pensions and linked this reform to the future development of salary scales, enabling millions of the elderly to participate in the economic miracle and removing the single greatest cause of poverty in the Federal Republic.[18] For twenty years thereafter, poverty occupied a marginal position within discussions concerning the West German welfare state.

Characteristic of the dominant conviction that poverty as a structural phenomenon of West German society had enduringly been defeated, and would never again determine the agenda of social policy, the Federal Law on Social Assistance (Bundessozialhilfegesetz), was passed without significant public attention, in 1961. The law created a differentiated policy of 'help in special life situations', which was tailored to individual life circumstances and intended in the future to represent the chief focus of public policy designed to combat poverty.[19] The law strengthened a constellation of actors, which was characteristic of the decentralized decision-making structures of the federal welfare state.

In contrast to the policies regarding national social insurance, which were primarily negotiated by both government and opposition at the central political level of parliamentary conflict, policies concerning poverty were shaped by a complex cooperation of various influential actors, such as: the representatives of local government; the individual federal states; charitable organizations (especially the Protestant Diakonie and Catholic Caritas), as well as ministerial bureaucracies. Political parties and trade unions, by contrast, barely played a role in these negotiations. Whereas overall legislative responsibility for social security was a prerogative of the federal government, the individual states (*Länder*) had responsibility for fixing its amounts and regulating it. These guidelines were drawn up for diverse social categories (families, single people, the elderly and, from 1985 onwards, single parents). They represented a central means of regulating social inequality, as: firstly, they defined the living standards appropriate for all individuals who could not pay their own way, or were not supported by the pre-existing systems of social insurance; and secondly, the standard rates of social assistance functioned as a form of unofficial minimum wage for the lowest income groups, and formed an important point of reference in the development of salary scales. Local authorities financed these benefits and were also responsible for the practical implementation of social assistance, enjoying extensive room for discretion in this regard, such as when distributing individual payments.

The German Association for Public and Private Welfare (Deutscher Verein für öffentliche und private Fürsorge), founded in 1880, brought together a range of actors in this field of social policy. The significance of its members for the implementation of poor relief and the expert knowledge assembled in this society ensured it could exert a considerable influence on the development of poverty policy, especially after one of its branches was awarded responsibility for fixing the standard rates of social assistance.[20] The German Association for Public and Private Welfare reconciled the partly contradictory interests of local government and welfare agencies through a technocratic culture of problem solving in which solutions to problems of poverty were developed in a non-political and consensual manner, and legitimized with reference to their focus on the problem at hand. Simultaneously, the society excluded other actors, (for example, self-help organizations of the poor and unemployed) from the field of poverty policy. Within this organization, representatives of local government set the tone. Its social experts retained the right to determine the implementation of poor relief according to 'objective' criteria, frequently in the interests of the poor themselves. Nevertheless, beneath these claims of objectivity were concealed demanding fiscal targets and far-reaching value judgements. The 'shopping basket' model (*Warenkorb-Modell*) devised by the German Association for Public and Private Welfare, which served as a reference system to calculate the amount of supplementary benefits and thereby defined the living standards of its recipients, was an attempt to provide a given quality of life on the basis of 'objective' definitions of what is necessary for an individual to enjoy a dignified life, and to protect him or her from falling below this level as a result of government cuts. Simultaneously, the society presented as 'normal', class- and gender-based patterns of consumption whose normative status was already contested in the early Federal Republic, and was increasingly challenged from the late 1960s onwards, but under the ongoing economic boom and constant inflow of taxes for funding social expenditure, the topic disappeared from political and public discussion. [21]

As the problem of poverty increasingly appeared to have been overcome, and the more poverty did not emanate from a single source but rather reflected a wide range of life situations frequently divergent from normative societal expectations, the less attention was paid to the poor as voters by political parties. This was particularly the case as both main West German parties, the SPD and the CDU, primarily saw themselves as representatives of working people's interests.

The marginality of poverty as a theme within the field of West German social policy was reflected in contemporary academic research. Prior to the 1970s, German sociologists rarely tackled questions of social inequality.[22] This neglect also applied to analysis of poverty. Rather, the subject was discussed in a sensationalist manner by journalism, such as Jürgen Roth's widely read poverty report. In an indirect fashion, poverty also played a role in discussions of 'underprivileged', 'marginal groups'. These terms referred to people who did not fulfil certain normative expectations, such as the homeless, drug addicts or juvenile criminals.[23] These studies overwhelmingly displayed a perspective which did not integrate poverty as a relevant social phenomenon into a description of West German society as a whole, but rather excluded it as an 'eccentric and peripheral exception to the rule'.[24]

One can also explain poverty's marginality on the research agenda of the social sciences with reference to the contemporary predominance of sociological models which primarily focused on the middle classes. Sociology was above all interested in the economically active part of the population. This trend ensured that groups of people not engaged in the labour market were largely ignored.[25] Another explanation for this state of affairs is that the culture of welfare state intervention in Germany was profoundly influenced by legal categories and based on administrative knowledge. In marked contrast to Great Britain, where social science expertise on poverty and social reform often went hand in hand, there were only a few points of exchange between academia and public-policy formation in the Federal Republic. Both these contexts changed progressively with the shifts in social science research on planning at the end of the 1960s.

The increasing relaxation of these boundaries was not without consequence for the position of social scientific experts in the field of welfare policy. Their knowledge concerning the welfare state had derived a considerable portion of its reputation from the claim that it was not bound to political targets. Typical in West Germany was the great influence of experts from welfare organizations who provided indispensable knowledge for the implementation of social policies and consultancy services to state authorities. The social scientific research on planning, which marked a height of the discipline's consultation by the state authorities, had gained its attractiveness because it claimed to offer politically 'neutral' information as the basis of its 'rational' policy recommendations.[26] Especially for the Social Democratic Party, with its optimistic belief in modernization, expert knowledge was the basis of hope for the future and simultaneously a source of political legitimation. Led by scholarship, man could, in the future, live 'free from hunger, free from poverty, free from fear', as public policy in the future would be 'bold, objective, sober and logical' due to its foundation on the advice of experts. Such was the declaration of the SPD's candidate for the chancellorship in 1962, Willy Brandt, at his party's annual conference.[27]

The Politicization of Poverty since the 1970s

Heiner Geißler's campaign was a radical rejection of the idea that the actions of the welfare state could be depoliticized through scholarly expertise. In tackling the 'new social question' Geißler cast doubt on the political neutrality of official statistics by countering the state's reports with documentation based on the opposition's own surveys. He questioned the knowledge of actors in the field of social policy about their actions' effects in a new, politicizing and polarizing manner. Geißler thereby transformed poverty from a category of social analysis into a term of party political struggle, directed against the Keynesian social democratic welfare state, and its basis on the normative category of male industrial workers.[28] His fundamental criticism was also directed against what he perceived to be a welfare state dominated by the interests of the trade unions, in which life situations that did not form part of a conflict between capital and labour lacked a voice. For the first time, poverty became the subject of hard political controversies.

The campaign initiated by Geißler concerning the 'new social question' was more than a mere attempt to rejuvenate the middle class parties of the centre right via discussion of topics with political traction.[29] His criticism drew upon classic elements of conservative criticism of the welfare state, such as its allegedly spiralling costs. Simultaneously, Geißler utilized social scientific arguments from North America concerning the place of social security within the political culture of capitalist democracies. He cited the arguments of conservative American political scientists who claimed the rising demands of welfare state clients would ultimately render parliamentary democracies ungovernable – as within the context of reduced fiscal possibilities, governments would not be able to implement policies against the material interests of voters.[30]

In making these arguments concerning the politicization of knowledge in the field of social policy matters, Geißler relied upon a younger generation of social scientific experts, who, after the CDU's departure from government in 1969, were recruited into the party's planning team, or later transferred to Geißler's own planning group concerning social policy within his ministry of the state of Rheinland-Pfalz. From 1970 onwards, these experts wrote a range of reports which were used as ammunition by the minister for social justice of Rheinland-Pfalz, and later CDU general secretary, in his battle for the supremacy of interpretation concerning social policy.[31]

In terms of their empirical claims and theoretical foundations, Geißler's arguments were thoroughly conservative. They overwhelmingly revealed concern for families with several children, and the elderly. In terms of social policy, he was deeply troubled by poverty's destruction of core family relationships. Beyond these conservative parameters, Geißler posed two fundamental questions. Firstly: what would happen if the industrial economy, so closely linked to the West German system of social insurance, eroded, and work could no longer form the basis of entitlement to welfare provision? Secondly: how could social security be organized in the context of an ageing population, changing gender roles and new family structures? Here, too, his policy recommendations were conservative. Geißler was committed to the preservation of the traditional two-parent family, in which the woman bore the burden of domestic work and childcare. His proposed solutions, were, however, thoroughly progressive in the eyes of contemporaries, and corresponded in certain respects to ideas which had been mooted by new social movements.

Geißler questioned the dominant understanding of the welfare system, which made the state solely responsible for the fulfilment of social needs, and availed itself of the funds necessary to achieve set targets. Instead, he advocated a partial retreat from the centralized welfare state, based on social insurance and social security contributions paid from wages, by suggesting that subsidiary forms of assistance in the proximity of families at the local level should be strengthened, that social service provision catering primarily for families should be expanded, and that familial care work should acquire legal recognition. As minister for social affairs in Rheinland-Pfalz, Geißler had himself made several moves in this direction, such as by commissioning pilot projects expanding social services.[32]

Geißler's thesis of the 'new social question' followed the logic of traditional debates in the field of social policy, as it addressed social problems primarily as ones of undersupply and the inadequate integration of persons in schemes of social insurance. What was new, by contrast, was the prominent use of social-scientific expertise in Geißler's arguments and the target of his criticisms, namely, the centrality of employment within the Keynesian welfare state. When the West German public debated the problem of the 'new poverty' with unusual sharpness in the mid-1980s,[33] it was the defence of precisely this model of welfare provision that was at stake. The 'new poverty' was, of course, hardly 'new'. The Protestant theologian Fritz Kern had already used the term in a decidedly anti-democratic context after the First World War in order to characterize the social position of the middle classes impoverished by inflation.[34] In its contemporary usage, the term had many progenitors. Feminist critics of the welfare state, who had been propelled since the early 1980s into political discussions by the Green Party, highlighted the deficit in social security for elderly women and single parents. The concept also alluded to inadequate welfare provision for other so-called 'marginal groups' (*Randgruppen*), especially immigrants, who were frequently affected by unemployment.[35]

Similarly to Geißler, the Greens developed a strategy of public mobilization, which made poverty the subject of political controversy. Additionally, they raised the topic through several parliamentary initiatives.[36] In so doing, the Green Party repeatedly highlighted the unsatisfactory state of West German social statistics, which provided a 'truly incomplete picture of poverty'.[37] Even if the Greens denounced the 'social dismantling of the CDU–FDP government'[38], their own criticism aimed at a yet more fundamental question. For the Green Party, the 'new poverty' stood as a symbol for the sum of all deficits of a model of social insurance primarily organized around the salaried employment of 'male breadwinners'. They called this model into question not only because of the emerging 'crisis of work-oriented society' (*Arbeitsgesellschaft*),[39] but also due to its lack of gender equality. The Greens did not therefore consider reforming the existing system of social insurance. In opposition to the compulsory national system of social insurances, they proposed the alternative model of a tax financed 'need orientated basic protection for all life situations'.[40] The inequalities caused by poverty within a system of social insurance linked closely to employment would thereby be avoided, and women afforded security in old age independently of their husbands or partners.

The most effective interpretation of the 'new poverty' was, however, presented by the German Trade Union Association, DGB. It saw the phenomenon as one primarily affecting the unemployed. The trade unions and social democratic opposition aimed to highlight the social declassification of the long-term unemployed, who, according to this interpretation, were increasingly falling through the welfare net due to the CDU–FDP government's budgetary cuts. With these arguments, representatives of the trade unions attempted to organize a line of defence against the feared 'social clearcutting'[41] it was anticipated that Helmut Kohl's Christian Democratic–Liberal coalition would implement after assuming power in October 1982. Simultaneously, the debate concerning the 'new poverty' was closely related to a trade union campaign for a societal redistribution of labour through a shortening of working hours without salary decreases, which resulted in 1984 in major strike action, especially in those sectors threatened by structural economic change, such as the metal and printing industries. For the social democrats, the debate about the 'new poverty' also represented an attempt to reclaim the party's status as a champion of the welfare state, which had suffered due to its implementation of budgetary cuts at the start of the 1980s. It also served to strengthen the party's alliance with the trade unions and to help it find its feet in opposition.[42]

Far more was at stake in this debate, however, than the consequences of welfare cuts. The trade union discussion of poverty in the 1980s termed it 'new' above all because in affecting the cyclically generated and growing group of the long-term unemployed, it impacted many (mostly male) individuals who had previously paid from their wages into the social insurance funds, and for whom it had previously been 'unimaginable, to become a recipient of social assistance'.[43] The trade union perspective thereby airbrushed out of the picture those groups among the poor whose plight resulted from socio-cultural transformations. This narrow perspective especially affected the rapidly growing number of single-parent-families among the recipients of social assistance. For this purpose, the trade unions directed public attention towards the question of how a society accustomed to the decades-long experience of full employment and increasing prosperity, should adjust to the profoundly changed economic parameters which had developed since the 1970s. In contrast to the discussion concerning 'marginal groups', the debate about the 'new poverty' put the problem of social inequality onto the agenda of social policy and challenged the dominant self-understanding of the Federal Republic. Previous political controversies concerning welfare had restricted themselves to arguments regarding the insufficient integration of special groups into the West German welfare state. Now, for the first time in the history of the Federal Republic, a general debate concerning the levels of social-political exclusion was being conducted, with the status of the long-term unemployed as its core battleground.

The trade unions and SPD interpreted the centre-right coalition's budgetary cuts as part of a conscious policy of wealth redistribution from 'the bottom to the top',[44] which would be brought about by cutting taxes on income and property on the one hand, while reducing social benefits on the other. The SPD and trade unions viewed this policy's interference with unemployment insurance and the tax-funded help of the unemployed as directly feeding growing social inequality. The principle established in the Federal Republic of Germany by the 'dynamic' pension of 1957, that in order to maintain living standards pensions should track economic growth and wage levels, had been expanded by the reformist policies of the 1960s and 1970s to include almost all branches of social insurance and care. Only the so-called 'poverty clientele' among the recipients of social assistance were explicitly exempt. In the 'last net' of social security, the principle predominated that payments should be dependent on the demonstrated need of the individuals in question, and that benefits from social assistance should be clearly lower than income from the lowest wages. By depriving the unemployed of payments from the unemployment insurance fund that were linked to standards of earlier income, and providing them instead with the lower support levels of social assistance, living standards were endangered on a grand scale. The DGB criticized the CDU–FPD government, claiming that the social decline of the unemployed had been consciously calculated to repair public finances.[45]

Even if the empirical evidence concerning the actual extent of such downward social mobility remained contested, and it took time before social scientists could give a detailed picture of these transformations of West, and after 1990, reunited German society (for details see the following chapter), it can neverthe-less be argued that through the expulsion of the long-term unemployed from unemployment insurance schemes into social assistance, constitutive elements of the post-war welfare state were for the first time being put into question. The principle of maintaining the living standard of those affected was surrendered and the equivalency of financial contribution to the system of social security and social security benefits was weakened.[46] Discussion of the trades unions' theses and their social-scientific data was therefore far more than an argument regarding the social impact of structural economic transformations. Until this point, the social peace embodied in the 'German model' was based on the principle that a high level of social security was sacrosanct. According to the SPD and trade unions, the mass transfer of the unemployed into social assistance placed this social consensus in doubt. The high value it had previously been accorded was firstly a reflection of social security's function as a guarantor of social stabil-ity and a provider of a competitive economic advantage over the strike-prone societies of Western and Southern Europe. Secondly, a strong welfare state was seen as insurance against political instability in the event of an economic crisis, as Germany had experienced during the early 1930s.[47] In order to underscore the dangers of this policy shift, the German Trade Union Association explicitly highlighted the connections between the cuts in social expenditure by the presi-dential governments of the early 1930s, and the subsequent collapse of Weimar democracy.[48]

The debate surrounding the 'new poverty' also represented a contestation of West German society's self-understanding as a society based on work. This perception had considerable consequences for state policies addressing poverty, which had traditionally been extensively based on a binary categorization of the poor as either 'deserving' or 'undeserving' on the basis of their willingness to work. In the 1980s, many local authorities reactivated compulsory work schemes as a test of need and willingness to work, which were felt to be discriminatory by the recipients of social benefits.[49]

Why, therefore, did the 'new poverty' become a leading topic of the trade union resistance to the Kohl government, but not for the SPD opposi-tion? One explanation lies in the SPD's conception of the welfare state, which, despite the growing levels of permanent unemployment, firmly held onto the idea of a working society, so that alternative models of social security, which had given up the close connection to salaried employment, were often unwelcome, as revealed by the harsh rejection of the plans for a minimum wage without condi-tions, by the party's general secretary.[50] The Green Party's criticisms, by contrast, focused specifically on this point and criticized the 'choiceless socialization by work or marriage' as a 'perpetuation of patriarchal petit bourgeois capitalism by the institutions of the welfare state'; in short, a model of social security they aimed to overcome.[51]

The Pluralization of Expertise in the Field of Social Policy

In the debate concerning the 'new social question', as well as that regarding the 'new poverty', social scientific knowledge about the welfare state played a prominent role. Geißler's effective instrumentalization of social statistics could only succeed because the CDU had built up a formidable team of researchers in this field, and employed young academics capable of conducting empirical social research. In the discussion surrounding the 'new poverty', figures evoked in opposition to those of government ministries played an important role. In this case it was think tanks closely affiliated with the trade unions as well, as social scientists, which provided the expertise to oppose official poverty statistics.[52]

The politicization of knowledge concerning poverty was further aided by the fact that in the second half of the 1970s, a new social scientific perspective on the welfare state emerged. It was developed in research projects which were originally partly financed by the federal government in order to provide a scientific basis for the social policies of the SPD–FDP coalition. Information was supposed to optimize social policy decision making and make up for deficits of focus in the political process.[53] In this manner, a form of social scientific knowledge developed in the late 1970s which, to a limited extent, became a critical voice in the debates on governmental social policies. The information generated by ministerial bureaucracies for social budgets possessed specific strengths, such as the figures' high levels of reliability, but in certain other regards their perspectives were limited. Among these deficiencies was the over-representation of social insurance characterized by financial benefits. Areas of the welfare state difficult to quantify statistically, such as social services and schemes to enable access opportunities to social and cultural facilities, such as care and education, were, by contrast, underrepresented. Areas of local government responsibility, such as poverty policy, were also comparatively neglected. The social budget served the political coordination of legislative action.

In this perspective, social policy meant above all one thing: regulating the sums of money flowing into the social insurance systems. Information which described the effects on life chances and on social stratification caused by the welfare state, by contrast, barely came into consideration. The social budget, along with official reports on social conditions (*Sozialbericht* and *Sozialbudget*), contained few indicators concerning these effects of social policy. From the 1970s onwards, they were brought under closer examination. In an age where welfare was starved of government funding, questions concerning the distributary effects of social transfer emerged with noticeably greater clarity, not least in the debates concerning the 'new poverty' and the 'new social question'.

At this point, the social indicator movement began, which since the early 1970s had established itself in various West German sociological institutes. It seized upon concepts which had already been discussed in the United States and Scandinavia since the 1960s. This new research methodology shared social scientific planning research's conviction, that modern societies are increasingly shaped by the distribution of public goods, and that they are both in need, and capable of, modernization. This research thereby reflected the influence of cybernetic models during the 1960s and 1970s.

In three clear respects, however, research into social indicators differed from previous approaches. Firstly, it had noticeably shifted its research perspectives. The institutions of the welfare state and the behaviour of governmental bureaucracies no longer stood as the chief focus of attention, but rather the welfare of individuals or households, which, secondly, in turn also changed research methodologies. Research into social indicatory factors employed an approach focused on effects. It paid less attention to the passage of legislation and social expenditures, but instead attempted to answer the question of which social consequences social policy produced, and how the development of social policy was perceived by the West German population. Thirdly, in order to do this, researchers employed an alternative measurement methodology: privileging questionnaires and qualitative, non-fiscal indicators, over the aggregated collections of data averages employed by government statistics. This created a more individualized and client centric picture of social policy and its effects.[54]

To what extent did this change of perspective influence the conduct of social policy? In a time of decreasing distributive possibilities, the legitimizing function of social reforms became prominent. This explains why considerable public funds were spent on research into public opinion, which gauged the social and political attitudes of West German citizens.[55] A new applied and private sector of social policy knowledge thereby emerged, one profoundly shaped by the austerity era and increasingly incorporated into political decision-making processes. Public opinion experts contrasted high levels of support for the West German system of national social insurance with an extremely differentiated criticism of cuts to social services. Reductions in social benefits and of social security in general were above all associated with the SPD administration in power prior to 1982, which undermined many voters' trust in the party, especially that of its traditional core supporters.[56]

It was only in a highly incomplete manner that the expansion of social policy knowledge embraced new challenges, such as poverty in an age of ongoing unemployment. Nevertheless, public opinion surveys clearly demonstrated that federal citizens were sensitive to demonstrations of poverty in the public realm, despite a poverty rate low by European standards.[57] A study commissioned by the Federal Ministry for Youth, Health and the Family provided numerous indications of the fact that the potential of social assistance to prevent the growth of poverty was not completely exhausted. Many of those entitled to receive its payments, especially the elderly, were reluctant to do so, since claiming such benefits still bore a certain social stigma in West German society.[58]

Sophisticated figures concerning income distribution among households were only available to a limited extent in the mid-1970s, with the Federal Statistics Office's policy of measuring income and consumption every five years hardly adequate to reveal the dynamics of poverty's development on the ground. Even if the opposition and committed social scientists repeatedly called for the establishment of regular reporting on poverty,[59] the number of supplementary benefit recipients was only published annually, with the result that information concerning poverty continued to be weakly represented within official statistics. It was only in 2001 that the SPD–Green coalition government established a regular report concerning poverty and wealth in the Federal Republic.[60]

Decisive expansions of political knowledge about poverty thereby emerged primarily outside the state administration and within university research clusters. Research into poverty formed the core of successful long-term research programmes. Stefan Leibfried's research project 'Risks of Reproduction, Social Movements and Social Policy' (1978–1988), at Bremen University, served as a precursor for the methodologically influential DFG special research cluster 186 'Passages of Status and Risk Situations in a Lifetime', as well as the Centre for Social Policy at Bremen University, one of the leading interdisciplinary research units concerning the theory and practice of the modern welfare state.[61] Wolfgang Zapf and Richard Hauser's working group at Frankfurt University developed the concept of the 'socio-economic panel' (SOEP), which today still provides the basis for a differentiated reporting of income development in the Federal Republic.[62]

Together with other academics within the working group 'Poverty and Deprivation', Leibfried and Hauser campaigned publicly and with considerable public resonance on questions of social policy addressing poverty.[63] These critics raised three key points: local government's erosion of the value of supplementary benefit payments by reducing their connection to demonstrable need and life situations; the social assistance basis on outdated costs of living and patterns of consumption; and inadequate reporting about poverty.[64]

Such criticism was directed against the closed expert culture of the German Association for Public and Private Welfare. The normative 'shopping basket' model (*Warenkorb-Modell*) was especially criticized, with the voices of charities and self-help organizations joining the chorus. This wave of criticism reached its first high point in 1980, when the celebrations marking the centenary of the German Association's foundation were disrupted by welfare recipients' protest actions and sympathetic media coverage. Social scientists from Bremen University orchestrated the protest with strategically targeted research findings.[65]

Publically engaged scholarly expertise thereby became the handmaiden of a development which led to the opening up of the field of political debate concerning poverty and placed the German Association's monopolistic claims to expertise in doubt. Further elements in this process were the increasing organization of welfare recipients in self-help groups, who, through the media, had access to the field of political discussion concerning poverty, and above all the German Association for Public and Private Welfare's own waning integrative force. The latent conflict between the representatives of local government on the one hand, who advocated a limiting of welfare costs, and those of charitable bodies on the other, who, due to the economic crisis, campaigned for an expansion of poor relief, dominated West German politics in this area from the late 1970s onwards. These tensions were exacerbated by the fact that public policy concerning poverty was simultaneously confronted with new problems resulting from processes of social and cultural transformation. Among these was the so-called 'care poverty', (*Pflegearmut*) whereby an increasing number of elderly people could not afford the costs of care at home or in medical institutions during their final years, becoming dependent on benefits from social assistance. A further source of conflict emerged from the fact that the federal government, as part of its attempts to cut welfare costs, extensively offloaded responsibility for the provision of unemployment relief onto local authorities and the supplementary benefits scheme they were obliged to provide.

At the start of the 1980s, these tensions within the field of poverty policy escalated to the extent that the German Association for Public and Private Welfare was no longer able to present a consensual reform of the standard rates of social assistance. From that point on, charitable bodies functioned increasingly outside the framework of the German Association; for example, by commissioning academic studies designed to prove the inadequacy of the financial provision provided under the law on social assistance (Bundessozialhilfegesetz). The Federal Council of Germany's consistent and uniform opposition was responsible for the failure of this reform, as its members represented individual federal states and acted as spokespeople for the interests of local authorities. The latter strictly rejected an adjustment of social benefits and instead recommended cuts, which would clearly accentuate the character of these payments as mere emergency help. It was only in October 1989, after protracted negotiations, that a new law was passed, which contained cuts for certain groups (young adults, for instance), thereby giving up the 'shopping basket' as a model for the calculation of benefits. The new statistical calculation method was less advantageous for the recipients of social assistance because it was based on the consumption patterns of the lowest income groups. Despite the increasing rates of inflation, levels of payment were only increased at intervals of several years so that the principle of welfare provision according to need was further eroded. Simultaneously, the German Association for Public and Private Welfare finally lost competency for the regulation of the social assistance rulebook and its central place in the actor constellation responsible for the formation and implementation of West German policies addressing poverty.[66]

Even if social scientists increasingly appeared as independent actors in the field of political debate concerning poverty, their influence on the formulation of government policy and party programmes was limited. The Green Party furnished a certain exception to this rule as it worked closely with leading social and political scientists. For example, the feminist sociologists Ilona Ostner, Uta Gerhardt and Georg Vobruba among others, engaged in internal party debates about the provision of basic social security; and Stefan Leibfried advised the party on their parliamentary interpellations of governmental social policy.

Nevertheless, the decisive arguments driving the Greens' programme of social reform were politically motivated, not the result of such academic consultations. The SPD was more cautious in its utilization of the findings produced by social scientific research on poverty, and attempted instead to draw upon the expertise of charitable bodies.[67]

A young generation of academic sociological entrepreneurs, including Hauser and Leibfried, could mobilize extensive research funds from public non-state bodies such as the German Research Community and the European Union. This is why one of the first substantial empirical investigations into poverty in the Federal Republic was included in the European Commission's report on the Community's first specific anti-poverty programme.[68]

The research commissioned by ecclesiastical associations was also important in increasing interest in research regarding poverty.[69] In the late 1980s, drawing on observations of their own social work in the field, the Catholic Caritas and Protestant Diakonie made the alleviation of poverty the basis of their charitable engagement. Catholic welfare associations had already addressed the topic in diverse ways since the 1970s in the context of the debate about familial poverty initiated by Heiner Geißler. In the 1980s, ecclesiastical forums such as academies and Church councils focused the debate on the relationship between poverty and unemployment. Influenced by Latin American Liberation theology and its concept of an 'option for the poor', both major Churches decided that the conduct of pastoral care should devote greater attention to combating poverty, and Church organizations should direct their resources to that end in order to provide a voice for the long unrepresented interests of the poor.[70]

Additionally, local government authorities, which were heavily affected by rising costs of poor relief, commissioned and published several studies. These studies wanted to draw attention to the consequences of offloading social expenditures from the federal to the local level.[71] In certain respects, these works established a counterculture to the social-political knowledge production commissioned by the federal government. Most studies which were published by ecclesiastical organizations or local government authorities combined empirical social scientific evidence with practical, applied knowledge derived from social work in the field.

This boom of social research concerning poverty since the 1980s has played a decisive role in the topic's politicization, even if the research's impact on public policy has remained limited due to the *Bundesrat*'s representation of local authorities' fiscally conservative agenda. In this sense the upsurge of research on poverty during the 1980s was not only closely connected with the politicization of the poverty question, but also with the appropriation of social-political knowledge by different groups and society in general. Overall, these developments led to a partial denationalization and pluralization, but also a polarization of social-political knowledge, as had first emerged during the mid-1970s in the debate surrounding the 'new social question', illustrated in this chapter's introduction.[72]

Notes

This chapter has been translated by Thomas Brodie.

1. Bundesministerium für Arbeit und Sozialordnung. 1992. *Statistisches Taschenbuch 1950 bis 1990. Arbeits- und Sozialstatistik.* Bonn, 7.4.

2. See, for example, SPD Bundestag member Max Seidel, Deutscher Bundestag, Stenographischer Bericht, VI/31, 19 February 1970, p. 1446.

3. For the difference between a 'social policy of the first order' aimed at social problems and a 'social policy of secondary order' striving to stabilize the social insurance system, see: F.-X. Kaufmann. 2002. *Sozialpolitik und Sozialstaat. Soziologische Analysen.* Opladen: VS Verlag für Sozialwissenschaften, pp. 136–44; for the shift from the era of welfare expansion to that of limited growth, see: W. Süß. 2011. 'Umbau am "Modell Deutschalnd". Sozialer Wandel, ökonomische Krise und wohlfahrtsstaatliche Reformpolitik in der Bundesrepublik Deutschland "nach dem Boom"', *Journal of Modern European History* 9:215–40; M.H. Geyer. 2008. 'Sozialpolitische Denk- und Handlungsfelder: Der Umgang mit Sicherheit und Unsicherheit', in M.H. Geyer (ed.). *Geschichte der Sozialpolitik in Deutschland seit 1945,* vol. 6, *Bundesrepublik Deutschland 1974–1982, Neue Herausforderungen, wachsende Unsicherheiten.* Baden-Baden: Nomos, pp. 111–231.

4. Deutscher Bundestag, Stenographischer Bericht, VIII/169, 13 September 1979, p. 13498.

5. A comprehensive discussion of the reform era is provided in: H.G. Hockerts (ed.). 2006. *Geschichte der Sozialpolitik in Deutschland seit 1945,* vol. 5, *Bundesrepublik Deutschland 1966–1974. Eine Zeit vielfältigen Aufbruchs.* Baden-Baden: Nomos; for these reformist policies' social priorities, see: H.G. Hockerts and W. Süß. 2006. 'Der Wohlfahrtsstaat in einer Zeit vielfältigen Aufbruchs. Zur sozialpolitischen Bilanz der Reformära', in H.G. Hockerts (ed.), *Geschichte der Sozialpolitik in Deutschland seit 1945,* 'vol. 5, *Bundesrepublik 1966–1974. Eine Zeit vielfältigen Aufbruchs.* Baden-Baden: Nomos, pp. 943–62.

6. Bundesministerium für Arbeit und Sozialordnung (ed.). 1969. *Sozialbudget 1968 der Bundesrepublik Deutschland.* Bonn; Bundesministerium für Arbeit und Sozialordnung (ed.). 1971. *Sozialbericht 1970.* Stuttgart: Kohlhammer, and later editions.

7. H. Berié. 1970. 'Das Sozialbudget: Instrument rationaler Sozialpolitik', *Die Sozialordnung der Gegenwart* 10:43–61.

8. Keßler, Note to Secretary of State Eicher, 17 November 1975, regarding the 'new social question', Bundesarchiv Koblenz, BArch, B 136/14954.

9. Poverty as part of the Federal Republic's social history has until now only been examined in individual studies. For an overview, see: H. Uerlings, N. Trauth and L. Clemens (eds). 2011. *Armut. Perspektiven in Kunst und Gesellschaft.* Darmstadt: Primus; for a discussion of the issue of poverty within the historiography of the Federal Republic, see: W. Süß. 2010b. 'Vom Rand in die Mitte der Gesellschaft. Armut als Problem der deutschen Sozialgeschichte 1961–1989', in U. Becker, H.G. Hockerts and K. Tenfelde (eds), *Sozialstaat Deutschland. Geschichte und Gegenwart.* Bonn: Dietz, pp. 123–39; for a British–German comparison, see: W. Süß. 2010a. 'Armut im Wohlfahrtsstaat', in H.G. Hockerts and W. Süß (eds), *Soziale Ungleichheit im Sozialstaat. Die Bundesrepublik und Großbritannien im Vergleich,* Munich: Oldenbourg, pp. 19–42; for the Federal Republic's early history, see: W. Rudloff. 2002. 'Im Schatten des Wirtschaftswunders: Soziale Probleme, Randgruppen und Subkulturen 1949 bis 1973', in Th. Schlemmer

and H. Woller (eds), *Bayern im Bund*, vol. 2, *Gesellschaft im Wandel 1949–1973*. Munich: Oldenbourg, pp. 347–467; Ch. Sachße and F. Tennstedt. 2012. 1988–2012. *Geschichte der Armenfürsorge in Deutschland*, 4 vols, Stuttgart: Kohlhammer; for the history of poverty images and discussions about poverty, see: L. Leisering. 1993. 'Zwischen Verdrängung und Dramatisierung. Zur Wissenssoziologie der Armut in der bundesrepublikanischen Gesellschaft', *Soziale Welt* 44:486–511; M.S. Graf. 2015. *Die Inszenierung der Neuen Armut im sozialpolitischen Repertoire von SPD und Grünen 1983–1987*, Frankfurt/Main: Peter Lang; C. Lorke. 2015a. 'Die Inszenierung des (Un-) Würdigen. "Armut" und Massenmedien im geteilten Deutschland (1949–1989)', in J. Ahrens, L. Hieber and Y. Kautt (eds), *Zur Theorie des Image. Visuelle Kommunikation in gesellschaftlichen Konfliktlagen*. Wiesbaden: Springer, pp. 271–93; for the empirical details of poverty in the Federal Republic, see Olaf Groh-Samberg's chapter in this volume.

10. Geyer, 'Sozialpolitische Denk- und Handlungsfelder', pp. 125–30.

11. Geißler had already publicized his arguments to the West German public in numerous interviews and documentaries. H. Geißler. 1976. *Die Neue Soziale Frage. Analysen und Dokumente*. Freiburg/Breisgau: Herder, p. 26.

12. M. Schüler, Secretary of State, writing to the social democratic Federal Minister, April 1976, with accompaniment: Analysis of the Federal Chancellery, Dep. V/1, regarding statements of the Geißler-study and political evaluation, 17 September 1976, BArch, B 136/14954.

13. Christmann, Note to the Secretary of State of the Federal Ministry of Labour and Social Affairs, regarding the New Social Question, 5 December 1975, BArch, B 136/14954; see also Kortmann's criticisms, which showed that Geißler's central indicators of the potential requirements of social assistance were systematically set too high: K. Kortmann. 1976. 'Zur Armutsdiskussion in der Bundesrepublik Deutschland. Kritischer Vergleich vorgelegter Studien und Berechnungen auf der Grundlage des Bundessozialhilfegesetzes', *Nachrichtendienst des Deutschen Vereins für öffentliche und private Fürsorge* 56:144–49.

14. For the rapidly growing contemporary German language historiography of the 'post boom' period, see: A. Doering-Manteuffel and L. Raphael. 2012. *Nach dem Boom. Perspektiven auf die Zeitgeschichte seit 1970*. 3rd edn. Göttingen: Vandenhoeck & Ruprecht; A. Wirsching and M. Lazar (eds). 2011. 'European Societies in the 1970s and 1980s', *Journal of European History* 9(2): 167–283; F. Bösch (ed.). 2015. *Geteilte Geschichte. Ost- und Westdeutschland 1970–2000*. Göttingen: Vandenhoeck & Ruprecht.

15. Lorke, 'Die Inszenierung des (Un-)Würdigen', p. 7.

16. Leisering, 'Zwischen Verdrängung und Dramatisierung', pp. 490–95.

17. H.G. Hockerts, 2011. 'Integration der Gesellschaft. Gründungskrise und Sozialpolitik in der frühen Bundesrepublik', in H.G. Hockerts, *Der deutsche Sozialstaat. Entfaltung und Gefährdung*. Göttingen: Vandenhoeck & Ruprecht, p. 23.

18. H.G. Hockerts, 2011. 'Wie die Rente steigen lernte: Die Rentenreform von 1957', in H.G. Hockerts, *Der deutsche Sozialstaat. Entfaltung und Gefährdung*. Göttingen: Vandenhoeck & Ruprecht, pp. 71–85; C. Torp. 2015. *Gerechtigkeit im Wohlfahrtsstaat. Alter und Alterssicherung in Deutschland und Großbritannien von 1945 bis heute*. Göttingen: Vandenhoeck & Ruprecht.

19. D. Giese, 1986. '25 Jahre Bundessozialhilfegesetz. Entstehung, Ziele, Entwicklung', *Zeitschrift für Sozialhilfe und Sozialgesetzbuch* 25:249–58, 305–14, 374–82; F. Föcking.

2007. *Fürsorge im Wirtschaftsboom: Die Entstehung des Bundessozialhilfegesetzes von 1961.* Munich: Oldenbourg.

20. T. von Winter. 2001. 'Vom Korporatismus zum Etatismus. Strukturwandlungen des armutspolitischen Netzwerks', *Zeitschrift für Politikwissenschaft* 11:1577–92; P. Trenk-Hinterberger. 2008. 'Sozialhilfe', in M.H. Geyer (ed.), *Geschichte der Sozialpolitik in Deutschland seit 1945*, vol. 6, *Bundesrepublik Deutschland 1974–1982. Neue Herausforderungen, wachsende Unsicherheiten.* Baden-Baden: Nomos, pp. 607–10.

21. For the contemporary criticism of the 'shopping basket' model, see: 'Einfaches Leben', *Der Spiegel*, 18 April 1980, pp. 257–60.

22. This textbook was reacting to the deficit in concise compilation works for the academic training of sociologists and social workers. Due to these deficiencies within contemporary German-language scholarship, the contributors above all referenced Anglo-Saxon studies; see: H. Colla. 1974. 'Armut im Wohlfahrtsstaat', in A. Bellebaum and H. Braun (eds), *Reader soziale Probleme.* Frankfurt/Main: Campus, pp. 19–33.

23. J. Roth. 1971. *Armut in der Bundesrepublik. Beschreibungen, Familiengeschichten, Analysen, Dokumentationen.* Frankfurt/Main/Main: Campus; Spiegel-Redaktion (ed.). 1973. *Unterprivilegiert. Eine Studie über sozial benachteiligte Gruppen in der Bundesrepublik Deutschland.* Neuwied: Luchterhand; A. Kögler. 1976. *Die Entwicklung von "Randgruppen" in der BRD. Literaturstudie zur Entwicklung randständiger Bevölkerungsgruppen.* Göttingen: Vandenhoeck & Ruprecht; Lorke, 'Die Inszenierung des (Un-)Würdigen', pp. 183–91.

24. H. Strang. 1970. *Erscheinungsformen der Sozialhilfebedürftigkeit. Beitrag zu Geschichte, Theorie und empirischen Analyse der Armut.* Stuttgart: Kohlhammer, p. 36.

25. S. Leibfried and W. Voges. 1992. 'Vom Ende einer Ausgrenzung? Armut und Soziologie', in S. Leibfried and W. Voges (eds), *Armut im modernen Wohlfahrtsstaat.* Opladen: VS Verlag für Sozialwissenschaften, pp. 14–18; compare to P. Nolte. 2000. *Die Ordnung der deutschen Gesellschaft. Selbstentwurf und Selbstbeschreibung im 20. Jahrhundert.* Munich: C.H. Beck, pp. 318–51.

26. W. Süß. 2004. '"Rationale Politik" durch sozialwissenschaftliche Beratung? Die Projektgruppe Regierungs- und Verwaltungsreform 1966–1975', in S. Fisch and W. Rudloff (eds), *Experten und Politik. Wissenschaftliche Politikberatung in geschichtlicher Perspektive.* Berlin: Duncker & Humblot, pp. 329–48; G. Metzler. 2005. *Konzeptionen politischen Handelns von Adenauer bis Brandt. Politische Planung in der pluralistischen Gesellschaft.* Paderborn: Schönigh.

27. Cited in T. Lütjen. 2007. *Karl Schiller (1911–1994). "Superminister" Willy Brandts.* Bonn: Dietz pp. 185–86.

28. 'Wir sind arm an Wissen über die Armut'. Dokumentation des Sozialministers Heinrich Geißler. Alter und Kinderreichtum sind die häufigsten Merkmale sozial Unterprivilegierter, *Frankfurter Rundschau*, 27 November 1975, in Geißler, *Die Neue Soziale Frage.*

29. F. Bösch. 2008. 'Krise als Chance. Die Neuformierung der Christdemokraten in den siebziger Jahren', in K. Jarausch (ed.), *Das Ende der Zuversicht? Die siebziger Jahre als Geschichte.* Göttingen: Vandenhoeck & Ruprecht, pp. 304–305.

30. J. Hacke. 2008. 'Der Staat in Gefahr. Die Bundesrepublik der 1970er Jahre zwischen Legitimationskrise und Unregierbarkeit', in D. Geppert and J. Hacke (eds), *Streit um den Staat - intellektuelle Debatten in der Bundesrepublik 1960–1980.* Göttingen: Vandenhoeck & Ruprecht, pp. 188–206.

31. Alongside elaborations regarding the 'new social question', the polarizing contrast of price stability on the one hand, and welfare state expansion on the other, was often invoked in the debate concerning the 'cost explosion' in the health service. See: Policy Planning Staff of the CDU/CSU parliamentary group of the German Bundestag, 'Domestic Reforms of the SPD/FDP government coalition. Domestic Reforms. Aspirations and reality', 18 March 1971, Archiv der Sozialen Demokratie (AdSD), Bonn, Herbert Wehner papers, 1/HWAA001590.

32. 'Sozialstationen in Rheinland-Pfalz. Broschüre des Ministeriums für Soziales, Gesundheit und Sport, 1974', printed in Geißler, *Die Neue Soziale Frage*, pp. 120–25.

33. For example, see: 'Kein Geld, kein Spaß. Wozu noch leben. *Spiegel*-Report über Neue Armut in der Bundesrepublik', *Der Spiegel*, 24 December 1984, pp. 52–69.

34. F. Kern. 1920. *Die neue Armut und die neuen Armen. Ein Zeitbild.* Berlin: Koehler. For the discussions about discourse surrounding the 'new poverty', see: Graf, *Die Inszenierung der Neuen Armut*, pp. 17–26; Lorke, 'Die Inszenierung des (Un-)Würdigen', pp. 312–38, as well as Groh-Samberg's contribution in Chapter 8 of this volume.

35. M.-L. Stiefel. 1986. *Armut in Baden-Württemberg. Eine Bestandsaufnahme.* Stuttgart: Kohlhammer, pp. 3, 73, 86; Graf, *Die Inszenierung der Neuen Armut*, pp. 100–9.

36. Große Anfrage der Abgeordneten Bueb, Wagner und der Fraktion DIE GRÜNEN, betr. Armut und Sozialhilfe in der Bundesrepublik Deutschland, 9 December 1985, Bundestagsdrucksachen X/4503 und X/4504.

37. Stiefel, *Armut in Baden-Württemberg*, p. 89.

38. Ibid, p. 4.

39. R. Dahrendorf. 1983. 'Wenn der Arbeitsgesellschaft die Arbeit ausgeht', in J. Matthes (ed.), *Krise der Arbeitsgesellschaft. Verhandlungen des 21. Deutschen Soziologentages in Bamberg 1982.* Frankfurt/Main/Main: Campus, pp. 25–37.

40. Die Grünen im Bundestag. 1988. *Freiheit von Armut.* Essen: Klartext, p. 3.

41. G. Muhr. 1984. 'Die neue Armut in Deutschland', *Metall*, 13 April.

42. Süß, 'Vom Rand in die Mitte der Gesellschaft', pp. 137–38, Lorke, 'Die Inszenierung des (Un-)Würdigen', pp. 314–23; Graf, *Die Inszenierung der Neuen Armut*, pp. 69–79.

43. A. Trube. 1986. *Arbeitslosigkeit und Neue Armut in Düsseldorf. Ein Bericht über Ursachen, Ausmaß und Folgen des sozialen Elends sowie Vorschläge für Gegenmaßnahmen.* Bochum: Schallwig, p. 9.

44. Vorstand der SPD (ed.). 1986. *Zukunft für alle – arbeiten für soziale Gerechtigkeit und Frieden. Regierungsprogramm der SPD 1987–1990 der Sozialdemokratischen Partei Deutschlands.* Bonn: Neue Gesellschaft, p. 6.

45. Memorandum for the press conference of the DGB about new poverty: G. Muhr, 'Unterlage zur Pressekonferenz des DGB zur Neuen Armut', 10 July 1984, p. 8, BArch, B 149/62371.

46. For the position of the trade unions, see: W. Adamy and J. Steffen. 1984a. 'Arbeitslos gleich arm. Ursachen und Lösungsansätze zur Beseitigung der neuen Armut', *WSI-Mitteilungen* 37:574–81; W. Adamy and J. Steffen. 1984b. 'Sozialer Abstieg durch Arbeitslosigkeit – Vom Arbeitnehmer zum Sozialhilfeempfänger', *Die neue Gesellschaft* 31:151–56. Members of the federal government's own Institute for the Labour Market and Occupational Research came to less clear-cut conclusions. See: C.F. Büchtemann. 1985. 'Soziale Sicherung bei Arbeitslosigkeit und Sozialhilfebedürftigkeit. Datenlage

und neue Befunde', *Mitteilungen aus der Arbeitsmarkt- und Berufsforschung* 18:450–66; 'Das traditionelle System der Sozialpolitik in Frage gestellt' *Frankfurter Rundschau*, 7 September 1984.

47. Herbert Ehrenberg, Deutscher Bundestag, Stenographischer Bericht, VIII/8, 20 January 1977, p. 252; Walter Arendt, ibid., VII/243, 14 May 1976, 17195.

48. G. Muhr, memorandum for the press conference of DGB about new poverty, 10 July 1984, p. 11, BArch, B 149/62371.

49. M. Willing. 2005. 'Sozialhilfe', in M.G. Schmidt (ed.), *Geschichte der Sozialpolitik in Deutschland seit 1945*, vol. 7, *1982–1989. Finanzielle Konsolidierung und institutionelle Reform*. Baden-Baden: Nomos, pp. 501–505.

50. P. Glotz. 1986. 'Freiwillige Arbeitslosigkeit? Zur neueren Diskussion um das "garantierte Grundeinkommen"', *Gewerkschaftliche Monatshefte* 36:180–92.

51. Michael Opielka, Armutsverhinderung als politisches Projekt, 9 June 1986, p. 4, speech notes, cited in Graf, *Die Inszenierung der Neuen Armut*, p. 150.

52. Adamy and Steffen, 'Arbeitslos gleich arm'; ibid. 'Sozialer Abstieg durch Arbeitslosigkeit'; S. Leibfried and F. Tennstedt (eds). 1985. *Politik der Armut und die Spaltung des Sozialstaats*. Frankfurt/Main: Campus.

53. W. Zapf, 1973. 'Gesellschaftliche Dauerbeobachtung und aktive Politik', *Allgemeines Statistisches Archiv* 57:149.

54. For example: W. Zapf. 1978. *Lebensbedingungen in der Bundesrepublik: Sozialer Wandel und Wohlfahrtsentwicklung*. Frankfurt/Main: Campus.

55. 'Sozialstaat und Reformpolitik. Einstellungen und Meinungen zum Sozialstaat in der Bundesrepublik – Wahrnehmung, Nutzung und mögliche Einschränkung des Angebots an Sozialleistungen, Infratest-Studie, 14.12.1975, BArch., B 136/14974; H. von Bielinski, B. von Rosenbladt and W. Ruhland. 1983. *Herausforderungen der Sozialpolitik. Maßnahmen zur Absicherung des Systems der sozialen Sicherung, zur Bekämpfung der Arbeitslosigkeit und zur Verkürzung der Arbeitszeit im Urteil der Bürger. Bericht über eine Repräsentativumfrage im Auftrag des Bundesministeriums für Arbeit und Sozialordnung*. Bonn: Bundesminister für Arbeit und Sozialordnung, Referat Presse und Information.

56. Furmaniak to the members of the Federal Cabinet, 1 June 1977, also, comment to the ongoing surveys of Infratest: Infratest Politikbarometer, 27 June 1977, AdsD, Manfred Matthöfer papers/78.

57. Commission of the European Communities. 1977. *The Perception of Poverty in Europe*. Brussels, pp. 66–70, 77.

58. H. Hartmann. 1981. *Sozialhilfebedürftigkeit und die Dunkelziffer von Armut. Bericht über ein Forschungsprojekt zur Lage potentieller Sozialhilfeberechtigter*. Stuttgart: Kohlhammer.

59. For example: '"Wir brauchen eine regelmäßige umfassende Armutsberichterstattung in der Bundesrepublik". Fachpolitische Stellungnahme der Arbeitsgruppe "Armut und Unterversorgung"'. 1987. *Soziale Sicherheit* 36:136–40; 'Armutsberichterstattung statt Tabuisierung von Armut: Fachpolitische Stellungnahme der Arbeitsgruppe "Armut und Unterversorgung"'. 1987. *Theorie und Praxis der sozialen Arbeit* 38:228–34.

60. 'Lebenslagen in Deutschland: Der erste Armuts- und Reichtumsbericht der Bundesregierung'. 2001. Berlin: Bundestagsdrucksache XVI/5992.

61. See Groh-Samberg's chapter 8 of this volume. For a summary of the 'dynamic poverty research', which, in contrast to class specific indicators of social inequality, granted more weight to particular crises of postmodern lifecycles as causes of poverty, see:

L. Leisering and S. Leibfried. 2000. *Time and Poverty in Western Welfare States: United Germany in Perspective.* Cambridge: Cambridge University Press.

62. The Frankfurt working group pursued at the start of the 1970s, in conjunction with the DFG-financed project 'Social policy decision making and indicatory systems', a research methodology which was interested in social policy impact evaluation and thereby closely coordinated with the planning department of the Federal Chancellor's Office. With the consent of special research cluster 3, 'micro analytical bases of social policy' by the DFG in 1979, their research interests shifted towards questions of income distribution and social inequality. The first wave of socio-economic panels (SOEPs) was financed as an auxiliary project of the special research cluster. After the latter's funding elapsed, the SOEP was permanently housed within the German Institute for Economic Planning.

63. For example, Leibfried and Tennstedt, *Politik der Armut.*

64. Das traditionelle System der Sozialpolitik in Frage gestellt, Armutsberichterstattung statt Tabuisierung von Armut.

65. '100 Jahre Deutscher Verein 1880–1980'. 1980 *Nachrichtendienst des Deutschen Vereins für öffentliche und private Fürsorge* 60: 220–66; regarding the protests: Der Deutsche Verein und die Regelsätze. 1980 *Nachrichtendienst des Deutschen Vereins für öffentliche und private Fürsorge* 60:397–406. The reporting by the mass media was strongly influenced: A. Hofmann and S. Leibfried. 1980. 'Warenkorb und Regelsatz – Zur historischen Durchsetzung der Rationalisierung in der Armenpflege und zum Ausblenden von Alternativen', *Neue Praxis. Zeitschrift für Sozialarbeit, Sozialpädagogik und Sozialpolitik* 10:260–85.

66. Winter, 'Vom Korporatismus zum Etatismus', 11:1588–95; Trenk-Hinterberger, 'Sozialhilfe', pp. 617–29; Willing 2005. Sozialhilfe', pp. 483–501.

67. Graf, *Die Inszenierung der Neuen Armut*, pp. 83–92, 132–36.

68. R. Hauser, H. Cremer-Schäfer and U. Nouvertné (eds). 1981. *Armut, Niedrigeinkommen und Unterversorgung in der Bundesrepublik Deutschland.*Frankfurt/Main Campus.

69. P. Frings, F. Schwarte and U. Thien. 1987. *Arme haben keine Lobby. Caritas-Report zur Armut.* Freiburg/Breisgau: Lambertus; C. Sellin and K. Besselmann. 1987. *Erscheinungsformen und Auswirkungen sozialer Not und Verarmung.* Cologne: ISG.

70. For the Catholic Church, see: W. Kerber, A. Deissler and P. Fiedler. 1981. 'Armut und Reichtum', in F. Böckle (ed.). *Christlicher Glaube in moderner Gesellschaft.* Freiburg im Breisgau: Herder, vol. 17, pp. 77–122; Deutscher Caritasverband (ed.). 1985. *Caritas '85. Jahrbuch des Deutschen Caritasverbandes.* Karlsruhe: Badenia; for the Protestant Church's stance, see: *Armut in einer reichen Gesellschaft. Diskussionspapier des kirchlichen Dienstes*, 1986, BArch, B 149/76708, pp. 16–17.

71. Trube, *Arbeitslosigkeit und Neue Armut in Düsseldorf*; H. Wupper. 1986. 'Soziale Umbruchtendenzen in Bochum. Arbeitslosigkeit, Armut, Selbsthilfe'. Bochum: Schallwig; Stadt München/Sozialreferat. 1987. *Neue Armut in München: Ursachen, Strukturen, Entwicklungstendenzen, sozialpolitische Konsequenzen.* Munich.

72. The extent to which the constellation of actors in the field of social policy was transformed over time, by this development, is revealed by contemplation of the SPD-Green Agenda policies since 2004, which strategically employed the study of an expert commission in advance of the legislative process, in order to structure political discourse around the proposed reforms' leitmotifs. See: A. Hassel and C. Schiller. 2010. *Der Fall Hartz IV. Wie es zur Agenda 2010 kam und wie es weitergeht/*

Frankfurt/Main: Campus; S. Hegelich, D. Knollmann and J. Kuhlmann. 2011. *Agenda 2010. Strategien - Entscheidungen - Konsequenzen.* Wiesbaden: VS Verlag für Sozialwissenschaften.

Works Cited

'100 Jahre Deutscher Verein 1880–1980'. 1980. *Nachrichtendienst des Deutschen Vereins für öffentliche und private Fürsorge* 60:220–66.

Adamy, W., and J. Steffen. 1984a. 'Arbeitslos gleich arm. Ursachen und Lösungsansätze zur Beseitigung der neuen Armut', *WSI-Mitteilungen* 37:574–81.

———. 1984b. 'Sozialer Abstieg durch Arbeitslosigkeit – Vom Arbeitnehmer zum Sozialhilfeempfänger', *Die neue Gesellschaft* 31:151–56.

'Armutsberichterstattung statt Tabuisierung von Armut: Fachpolitische Stellungnahme der Arbeitsgruppe "Armut und Unterversorgung"'. 1987. *Theorie und Praxis der sozialen Arbeit* 38: 228–34.

Berié, H. 1970. 'Das Sozialbudget: Instrument rationaler Sozialpolitik', *Die Sozialordnung der Gegenwart* 10:43–61.

Bielinski, H. v., B. v. Rosenbladt and W. Ruhland. 1983. *Herausforderungen der Sozialpolitik. Maßnahmen zur Absicherung des Systems der sozialen Sicherung, zur Bekämpfung der Arbeitslosigkeit und zur Verkürzung der Arbeitszeit im Urteil der Bürger. Bericht über eine Repräsentativumfrage im Auftrag des Bundesministeriums für Arbeit und Sozialordnung.* Bonn: Bundesminister für Arbeit und Sozialordnung, Referat Presse und Information.

Bösch, F. 2008. 'Krise als Chance. Die Neuformierung der Christdemokraten in den siebziger Jahren', in K. Jarausch (ed.), *Das Ende der Zuversicht? Die siebziger Jahre als Geschichte.* Göttingen: Vandenhoeck & Ruprecht, pp. 296–309.

——— (ed.). 2015. *Geteilte Geschichte. Ost- und Westdeutschland 1970–2000.* Göttingen: Vandenhoeck & Ruprecht.

Büchtemann, C.F. 1985. 'Soziale Sicherung bei Arbeitslosigkeit und Sozialhilfebedürftigkeit. Datenlage und neue Befunde', *Mitteilungen aus der Arbeitsmarkt- und Berufsforschung* 18:450–66.

Bundesministerium für Arbeit und Sozialordnung (ed.). 1969. *Sozialbudget 1968 der Bundesrepublik Deutschland.* Bonn.

——— (ed.). 1971. *Sozialbericht 1970.* Stuttgart: Kohlhammer.

———. 1992. *Statistisches Taschenbuch 1950 bis 1990. Arbeits- und Sozialstatistik.* Bonn.

Deutscher Caritasverband (ed.). 1985. *Caritas '85. Jahrbuch des Deutschen Caritasverbandes.* Karlsruhe: Badenia.

Colla, H. 1974. 'Armut im Wohlfahrtsstaat', in A. Bellebaum and H. Braun (eds), *Reader soziale Probleme.* Frankfurt/Main: Campus, pp. 19–33.

Commission of the European Communities. 1977. *The Perception of Poverty in Europe*. Brussels: European Communities.

Dahrendorf, R.1983. 'Wenn der Arbeitsgesellschaft die Arbeit ausgeht', in J. Matthes (ed.), *Krise der Arbeitsgesellschaft. Verhandlungen des 21. Deutschen Soziologentages in Bamberg 1982*. Frankfurt/Main: Campus, pp. 25–37.

'Das traditionelle System der Sozialpolitik in Frage gestellt'. 1984. *Frankfurter Rundschau*, 7. September.

'Der Deutsche Verein und die Regelsätze'. 1980. *Nachrichtendienst des Deutschen Vereins für öffentliche und private Fürsorge* 60:397–406.

Die Grünen im Bundestag. 1988. *Freiheit von Armut*. Essen: Klartext.

Doering-Manteuffel, A., and L. Raphael. 2012. *Nach dem Boom. Perspektiven auf die Zeitgeschichte seit 1970*. 3rd edn. Göttingen: Vandenhoeck & Ruprecht.

'Einfaches Leben'. 1980. *Der Spiegel*, 18 April, pp. 257–60.

Föcking, F. 2007. *Fürsorge im Wirtschaftsboom: Die Entstehung des Bundessozialhilfegesetzes von 1961*. Munich: Oldenbourg.

Frings, P., F. Schwarte and U. Thien. 1987. *Arme haben keine Lobby. Caritas-Report zur Armut*. Freiburg im Breisgau: Lambertus.

Geißler, H. 1976. *Die Neue Soziale Frage. Analysen und Dokumente*. Freiburg/Breisgau: Herder.

Geyer, M.H. (ed.). 2008. *Geschichte der Sozialpolitik in Deutschland seit 1945, Bd. 6: Bundesrepublik Deutschland 1974–1982. Neue Herausforderungen, wachsende Unsicherheiten*. Baden-Baden: Nomos.

Geyer, M.H. 2008. 'Sozialpolitische Denk- und Handlungsfelder: Der Umgang mit Sicherheit und Unsicherheit', in M.H. Geyer (ed.), *Geschichte der Sozialpolitik in Deutschland seit 1945*, vol. 6, *Bundesrepublik Deutschland 1974–1982. Neue Herausforderungen, wachsende Unsicherheiten*. Baden-Baden: Nomos, pp. 111–231.

Giese, D. 1986. '25 Jahre Bundessozialhilfegesetz. Entstehung, Ziele, Entwicklung', *Zeitschrift für Sozialhilfe und Sozialgesetzbuch* 25:249–58, 305–14, 374–82.

Glotz, P. 1986. 'Freiwillige Arbeitslosigkeit? Zur neueren Diskussion um das "garantierte Grundeinkommen"', *Gewerkschaftliche Monatshefte* 36:180–92.

Graf, M.S. 2015. *Die Inszenierung der Neuen Armut im sozialpolitischen Repertoire von SPD und Grünen 1983–1987*. Frankfurt/Main: Peter Lang.

Hacke, J. 2008. 'Der Staat in Gefahr. Die Bundesrepublik der 1970er Jahre zwischen Legitimationskrise und Unregierbarkeit', in D. Geppert and J. Hacke (eds), *Streit um den Staat - intellektuelle Debatten in der Bundesrepublik 1960–1980*. Göttingen: Vandenhoeck & Ruprecht, pp. 188–206.

Hartmann, H. 1981. *Sozialhilfebedürftigkeit und die Dunkelziffer von Armut. Bericht über ein Forschungsprojekt zur Lage potentieller Sozialhilfeberechtigter*. Stuttgart: Kohlhammer.

Hassel, A., and Schiller, C. 2010. *Der Fall Hartz IV. Wie es zur Agenda 2010 kam und wie es weitergeht*. Frankfurt/Main: Campus.

Hauser, R., H. Cremer-Schäfer and U. Nouvertné (eds). 1981. *Armut, Niedrigeinkommen und Unterversorgung in der Bundesrepublik Deutschland.* Frankfurt/Main: Campus.

Hegelich, S., D. Knollmann and J. Kuhlmann. 2011. *Agenda 2010. Strategien – Entscheidungen – Konsequenzen.* Wiesbaden: VS Verlag für Sozialwissenschaften.

Hockerts, H.G. (ed.). 2006. *Geschichte der Sozialpolitik in Deutschland seit 1945,* vol. 5, *Bundesrepublik Deutschland 1966–1974. Eine Zeit vielfältigen Aufbruchs.* Baden-Baden: Nomos.

———. (2010). 'Wie die Rente steigen lernte: Die Rentenreform von 1957', in H.G. Hockerts, *Der deutsche Sozialstaat. Entfaltung und Gefährdung.* Göttingen: Vandenhoeck & Ruprecht, pp. 71–85.

———. 2011. 'Integration der Gesellschaft. Gründungskrise und Sozialpolitik in der frühen Bundesrepublik', in H.G. Hockerts, *Der deutsche Sozialstaat. Entfaltung und Gefährdung.* Göttingen: Vandenhoeck & Ruprecht, pp. 23–42.

———, and W. Süß. 2006. 'Der Wohlfahrtsstaat in einer Zeit vielfältigen Aufbruchs. Zur sozialpolitischen Bilanz der Reformära', in H.G. Hockerts (ed.), *Geschichte der Sozialpolitik in Deutschland seit 1945,* vol. 5, *Bundesrepublik Deutschland 1966–1974. Eine Zeit vielfältigen Aufbruchs.* Baden-Baden: Nomos, pp. 943–62.

Hofmann, A., and S. Leibfried. 1980. 'Warenkorb und Regelsatz – Zur historischen Durchsetzung der Rationalisierung in der Armenpflege und zum Ausblenden von Alternativen', *Neue Praxis. Zeitschrift für Sozialarbeit, Sozialpädagogik und Sozialpolitik* 10:260–285.

Kaufmann, F.-X. 2002. *Sozialpolitik und Sozialstaat. Soziologische Analysen.* Opladen: VS Verlag für Sozialwissenschaften.

Kerber, W., A. Deissler and P. Fiedler. 1981. 'Armut und Reichtum', in F. Böckle (ed.), *Christlicher Glaube in moderner Gesellschaft.* Freiburg im Breisgau: Herder, vol. 17, pp. 77–122.

'Kein Geld, kein Spaß. Wozu noch leben. *Spiegel*-Report über Neue Armut in der Bundesrepublik'. 1984. *Der Spiegel,* 24 December, pp. 52–69.

Kern, F. 1920. *Die neue Armut und die neuen Armen. Ein Zeitbild.* Berlin: Koehler.

Kögler, A. 1976: *Die Entwicklung von "Randgruppen" in der BRD. Literaturstudie zur Entwicklung randständiger Bevölkerungsgruppen.* Göttingen: Vandenhoeck & Ruprecht.

Kortmann, K. 1976. 'Zur Armutsdiskussion in der Bundesrepublik Deutschland. Kritischer Vergleich vorgelegter Studien und Berechnungen auf der Grundlage des Bundessozialhilfegesetzes', *Nachrichtendienst des Deutschen Vereins für öffentliche und private Fürsorge* 56:144–49.

'Lebenslagen in Deutschland: Der erste Armuts- und Reichtumsbericht der Bundesregierung'. 2001. Berlin: Bundestagsdrucksache XVI/5992.

Leibfried, S., and F. Tennstedt (eds). 1985. *Politik der Armut und die Spaltung des Sozialstaats.* Frankfurt/Main: Campus.

————, and W. Voges. 1992. 'Vom Ende einer Ausgrenzung? Armut und Soziologie', in S. Leibfried and W. Voges (eds). 1992. *Armut im modernen Wohlfahrtsstaat*. Opladen: VS Verlag für Sozialwissenschaften, pp. 9–33.

Leisering, L. 1993. 'Zwischen Verdrängung und Dramatisierung. Zur Wissenssoziologie der Armut in der bundesrepublikanischen Gesellschaft', *Soziale Welt* 44:486–511.

————, and S. Leibfried. 2000. *Time and Poverty in Western Welfare States: United Germany in Perspective*. Cambridge: Cambridge University Press.

Lorke, C. 2015a. 'Die Inszenierung des (Un-)Würdigen. "Armut" und Massenmedien im geteilten Deutschland (1949–1989)', in J. Ahrens, L. Hieber and Y. Kautt (eds), *Zur Theorie des Image. Visuelle Kommunikation in gesellschaftlichen Konfliktlagen*. Wiesbaden: Springer, pp. 271–93.

————. 2015b. *Armut im geteilten Deutschland. Die Wahrnehmung sozialer Randlagen in der Bundesrepublik Deutschland und der DDR*. Frankfurt/Main: Campus.

Lütjen, T. 2007. *Karl Schiller (1911–1994). "Superminister" Willy Brandts*. Bonn: Dietz.

Metzler, G. 2005. *Konzeptionen politischen Handelns von Adenauer bis Brandt. Politische Planung in der pluralistischen Gesellschaft*. Paderborn: Schönigh.

Muhr, G. 1984. 'Die neue Armut in Deutschland', *Metall*, 13 April.

Nolte, P. 2000. *Die Ordnung der deutschen Gesellschaft. Selbstentwurf und Selbstbeschreibung im 20. Jahrhundert*. Munich: C.H. Beck.

Roth, J. 1971. *Armut in der Bundesrepublik. Beschreibungen, Familiengeschichten, Analysen, Dokumentationen*. Frankfurt/Main: Campus.

Rudloff, W. 2002. 'Im Schatten des Wirtschaftswunders: Soziale Probleme, Randgruppen und Subkulturen 1949 bis 1973', in Th. Schlemmer and H. Woller (eds), *Bayern im Bund*, vol. 2, *Gesellschaft im Wandel 1949–1973*. Munich: Oldenbourg, pp. 347–467.

Sachße, Ch., and F. Tennstedt. 2012. *Geschichte der Armenfürsorge in Deutschland*, 4 vols. Stuttgart: Kohlhammer.

Sellin, C., and K. Besselmann. 1987. *Erscheinungsformen und Auswirkungen sozialer Not und Verarmung*. Cologne: ISG.

Spiegel-Redaktion (ed.). 1973. *Unterprivilegiert. Eine Studie über sozial benachteiligte Gruppen in der Bundesrepublik Deutschland*. Neuwied: Luchterhand.

Stadt München/Sozialreferat. 1987. *Neue Armut in München: Ursachen, Strukturen, Entwicklungstendenzen, sozialpolitische Konsequenzen*. Munich.

Stiefel, M.-L. 1986. *Armut in Baden-Württemberg. Eine Bestandsaufnahme*. Stuttgart: Kohlhammer.

Strang, H. 1970. *Erscheinungsformen der Sozialhilfebedürftigkeit. Beitrag zu Geschichte, Theorie und empirischen Analyse der Armut*. Stuttgart: Kohlhammer.

Süß, W. 2004. '"Rationale Politik" durch sozialwissenschaftliche Beratung? Die Projektgruppe Regierungs- und Verwaltungsreform 1966–1975', in S. Fisch and W. Rudloff (eds), *Experten und Politik. Wissenschaftliche*

Politikberatung in geschichtlicher Perspektive. Berlin: Duncker & Humblot, pp. 329–48.

———. 2010a. 'Armut im Wohlfahrtstaat', in H.G. Hockerts and W. Süß (eds), *Soziale Ungleichheit im Sozialstaat. Die Bundesrepublik und Großbritannien im Vergleich*. Munich: Oldenbourg, pp. 19–42.

———. 2010b. 'Vom Rand in die Mitte der Gesellschaft. Armut als Problem der deutschen Sozialgeschichte 1961–1989', in U. Becker, H.G. Hockerts and K. Tenfelde (eds), *Sozialstaat Deutschland. Geschichte und Gegenwart*. Bonn: Dietz, pp. 123–39.

———. 2011. 'Umbau am "Modell Deutschland". Sozialer Wandel, ökonomische Krise und wohlfahrtsstaatliche Reformpolitik in der Bundesrepublik Deutschland "nach dem Boom"', *Journal of Modern European History* 9:215–40.

Torp, C. 2015. *Gerechtigkeit im Wohlfahrtsstaat: Alter und Alterssicherung in Deutschland und Großbritannien von 1945 bis heute*. Göttingen: Vandenhoeck & Ruprecht.

Trenk-Hinterberger, P. (2008). 'Sozialhilfe', in M.H. Geyer (ed.), *Geschichte der Sozialpolitik in Deutschland seit 1945*, vol. 6, *Bundesrepublik Deutschland 1974–1982. Neue Herausforderungen, wachsende Unsicherheiten*. Baden-Baden: Nomos, pp. 607–35.

Trube, A. 1986. *Arbeitslosigkeit und Neue Armut in Düsseldorf. Ein Bericht über Ursachen, Ausmaß und Folgen des sozialen Elends sowie Vorschläge für Gegenmaßnahmen*. Bochum: Schallwig.

Uerlings, H., N. Trauth and L. Clemens (eds). 2011. *Armut. Perspektiven in Kunst und Gesellschaft*. Darmstadt: Primus.

Vorstand der SPD (ed.). 1986. *Zukunft für alle – arbeiten für soziale Gerechtigkeit und Frieden. Regierungsprogramm der SPD 1987–1990 der Sozialdemokratischen Partei Deutschlands*. Bonn: Neue Gesellschaft.

Willing, M. 2005. 'Sozialhilfe', in M.G. Schmidt (ed.), *Geschichte der Sozialpolitik in Deutschland seit 1945*, vol. 7, *1982–1989. Finanzielle Konsolidierung und institutionelle Reform*. Baden-Baden: Nomos, pp. 481–516.

Winter, T. 2001. 'Vom Korporatismus zum Etatismus. Strukturwandlungen des armutspolitischen Netzwerks', *Zeitschrift für Politikwissenschaft* 11:1573–608.

'"Wir brauchen eine regelmäßige umfassende Armutsberichterstattung in der Bundesrepublik". Fachpolitische Stellungnahme der Arbeitsgruppe "Armut und Unterversorgung"'. 1987. *Soziale Sicherheit* 36:136–40.

Wirsching, A., and M. Lazar (eds) 2011: 'European Societies in the 1970s and 1980s', *Journal of European History* 9(2):167–283.

Wupper, H. 1986. '*Soziale Umbruchtendenzen in Bochum. Arbeitslosigkeit, Armut, Selbsthilfe*'. Bochum: Schallwig.

'Wir sind arm an Wissen über die Armut'. Dokumentation des Sozialministers Heinrich Geißler. Alter und Kinderreichtum sind die häufigsten Merkmale sozial Unterprivilegierter, *Frankfurter Rundschau*, 27 November.

Zapf, W. 1973. 'Gesellschaftliche Dauerbeobachtung und aktive Politik', *Allgemeines Statistisches Archiv* 57:143–164.

————. 1978. *Lebensbedingungen in der Bundesrepublik: Sozialer Wandel und Wohlfahrtsentwicklung.* Frankfurt/Main: Campus.

Winfried Süß is a senior research fellow and project director at the Zentrum für Zeithistorische Forschungen Potsdam. His recent publications include: *Der 'Volkskörper' im Krieg. Gesundheitspolitik, medizinische Versorgung und Krankenmord im nationalsozialistischen Deutschland 1939–1945*, (2003); *Das 'Dritte Reich'. Eine Einführung* (co-edited with Dietmar Süß, 2008); *Soziale Ungleichheit im Sozialstaat. Die Bundesrepublik Deutschland und Großbritannien im Vergleich.* (co-edited with H.G. Hockerts, 2010); 'The Centre of the Party – Munich and the Reich Leadership of the Nazi Party', in Winfried Nerdinger et al. (eds), *Munich and National Socialism*, (2015), pp. 139–49, 594–95.

CHAPTER 8

The New Poverty

Trends and Debates in Contemporary Germany

Olaf Groh-Samberg

In Germany, poverty has been increasing for almost three decades. Poverty rates have been on the rise since the late 1970s, following a period of prosperity – or *Wirtschaftswunder* – characterized by a rapid decline of the high levels of post-war poverty. The return of poverty after the 1970s has led to intensive public and scientific debates about the so-called 'new poverty'. Poverty was judged to be 'new' because it re-entered the stage under the new historical conditions of a well-developed welfare state and a post-industrial system of social stratification. It essentially re-entered the scene with a new profile of vulnerable social groups, new causes and consequences of poverty in individual lifecycles, new divisions between societal insiders and outsiders, and, as a consequence, new challenges for social policy to address. Since the mid-1970s, a discourse within the social sciences and social policy has arisen on how to understand the nature of the 'new poverty', how to explain its almost constant growth despite the major policy reforms implemented over the past few decades, how to conceptualize and meas-ure its extent, and how poverty amidst affluence affects the social cohesion and democratic functioning of society as a whole.

This discourse has seen various concepts and terms emerge, spread and sometimes fade away: the term 'new poverty' is used here to describe the entire historical discourse since the 1970s (for reasons that I hope will become clear throughout this chapter) and has, in fact, been used differently throughout this discourse. Various terms and concepts have been coined to introduce new definitions of the situation: relative deprivation, social exclusion, underclass, poverty dynamics, precariousness and service proletariat – along with German terms, such as *Zweidrittelgesellschaft* (meaning a division of the society between the lowest third and the upper two-thirds of the population) or *Überflüssige* ('the superfluous', borrowed from Lenski's class of the expendables). This obsession with inventing new concepts reflects the irritating intractability of the phenomenon of rising poverty rates in modern welfare societies, signifying an epochal change in the social stratification system that, to date, seems to withstand all attempts to recognize and integrate this 'new' social reality into the self-representation of modern welfare societies.

This is indeed the argument that shall be developed in this chapter. The aim is to demonstrate that the discourse concerning the new poverty has largely failed to adequately describe the phenomenon and capture the social changes that lie behind it. This stark claim shall be supported by confronting the discourse of new poverty with empirical analysis on the developments of poverty in Germany. To give an empirical overview of poverty trends in contemporary Germany, this chapter analyses poverty based on a typological poverty indicator that combines multi-dimensional and longitudinal perspectives. Making use of the advantages of long-running household panel data – the German Socio-Economic Panel (SOEP) – this indicator allows the disentangling of different forms of poverty and vulnerability and, hence, the testing of the various interpretations of 'new poverty'. I show that the increase of poverty is mainly due to an increase in persistent poverty, i.e. long-term multiple poverty spells. No evidence exists for any trend towards more short-term poverty spells (as the contemporary thesis of 'temporalization' of poverty suggested) or for the idea that poverty has spread across the social stratification. The empirical investigation of poverty trends in Germany is important because it shows that many of the diagnoses that have been formulated in the discourse of the new poverty have not proven to be valid. In confronting the discourse with the empirical reality of poverty in Germany, I highlight the misunderstandings and misconceptions that have accompanied the discourse surrounding the new poverty in Germany.

The chapter proceeds in five steps: the first section gives a very brief overview of long-term trends of poverty in West Germany after the Second World War. The second section is devoted to the discourse of the new poverty that has been developing since the 1970s. The third section briefly turns to the problems of empirical poverty measurement. In section four, poverty trends will be analysed based on a more comprehensive measurement concept of poverty and data drawn from the SOEP. Section five concludes the article.

Poverty Trends in the Federal Republic of Germany

Poverty rates in the Federal Republic of Germany, as far as they can be traced in survey and administrative time series data, have been following a U-shaped pattern.[1] After a sharp decrease of the high levels of post-war poverty, poverty rates seemed to stabilize at their lowest historical levels during the 1960s and early 1970s. Since then, however, indicators show a gradual increase in poverty, starting in the late 1970s, and these rates entered a period of accelerated growth beginning around the turn of the millennium.

Figure 8.1 shows a range of indicators for West Germany that are available for longer time spans. The number of persons receiving social assistance (according to the Bundessozialhilfegesetz introduced in 1961) has risen from less than 1 per cent in the 1960s to 3.5 per cent of the population in 2004, when a major policy reform (the so-called Hartz reforms) took place. This increase of persons who received social assistance would have been even greater if asylum seekers and persons who needed nursing care had not been left out, if no ceiling had been put on adjustments in the standard rates, and if the restrictions on drawing social assistance had not been strengthened. Given that social assistance is a politically defined, means-tested benefit, the long-term development of persons who receive this benefit is typically flattened: in times of prosperity, social assistance

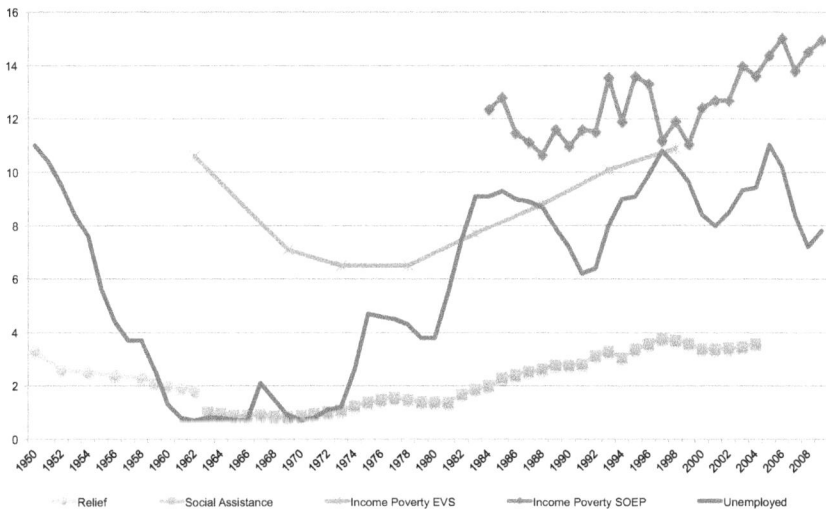

Figure 8.1 Long-term Trends of Poverty in Western Germany.

Sources and Notes: Relief: Persons receiving social assistance in % of Population; source: Hauser, R., H. Cremer-Schäfer and U. Nouverté. 1981, p. 36. Social Assistance: Recipients of *laufende Hilfe zum Lebensunterhalt außerhalb von Einrichtungen*, in % of the population at the end of each year; source: Statistisches Bundesamt, Fachserie 13, Reihe 2.1 (since 2001 only West-Germany Incl. Berlin). Income poverty EVS: persons below 50% of mean income (post-government or net household income including imputed rent, equivalized using old OECD scale), private households with German head only, very high incomes truncated, 1973–1988: without households of more than 6 persons. Data: EVS; source: Bundesanstalt für Arbeit und Sozialordnung (BMAS) 2001, p. 26. Income poverty SOEP: persons below 50% of mean income (post-government household income of previous year, including imputed rent, equivalized using old OECD scale) in % of the population. Data: SOEP (1984–2009); source: own calculations. Unemployed: persons in % of workforce population; source: Statistik der Bundesagentur für Arbeit. Arbeitslosigkeit im Zeitverlauf, Nürnberg.

is granted more generously to people who are in need, whereas in times of economic and fiscal crisis, when more people become needy but state budgets are tightened, access to social assistance becomes more restrictive, and the level of benefits is cut – at least in relation to the society's median welfare level. This has clearly happened to social assistance in Germany.

During the same period, the percentage of persons who were in relative income poverty rose from 6.5 per cent (1973) to 10.9 per cent (1998) and even further beyond 1998. This rate is calculated using data from the Income and Consumption Surveys (EVS), which the German Statistical Office conducts every five years. Foreigners and very high income(s) are under-represented in the EVS survey, which means that poverty is somewhat understated.[2] Poverty rates calculated on the basis of the German micro census from 1950 to date show the same pattern.[3] The development of income poverty can be traced more comprehensively in the SOEP longitudinal study that DIW Berlin carried out in cooperation with Infratest Sozialforschung.[4] The income poverty rate as calculated based on the SOEP is always higher than that based on EVS, mainly because a representative sample of foreigners is included, because high incomes are not truncated and because of some technical differences. Income poverty rates have risen in almost each of the seven years from 11.1 per cent in 1999 to 15.0 per cent in 2006. The decline from 2006 to 2007 was not sustainable; in 2009, the poverty rate caught up with the high level of 15.0 per cent.[5]

Additionally, the official unemployment rate is also shown in Figure 8.1. As can be seen, mass unemployment returned after a period of full employment in three sharp steps: after the oil price shock and world economic crisis of the early 1970s; at the beginning of the 1980s (de-industrialization in West Germany); and at the beginning of the 1990s (post reunification crisis with de-industrialization of the former GDR's industrial economy).

Long-term poverty trends run remarkably parallel to unemployment rates. However, during the most recent years, it seems as though the relation between unemployment and poverty has weakened, if not totally diminished. The number of unemployed people decreased after the introduction of the so-called Hartz IV reforms, but poverty did not stop growing. In other words, the poor did not profit any more from the recent economic prosperity and increasing employment rates. This remains to be explained. However, it may indicate a major change in the relation between poverty, labour markets and economic growth.

The Discourse of New Poverty

Given these figures, there can be no doubt that poverty has been on the rise in Germany for long periods of time and that a particularly strong increase occurred during the past ten years – since around the turn of the millennium. However, the causes, consequences and nature of this poverty increase have been and are still hotly debated. Since the 1970s – when poverty reached its lowest level – discourse emerged around the topic of a new poverty. Paradoxically, the term 'new poverty' was invented and basically coined at the very time when poverty rates rested on the tail of the U-shaped historical development. The basic idea of the new poverty was the commonly held view that the system of social stratification underwent an epochal shift during the period of welfare expansion: the shift from the traditional working class poverty that characterized the industrial era for almost two centuries, towards the new poverty of modern welfare societies. However, this basic point of position remained unchallenged during the period of rising poverty after the late 1970s.

The Invention of New Poverty: the 1970s

After the Second World War, poverty was a common experience for the majority of the population in Germany. However, in the course of the so-called *Wirtschaftswunder*, poverty declined at a rapid pace. In the late 1960s and the 1970s, poverty was deemed to have almost completely vanished from the social landscape of the German welfare state. When the new social assistance scheme was introduced in 1961/63, policy makers expected that regular (permanent) social assistance *'Hilfe zum laufenden Lebensunterhalt'* (HLU) would soon lose significance and relevance, whereas the temporary strand of social assistance, the assistance in special circumstances *'Hilfe in besonderen Lebenslagen'* (HBL), would become the most important tier of social assistance. Within the history of public views on poverty, the 1960s have been judged as the 'period of latency'.[6] During that decade, full employment was in place, and income poverty rates were at the lowest levels ever measured in German history (see Figure 8.1, above). If poverty was at all addressed, it was done so as a rather individual problem or as a vestige of outdated times. The term *Randgruppen* (i.e. marginal social groups) was invented to label a rather heterogeneous range of groups, such as beggars, people who lived in small shanty towns, or inmates of an orphanage.

In the 1970s, the observation that the traditional patterns of social inequality were in an almost epochal change was widespread among left-wing as well as conservative social scientists and social policy makers. The rapidly developing welfare state was seen at the core of this change. At the 1968 congress of the German Sociological Association, a group of young sociologists (amongst others, Claus Offe and Reinhard Kreckel) suggested that the welfare state was transforming the traditional system of social stratification from a vertically stratified class system into a new system where a horizontal axis of political organization and representation in the corporatist triangle of capital, labour and the state gains increasing importance. At the very same time, Kurt Biedenkopf and the general secretary of the Christian Democratic Party, Heiner Geißler, posed the thesis of a 'new social question' at the CDU's Mannheim Party congress in 1975 and later published it as a book.[7] From a very different angle, and with markedly different conclusions, Geißler argued in a way that was similar to his neo-Marxist opponents: that the integration of the working classes into welfare capitalisms had completely altered the system of social stratification and that the major social division henceforth ran between the unproductive classes and the productive classes represented in the corporatist triangle of the state, the industrial capitalist class and the working classes. Geißler, of course, criticized the socio-democratic and socio-liberal governments and the unions for their expansive welfare policies, attacking them as clientelistic and beneficial only to either the large capitalists or the industrial workforce. He argued that this policy came at the expense of those lacking political organization and not represented by the corporatist triangle – namely the non-working population: women, the elderly, the (families with many) children and the disabled. He claimed that these formed the 'new poor' and lay at the core of the 'new social question'. On the contrary, he claimed that the traditional poor – the working classes – were doing rather well thanks to German welfare capitalism and no longer needed to be seen as exploited or even disadvantaged as classes.

Heiner Geißler was the first to bring poverty back to the agenda of German social policy. He provided empirical estimates of poverty rates and claimed that almost 5.8 million Germans were living in poverty. Although his empirical estimations were strongly criticized, the general topic of a new poverty, (*neue Armut*), hitting a heterogeneous range of people instead of the working classes has subsequently remained unchallenged. The historical irony of this diagnosis is that it was born at the very time when poverty was at its lowest level in post-war German history, but it became an unquestioned pattern of interpretation of the new poverty cycle that began at the end of the 1970s. What Geißler termed the 'new poor' was, in fact, the poverty that had remained during the 'golden age' of prosperity: It was mainly the poverty of those generations and families that were not able to benefit either from economic growth and full employment, because they were not participating in the labour market, or from the social policy reforms, and in particular the pension reforms – mostly the elderly, and war widows in particular. The irony is that the emerging new poverty that started growing before the end of the 1970s was, in many respects, a recurrence of allegedly outdated social class inequalities. Instead of recognizing and analysing the legacies and the transformations of industrial class inequalities into post-industrial (i.e. de-industrialized) class inequalities, the debate around the emerging new poverty was pre-occupied and almost obsessed by the search for, and the prejudice of, the novelty of this unexpected phenomenon.

The Spreading of the 'New Poverty' and the Formation of Poverty Research in Germany: the 1980s

The term 'new poverty' was taken up and coined differently in the face of the strong increase in unemployment at the beginning of the 1980s. Bahlsen et al.

(1984) drew historical parallels between the demolition of unemployment insurance during the Weimar Republic and what happened in the FRG when mass unemployment returned after 1981.[8] While unemployment became the most important 'face' of the new poverty in the 1980s, and despite this historical argumentation, the term 'new poverty' continued to refer to a historical cut rather than continuity or transformation. The main argument was that the 'new poor' consisted of those who were expelled and excluded from 'employment society' (*Arbeitsgesellschaft*). The new social division was seen as drawn between the employed and unemployed, the insiders and outsiders of employment society, rather than between different groups of employed, i.e. occupational classes. This division was arguably re-enforced by the structure of West Germany's Bismarckian welfare state, with a strong emphasis on employment-based social insurance schemes and the corporate system of interest representation.

During the 1980s, important shifts in the demographic characteristics of the poor population took place. In the 1970s, the majority of beneficiaries of social assistance were older women, mostly (war) widows. However, the social assistance rates of the elderly decreased significantly during the 1980s, while the rates of younger families and children in particular started to rise. Also, single-parent households – and more precisely, single-mother households – increased in numbers and became one of the most prominent populations at risk. Moreover, households of migrants – mostly former 'guest-worker' (*Gastarbeiter*) immigrants – who experienced disproportionally low poverty rates before the 1980s, now became a risk population as well. These shifts were reflected in the concepts of the 'feminization' and 'infantilization' of poverty and taken as a further indication of a structural change in the nature and risk populations of the new poverty. While these demographic shifts were not yet recognized as long-term changes that reflected cohort-specific exposure to historical cycles of poverty, in the 1990s, the term 'new poverty' was used in a very unspecific and broad sense to denote the seemingly increasing social heterogeneity of the new poor.[9] Referring to Simmel's' (misleading) observations of the social heterogeneity of the poor, the new poor were sharply contrasted to traditional working class poverty – however, without any empirical evidence to substantiate this claim.

It was only during the 1980s that poverty research developed in Germany. Triggered by the European Commission's 'First Program on Combating Poverty and Social Exclusion in Europe' (1976–1980), Hauser et al. provided the first poverty report for Germany in 1981.[10] In 1984, a report published by a joint initiative of the German welfare organizations and the unions followed.[11] Despite the interests and pressure exerted by researchers, welfare organizations, unions and local government agencies that launched local poverty reports at this time, the German government withstood the pressure to accept poverty as a social policy problem and to establish an official poverty-monitoring and reporting system. The liberal–conservative government's main argument was that the social assistance scheme in Germany eliminated poverty. The increasing numbers of social assistance beneficiaries were not recognized as being poor because, as the argument goes, they received benefits that aimed to guarantee the minimum subsistence. Thus, because they received social assistance, they could no longer be poor. This argument, among other weaknesses, simply ignored the fact that almost 50 per cent of the population that was eligible to receive social assistance did not claim it.[12]

Given the ignorance of the German government towards increasing poverty, poverty research at that time was basically 'critical' in Germany. On the one hand, this critical impetus explicitly targeted neo-liberal and neo-conservative policies.[13] On the other hand, this was even more the case, as the sociological debates in the 1980s and 1990s were mainly concerned with the disappearance of social class inequalities due to the epochal overall increase in material welfare, and even affluence. In turn, it was argued that socio-economic inequalities were seen as having decreasing impact on everyday life and social identities. Rather, an individualization and pluralization of postmodern lifestyles 'beyond' social stratification was generally assumed and became popular – for instance, through the influential book *Risikogesellschaft* (*Risk Society*) by Ulrich Beck.[14] This view was hardly compatible with the empirical evidence of the existence and even the increasing trend of economic poverty and material deprivation. Against this background, the term *Zweidrittelgesellschaft* claimed that this idealistic view was, at best, valid only for the upper two-thirds of the society, whereas roughly a third of the population was seen as being exposed to the risk or reality of poverty. The concept of the two-thirds-society is thus a good illustration of how powerful both of these views have been: the view that traditional class inequalities were diminishing due to the welfare state, a mass culture of affluence and new life-styles, and the inclusiveness of standard employment regimes; and the view that a new poverty was emerging in the sense of a new social division between the insiders and the outsiders of employment society.

Only in 2000 did the new social democratic and green government intro-duce a regular national reporting of poverty and wealth in Germany. This was a breakthrough and a major success of the recently established poverty research that consisted of a broad variety of researchers and social policy experts at uni-versities, research institutes, municipalities and political organizations, such as unions and welfare organizations. Indeed, in a retrospective perspective, this success might also be seen as a Pyrrhic victory. The establishment of a national reporting system on poverty and wealth changed the scene in such a way that poverty research at universities and research institutes was increasingly chan-nelled into the position of a 'supply industry'. It became funded and involved in the expertise that entered the national reports, but it also became less of an independent research topic. The power over the legitimate definition of poverty moved to the German Federal Ministry of Work and Social Policy (BMAS). Interestingly, the term 'new poverty' and the debate around it were no longer reflected in the so-far four national poverty and wealth reports. However, this is already an outlook.

Dynamic Poverty Research and Social Exclusion: the 1990s

During the late 1990s, and before the national reporting system on poverty and wealth was launched, research on poverty increased rapidly. Two new approaches entered the agenda and transformed the discourse on 'new poverty'. On the one hand, the dynamic approach enriched the scientific perspectives on poverty and challenged the more or less implicitly held assumption of poverty as being permanent (or at least lasting). On the other hand, the social exclusion and the underclass debates swept over from France and the United States. The debates around these new concepts invoked a broader theoretical reconceptualization of poverty.

Until longitudinal data became available, most poverty was generally assumed to be persistent, that the same people stayed poor year after year. This appeared to be a natural and obvious inference from the fact that cross-sectional surveys showed that about the same number of people were poor every year. However, then longitudinal data, starting with panel surveys in the US in the late 1960s, began to show that despite unchanging cross-sectional poverty rates, it was not true that the same people were persistently poor.[15] Instead, the population in poverty consisted of a majority of people who were short-term poor (some of whom rotated in and out of poverty) and a minority of people who were long-term poor. In every Western country, including Germany, where panel surveys have been conducted, a similar pattern has been found.[16]

In Germany, a dynamic perspective was not applied in poverty research until the influential Bremen long-term study of social assistance; and until longitudinal income poverty data became available thanks to the Socio-Economic Panel Study (SOEP) that was annually collecting income data since 1984.[17] Based on longitudinal analysis of entering cohorts in the Bremen social assistance, the Bremer research team aimed to develop a new view on poverty. The basic empirical finding was that poverty spells are usually rather short. About 50 per cent of first-time recipients of social assistance managed to escape from welfare dependency within one year, and only very few remained on welfare for the entire observation period of six years. This finding was soon echoed by dynamic income poverty analysis showing that within a period of five years almost half of the persons who became income-poor during that period were only poor for exactly one year out of these five years. The discovery of the surprisingly high dynamic of poverty allowed scholars to overestimate the dynamics of poverty and to believe that a general trend existed towards a temporalization of poverty (i.e. a faster increase of short-term poverty spells as compared with a lower increase of long-term poverty spells).[18]

Drawing on the so-called individualization thesis of Beck, the Bremer poverty researchers argued that poverty is increasingly associated with risky status passages in individual life-courses rather than a structural risk belonging to the lower social classes. Poverty in contemporary Germany, they argued, has become 'temporalized, individualized and to a large degree also socially disembedded'.[19]

These three characteristics are closely interlinked. Together, they form part of a new form of poverty that is no longer class specific but rather an inherent, although dynamic, part of postmodern life courses in general.

In contrast, the reception of the French social exclusion and the Anglo-Saxon underclass literature gave rise to a more structural interpretation of the rising poverty. The French social exclusion literature focused on the de-regulation of labour market policies and the increasing forms of precarious employment along with the weakening of social ties.[20] Social exclusion was meant as a multi-dimensional process of detachment from inclusive institutions, such as regular employment, social security, family and wider social network integration. There are obviously contradictory but also common aspects in the dynamic poverty and social exclusion approaches. Both models see a generalized increase of social risks – life-course risks or precarious employment – in contemporary market societies that go beyond traditional class boundaries. Thus, they share with the 'new poverty' discourse the argument that the contemporary poor or socially excluded are no longer only the traditional working classes – this is different from the underclass concept. Although the social exclusion concept addressed similar issues of new social risks, it was more politically coined against the policies of neo-liberal de-regulation of employment and social security.

One particular dimension of social exclusion was urban segregation. This topic was core to the underclass concept in the US. As the term 'underclass' already denotes, this concept was distinct and even opposed to the European discourse of a new poverty and social exclusion due to its roots in a class perspective. Indeed, this also invoked hotly debated issues. One issue was the intersection of class and race, because America's urban ghettos were predominantly black. Moreover, the underclass concept was picked up and turned into a rather moral concept of a (class specific) 'culture of poverty'. Due to these debates and issues, coupled with the striking differences between the degree and racial component of urban segregation in the US compared with European cities, the underclass concept did not find its way into the European and German debate. However, from a more structural perspective, it highlighted the consequences of de-industrialization and mass unemployment on the restructuring of working class disadvantages.

The Ahistorical Nature of the New Poverty

Summing up, in the history of the discourse on new poverty, a variety of interpretations have been developed in order to understand the nature and driving forces of the new poverty cycle. However, most of the leading assumptions that are widely shared in this discourse have never been tested empirically. This pertains to the idea that the new poverty was categorically different from the class-based 'old poverty' rooted in the industrial system of social stratification, that it reflected new insider–outsider cleavages in the labour market, that it became increasingly heterogeneous in terms of social groups, that it was mainly and increasingly composed of short-term poverty spells rooted in individualized lifecycle risks, and that it would spread out more and more to the middle classes and the entire society, independent of social class. What is most important is that the discourse on new poverty was so preoccupied with the novelty of this phenomenon that it completely failed to assess and to understand the historical paths of the suggested epochal change. The discourse of the new poverty is basically ahistorical. This may already be concluded from the simple fact that the concept of new poverty was coined even before poverty actually started to rise again. It is also ahistorical because the counterpart of new poverty – the image of traditional, working class poverty – is much more a stereotype, echoing historical misunderstandings of vulgar Marxist class theories, than it is an empirically grounded understanding of the complex relation between poverty and social stratification in industrial capitalism. However, most important, the discourse regarding the new poverty was simply misleading in its core assumptions, as will be shown in the following sections.

Measuring Poverty: Income, Deprivation and Time

Besides the conceptual and theoretical debate on how to interpret and understand increasing poverty, a major issue in poverty research has always been measurement. Measuring poverty empirically is quite demanding. The more complex the theoretical concept of poverty, the more difficult it is to operationalize and measure. Any measure of poverty entails a range of decisions to be made that might appear to be rather technical measurement issues but, in fact, are highly consequential for the empirical results and can ultimately only be justified on normative grounds. This is basically due to the binary logic of the distinction between poor and non-poor, which itself points back to social policy and the basic decision of whether to help or not to help an individual who claims the need for support. Because of these unavoidable normative decisions, it has become a convention in poverty reports to use a set of different poverty concepts and measures in order to provide a variety of different possible views. Finally, poverty measurement requires detailed and high-quality data on economic resources, household needs and living conditions that are often not available.

It is beyond the scope of this chapter to provide an overview on the various concepts of poverty and the measurement issues involved. However, taking the widely accepted definition of poverty as a starting point, two important features of this definition stand out: the combination of economic resources/material deprivation and the consideration of time.

According to a definition proposed by the European Commission, which the German Federal Government has accepted in its poverty and wealth reports, individuals and families are regarded as poor if they have so little (material, social and cultural) means that they are excluded from the lifestyle or standard of living that is the minimum acceptable in the member state in which they live.[21] This definition of poverty is borrowed from Peter Townsend, who was the first researcher to provide a clear definition of poverty based on the concept of relative deprivation.[22] Thus, a fundamental distinction is made between absolute poverty and relative poverty. To be in absolute poverty means to lack the basics: food, clothing and shelter. Few people in Germany or in other Western countries are in that condition – and those are usually not entailed in surveys. Thus, in practice in European research, the definition of poverty is typically relative: an individual or household is viewed as poor compared with the average person or household in the same society. In other words, poverty is defined as a specific form of social inequality at the lower part of the inequality distribution.

Empirically, Townsend sought to identify a threshold within the income distribution such that deprivation – measured in terms of lacking goods or failing to participate in widely shared activities – would disproportionately increase once incomes fell below the threshold. Although Townsend's concept of poverty is widely endorsed, his empirical approach of attempting to identify an income threshold was widely regarded as unconvincing.[23] However, his work was influential for the further development of the deprivation approach to poverty that combines direct measures of living conditions (based on item scales on affordable goods and services) with indirect measures of economic resources. This approach was also implemented in the European household panel surveys (ECHP and EU-SILC) and thus widely used in European poverty research.[24] In Germany, only Hans-Jürgen Andreß et al. applied this approach.[25] In contrast, the so-called *Lebenslagen* (life domains) approach that has longer roots in German social policy research was more influential. This approach is based on a rather descriptive assessment of various, multi-dimensional life domains, such as housing, health, economic resources, education and social networks, and the distributions of undersupply in these domains.

In practice, however, and despite lip service to Townsend's definition of poverty, the concept of poverty most widely used in European research is that of relative income poverty. According to the current European Union definition of relative poverty, adopted by the list of Laeken indicators in 2001, a person who lives in a household with an equivalent income of less than 60 per cent of the national median income is regarded as poor – assuming that on such an income he/she is at risk of deprivation and social exclusion. This is why the European Commission changed the terminology from 'poverty rates' to 'at-risk poverty rates' when referring to the concept of relative income poverty. Household income is measured after social transfers and taxes (i.e. disposable or net income) and is tailored to account for household needs.[26] Clearly, a poverty line set at 60 per cent of median income is arbitrary; prior to the Laeken agreement, poverty lines of 50 per cent of mean income were commonly used.

However, considering disposable income alone gives only a very limited picture of the degree to which a person is at risk of material deprivation. First of all, the measurement of net equivalized incomes is afflicted by measurement error, and it usually does not cover assets and debts. Furthermore, it is quite possible for households to maintain standards of living that are regarded as socially acceptable even when they are on low incomes, either because income poverty is only temporary or because they have access to other resources – for example, savings or home production. On the other hand, households may live in deprivation although they receive rather high incomes – for example, because they have above-average needs due to health problems, are indebted, or spent their money without addressing their basic needs first. In the European literature, it has therefore long been argued that the measurement of poverty based on disposable income should be supplemented with direct measurements of standard of living in order to determine the extent to which those affected by income shortages fall below the minimum standard.[27] The literature on multi-dimensional poverty measurement has shown that the overlap of income poverty and material deprivation is substantial, yet it is far from perfect. One reason for this is that the relation between resources and deprivation is subject to time delays: i.e. households tend to anticipate future income fluctuations and distribute income resources over time in order to maintain smoother standards of living.[28]

As the dynamic approach to poverty highlights, the extent of material deprivation that is due to lacking resources is clearly dependent on the duration of living on low economic resources. Clearly, from a public policy and humanitarian point of view, medium- and long-term poverty matter a great deal more than does short-term poverty. Indeed, very short-term poverty may be of no significance at all. However, medium- and long-term poverty can be assumed to seriously affect the current lives and future prospects of adults and of children who grow up in poor households.

One methodological problem for longitudinal poverty analysis is the fact that measurement errors that might cancel out, at least to some extent, in a cross-sectional perspective will always appear as (artificial) poverty dynamics in a longitudinal perspective. Moreover, when using single poverty indicators, such as income poverty or social assistance receipt, equating changes in this single indicator with mobility into and out of poverty is misleading unless other life domains are taken into account. For instance, escaping from social assistance does not necessarily imply escaping from poverty unless resources and living standards rise above a certain threshold. In the same vein, income dynamics might not affect living conditions, as households tend to redistribute resources over time in order to maintain a constant standard of living.

The Solidification of Poverty – Empirical Analysis of Poverty Trends 1984–2013

Based on the discussion concerning poverty measurement, a robust poverty measure needs to take into account multi-dimensionality (i.e. indirect and direct measures of poverty) and time simultaneously. So far, however, multi-dimensional and longitudinal perspectives on poverty have seldom been combined. A more comprehensive measure of poverty is particularly needed in order to empirically test the various hypothesis and diagnosis of the new poverty. This concept should allow for a more differentiated assessment of 'strong' forms of poverty, in terms of permanent income poverty and material deprivation, and of temporal and inconsistent forms of poverty and/or precarious living conditions that reflect new social risks. In the following, such a measure will be proposed and used to analyse trend changes in the forms of poverty and precarious living conditions in West and East Germany from 1984 to date. The data are drawn from the German Socio-Economic Panel Study (SOEP).[29]

A Multi-dimensional and Longitudinal Measure of Poverty

To give a fuller picture of standards of living than would be obtained from considering income alone, three additional life domains are chosen. These relate to housing, financial assets and unemployment. Minimum standards are defined for each of these three domains. For each individual, information on incomes and material deprivation in these three life domains will be considered for five consecutive years. Based on this information, different forms and types of poverty, precarity and prosperity can then be distinguished.

In a first step, information on incomes and material deprivation is evaluated for each single year. Three income situations are defined. Individuals who live in households with disposable (equivalized) incomes of less than 50 per cent of the mean are defined as 'income poor'. Those with incomes between 50 per cent and 75 per cent of the mean income are viewed as 'low income', and those above 75 per cent of the mean are viewed as having an 'adequate' income. Similarly, three deprivation situations are defined according to the number of deprivations in the three life domains (no, one, multiple). Deprivation indicators that relate to the three life domains are defined in the following way: in housing, insufficient room (less than one room per persons aged three and above) and lack of basic equipment (e.g. warm water, central heating, balcony, terrace or garden) are regarded as deprivation; in the formation of financial reserves, households are regarded as deprived if they have no assets and no significant savings; finally, unemployment is included as a state of deprivation because it can be regarded as the most important non-monetary dimension of social exclusion. Many analyses on the basis of SOEP and corresponding databases in other countries show that unemployment hugely lowers satisfaction in life.[30] Multiple combinations of income poverty and deprivation are possible. In the worst-case scenario, an individual or household can be both in income poverty and suffering from multiple (i.e. two or three) deprivation(s). At the other extreme are adequate incomes (above 75 per cent of mean income) and zero (indicators of) deprivation. However, intermediate combinations of income and deprivation levels are quite common as well.

Table 8.1 Combined Poverty Indicator (2005–2009)

	per cent of population	averaged income position	averaged no. of deprivations/ year (max: 3)
Stable prosperity	44.1	1.32	0.08
Fragile prosperity	28.0	0.91	0.53
Temporary poverty	4.7	0.72	0.98
Inconsistent poverty	3.1	0.74	1.17
Zone of vulnerability	9.9	0.61	1.16
Zone of persistent poverty	10.1	0.45	2.05
Total	**100.0**	**1.00**	**0.59**

SOEPv30, 2005–2009, 5-years balanced panel, weighted results.

In a second step, the income and deprivation levels are considered across five years. The information of income and deprivation across five years is classified into a typology of various forms of exposure to material hardship. Table 8.1 gives the results for the period from 2005 to 2009. The database is SOEP, using a balanced sample of persons who took part in the survey continuously in the five years from 2005 to 2009.[31]

Between 2005 and 2009, about 10.2 per cent of the population lived in the zone of persistent poverty. The average disposable income at this group's disposal over the five years from 2005 to 2009 was only 45 per cent of mean income, which is clearly below the poverty threshold. Furthermore, this group averaged two (out of a maximum of three) states of deprivation during these years. Thus, a considerable number of people in Germany at this time were living in persistent multiple poverty. It is questionable whether this can be regarded as compatible with the view of Germany as a 'social' or 'welfare' state. In fact, a figure of 10.2 per cent in persistent poverty probably underestimates the actual situation because certain groups of people, such as the homeless, illegal migrants and many persons in institutions, are not covered in surveys such as SOEP or are at least clearly under represented.

Above the zone of persistent poverty, a zone of vulnerability can be identified, in which people persistently experience low incomes and single deprivations and repeatedly experience income poverty or multiple deprivations (although the two seldom occur together). This zone is almost as large as that of persistent poverty. The incomes of these individuals average around 61.5 per cent of the mean income, and on average individuals in this zone of vulnerability experience material deprivation in one of the three life domains. In other words, poverty has not yet become persistently strong, but that danger is always present. Households in this zone of vulnerability just about manage to avoid the worst scenario, but they scarcely experience periods of prosperity. For them, precarity has become a more or less permanent state.

Above the zone of vulnerability, there is a zone of fragile prosperity. Individuals in this zone are mostly on normal or higher incomes and show no signs of deprivation in the three life domains considered. However, in some years, they fall to low incomes or experience single deprivations. Thus, prosperity has become fragile in this zone, and some sort of precariousness seems to be around. This might be due to 'new social risks', temporal unemployment, health-related problems or simply financial strain. Embracing 28 per cent of the population, this zone covers more than its quarter.

At the top of the distribution, we find the zone of secure prosperity, which is characterized by normal or higher incomes and the absence of any deprivations in the three life domains. This zone of prosperity does by no means equate to wealth or possession of considerable riches. It is simply the absence of economic and material risks. A little under half of the population lives in this zone of secure prosperity.

In addition to this vertical stratification ranging from persistent poverty to persistent prosperity, with two intermediate zones of fragile prosperity and vulnerability, we also find a horizontal differentiation marked by the two categories of temporary and inconsistent poverty. These rather atypical or new occurrences of poverty are marked by combinations of poverty *and* prosperity. Temporary poverty means that experiences of prosperity and poverty (in both dimensions of incomes and living conditions) follow each other over time within the five-year period, whereas inconsistent poverty denotes stable situations of either poor incomes with no deprivations or multiple deprivations with higher incomes. It is often believed that temporary and inconsistent poverty–prosperity situations are typical of the new poverty that can no longer be regarded as structural and should rather be seen as the expression of the risks inherent in individualized lifestyles. In order to obtain a more robust measure of temporary poverty, we identify individuals who experience a simultaneous fluctuation in incomes and deprivation, i.e. good years and bad years; accordingly, inconsistent poverty here means stable inconsistent poverty across five years. Although averaged incomes and deprivations are similar for temporary poverty, inconsistent poverty and the zone of vulnerability, the experiences or forms of poverty are very different. However, it is evident that extreme shifts between poverty and prosperity as well as long-term inconsistencies between incomes and deprivation occur less often than the argument of the 'temporalization of poverty' suggests.[32]

Clear Increase in Persistent Poverty: Poverty Trends since 1984

The main goal of poverty measures is to monitor trends over time. Given that the SOEP already started in 1984 (and in 1989 for East Germany), it is possible to compute the poverty indicator described above for each successive five-year period. This means that poverty trends are smoothed because a large overlap of individuals and information is considered from one five-year period to the next. Figure 8.2 shows the distribution of the combined poverty indicator for West

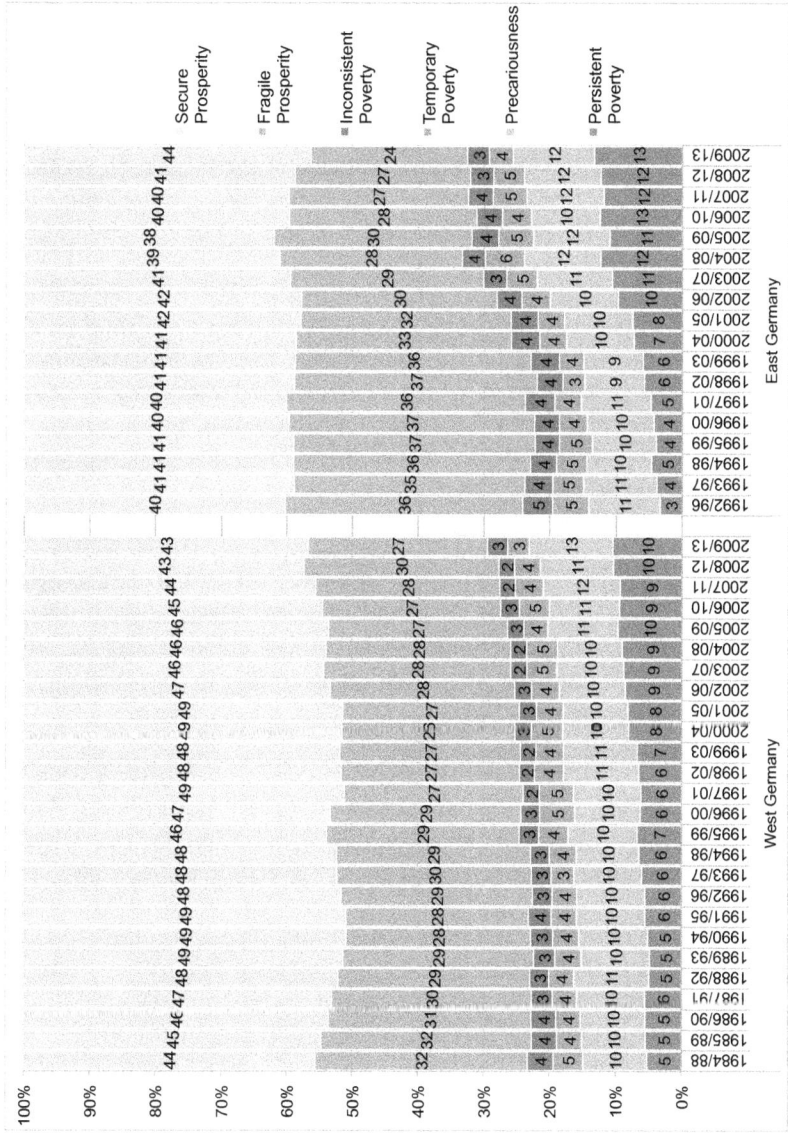

Figure 8.2 Poverty Trends in West and East Germany. SOEPv30, 1984–2013, five-year balanced panels, weighted results.

and East Germany. Given the stark differences between the two parts of reunified Germany, the poverty indicator is constructed separately for each region.

When looking at the trends over time, two trends predominate in both regions: the zone of unstable prosperity declines steadily over the entire period, and the zone of persistent poverty has been clearly increasing since the start of the 1990s. Temporary and inconsistent poverty along with the zone of vulnerability, on the other hand, prove largely stable, as does the zone of secure prosperity.

These trends are informative for the assumptions and hypothesis about the new poverty. First of all, the increase of poverty that can be observed from cross-sectional, time-series data is almost completely due to the increase of *persistent* poverty. All other forms of 'precarious' living conditions, such as temporary poverty experiences, inconsistent poverty and even the zone of vulnerability, are almost stable over time.

Secondly, during this period poverty is not increasingly spreading into the broad middle of society. Almost the entire upper half of the population lives in secure prosperity. Some fluctuations occur over time, but these reflect economic cycles rather than a stable trend over time. Even more so, what compensates for the increase in persistent poverty is the decline of the zone of fragile prosperity. Instead of increasing 'new social risks' that might lead to precarious living conditions, at least temporarily, these temporal economic strains are even decreasing over time.

Thirdly, as can be shown by more in-depth analysis, poverty becomes more persistent over time in the straightforward sense that it lasts for more years on average, and its cumulative effect continues through various stages of life so that its concentration within certain population groups is increasing.[33] Material disadvantages are accumulating in specific groups rather than spreading rapidly to the whole population. When analysing individuals over ten successive years, one can see no increase over time for downward mobility, e.g., from unsecure prosperity into persistent poverty, but rather, we observe a decreasing rate of upward mobility from the zone of persistent poverty into higher social strata. Thus, for those who are already poor, it became increasingly difficult to escape poverty. This trend is driving the overall increase in persistent poverty.

Fourthly, these trends are even more pronounced in the territories of former East Germany after reunification. Although starting from a much lower level of inequality and general standards of living – as can be seen from the lower shares of individuals in the zones of secure prosperity and of persistent poverty – the zone of persistent poverty has continuously increased since the start of reunification and almost skyrocketed since the turn of the millennium. In turn, the shrinking of the zone of fragile prosperity is more pronounced.

These results already clearly contradict basic assumptions about the new poverty. Where forms of material deprivations due to financial constraints are concerned, we do not find a tendency of these material risks to increasingly affect larger proportions of society. On the contrary, we find that poverty is increasingly concentrated amongst already disadvantaged groups and that it becomes more and more persistent over time.

Workers Most Affected by Persistent Poverty

Besides the development of levels of poverty over time, the question of the groups affected is of particular interest. During the period of rising poverty, a shift in the demographic profile of the poor took place, with children and females – in particular, single mothers – and migrants and their descendants being most affected. However, as already mentioned above, much of the demographic shifts are simply due to cohort-specific risks of exposure to historical poverty cycles.

One basic assumption of the discourse on new poverty was that it can no longer be seen as traditional, working class poverty. This assumption was rarely empirically tested. Figure 8.3 shows the ratios of persistent poverty for different social classes, using a collapsed version of the Erikson-Goldthorpe-Portocarero (EGP) class scheme.[34] As can be seen, the group chiefly affected by poverty are workers, especially the low skilled.

In West Germany, the poverty rates of unskilled and skilled workers moved slightly closer together during the brief post-reunification boom, owing to the decline in poverty among unskilled workers. However, in the ensuing recession, persistent poverty among unskilled workers began to rise continuously. With a slight delay, poverty rates for skilled workers have increased since around the turn of the millennium. For the intermediate classes, poverty rates increased as well but to a lower extent, and they increased even less for the service classes.

For East Germany, the picture is largely similar, but again, much more pronounced and with some notable special features. Until the turn of the millennium, the overall increase in persistent poverty was almost completely due to the further increase in the already higher poverty rates of unskilled workers. Skilled workers actually recorded under-average poverty rates in the post-reunification period. However, at the turn of the millennium, poverty sharply increased among the skilled working class, and it has continued to do so during the past few years. In contrast, the increase of poverty for the intermediate classes slowed down again. For the service classes, poverty risks increased only slightly, at least until recently.

Altogether, poverty is tending to increase in all occupational groups, but there is no evidence that social class is becoming less significant. On the contrary, the rapid rise in poverty ratios among unskilled workers suggests that differences of social class are largely stable in regard to the risk of persistent poverty. In the entire period covered by Figure 8.3, around three-quarters of all individuals in the zone of persistent poverty belong to the working classes (skilled and unskilled).

Of course, many other factors influence the risk of poverty as well. It is particularly high for persons with immigrant backgrounds, for single parents and for families with more than two children, and it accumulates if more than

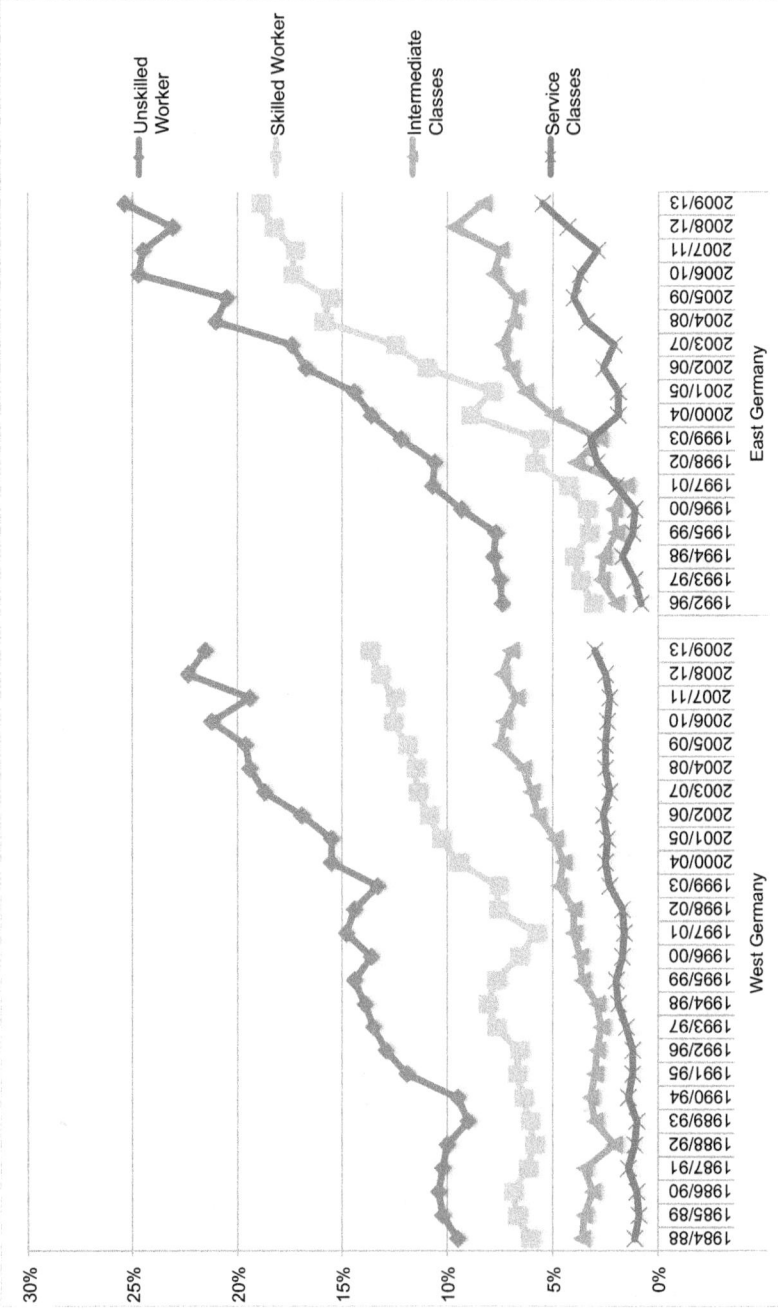

Figure 8.3 Rates of Persistent Poverty by Social Class. SOEPv30, 1984–2013, five-year balanced panels, weighted results.

one of these risk factors is present. Moreover, regional disparities of poverty within Germany between east and west, but also between north and south, have strongly increased over the past few decades – again, following the path dependencies of industrialization and de-industrialization.

Conclusion: the Legacies of De-industrialization

Since the late 1970s, Germany has experienced a dramatic increase in poverty. However, as this chapter has shown, this major change of social stratification has not previously been properly understood. The discourse of new poverty that accompanied the new poverty cycle has not managed to disentangle the continuities and changes of poverty in the historical process of de-industrialization. At the core of this failure stands the opposition of the new poverty against a traditional, working class poverty that has served as a guiding line of vision within this discourse. This has permitted scholars to empirically and conceptually account for the legacies of the industrial system of class stratification that have obviously still been at work during the period of de-industrialization since the 1980s in West Germany, and after reunification in former East Germany.

A sound understanding of the rising poverty will not be possible without uncovering the long arms of the history of industrial class stratification that have been abandoned and ignored much too early and rigorously. This is surely not to say that there are no 'new' emerging features of poverty and social stratification after the epochal break of the 1970s. Rather, only if we understand the continuities and legacies of the 'old' we are able to understand these new features.

The failure to trace historical changes, rather than to claim and presuppose the novelty of poverty in capitalist welfare societies, has strong implications. The argument that I want to pose is that poverty must always been understood within the framework of social stratification and its often complex patterns. However, what is most striking is that the (sociological) debate on social inequality has only very little intersection with the debate and research on poverty. Poverty has, until now, not become a mainstream topic in social inequality research – at least in sociological research. In Germany, it has remained a topic that is predominantly addressed by economists. This is not to say that poverty research should be streamed into oftentimes useless disciplinary divisions. In fact, the research on poverty is a good example of the rather rare but well-functioning interdisciplinary enterprises between economics, sociology and political science. My main point here is that the increase of poverty in recent decades in Germany marks probably the most dramatic change in the system of social stratification, but it has not been recognized as such because it did not find its way into historically well-informed and interdisciplinary research on social stratification.

Distinctions of social class are particularly marked in Germany. The picture drawn by international comparisons in research is clear: in scarcely any other Western country do educational attainment and the chances of social mobility depend as strongly on social background as they do in Germany.[35] Students from working class backgrounds have increased their participation in higher education due to an expansion of the entire sector, but the relative gap between them and the middle and upper classes has remained largely unchanged. More recent studies of school performance, such as PISA, only confirm that working class children lag behind the children of higher social classes in performance and competences. In part, this is presumably because they start from worse positions, with lower family educational backgrounds. Even more alarming is the finding that even with the same cognitive and schooling competences, they clearly perform worse in terms of school choice and certificates obtained than do children from more privileged family backgrounds. Thus, the expansion of education has not fully achieved its aim of mobilizing the 'educational reserves' of the lower social classes.

The increase in (persistent) poverty during the past thirty years is largely due to the massive loss of traditional jobs for unskilled and semiskilled workers – jobs that once offered good pay and security. Germany is suffering a particularly acute rise in poverty rates and poverty persistence due to the interaction of rigid class and status differences in the educational, employment and social security systems, coupled with increasing material risks. The recent labour market and social policy reforms may have attained their goal of fostering employment rates and economic growth, but they did not succeed in eliminating poverty or even stopping it from growing.

Developing a more comprehensive understanding of the increase in persistent poverty will continue to pose a major challenge to the social sciences, and historians will have to play an important role in this regard.

Notes

1. W. Voges. 2013. *Armut – zur extrem ungleichen sozialen Teilhabe*. Opladen: Barbara Budrich; O. Groh-Samberg and W. Voges. 2012. 'Armut und soziale Ausgrenzung', in S. Mau and N.M. Schöneck (eds), *Handwörterbuch zur Gesellschaft Deutschlands*. VS Verlag für Sozialwissenschaften, pp. 58–79; O. Groh-Samberg, 2009. *Armut, soziale Ausgrenzung und Klassenstrukturen. Zur Integration multidimensionaler und längsschittlicher Perspektiven*. Wiesbaden: VS Verlag für Sozialwissenschaften.
2. Bundesministerium für Arbeit und Sozialordnung (BMAS). 2001. 'Lebenslagen in Deutschland – Der 2. Armuts- und Reichtumsbericht der Bundesregierung'. Bonn.
3. Groh-Samberg and Voges, 'Armut und soziale Ausgrenzung'.
4. www.diw.de/soep (accessed 22 May 2016); G.G. Wagner, J.R. Frick and J. Schupp. 2007. 'The German Socio-Economic Panel Study (SOEP) – Scope, Evolution and Enhancements', *Schmollers Jahrbuch* 127(1):139–69.
5. J.R. Frick et al., 2005. *DIW Wochenbericht*, No. 4/2005.
6. S. Leibfried and L. Leisering. 1995. *Zeit der Armut: Lebensläufe im Sozialstaat*. Frankfurt/Main: Suhrkamp.
7. H. Geißler. 1976. *Die neue soziale Frage*. Freiburg: Herder.

8. W. Bahlsen et al. 1984. *Die neue Armut. Ausgrenzung von Arbeitslosen aus der Arbeitslosenunterstützung.* Cologne: Bund.

9. K.-J. Bieback and H. Milz. 1995. 'Zur Einführung: Armut in Zeiten des modernen Strukturwandels', in K.-J. Bieback and H. Milz (eds), *Neue Armut.* Frankfurt/Main, New York: Campus, pp. 7–27.

10. R. Hauser, R., H. Cremer-Schäfer and U. Nouvertné. 1981. *Armut, Niedrigeinkommen und Unterversorgung in der Bundesrepublik Deutschland. Bestandsaufnahme und sozialpolitische Perspektiven.* Frankfurt/Main, New York: Campus.

11. W. Hanesch et al. 1994: *Armut in Deutschland* (Armutsbericht des DGB und des Paritätischen Wohlfahrtsverbandes). Reinbeck/Hamburg: Rowohlt.

12. J.R. Frick and O. Groh-Samberg. 2007. *To Claim or Not to Claim: Estimating Non-Take-Up of Social Assistance in Germany and the Role of Measurement Error.* SOEP papers on Multidisciplinary Panel Data Research at DIW Berlin, No. 53/2007. Berlin: DIW Berlin.

13. C. Butterwegge. 2012. *Krise und Zukunft des Sozialstaates*, 4th edn. Wiesbaden: VS Verlag für Sozialwissenschaften.

14. U. Beck. 1986. *Risikogesellschaft.* Frankfurt/Main: Suhrkamp.

15. M.J. Bane and D.T. Ellwood. 1986. 'Slipping into and out of Poverty: The Dynamics of Spells', *The Journal of Human Resources* 21:1–23.

16. L. Leisering and S. Leibfried. 1999. *Time and Poverty in the Welfare State.* Cambridge: Cambridge University Press.

17. Ibid; it should be noted that longitudinal analysis of administrative social assistance data was also done at Bielefeld by Hans-Jürgen Andreß.

18. Leisering and Leibfried, *Time and Poverty.*

19. Author's translation. S. Leibfried et al. 1995. *Zeit der Armut. Lebensläufe im Sozialstaat.* Frankfurt/Main: Suhrkamp.

20. S. Paugam. 2005. *Les formes élémentaires de la pauvreté.* Paris: Presses Universitaires de France.

21. Bundesministerium für Arbeit und Sozialordnung (BMAS), 'Lebenslagen in Deutschland'.

22. P. Townsend. 1979. *Poverty in the United Kingdom. A Survey of Household Resources and Standards of Living.* Harmondsworth: Penguin Books.

23. J. Mack and S. Lansley. 1985. *Poor Britain.* London: Allen & Unwin; S. Ringen. 1988. 'Direct and Indirect Measures of Poverty', *Journal of Social Policy* 17(3):351–65. For a review, see: B. Nolan and C.T. Whelan. 1996. *Resources, Deprivation and Poverty.* Oxford: Clarendon Press.

24. C.T. Whelan et al. 2003. 'Persistent Income Poverty and Deprivation in the European Union: An Analysis of the First Three Waves of the European Community Household Panel', *Journal of Social Policy* 32(1):1–32.

25. H.-J. Andreß et al. 1999. *Leben in Armut. Analysen der Verhaltensweisen armer Haushalte mit Umfragedaten.* Wiesbaden: Westdeutscher Verlag.

26. Household income is used rather than individual income because in most households the incomes of members are pooled, and they have a roughly equal material standard of living. Equivalizing income to take into account household needs is based on the proposition that a larger household profits from economies of scale. Further, equivalent scales assign different needs to children than they do to adults. Researchers have proposed many different equivalent scales. The one used today is the 'new OECD scale' in

which the household reference person (or 'head') has a weight of 1.0, every other adult is weighted 0.5 and children are each weighted 0.3.

27. Ringen. 1988. 'Direct and Indirect Measures of Poverty'; B. Halleröd. 1995. 'The Truly Poor: Direct and Indirect Consensual Measurement of Poverty in Sweden', *Journal of European Social Policy* 5(2):111–29.

28. C.T. Whelan, R. Layte and B. Maitre. 2004. 'Understanding the Mismatch between Income Poverty and Deprivation: A Dynamic Comparative Analysis', *European Sociological Review* 20(4):287–302; Nolan and Whelan, *Resources, Deprivation and Poverty*.

29. Wagner, Frick and Schupp, 'The German Socio-Economic Panel Study'.

30. A.E. Clark, Y. Georgellis, R.E. Lucas and E. Diener. 2004. 'Unemployment Alters the Set-Point of Life Satisfaction', *Psychological Science* 15(1):8–13.

31. This is what is known as a balanced panel. All of the following descriptive analyses are weighted using the weighting factors supplied in SOEP. For a balanced panel from 2005 to 2009, the individual weight is calculated by multiplying the cross-sectional weight for the wave 2005 by the longitudinal weights for the years 2006, 2007, 2008 and 2009.

32. Leisering and Leibfried, *Time and Poverty*.

33. Groh-Samberg, *Armut, soziale Ausgrenzung und Klassenstruktur*; O. Groh-Samberg and F.R. Hertel. 2016. 'Abstieg der Mitte? Zur langfristigen Mobilität von Armut und Wohlstand', in P.A. Berger and N. Burzan (eds), *Dynamiken (in) der gesellschaftlichen Mitte*. Wiesbaden: Westdeutscher Verlag (forthcoming).

34. All persons are assigned to a social class based on their current or last occupations. In the case of children or adults who have never worked, they are assigned to the social class of the male (or otherwise female) household head.

35. R. Breen (ed.). 2004. *Social Mobility in Europe*. Oxford: Oxford University Press.

Works Cited

Andreß, H.-J., et al. 1999. *Leben in Armut. Analysen der Verhaltensweisen armer Haushalte mit Umfragedaten.* Wiesbaden: Westdeutscher Verlag.

Bahlsen, W., et al. 1984. *Die neue Armut. Ausgrenzung von Arbeitslosen aus der Arbeitslosenunterstützung.* Cologne: Bund.

Bane, M.J., and D.T. Ellwood. 1986. 'Slipping into and out of Poverty: The Dynamics of Spells', *The Journal of Human Resources* 21:1–23.

Beck, U. 1986. *Risikogesellschaft.* Frankfurt/Main: Suhrkamp.

Bieback, K.-J., and H. Milz. 1995. 'Zur Einführung: Armut in Zeiten des modernen Strukturwandels', in K.-J. Bieback and H. Milz (eds), *Neue Armut.* Frankfurt/M., New York: Campus, pp. 7–27.

Breen, R. (ed.). 2004. *Social Mobility in Europe.* Oxford: Oxford University Press.

Bundesministerium für Arbeit und Sozialordnung (BMAS). 2001. 'Lebenslagen in Deutschland – Der 2. Armuts- und Reichtumsbericht der Bundesregierung', Bonn.

———. 2005. 'Lebenslagen in Deutschland – Der 3. Armuts- und Reichtumsbericht der Bundesregierung', Bonn.

Butterwegge, C. 2012. *Krise und Zukunft des Sozialstaates*, 4th edn. Wiesbaden: VS Verlag für Sozialwissenschaften.

Clark, A.E., Y. Georgellis, R.E. Lucas and E. Diener. 2004. 'Unemployment Alters the Set-Point of Life Satisfaction', *Psychological Science* 15(1):8–13.

Frick, J.R., and O.Groh-Samberg. 2007. *To Claim or Not to Claim: Estimating Non-Take-Up of Social Assistance in Germany and the Role of Measurement Error.* SOEP papers on Multidisciplinary Panel Data Research at DIW Berlin, No. 53/2007. Berlin: DIW Berlin.

———, et al. 2005. *DIW Wochenbericht*, No. 4/2005.

Geißler, H. 1976. *Die neue soziale Frage.* Freiburg: Herder.

Groh-Samberg, O. 2009. *Armut, soziale Ausgrenzung und Klassenstrukturen. Zur Integration multidimensionaler und längsschittlicher Perspektiven.* Wiesbaden: VS Verlag für Sozialwissenschaften.

———, and F.R. Hertel. 2016. 'Abstieg der Mitte? Zur langfristigen Mobilität von Armut und Wohlstand', in P.A. Berger and N. Burzan (eds), *Dynamiken (in) der gesellschaftlichen Mitte.* Wiesbaden: Westdeutscher Verlag (forthcoming).

———, and W. Voges. 2012. 'Armut und soziale Ausgrenzung', in S. Mau and N.M. Schöneck (eds), *Handwörterbuch zur Gesellschaft Deutschlands.* VS Verlag für Sozialwissenschaften, pp. 58–79.

Halleröd, B. 1995. 'The Truly Poor: Direct and Indirect Consensual Measurement of Poverty in Sweden', *Journal of European Social Policy* 5(2):111–29.

Hanesch, W., et al. 1994. *Armut in Deutschland* (Armutsbericht des DGB und des Paritätischen Wohlfahrtsverbandes). Reinbeck/Hamburg: Rowohlt.

Hauser, R., H. Cremer-Schäfer and U. Nouverté. 1981. *Armut, Niedrigeinkommen und Unterversorgung in der Bundesrepublik Deutschland. Bestandsaufnahme und sozialpolitische Perspektiven.* Frankfurt/Main, New York: Campus.

Leibfried, S. and L. Leisering. 1995. *Zeit der Armut: Lebensläufe im Sozialstaat.* Frankfurt/Main: Suhrkamp.

———, et al. 1995. *Zeit der Armut. Lebensläufe im Sozialstaat.* Frankfurt/Main: Suhrkamp.

Leisering, L., and S. Leibfried. 1999. *Time and Poverty in the Welfare State.* Cambridge: Cambridge University Press.

Mack, J., and S. Lansley. 1985. *Poor Britain.* London: Allen & Unwin.

Nolan, B., and C.T. Whelan. 1996. *Resources, Deprivation and Poverty.* Oxford: Clarendon Press.

Paugam, S. 2005. *Les formes élémentaires de la pauvreté.* Paris: Presses Universitaires de France.

Ringen, S. 1988. 'Direct and Indirect Measures of Poverty', *Journal of Social Policy* 17(3):351–65.

Townsend, P. 1979. *Poverty in the United Kingdom. A Survey of Household Resources and Standards of Living.* Harmondsworth: Penguin Books.

Voges, W. 2013. *Armut – zur extrem ungleichen sozialen Teilhabe.* Opladen: Barbara Budrich.

Wagner, G.G., J.R. Frick and J. Schupp. 2007. 'The German Socio-Economic Panel Study (SOEP) – Scope, Evolution and Enhancements', *Schmollers Jahrbuch* 127(1):139–69.

Whelan, C.T., et al. 2003. 'Persistent Income Poverty and Deprivation in the European Union: An Analysis of the First Three Waves of the European Community Household Panel', *Journal of Social Policy* 32(1):1–32.

———, R. Layte and B. Maitre. 2004. 'Understanding the Mismatch between Income Poverty and Deprivation: A Dynamic Comparative Analysis', *European Sociological Review* 20(4):287–302.

Olaf Groh-Samberg is Professor of Sociology at the Bremen University. He is a member of the SOCIUM research group Inequality Dynamics in Welfare Societies. His recent publications include: together with Wolfgang Voges, 'Precursors and consequences of youth poverty in Germany', *Longitudinal and Life Course Studies* 5(2):151–72 (2014); with Florian R. Hertel, *Class Mobility Across Three Generations in the US and Germany. Research in Social Stratification and Mobility* (2013); together with Joachim R. Frick and Markus M. Grabka, 'The Impact of Home Production on Economic Inequality in Germany' *Empirical Economics* 43:1143–69 (2013).

Index

www.ingramcontent.com/pod-product-compliance
Lightning Source LLC
Chambersburg PA
CBHW070916030426
42336CB00014BA/2442